Public Sector Communication: How Organizations Manage Information

Public Sector Communication: How Organizations Manage Information

Doris A. Graber
University of Illinois at Chicago

Congressional Quarterly Inc.
Washington, D.C.

Cover design: Ben Santora
Book design: Kaelin Chappell

Copyright © 1992 Congressional Quarterly Inc.
1414 22nd Street, N.W., Washington, D.C. 20037

Printed in the United States of America

Library of Congress Cataloging-in-Publication Data

Graber, Doris A. (Doris Appel)
 Public sector communication : how organizations manage information
/ Doris A. Graber
  p. cm.
 Includes bibliographical references and index.
 ISBN 0-87187-685-X (hard) -- ISBN 0-87187-560-8 (paper)
 1. Communication in public administration. I. Title.
JF1525.C59G73 1991   91-40338
 353.007—dc20   CIP

**For Jane, Lance, Ellen, Mary Beth, and Violet
who know firsthand
the manifold challenges presented by
organizational communication**

Contents

Tables, Figures, and Boxes

Tables

Figures

Boxes

Preface

All human beings live in organized groups, ranging from the family to the state to the world community. All of these groups function through communication which is the transmission and exchange of information. In 1966 Karl Deutsch, a renowned scholar of politics, wrote a book entitled *The Nerves of Government: Models of Political Communication and Control*.[1] In it he argued that the essence of governmental organizations is decision making, and the essence of decision making is communication. Politics is a struggle to control the messages and commands that allocate human and material resources within human organizations. Understanding how government at all levels operates and what prompts it to act or refrain from action requires studying how messages of various types are composed and how they travel the nerve paths of the body politic.

I share Deutsch's view. The major premise on which this book rests is the belief that communication steers the activities of all organizations. Every organization takes in, generates, and uses information. Every organization transmits information to its members and outsiders. Scholars interested in analyzing how organizations operate, administrators eager to build organizations with a high potential for effective functioning, employees who seek to work effectively in such organizations, and clients who deal with these organizations all need to be concerned about information management. Since one out of every six citizens works in the public sector and nearly every American deals with public organizations, the quality of public sector communication affects all of us.

Concern about public sector communication is especially necessary because communicating has become increasingly difficult in all types of organizations, private as well as public. Public agency insiders—as well as outsiders concerned about bureaucracies—are asking more questions and are more willing and often more eager to express dissenting views. Governmental agencies now administer more controversial programs than ever before, which affect ever larger numbers of people. Programs dealing with environmental protection, nuclear energy, and immigration policy are examples. The messages disseminated by agencies concerned with these programs are increasingly complex at a time when many clients of these programs are less competent than ever before to cope with written instructions in English.

Many scholars have addressed information-management issues in the past thirty years, but they have focused largely on communication within business organizations, neglecting organizational communication in the public sector. Such neglect is unfortunate because effective information management in the public sector poses many unique problems for public officials. When one considers national, state, and local governments and their activities throughout the United States, the number of public organizations conducting important business is huge. If these institutions are to benefit from advanced knowledge in information management and organizational communication, it must be adapted to public sector conditions and needs. It must be presented to practitioners and students within the context of communication theories to foster an understanding of what is happening and to enable them to cope with the many public sector communication problems. That is why this book was written.

What the Book Will Cover

Chapter 1 presents a brief overview of the importance of organizational communication and the various theories that have guided investigations into the field. The technical and ethical problems faced by organizational communication in the public sector will be emphasized. To keep the discussion close to operational realities, a number of examples drawn from the public sector will be presented. The problems of information gathering faced by governmental organizations will be discussed in Chapter 2. How can administrators collect sufficient information to make well-rounded decisions without drowning in an excess of information? How can regulatory agencies extract "truth" from reluctant and often obstreperous sources in the private sector? Such questions relate to the issue of intelligence needs in the public sector and to the quality of organizational intelligence. Problems of publicity and secrecy in democratic societies will also be included here.

The focus will then shift in Chapter 3 to the structural arrangements that shape the flow of information within organizations. Various ways of organizing decision-making flows will be discussed in Chapter 4, including models and examples of information flows characterizing decision making in various governmental bodies. Network impact on the flow and substance of communication will receive attention in Chapter 5, as will the political implications of selecting particular formal and informal network structures.

Chapter 6 will be devoted to communication styles and climates and the extent to which they foster and diffuse innovations. The discussion will focus on techniques ensuring that upward, downward, and lateral communication flows will be structured to support organizational objectives and programs and to maintain internal functioning at high levels of morale.

Attention will then switch from internal to external communication, sometimes called marketing communication. In Chapter 7 various activities, such as lobbying and public relations, which are designed to enhance the image of an organization, will be analyzed. Principles of persuasion will be discussed as they pertain to the conduct of public relations campaigns, relations with the mass media, and the work of lobbying groups.

Many public agencies deal directly with individual citizens. The Internal Revenue Service, the Social Security Administration, and the Immigration and Naturalization Service are examples. Agency-client relations in the public sector differ vastly from their counterparts in private business. A welfare client or a taxpayer has a dependency relationship with the relevant government agency, which creates unique problems that do not arise when clients have a choice among providers of services and pay money as a quid pro quo. Chapter 8 will deal with these and similar problems.

Various techniques for detecting communication problems in organizations and methods for devising remedial procedures are covered in Chapter 9. To familiarize readers with analytic tools designed to assess the quality of internal and external communications, major evaluation techniques, such as network analysis and communication audits, will be discussed briefly. However, for nuts-and-bolts details, the reader will be referred to the appropriate literature.

The concluding Chapter 10 reflects on the arguments presented throughout the book and what they tell us about the past, the present, and the future of public sector organizational communication. It examines once more the trade-offs between efficiency in the economic sense and effectiveness in terms of satisfying human needs and political aspirations. This chapter attempts to map out areas where widely accepted improvements seem possible and also acknowledges barriers that currently seem insurmountable.

The book has a dual focus throughout. On one hand, it presents an analysis of organizational communication and information management as viewed from various theoretical perspectives. Political organizations are studied in terms of communication flows among structural parts of the system. Like Karl Deutsch, I view communication as the "nerves of government" that determine how political organizations function, but I am also concerned with a practical view of the subject. I want to show how an understanding of organizational communication can contribute to designing institutions in which well formulated messages circulate in ways that enhance the performance of these institutions and allow them to reach their goals more efficiently.

The sources used for this book reflect this duality, and also reveal the interdisciplinary roots of organizational behavior studies. Accordingly, the book blends findings from the organizational behavior and decision-making literature in sociology, communication, and, above all, political science.

Acknowledgments

I consider this book, in the truest sense, a product of extensive collaboration. My many collaborators are listed in the bibliography and in various and sundry references throughout the chapters. Without the work done by these scholars, mine would have been impossible. By completing important research and publishing it, they allowed me and others to benefit from their findings and interpretations. I thank them all.

Special thanks are due to four scholars whose works and thoughts not only pervade the book but who also took the time to read the draft manuscript and give me the benefit of their counsel. They are Dr. Naomi B. Lynn, president of Sangamon State University; Professor Everett Rogers, Annenberg School of Communications, University of Southern California; Professor Aaron Wildavsky, Survey Research Center, University of California at Berkeley; and Professor James Q. Wilson, Graduate School of Management, University of California, Los Angeles. All of them have studied public sector organizational communication for many more years than I, so that their advice and support were extraordinarily important. That holds true also for Professor James Danowski, University of Illinois at Chicago, who read the materials on networking, and Professor Susan McManus, University of South Florida, who made several important suggestions about the ideal scope of a book of this sort.

The book has also benefited from the careful work of many research assistants. Among them, Edward Tverdek was outstanding in his diligence in finding elusive information sources and his helpful annotations of articles from the social science literature. Israel Reyes made a major contribution through collecting and analyzing publications from various public agencies. Others who stood out in this very large group are Terry Feinberg, Thomas Burke, Pamela Sinclair, Rosie Balk, and Laurent Pernot.

As usual, the CQ staff has given me outstanding support. It began with Joanne Daniels, then director of CQ Press, who presided at the launching of this book and passed the project on to developmental editor Margaret Benjaminson, and finally acquisitions editor Brenda Carter. All of them provided me with thoughtful critiques about the project as a whole as well as individual chapters. Freelance editor Janet Wilson took on the task of polishing the finished manuscript with an eagle eye for finding flaws and a great talent for clarifying murky points. Nancy Lammers ably guided the editing process, and Ann O'Malley guided the book through the production phase. I am very grateful to these talented "book people."

Finally, saving matters closest to my heart for last, I want to thank Tom and the rest of my family once again for their never-ending support for all my time-consuming ventures and, above all, for their love.

Doris A. Graber

Note

1. Karl Deutsch, *The Nerves of Government: Models of Political Communication and Control* (New York: Free Press, 1966).

Public Sector Communication: Perspectives and Theories

Importance of Information Management

On January 28, 1986, the space shuttle *Challenger* exploded ninety seconds after take-off, killing all on board. The disaster rocked the nation and severely disrupted America's space program. Shuttle launches were halted for more than two years. Meanwhile, a thorough investigation tried to pinpoint the causes of the tragedy. The verdict, as stated in the investigating committee's report, was "chronic failure in the space agency and its contractors to communicate life and death problems up the chain of command." Other comments pointed out the "general ignoring of urgent memos seeking redesigning of critical booster-rocket joints" and the fact that "red flags were simply obscured in paper work." [1]

Figure 1-1 shows the chain of command through which information should have traveled from the contractors to the mission management team during final pre-flight readiness reviews. But the plans for sound communication went awry. Records show that during the summer preceding the launch two engineers at Morton Thiokol—the private contractor who was building the shuttle (level 4 in the figure)—had warned that its parts called O-rings were a potential source of trouble that might cause the spacecraft to crash. Their memos never left the company. William Lucas, director of the Marshall Space Flight Center in Alabama (level 3 in the figure), was aware that O-rings might cause problems but did not know that they were critical to flight safety. The engineers' memo had not been made available to him, nor had he been alerted that the National Aeronautics and Space Administration (NASA), in Washington, D.C., had documents alluding to the potential seriousness of the problems. NASA officials, eager to proceed with the launch, had raised questions about the accuracy of these reports.

Figure 1-1   Launch Readiness Review Outline

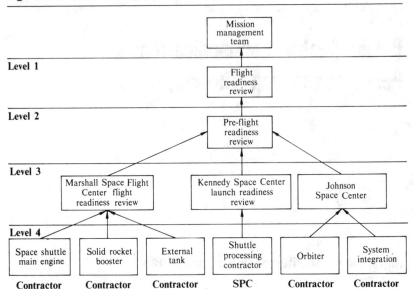

Source: U.S. Congress, House, Committee on Science and Technology, *Investigation of the Challenger Accident*, Report, 99th Congress, 2d session (Washington, D.C.: Government Printing Office, 1986), 83.

Note: Readiness reviews for both the launch and the flight of a shuttle mission are conducted at ascending levels that begin with contractors.

The night before the launch, Lucas was informed that cold weather might bring trouble with the O-rings. He explained that he did not relay this information to NASA to warn about dangers of launching *Challenger* because "he was not in the chain of command to approve a launching." [2] Furthermore, he believed that Morton Thiokol had approved the launch because he had not seen their memo expressing numerous reservations.

On the fateful night before the launch, lower-level NASA officials met with the manufacturer of the booster rockets and were told that the O-rings were a potential source of trouble. They failed to convey this information to top-level NASA officials the next morning during a meeting. The reason they gave was that the manufacturer, using available research data, had mentioned the problem only as a possibility, *not* as a certainty, so the warning message did not seem to them important enough to mention.

Meanwhile, Rocco Petrone, director of shuttle operations at the Marshall Space Flight Center, had become concerned about potential O-ring problems in cold weather. He directed his subordinates to tell NASA officials at Cape Canaveral to cancel the launch because of the cold weather. His message indicated that ice damage might endanger the reentry of the vehicle into the earth's atmosphere. This message was misinterpreted. Because it mentioned reentry, rather than the launching of the vehicle, the message was downgraded and NASA officials continued to think that personnel at the Marshall facility considered the launch to be safe.

The shuttle disaster is a graphic example of the difficulty of establishing good communication patterns in a complex public organization and the serious consequences that may ensue when communication is mishandled. It certainly is not intended to suggest that public agencies routinely mismanage information. Somehow, in the *Challenger* case, the channels leading from Morton Thiokol to the Marshall Space Flight Center and from the center to NASA officials were not functioning properly. Important information did not reach the appropriate receivers, and a number of misunderstandings were not detected until it was too late.

The *Challenger* case also illustrates that it is possible to learn from mistakes and to take precautions to avoid or lessen such problems. For example, the Presidential Commission on the Space Shuttle *Challenger* Accident, under the chairmanship of former Attorney General William Pierce Rogers, recommended that the Launch Readiness Review Process, shown in Figure 1-1, be revised to ensure better upward communication of potentially crucial information. In accordance with this suggestion, the reviews are no longer buried within the agency's bureaucracy, where safety concerns are likely to be subordinated to the pressures to launch the shuttle at specified times. Rather, reviews are to be performed by a larger, better-financed staff, separate from the general bureaucracy, with a co-equal top manager who can draw attention to concerns that previously fell by the wayside. NASA has also created an anonymous problem-reporting system, encouraging workers to point out danger signs. These reports are then investigated by NASA, and management is notified.[3]

The study of communication in public organizations is important precisely because communication flows that are essential to the life of organizations are amenable to human control. In the United States today, nearly 20 percent of the population works for some type of public organization, and every person's life is affected by the activities of many public agencies. All these public organizations are generators, receivers, and users of information. All transmit information internally as well as to people outside the agency. In fact, government's ability to collect, store, process, and use information is at a historical peak, thanks to the new communication technologies. A grid of often interlocking data systems covers the nation, making more information available for communication.

The complex activities that involve gathering information for collective purposes, processing it, and passing it on to others are encompassed under the label "organizational communication" or "information management." As social psychologists Daniel Katz and Robert Kahn point out, "Communication—the exchange of information and the transmission of meaning—is the very essence of a social system or an organization." [4]

Knowledge about organizational communication is increasingly needed because transmitting information and meaning is becoming more difficult. There are several reasons. It is now harder to formulate clear messages because the subject matter to be communicated has not only multiplied but also is vastly more technical. Public agencies, for example, must send messages about complex matters such as chemical hazards in homes, eligibility for Individual Retirement Accounts (IRAs), or diseases such as AIDS. A second problem is the growing diversity of the audiences for whom these messages must be formulated. The personnel of public agencies, as well as public agency clienteles, reflect greater ethnic and cultural diversity than ever before. This is especially true in the largest public agencies, such as the Social Security Administration and the Internal Revenue Service. Governments at all levels are also widening the scope of their activities and performing many new functions that intrude on the lives of citizens. These new activities may embroil public agencies in controversy. Dissidents tend to be more numerous and better organized than in the past. Their communications may interfere with the objectives of government communications. Remedial measures may become necessary.

It seems reasonable to argue that the complex tasks facing governments at all levels require skilled information management. Information needs must be assessed wisely and information flows must be guided properly. Without effective and responsible information management, the flood tide of information can become a menace rather than an asset to good government.

Defining the Scope of the Study

To delineate the main focus of this book, several major concepts must be defined and explained. Communication, the transfer of meaningful information from a source to a receiver, is the most important. The raw material for communication is *information*—data about various occurrences that have been collected and arranged to serve a purpose. That purpose may be to answer a question, to direct an activity, or to describe what has happened.[5] The carefully planned and controlled steps taken to achieve such purposes constitute *information management*. Once information has been shaped into an organized body of thought, it becomes *knowledge*.

Communication occurs because people in organizations need to receive and transmit information to coordinate their activities and perform their jobs. When messages are sent, they are intended to change the receiver's knowledge, attitude, or overt behavior in some predetermined manner. In fact, communication has been defined as "a process in which there is some predictable relation between the message transmitted and the message received." [6] Communication can take many different forms, such as words, gestures, or symbols, and senders and receivers can be individuals or groups.

The renowned social scientist Harold Lasswell, in a now classic conceptualization of the communication process, grounded in the work of mathematician Claude Shannon and electrical engineer Warren Weaver, identified five major elements that deserve attention: sources, messages, channels, receivers, and effects. Scholars have subsequently added feedback as a sixth element.[7] Communications are originated by *sources,* or senders. It is important to ascertain the sources of messages because message meanings and authoritativeness vary, depending on the source. When President Bush declares that the U.S. economy is in trouble, the impact is far more profound than if the same message comes from Communist Cuba's President Fidel Castro. Sources shape the information being transmitted into *messages* to carry the meanings that the sources wish to convey. The messages are then sent through *channels,* such as telephone calls, electronic mail, letters, or stories publicized in the mass media. We shall examine this message-transmission process to pinpoint problems in obtaining good information for transmission, formulating it into effective messages, and choosing appropriate channels for sending the message to designated *receivers.* Sometimes messages may miss their targets entirely or they may be conveyed to unanticipated receivers.

We shall also examine why messages intended to produce predetermined *effects* on receivers often fail to do so or have unexpected effects. These may manifest themselves as changes in behavior, knowledge, or attitudes. A presidential warning that the economy is in trouble may lead investors to sell off assets, producing stock-market declines. It may enlighten the public about the nation's economic status and may generate feelings of pessimism and despair. To discover the precise effects produced by messages, organizations need *feedback.* Feedback—information about the impact produced by the message and the consequences attributable to the impact—permits people to learn from their past actions and to incorporate this new knowledge into future actions. Because it may be the key to organizational effectiveness, communications should be structured so that they will elicit good feedback. Requiring responses to policy proposals or formal impact evaluations of existing programs are examples.

Effective communication requires framing messages—*encoding* is the technical term—so that they are comprehensible to the receivers who *decode* them. Message senders must therefore know the culture and comprehension levels of receivers. It seems ill advised, for instance, to couch welfare application forms in legal lingo that is incomprehensible to most of the people who must complete these forms. Throughout this book we will discuss a number of aspects of message production that enhance or detract from its effectiveness. For example, in many cases, *homophily*—cultural uniformity between source and receiver—makes it easier to formulate effective messages; *heterophily*—cultural diversity of sender and receiver—makes it harder. Effectiveness suffers if there are distortions in messages, delays in transmission, or restrictions in the use of various transmission channels.

Conflicting or unrelated messages in the transmission channels may interfere with the transmission and effects of desired messages. These extraneous messages are often called *noise*. Repetition of essential message elements—*redundancy*—is commonly used as a means to compensate for noise. A simple example would be a military pilot's repetition of messages concerning the precise location of bombing targets when talking to his headquarters. Redundancy is time-consuming and may seem wasteful, but it often is essential for comprehension. In normal conversations, half of the messages usually are redundant.

What do we mean by *organizations*? In general, organizations are stable systems of individuals who coordinate their work through communication to achieve collective goals. Working collaboratively usually involves a division of labor and an organizational hierarchy. Some individuals are designated as superiors; others become subordinates. As the cartoon here suggests, these roles strongly affect communication behavior. People acting as superiors are generally authorized to transmit messages that their subordinates are expected to obey. At the top levels, superiors at the centers of decision-making and control are often the information managers par excellence within the organization. Control over information flows makes them powerful. The ranking systems that are established and maintained through communication institutionalize inequality in organizations, even between people who may be social equals otherwise.

Division of labor, the hallmark of bureaucratic organizations, creates many communication problems that are absent in less differentiated organizations in which individuals do the whole job without needing to consult with others. Division of labor within organizations often requires the establishment of subunits. Communication is needed to keep these subunits integrated with the larger whole.

Organizations develop elaborate sets of interconnected communication channels for receiving and processing information from their environment and for sending internal and external messages. These channels constitute the organizational communication structure through which information can be managed. Communication permits organizations to make decisions, to get feedback about the wisdom of these decisions and their implementation, and to make corrections. Exchanging information with the external environment embeds the organization in that environment.[8]

The Organizational Hierarchy

Source: Adapted from Gerald M. Goldhaber, *Organizational Communication,* 3d ed. (Dubuque, Iowa: Wm. C. Brown, 1983), 23. Illustration by Patt Chisholm.

Since good information is crucial to the sound functioning of organizations, they must devise ways to secure it, process it, and disseminate it to the appropriate receivers within the organization. This raises a number of issues relating to communication policy and information management. Organizations must make sure that they will obtain essential information both internally and externally at the appropriate time. This includes feedback about the organization's own activities. Administrators must ascertain that the information received is accurate and complete enough to manage the organization effectively. It must be information obtainable without undue cost of money and effort and without invading the rights of people to whom the information relates. Given the surfeit of information— over one-third of the Gross National Product now represents knowledge production and distribution—administrators must be selective about what information they gather and what they produce and disseminate. They must decide what information should be stored in organizational memories and what should be discarded after it has been used. Effective internal information retrieval mechanisms must be developed.

The Public Sector—A Different World

The special focus of this book is on *public* organizations—institutions established by governments at various levels to carry out governmental functions. This means primarily, but not exclusively, administrative departments and agencies, such as the Department of Defense and the Environmental Protection Agency at the federal level, the Insurance Department or the Auto License Division at the state level, or the Police Department or City Clerk's Office at the local level. Although legislative bodies or top-level executive staffs are not the main focus of this book, examples relating to the presidency and Congress have been included to make use of a number of interesting studies for which, unfortunately, no counterparts exist in the literature covering administrative agencies.

Communication in public sector agencies has been largely ignored despite the fact that public organizations have a tremendous impact on the life of every American. This oversight is puzzling, as well as unfortunate, because the communication problems of public bodies differ from those in the private sector in many important ways. This book focuses on these differences and their implications.[9] Table 1-1 summarizes major differences between public and private organizations in terms of internal structures and processes, environments, and interaction with their environments. The table presents a resumé of the major differences reported in the scholarly literature under three headings: Environmental Factors, Organization-Environment Transactions, and Internal Structures and Processes.

Above all, as Table 1-1 indicates under the Environmental Factors heading, public agencies are part of the political system. Their structure, resources, personnel, goals, and even day-to-day decisions are shaped by political events. This forces public agencies to structure their activities and communications to stay afloat in the sea of politics. Professional and technical goals that clash with political requirements must be adjusted in a series of often uncomfortable compromises. If possible, public agencies try to channel the political currents so that they are favorable to the course that the agency's changing captains would like to steer. More often, the political currents dominate.

When agencies manage to ingratiate themselves with political leaders and crucial publics, they tend to be well financed, regardless of their past efficiency or effectiveness. Agencies are therefore greatly concerned about the images they present to important leaders. Agency heads strive for fast

Table 1-1 Summary of Literature on the Attributes of Public Organizations Relative to Private Organizations

Environmental Factors

Degree of market exposure (reliance on appropriations)
- Less market exposure results in less incentive to cost reduction, operating efficiency, and effective performance.
- Less market exposure results in lower allocational efficiency (reflection of consumer preferences, and proportioning supply to demand).
- Less market exposure means lower availability of market indicators and information.

Legal, formal constraints (courts, legislature, hierarchy)
- More constraints on procedures and spheres of operations (less autonomy of managers in making such choices).
- Greater tendency to proliferation of formal specifications and controls.
- More external sources of formal influence and greater fragmentation of those sources.

Political influences
- Greater diversity and intensity of external informal influences on decisions.
- Greater need for support of "constituencies."

Organization–Environment Transactions

Coerciveness
- More likely that participation in consumption and financing of services will be unavoidable or mandatory. (Government has unique sanctions and coercive powers.)

Breadth of impact
- Greater symbolic significance of actions of public administrators. (Wider scope of concern, such as "public interest.")

Public scrutiny
- Greater public scrutiny of public officials and their actions.

Unique public expectations
- Greater expectations that public officials act with more fairness, responsiveness, accountability, and honesty.

(continues)

Table 1-1 *(continued)*

Internal Structures and Processes

Complexity of objectives, evaluation, and decision criteria
- Greater multiplicity and diversity of objectives and criteria.
- Greater vagueness and intangibility of objectives and criteria.
- Greater tendency of goals to be conflicting (more "tradeoffs").

Authority relations and the role of the administrator
- Less decision-making autonomy and flexibility.
- Weaker, more fragmented authority over subordinates and lower levels.
- Greater reluctance to delegate, more levels of review, and greater use of formal regulations.
- More political, expository role for top managers.

Organizational performance
- Greater cautiousness and rigidity. Less innovativeness.
- More frequent turnover of top leaders due to elections and political appointments results in greater disruption of implementation of plans.

Incentives and incentive structures
- Greater difficulty in devising incentives for effective and efficient performance.
- Lower valuation of pecuniary incentives by employees.

Personal characteristics of employees
- Variations in personality traits and needs, such as higher dominance and flexibility, and a higher need for achievement on the part of government managers.[a]
- Lower work satisfaction and lower organizational commitment.[a]

Source: Hal G. Rainey, Robert W. Backoff, and Charles H. Levine, "Comparing Public and Private Organizations," *Public Administration Review* 36 (March/April 1976): 236-237. Reprinted with permission.

[a] Represents results of individual empirical studies, rather than points of agreement among authors.

and visible demonstrations of progress, particularly ones that can be used to attract favorable publicity. This focus on immediate success may lead to neglect of long-range problems. In the *Challenger* situation, for example, the desire to demonstrate success to critics of the program in and out of government and thereby assure continued support was cited as one reason for making light of safety concerns. The fact that the mass media had repeatedly publicized delays in the program also created pressures to proceed.[10]

Public agencies are also far more vulnerable than private organizations to having unwanted communication tasks thrust upon them. External political actors, such as Congress or the executive branch, often prescribe major policy directions and make personnel and budget decisions. For instance, when Congress passed the Freedom of Information Act in 1966, many agencies were flooded with requests for time-consuming searches of their records. Since Congress provided no additional funds for handling these tasks, agencies were forced to reassign personnel. Even these reassignments proved difficult because laws governing personnel decisions sharply reduce options that would be available in the private sector.

Another major difference between private and public agencies that has a bearing on communications is the absence of widely accepted yardsticks for gauging and publicizing a public agency's success. This is usually not reflected in the monetary profits they earn. For instance, if the sale of tax-delinquent housing is designed to provide homes for the poor, selling such housing at auction at a very high price to large real estate operators would be counterproductive. Public agencies measure their success in terms of the scope of the mission entrusted to them, the financial resources allocated to them, the size of their staffs, and the satisfaction of their clienteles. These indicators of successful operations are poor weapons for defending an agency if it comes under fire for high costs or low revenues. In fact, unlike the private sector, incentives to limit service are strong. Fewer services usually mean saving scarce public resources. In the private sector it would mean a costly loss of business.[11]

Under the heading Organization-Environment Transactions, Table 1-1 lists the breadth of impact of public agencies. In addition to mentioning their impact on major aspects of life in the United States, one must also note the multiplicity of public agencies that affect our lives. Coordination of their activities is an almost insurmountable challenge. It is therefore not surprising that conflicts between personnel in different departments are quite common in the public sector. Congress and state legislatures act like remote boards of directors, making little effort to integrate the operations of diverse agencies. They know that proposals for changes invariably stir a hornets' nest of vested interests whose claims are difficult to accommodate. Reorganizations of agencies may entail major revisions of communication patterns.

Failure to coordinate the work of various agencies is particularly serious because their duties frequently overlap. For political reasons, public agencies often represent strange aggregations of tasks and goals that one might not expect under one organizational roof. Accordingly, agencies may have to generate very diverse types of information and messages to meet internal and external needs.[12] Management of public agencies is also made more difficult because decisions about funding, personnel, and policies frequently are dictated by partisan concerns rather than the merits of the case that agency officials may plead.

Many political concerns that shape the public sector are also shared by the private sector. Private firms operate subject to rules issued by the government and must therefore respond to political pressures. Like public agencies, they may have to expose their activities to public scrutiny through reports to the government or public relations releases. But, as Table 1-1 suggests, the differences remain major.

From an organizational communications perspective, a crucial difference between public and private organizations springs from the fact that public organizations operate or are presumed to operate in an atmosphere of openness. Internal and external communications of public agencies, unlike private sector organizations, are potentially, if not always actually, subject to public scrutiny. This is performed most frequently by hostile press and public interest groups. Scrutiny may also come from members of legislatures who eagerly seek plaudits for spotlighting what appear to be bureaucratic failings. In most instances, humiliating administrators is "not so much an exercise in sadism as a byproduct of pursuing other goals," such as self-glorification.[13]

Open organizational communication in the public sector is particularly important in democratic societies, which glorify the full and free flow of information. This is partly a matter of principle, springing from the belief that democracy must conduct its business openly so that all citizens can know what is going on. It is also partly an efficiency issue, grounded in the belief that open communication is beneficial because it exposes a multiplicity of concerns and opinions that then become available for decision making. Based on these beliefs, promotion of open communication has become enshrined in America's fundamental laws, such as the constitutionally protected rights of freedom of assembly, speech, and the press. Access to information has been eased through sunshine laws that open the meetings of public bodies to the citizenry and through freedom of information laws that permit private citizens to scan information files collected by the government. Of course, there are also laws that impede free access to information. Privacy laws, which prohibit government agencies from unauthorized disclosure of personal information, are an example.

Freedom and openness have a price. Upholding the principle of the free flow of information has posed many difficult problems for governmental organizations. The most dramatic of these involve the conflict between protecting national security secrets from the nation's enemies and at the same time not placing undue limits on access to and circulation of information. But even when national security is not involved, disclosure of information can be troublesome. When public agencies negotiate agreements internally or with outside agencies, full control over information can be a significant asset. Having to share information with the opposing side may severely limit the ability to strike favorable bargains. It may foster conflict by publicizing clashing values and alerting opponents, as has happened in the areas of environmental and nuclear safety. It may also lead to a dual decision-making process, with the formal level out in the open, accessible to the public, and the informal level taking place behind closed doors.

To avoid the risks of potentially dangerous adverse publicity, public managers tend to adopt cautious, conservative operating styles. They prefer stability and adherence to the letter of the law to flexibility and innovativeness. To assure accountability, managers in the public sector emphasize strict controls and rules for employees. They are less inclined to delegate authority or to solicit group decisions. If they follow the rules closely, they are less likely to be blamed when things go wrong. This type of management often creates an atmosphere of hostility and mistrust that can hamper agency achievements.

The size and diversity of public institutions and the requirements of checks and balances of power built into these institutions create unique challenges for public sector managers. As Table 1-1 records, these top executives enjoy far less control over their organizations than is true of their private sector counterparts. In a 1979 *Fortune* article, W. Michael Blumenthal, then secretary of the Treasury, voiced a typical complaint about how much more power he had enjoyed as a corporation president than as a cabinet secretary: "Even though I'm technically the chief executive of the Treasury, I have little real power, effective power, to influence how the thing functions." [14] As a public official, he felt helpless and exasperated about responsibility unmatched by powers of control.

Anthony Frank, postmaster general, recruited from running the nation's sixth largest savings institution, told reporters how the disparities of scale between private and public bodies make control difficult.[15] Instead of 2 million customers, he now served 200 million in the public sector. Instead of 400 branches, there were 40,000. Instead of a work force of 8,000 employees, he now headed an army of 800,000. Instead of making policies independently, he now had to be sensitive to the ideas of 15 different constituencies, including members of Congress and their staffs, the Postal Rate Commission, and four unions and three management associations. Most troubling, he found that independent commissions control the pricing of products and services sold by the Postal Service and that it took up to a year to get rate changes to match the activities of private competitors.

Because superior-subordinate relations are vastly more complex in public agencies, top personnel do not have the strong control over organizational communication flows enjoyed by their private sector counterparts. As the literature summarized in Table 1-1 indicates, administrators in the public sector usually lack major controls over their personnel. They have limited power to hire and fire because employees are either protected under a merit system or selected on a patronage basis, putting them under the wing of a political angel. Many employees who perform important support services belong to central staff agencies that are beyond the control of the organizations they serve. Examples are the federal Office of Personnel Management and the Office of Management and Budget. These agencies have their own priorities, which may differ sharply from their client organizations. Communication efforts to bring about mutual understanding and cooperation are rarely entirely successful.

Promotions and pay may be predetermined by seniority or other rules. This makes it difficult to reward merit or take disciplinary action except for the most serious infractions. Preferences for minorities and veterans further remove control over personnel and may produce resentment among people who do not enjoy these special benefits. Morale at the lower levels of government service also frequently suffers because jobs lack prestige; pay may be poor compared with unionized jobs in the private sector. As discussed more fully in Chapter 6, this limits the possibility for leadership and makes it more difficult to use various communication techniques to generate high levels of morale.

Control over information is also difficult because information needs are extremely diverse in public agencies. Information is required for policy formulation, planning, decision making, and implementation and control in a vast number of areas such as international trade, education, and public safety.[16] Political considerations may force top-level administrators to structure their information intake and use in ways that run counter to their preferences and often counter to the norms of professionalism, which are based on nonpolitical criteria.

Another reason for lack of control over information and poor morale is the fact that many top administrators are political appointees who are unlikely to stay a long time compared to the tenure of subordinates with civil service protection. The average political executive in the United States at the cabinet or sub-cabinet level remains in office for a scant twenty-two months—scarcely enough time to know the agency intimately, let alone gain control over information flows. The *Challenger* crash provides an example. The problems posed by O-rings were to be the focus of a high-level meeting in the spring of 1984. That meeting was never held because the two main organizers had left or were in the process of leaving NASA, and their successors were never alerted to these pending concerns.[17]

From a broader perspective, organizational communication issues in the public sector, to a greater extent than in the private sector, involve much more than concerns about operating organizations efficiently. They entail the distribution of power in government and society. People who control important messages circulating within an organization have the opportunity to be powerful within that organization. This may allow them to determine policies that have major societal consequences. For this reason, political concerns often dominate at the expense of efficiency and equity concerns when administrators structure and channel communication flows and map out communication patterns.[18]

While the challenges faced by public sector communicators seem daunting, steady improvements have been made. Numerous commissions at all levels of government have tackled public sector communication problems. In the past, such efforts usually drew on private sector experts assembled in blue-ribbon commissions, such as the Grace Commission created by President Reagan in 1982 to examine federal government operations from a private business perspective. When it became clear that public business cannot be run like private business, a new combination approach, called quality management, became popular. It tempered the business knowhow of the private sector with the sense of political realism of public sector officials.

In the state of Washington in 1990, for example, a mail flow problem involving operations in the state capital, was ameliorated through the combined efforts of managers from the public and private sectors. At the time, state agencies were sending out an average of 47 million pieces of mail annually and circulating 15 million pieces of mail internally. Incoming mail averaged 36 million pieces.[19] Nearly half the states, as well as the federal government and many localities, now have programs and institutions to improve all phases of their operations, including communication, through private/public quality management operations. Among them are large states such as California, New York, and Florida, as well as smaller ones such as Minnesota, Iowa, South Carolina, and Washington.

The Antecedents of Organizational Communication Studies

Problems in the Broader Field

The study of organizational communication and the analysis of difficulties are plagued by a number of problems typical of a young field. As yet, it lacks an overarching theory. In fact, there are heated disputes about what theoretical approaches are best. Unfortunately, much of the research has been static, looking at organizational communications at one point in time. Dynamic approaches, using time-series analyses to discover long-range patterns, have been relatively rare. Field studies involving observations of types of actual communication behavior have also been scarce. There has been little "soaking and poking" in the vein of Richard Fenno's intensive observations of members of Congress.[20] The validity of the few controlled experiments that have been conducted can be questioned because laboratory studies cannot effectively simulate the social structure in which organizational communication takes place. Samples of organizations that were observed have been too small to establish norms. Case studies of individual organizations, which predominated before the 1970s, were not conducive to building generalizations because they dealt mainly with specific communication problems. In most of these studies, insufficient attention was paid to the internal structures of organizations and to situational variables that might affect their communication behavior. As mentioned, no special efforts were made to delineate organizational communication problems in public institutions. Nonetheless, these earlier studies provide precedents.

Contributions of Political Communication Studies

Systems Level Studies.   Many studies of various aspects of political communication have helped lay the groundwork for understanding organizational communication in the public sector. Among the earliest were a number of language studies by philosophers, and later studies by social and behavioral scientists of the impact of verbal pronouncements on politics. The work of scholars such as Harold Lasswell, Edward Sapir, Kenneth Burke, Ernst Cassirer, Alfred North Whitehead, Susan Langer, Kenneth Boulding, and Murray Edelman has provided information about the many different ways in which human beings can and do communicate symbols to achieve political objectives.[21] As discussed more fully in Chapter 7, messages emanating from the public sector provide many examples. Advertising and public relations studies and propaganda analyses are all offshoots of this political linguistics research.

The most important contributions made by general political communication studies to an understanding of organizational communication in the public sector are the analyses of communication flows that trace how messages are generated and circulated in political systems and how they continuously guide operations of the system. As previously noted, Karl Deutsch's pathbreaking study, *The Nerves of Government: Models of Political Communication and Control,* is the prime example.[22] Deutsch argued that the functions of the body politic, like those of the human body, are triggered by its communication system—the *nerves* of government.

The study of communication flows in entire political systems was widely used by scholars of comparative government interested in factors that might influence the development of the many newly independent nations that were emerging in the 1960s. These scholars believed that the major political processes that should concern leaders eager to develop their countries, such as political socialization and participation and the free circulation of information throughout the country, all hinged on the nature and quality of a state's political communication system.[23]

The fact that many of these early studies dealt with the largest political body—the state—does not diminish their relevance for smaller types of organizations, such as public agencies within states. A few examples from these analytical studies will indicate their thrust and relevance to organizational communication at all levels. Deutsch, for instance, pointed out the importance of constant flows of information into political systems if they are to function well.[24] Information must cover not only what is going on inside the system but also what is happening in the external setting within which it operates. As shown in Figure 1-2, Information Flow in Foreign Policy Decisions, adapted from Deutsch's work, new information entering a system is combined with information already present in the system's organizational memory so that organizational decisions represent an amalgamation of old and new information. When messages are communicated to various receivers within a political system, they generate further communications as well as actions. All messages that pass through a system must be encoded in ways that are comprehensible to the intended recipients. In the process of preparing appropriate messages, much information may be lost. The original meaning intended by the sender may also become distorted when it is filtered through screens of various innate prejudices and preferences, as exemplified by Deutsch's screen of selective attention or screen of repression from consciousness. The combination of new information with that stored in both deep and current organizational memory may also alter the message so that it no longer accurately reflects the original communication.

To permit actors in a political system to learn from past decisions and to adjust their actions accordingly, feedback messages must be generated about the impact of past decisions. Figure 1-2 labels these as information about consequences of output. Policy evaluation studies in public agencies are examples of feedback procedures. They have become increasingly common in recent decades. When feedback messages reveal performance faults, it becomes possible to correct past errors and steer the system in the right direction. The term *cybernetic system* is used to describe the role played by feedback in organizations. Instead of striving for static maintenance of the organization, the goal is conscious guidance toward an improved social system. Cybernetic information flows in political and other types of organizations are circular. Information reaching the organization produces action, which in turn generates information that is reintroduced into the system to adjust subsequent action for past errors. Feedback becomes a means for constant adaptation. The model suggests that

Figure 1-2 A Crude Model: Functional Diagram of Information Flow in Foreign Policy Decisions

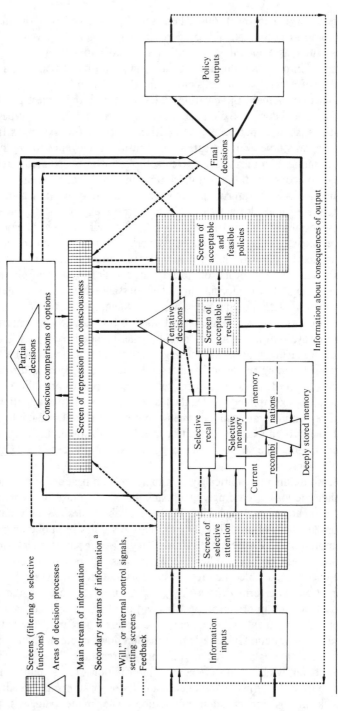

Screens (filtering or selective functions)

Areas of decision processes

Main stream of information

Secondary streams of information [a]

"Will," or internal control signals, setting screens

Feedback

Source: Adapted from Karl W. Deutsch, *The Nerves of Government: Models of Political Communication and Control* (New York: Free Press, 1966), 218. Reprinted with permission of the Free Press, a division of Macmillan, Inc.

[a] Secondary streams of information make minor contributions to the decision, but may be voluminous. Functions subject to the perceivers' mental process include filtering screens, consciousness, and deliberate choices made as part of the "Will" system.

information flows do more than initiate and guide activities within the system. They also permit a system to learn and to change its goals in accordance with changing needs and human and material resources.

To allow for the fact that political systems are in constant flux—rather than in equilibrium as postulated by earlier theories—Deutsch explained that political messages must anticipate developments rather than dealing with situations existing at the time decisions are made. In fact, decision makers in organizations must take into account that there are always time *lags* between the generation and receipt of feedback and other information on the one hand and the response to this information on the other. If no adjustments are made for these time lags, decisions may provide solutions geared to conditions that no longer exist. A plan to abandon tuberculosis hospitals, for example, may come years too late to save the cost of maintaining empty hospitals. It may fail to anticipate the renewed need for such hospitals because the disease is reemerging as a public health menace.

To compensate for unavoidable lags in the communication process, decisions must *lead,* or be ahead of, current goals. Most of the time, governments are not very effective in anticipating the leads needed to solve problems. Frequently there are gaps between information available to intelligence-gathering agencies and information available to operating agencies. When leads are excessive, overly large *gains* may ensue so that the target is missed. Such oversteering is uncommon in the United States, where most changes are incremental because bureaucrats lean toward excessive caution and because the wishes of numerous conflicting pressure groups need to be considered in many public policy decisions.

Deutsch's analysis of communication flows in public organizations also points out that information passes through a variety of channels whose configuration is highly significant. Messages cannot reach their destination if communication channels are unavailable or if they lack the capacity to handle the flow of essential messages. This is well illustrated in crises such as earthquakes or floods when rescue services may be unable to communicate with victims because telephone channels are jammed or disrupted and roads are too clogged to permit messengers to reach their destination. During the stock-market crash of 1987, when an exceptionally large number of investors tried to reach their brokers quickly to conserve their funds in a rapidly plunging market, phone lines were so jammed that many investors were unable to make connections. Millions of dollars were lost as a consequence.

If units within a political system are improperly connected, messages may miss the appropriate target. In the space-shuttle disaster, for example, connections were faulty between the three relevant units—the subcontractor for the booster rockets, the Marshall Space Flight Center, and NASA officials at the launch site. Messages about possible launching problems never reached the officials actually in charge of the final launching of the spacecraft.

The structure of the network of communications within an organization determines the patterns through which messages are diffused. Generally, leaders are at the hub of communications and therefore receive comparatively large amounts of information for decision making. If important information fails to reach them, their decision making is apt to suffer. People who are not connected to the channels through which essential information flows may be unable to participate effectively in organizational decision making. Channels of communication vary in the number of people they connect and in the character of the information flow they carry. Flow may be predominantly in one direction, taking the form of commands, or it may be reciprocal, involving exchanges of information among individuals.

Communication factors can be used as indicators of how well political organizations function. For instance, performance is affected by the time it takes for policy makers to become aware of new conditions. Once aware, how fast can and do they make appropriate decisions? How fast do different parts of the organization respond? Do communication lags vary depending on the configuration of transmission channels? Would changes in channel configurations improve the situation?

Deutsch also addresses the issue of the quality of information available to public officials, which we shall encounter again in the next chapter. To be useful, messages circulating throughout the system must be clear so that the sender's intended meanings are transmitted to receivers. Information must also be timely. It is useless if it reaches its destination too late. An announcement that research money is available for projects of interest to an agency is worthless if it arrives after the deadline is passed or can no longer be met. Furthermore, information must be complete, accurate, and reliable. Much that circulates through the halls of government is not. Congressional hearings during the Reagan administration exposed many instances of incomplete, inaccurate, and unreliable foreign affairs information circulating at the highest levels of government. National Security Council personnel withheld information from the president about diversion of proceeds from arms sales to Iran to Nicaragua's anti-Communist contra fighters. Similarly, Congress was kept uninformed and misled by false testimony, and important documents were shredded so that they would be unavailable once an investigation had gotten underway.

Whether or not messages will have an impact hinges on a number of conditions. Deutsch pointed out that impact requires that the organization be receptive to the communication. This means that it should be flexible enough to permit new information to trigger change and that existing knowledge within the organization allows it to attend to the new message in appropriate ways. It is also important that the organization not be overloaded with messages. Impact also hinges on available resources. If all resources within an organization are committed and cannot be reallocated, no new goals can be achieved. Much information is lost in the transmission process as such and in the decoding process. Good communication systems minimize such losses.

One of the most potentially fruitful aspects of Deutsch's analysis of political communication systems is his discussion of problems likely to plague these organizations. Problems can be discovered by tracing the paths of communication flows through political systems, examining the substance of meanings conveyed and analyzing how the information is used. Communication problems spring from the structural characteristics of public organizations as well as from imperfect functioning. Functional problems are often caused by the manner in which people ordinarily process information.

One of the most common problems, both structural and functional, relates to channel capacity. There may be too few channels to carry all necessary messages, or the capacity of individual channels for carrying messages may be unduly limited. Inadequate channel capacity produces message overloads that clog the system. Inadequate telephone lines to public agencies to handle peak demands are common despite new technologies for automatic channeling of messages and computerized responses to routine inquiries. For instance, lines to the Internal Revenue Service commonly are overloaded when the filing deadline approaches. The overload problem is compounded by the fact that few organizations have been able to develop satisfactory ways to screen incoming messages so that those deserving priority can be identified and channeled accordingly. The common practice of giving automatic priority to messages by technical experts, ignoring the insights of policy experts and politically knowledgeable insiders, can be disastrous. When channel capacity is insufficient, priority tends to be given to immediate problems that surface first, while long-range problems languish until they have become pressing emergencies.

Another serious problem that is largely structural is the scarcity of channels for funneling citizen communications into the decision-making system. This problem is prevalent in both democratic and authoritarian countries. Despite recent efforts to ease access to government agencies, disadvantaged groups in particular often find it difficult to route their concerns appropriately so that they receive consideration. In most instances, elections are the only publicly provided channel through which these groups are heard. Compared with resource-rich groups, they lack the alternative to create effective lobbies.

Among functional problems, message distortion due to faulty encoding or decoding of messages ranks high. Opportunities to misunderstand and be misunderstood are legion in a society where the contexts in which messages are framed and received vary greatly and may be in constant flux. Since meanings often depend on context, misinformation or lack of information about context usually leads to faulty message interpretation. A complaint about gasoline fumes penetrating residences usually signals a nuisance that can wait for action by appropriate agencies. But the context in which the complaint is made may alter the situation radically. When such a complaint follows an explosion and fire in a nearby refinery, it may constitute an emergency requiring immediate attention. A misunderstanding of this context could prove fatal.

Finally, human psychological propensities get in the way of accurate perception of meanings. "Group think" is a common organizational manifestation that often impairs decision making. Psychological pressures to conform to beliefs presumed to be held in common by the group may lead individuals to structure their perceptions accordingly. When that happens, screening of information becomes biased so that elements supporting the tenor of the group's beliefs are given priority in selection and emphasis.

The characteristics and problems identified by Deutsch suggest major aspects of organizational communication systems that need to be examined to ascertain the nature, capacity, and problems of the system and the potential for improvement. Analysts need to know the substance and format of the information that travels through the organization, the points where messages originate and are delivered, the adequacy of the channels, the actual and potential bottlenecks, and the impact of human information processing on message meanings circulating within an organization. Information about these matters should permit improvements in the organizational communication system.

Richard Fagen, in *Politics and Communication,* illustrates another approach to using communication factors to assess how well political organizations function.[25] His approach can be readily adapted to judge the degree of democracy in public agencies. Fagen asked questions about the quantity and quality of communications bearing on crucial governmental decisions and about popular participation in the political dialogue. The underlying assumption is that democratic governance requires open communication systems to which citizens have ready access. Fagen's inquiry is based on six questions:

1. What role does communication play in the initial choice of leaders and in subsequent changes of leadership?
2. Who defines political problems and ways to deal with them?
3. Who participates in making public policy?
4. What is the scope of allowable criticism?
5. How do citizens become informed about the political world?
6. Who may choose to become isolated from politics?

The first question obviously relates to the extent of debate at the time of choosing leaders to guide the policies of the organization. Wide-ranging

discussion and broad participation are considered the hallmarks of democratic governance. If they are lacking, the organization cannot claim to be
genuinely democratic. The second question asks who sets the agenda for an
organization's work by defining its mission. This is a particularly important
question in public bodies because their mandate is rarely clearly defined.
Stating that an agency must protect public safety or enhance public
welfare carries little concrete meaning. Officials who control the agenda
therefore enjoy great power through determining the thrust of the agency's
activities. The third question probes a bit more deeply to ascertain which
organization members contribute ideas to decision making within the
organization after the basic guidelines and goals have been set. This relates
to issues of internal network structure, to be discussed in Chapter 5, and to
issues of internal influence patterns reflected in networks. Question 4 raises
concerns about freedom to express dissent and about formal and informal
censorship. The prospects for good governance are better when organizations permit and even encourage the expression of dissenting views.
Question 5 relates to the availability and use of communication channels
between public agencies and the citizenry. Question 6, which is somewhat
less germane to communication issues within organizations, concerns
compulsory participation. This issue tends to be crucial in totalitarian
societies, which often deny the freedom to remain passive.

It should be readily apparent that the systems approach used by
Deutsch, Fagen, and others lends itself nicely to the comparison of
communication patterns in various types of political organizations. One
may judge how simple or complex these patterns are, relative to other
organizations, and how cultural, social, economic, and political factors
affect the nature of organizational communication systems. One can
compare how organizations allot resources to communication functions and
how they distribute them among information production, reception, and
dissemination. Allocation patterns thus reveal where the organization's
priorities lie. One can also assess differences among various organization
members in access to information and ability to disseminate their views to
various potential receivers. The findings may provide clues to the degree of
democracy within the organization and the extent of internal cohesion.
Cohesive organizations are able to transmit information accurately about a
wide variety of topics to most of their members without major losses or
distortions and without a great deal of noise.

Decision-making Studies. A second branch of political communication studies
that deserves credit for major contributions to the field of organizational
communication focuses on information management at top levels of
government. Here one must include Richard Neustadt's *Presidential
Power,* published in 1960, which relates presidential power to access to
information and to control of information flows. In fact, Neustadt states

categorically that "presidential power is the power to persuade."[26] One should also include studies by Robert Kennedy, Graham Allison, and Irving Janis, which analyze information flows and decision making during the Cuban missile crisis in 1962.[27] Other pioneering works dealing with information management when major decisions must be made are Alexander L. George's *Presidential Decisionmaking in Foreign Policy* and Lloyd S. Etheredge's *Can Governments Learn?*[28] All of these studies focus on ways in which information is collected, processed, and guided to assure that the appropriate people are involved, the right kind of information is conveyed at the proper time, and various common problems that lead to information distortion and faulty decisions are avoided. This work provides the foundation for the analysis of decision making presented in Chapter 4.[29]

Information-management concerns also guide decision-making studies dealing more specifically with organizational communication, although most of them do not focus on problems encountered in the public sector. Organizational communication studies relevant to situations in the public sector include Herbert Simon's pioneering work, *Administrative Behavior,* and studies by Everett and Rekha Rogers, R. Wayne Pace and Don Faules, and Gerald Goldhaber, which focus more specifically on organizational communication.[30] Several major organizational behavior studies also devote substantial attention to organizational communication. They include Daniel Katz and Robert Kahn's *The Social Psychology of Organizations,* Jeffrey Pfeffer's *Power in Organizations,* and Karl Weick's *The Social Psychology of Organizing.*[31]

Studies of Intraorganizational Communication

Most studies dealing with organizational communication in general focus primarily on internal communication. Their major concerns relate to managing internal information flows in individual institutions in ways that will motivate workers to perform well. Historically, three major theoretical approaches have dominated these studies of intraorganizational communication patterns, each based on a different view of the human motivations and types of behavior that should be considered in devising effective internal communication systems. The main approaches to intraorganizational communication are the Scientific Management School launched by Frederick Taylor in 1911; the Human Relations School started by Chester Barnard and Elton Mayo in the 1930s; and the Systems School, which combines elements of its two predecessors. Its godparents were biologist/philosopher Ludwig van Bertalanffy, logician Anatol Rapoport, philosopher/economist Kenneth Boulding, and sociologist Talcott Parsons. Table 1-2 outlines the basic features of these schools.[32] Based on these theories and their ethical implications, organization leaders have adopted different management and communication strategies and styles. For exam-

Table 1-2 Three Main Schools of Organizational Behavior

	Scientific Management	Human Relations	Systems
Basic principles and assumptions about human behavior	A mechanistic view of behavior: man is economically motivated and will respond with maximum performance if material rewards are closely related to work efforts. Favors human engineering of worker effort and time to achieve maximum production, efficiency, and profit for the managers/owners.	A social view of man: informal groups affect production rates; attention to workers' needs and job satisfaction can motivate higher performance; worker participation in decision making; realization that the individual's goals may differ from the organization's goals; workers motivated by social needs and by their peer relationships.	The organization is an open system in continuous interaction with its environment; the system and its environment codetermine each other. The system must be analyzed as a whole in order to be understood properly. The organization is composed of subsystems, which are interdependent; individuals are the carriers of the organization.
Main research methods	Observation (including time-and-motion studies); participation; some surveys.	Survey interviews and questionnaires; observation; participation; diary keeping; sociometric analysis of leadership and communication patterns.	Network analysis of sociometric data from survey interviews and questionnaires; systems analysis; computer simulation
Main types of organizations	Industrial firms and public utilities.	Manufacturing plants (especially assembly-line operations), including some outside the United States.	Industrial, military, and government organizations; hospitals; educational and mental institutions; prisons.
Bias of the school	Pro-management; "management knows best."	Pro-workers; sympathetic to them.	Pro-"organization"; the organization exists as an entity that consists of more than just its present individual members.
View of organizational communication	Emphasis on written, formal channels of communication: impersonal, work-related messages initiated by higher-ups and sent down the chain of command.	Informal communication as well as formal; stress on interpersonal channels, especially with peers. Rumor and the grapevine exist.	Communication interrelates the subsystems. Communication across the organization's boundary with its environment is also important.

(continues)

Table 1-2 (continued)

	Scientific Management	Human Relations	Systems
Importance of communication	Relatively unimportant and largely restricted to downward communication from management to workers.	Relatively important, but mainly limited to peer communication; some attention to communication of needs from workers to management.	Very important; communication is considered the cement that holds the units in an organization together.
Purpose of communication	To relay orders and information about work tasks and to achieve obedience and coordination in carrying out such work.	To satisfy workers' needs, to provide for lateral interaction among peers in work groups, and to facilitate the participation of members in organizational decision making. A high degree of receiver orientation in communication from management.	To control and coordinate; to provide information to decision makers; and to adjust the organization to changes in its environment.
Direction of communication flows	Downward from management to workers, in order to persuade or convince them to follow instructions.	Horizontal among peers who belong to informal work groups; vertical between workers and management to assess worker needs and to make possible participatory decision making.	All directions within the system, including downward and upward across hierarchical levels, and across the organization's boundary with the environment.
Main communication problems thought to exist	Breakdown in communication due to bypassing a hierarchical level and a too-large span of control.	Rumors communicated through the "grapevine"; a partially ineffective formal communication structure.	Overload, distortion, and omission; unresponsiveness to negative feedback.

Source: Adapted from Everett M. and Rekha Agarwala Rogers, *Communication in Organizations* (New York: Free Press, 1976), 30-31, 56. Reprinted with permission.

ple, Theory X managers, who believe that people perform best in a restrictive, rule-dominated environment, provide close supervision and restrict communication flows. Theory Y managers, who believe that an environment fostering personal growth is best, strive to humanize the workplace by encouraging communication between superiors and subordinates. They also permit subordinates to share in decisions about their work.

The Scientific Management School, also called Taylorism, introduced scientific methods into the management of organizations. Taylor believed that workers were predominantly motivated by financial rewards. It was therefore important to analyze each job scientifically so that performance standards could be set and achievement of these standards measured accurately. Pay scales were to reflect performance achievements. Taylor viewed intraorganizational communication purely from a task-performance perspective, ignoring humanistic considerations. He recommended that communication be structured so as to be impersonal and task oriented. Messages were to be used largely to inform workers about their jobs and to coordinate the work performed by members of the organization. There was no need to consider that workers might feel alienated by such an impersonal environment.

Taylor emphasized written, formal channels, hierarchically organized so that authoritative messages relaying instructions to the work force would travel from top to bottom. To avoid too many links in a hierarchy, which might lead to breakdowns in communication, Taylor recommended that each superior have no more than five or six subordinates. Top management should be kept fully informed about everything in the organization. *Staff* officials engaged in organizational support functions such as personnel administration, financial management, or research should therefore communicate their expertise upward. *Line* officials, charged with overseeing the basic work, should pass task-related information downward.

To get around channeling all messages through the top and risking information overload, management theorist Henri Fayol later suggested that it might be useful to relay messages horizontally in emergency situations. However, higher-ups were to be informed about this deviation from hierarchical flows. These horizontal links among officials at similar levels in the organization's hierarchy became known as Fayol's Bridge.[33]

Taylorism became the target of union wrath because it was perceived as treating people as if they were machines. Managers seemed to be concerned only with high rates of production and to care little about the well-being and communication needs of subordinates. Eventually the pendulum swung in the opposite direction. The classical theories of organization and management were replaced by modern behavioral and systems theories.

Chester Barnard's experiences while working at New Jersey Bell Telephone Company and Elton Mayo's studies of employees' responses to making the workplace more interesting at Western Electric's Hawthorne plant in

Cicero, Illinois, demonstrated the importance of psychological factors in the workplace. Concern about people seemed more important for stimulating productivity than concern about organizational structures and positions. The Human Relations School demonstrated that workers' performance improved if jobs were made exciting and humanly rewarding in terms of interpersonal relationships. Moreover, individual performance norms tended to reflect group performance norms. In fact, the Hawthorne studies demonstrated that morale and productivity hinged more on intergroup communication than on the quality of the workplace surroundings. Accordingly, organizational communication, at formal as well as informal levels, had to address the needs of workers as individuals and as members of informal groups. It had to be couched in language that would appeal to workers. The study and assessment of intraorganizational communication factors became an important facet of any assessment of organizational effectiveness.

To increase their satisfaction with the job, workers' input into decision making was essential, even though it was clear that individual goals would often differ from organizational goals. Barnard, in his book *The Functions of the Executive,* pointed out that authority is most effective when it rests on willing cooperation by subordinates.[34] He called this the *acceptance theory of authority.* Good message systems are necessary to elicit willing cooperation. Barnard also noted that effective communication can widen what he called the *zone of indifference.* This is the range of options that people are quite willing to accept because they have no strong preferences.

A Human Resources Subschool argued that all human resources within an organization must be marshaled through formal and informal communications traveling upward, downward, and horizontally, so that managers, as well as workers, can benefit from better relations. The chief proponents of this Human Resources group were Douglas McGregor of the Massachusetts Institute of Technology, Rensis Likert of the University of Michigan, and Chris Argyris, who was affiliated with both Yale and Harvard Universities. Likert advocated participatory management. Commitment to the organization and maintenance of group cohesion were important goals. To achieve them, organizational leaders must move beyond attention to formal communication and concern themselves with informal communication as well. For example, rumors and grapevine messages deserve attention, especially when they deal with serious issues such as the possibility of plant closings.[35]

The Human Relations School as well as its Human Resources Subschool were criticized for overemphasizing people and disregarding other organizational resources. To correct this perceived imbalance, E. Wight Bakke and Chris Argyris proposed the "fusion theory," arguing that the influence between people and organizations is reciprocal. Individuals become socialized to accept organizational norms, and these norms are personalized by the people who make up the organization. Their efforts are closely related to those of the scholars discussed next.[36]

The Systems School combined many elements of the Scientific Management and Human Relations schools but put them into a broader systems perspective, akin to the approaches of Deutsch, Fagen, and others already discussed. The organization must be considered as a whole and from all aspects including structural features and human relations. The ongoing relationships among subunits and among structures and functions are crucial. Organizations can be studied either as "closed" systems, largely ignoring their environment, or as "open" systems whose functioning depends on the environment in which they operate. As discussed more fully in Chapter 5, since every system is part of a larger system, it is often difficult to define its boundaries. Frequency of communications may provide clues. Frequencies tend to be greater inside the boundaries than across boundaries.

The early studies called everything outside an organization's boundary its *environment*. Later studies restricted the term to other individuals and organizations with which systems interact in making decisions. This is the *relevant environment*. It encompasses all physical and social factors outside the system's boundary that individuals within the system consider in decision making.[37] The limits of the environment are set by the perceptions of organization insiders. They can be detected by examining the external communication relationships that insiders report or by analyzing communication patterns to detect interactions with other organizations.

Proponents of a systems approach contend that organizations must be analyzed as a whole to understand relationships among the component parts, which may constitute subsystems in their own right, and to understand the interrelations among various functions. For example, decision making within a system must be viewed from technical and legal, as well as political, perspectives. Organizations are systems that perform work, set goals, settle conflicts, and allocate costs and benefits in a seamless web of activities.[38] Because open systems must continually adapt to their environment, they are in a constant state of more or less rapid flux. Studies must be repeated to capture these changes. While systems theorists acknowledge that the role of individuals is critical in organizations, they also contend that organizations have lives of their own that continue even when personnel changes.

Systems theorists such as Deutsch consider information processing to be the main function of organizations. As Daniel Katz and Robert Kahn note in their 1966 landmark book, *The Social Psychology of Organizations,* systems theorists view communication as the basic mechanism by which the work of many people can be coordinated within and among organizations. Communication is essential to sound, information-based decision making.[39]

Two subschools developed from the systems school. One was the technology subschool, which focused on the relationship between communication patterns and specific technologies used by organizations to perform tasks. Different patterns would evolve, for instance, depending on whether piecework or assembly-line performance was used. The second subschool focused on decision-making processes. Its chief proponents were people like Herbert Simon, whose books *Models of Man* and *Administrative Behavior* deal with rational human behavior in social settings, and Richard Cyert and James March, who developed *A Behavioral Theory of the Firm.*[40]

A final type of system, which is almost a nonsystem, has been called "ad-hocracy." [41] It refers to the fact that many communication structures are temporary, centered around specific tasks, in post-bureaucratic societies. New organizations are created whenever new tasks arise. The professionals who work in these temporary organizations are loyal to their professional creeds but not necessarily to the personnel in these agencies or the agencies themselves. Constant changes in organizations, which have become commonplace, make adaptation to new patterns a continuous burden.

Analysis of organizational communication may encompass all three intraorganizational theories simultaneously. The Senate's investigation of the Watergate scandal is a case in point. As communications scholar Gerald Goldhaber has pointed out, like adherents of the scientific management school, senators looked into the hierarchical communication structure of the White House, the formal duties assigned to White House aides, and the nature and flow of directives from the president's office. The Senate used the human relations approach when it asked various defendants about the personal motives that prompted their actions. The social systems approach was evident in questions probing the relation between the burglary at Watergate and other issues, such as who ordered the burglary and who was attempting to cover it up. The answers revealed a complex web of interrelationships at the highest levels of the political system.[42]

Interpretive Approaches

The pendulum of communication theories has swung once again. The Systems School has been found wanting by many scholars and administrators who decry the fact that it is anchored in capitalist notions of efficiency, with human relations concerns merely a tool to realize maximum production. Interpretive and critical theories make human beings and their welfare, as they perceive it, once again the focus of organizational concern as well as the chief object of organizational communication studies. Organizational health and efficiency are secondary. These theorists are chiefly interested in ascertaining the meanings created through human interaction. They believe that greater sensitivity and responsiveness to workers' feelings and perceptions will lead to more egalitarian organizational relationships and to a better society overall.[43] Since communication patterns must vary depending on the goals to be achieved, information flows and research that seem ideal from an interpretist or critical perspective are unlikely to be seen as ideal from other perspectives.

According to interpretive theories, organizations develop from social relationships in which people integrate their behavior to achieve shared goals. There is no organizational reality, as positivist theorists, who focus inquiry on observable phenomena, would argue. Rather, organizational reality is whatever members of the organization believe it to be. It is socially constructed through verbal and nonverbal communication among the members of the organization. Unlike the theories discussed earlier, which view communication as a conduit of task-related information to maintain existing structures and motivate personnel to achieve organizational goals, the focus in interpretive studies is on the ways in which shared understanding affects workers whose interaction constitutes the organization.

Roles, norms, and values must be studied subjectively by observing and interacting with workers rather than by so-called objective criteria interpreted from the researcher's perspectives. Descriptions and interpretation are deemed more significant than traditional hypothesis testing. Moreover, managerial perspectives should not be accorded preferential status, compared with the perceptions of ordinary workers, as has been customary in the past. The fact that subordinates must balance their organizational goals against private and community goals, which are equally or more important, must also be considered.

Among those who have been active in bringing these ideas to the fore in the scholarly community are Karl Weick, author of *The Social Psychology of Organizing,* and David Silverman, who wrote *The Theory of Organisations.*[44] Weick argues that interactive communication behaviors, rather than static institutions, are the keys to understanding organizational behavior. Human beings organize because they need information to cope with a complex and uncertain environment, as they perceive it. The exchange of information, in which senders convey messages to receivers who respond in ways that indicate whether shared meanings have been transmitted, is called a *double interact.* Weick deems this interpersonal feedback process crucial to the creation of shared meanings.

Silverman, too, points out that institutions are symbolic artifacts created through shared meanings, even though people experience them as social facts. Contrary to the assertion by positivistic scholars, action is not determined by external forces; rather, it is determined by the meanings that people assign to their acts. Survival of the organization becomes a desirable goal only if it evolves from the meshed goals of organization members. Organizational survival, for its own sake, or for various capitalist objectives that run counter to the goals of organization members, becomes a form of intolerable repression of workers.[45]

Interpretists have used many research approaches to study organizations. These include hermeneutics, the study of the verbal construction of social meanings; ethnomethodology, the study of how people explain their daily experiences; phenomenology, the study of observable happenings; and symbolic interactionism, the study of how people use symbols to communicate with one another. In each of these approaches, the study of verbal interaction is central. For instance, interpretists can study how people interact in organizations by paying attention to the meanings they assign to verbal interactions or by studying the symbols they commonly use during discourse.

The interpretive school is bifurcated into naturalistic and critical approaches. Naturalists are concerned with recording existing interactions and the perceptions they generate. They observe actual organizational behavior much as anthropologists would, and then describe and explain what they have seen. Critical researchers are concerned with what interactions ought to be. The Institute for Social Research at the University of Frankfurt in Germany has been the intellectual fountainhead of critical theory. It became the home of the Frankfurt School in the 1920s, guided by philosophers such as Jürgen Habermas, author of *Toward a Rational Society,* and scholars such as Max Horkheimer, who wrote *Critical Theory.*[46] In the late 1970s Robert B. Denhardt and several colleagues applied Habermas's ideas to the field of public administration.[47] The Denhardt group argued that the public's distrust of bureaucracies was largely due to faulty communication, resulting from insufficient input by citizens into decision making and insufficient concern about their views.

Many critical researchers believe that current approaches to studying and practicing organizational communication serve to perpetuate a repressive capitalist system. Alleging that organizations are structured to generate norms that support submission to established authorities, they advocate a change to various types of socialism, including Marxism, where presumably communication patterns are designed to enhance the workers' freedom.

A critical perspective encourages the questioning of prevalent practices and assumptions and attempts to pinpoint false understandings. It looks at communication from the perspectives of the organization's workers and clients rather than its managers. It also examines constraints on the communication process that are undemocratic because they affect individuals within the organization unequally. Critical researchers allege that current organizational communication flows lead to distortions of reality and suggest ways in which such distortions can be eliminated.

An Embarrassment of Riches

The various theories discussed add up to an embarrassment of riches. There are unbridgeable disagreements about many fundamental issues. Theorists disagree about the focus of research, advocating a range of perspectives from the individual to the group to the entire organization to the total system in which it is embedded. They differ on whether the organization's welfare should be more important, or whether one can even regard organizations as having an existence aside from the perceptions of their members.

They also disagree about whether social scientists should be neutral observers of the phenomena they study or whether, as critical theorists argue, they should be concerned with making value judgments and suggesting changes in accordance with these judgments. If the recommendations of critical theorists were put into practice, organizational communication in the public sector would take on totally new forms. What are now the lower levels of organizational hierarchies would become dominant in decision making, and the focus would be on humanistic values rather than current notions of efficiency, impartiality, and rule predictability. Democracy in social relationships would be deemed more important than technical efficiency and outputs of goods and services.

As Michael Harmon and Richard Mayer note, "[T]he relationship of the individual to the organization . . . is perhaps the most problematic issue for a theory of public organization." [48] The early theorists assumed that organizational and individual needs were compatible and looked for ways to integrate these needs. Critical theorists view organizations as sources of repression. However, while their critiques are devastating, they have drafted few blueprints for building the ideal organization that they envision.

Summary and Conclusions

Every study needs a historical and theoretical context to provide an appropriate perspective for the ensuing analysis and a definition of terms to tune the author and readers to compatible intellectual frequencies. Accordingly, this chapter opened with a discussion of the importance of organizational communication in public sector agencies and the need for effective communication management.

In discussing the major differences between the private and the public sectors, it was pointed out that public agencies are an integral part of a political system that puts a premium on divided authority, stresses open communication, and deprives public agencies of major control over their personnel. Public agencies must therefore structure their messages to keep a host of diverse constituencies appeased. They must also coordinate their work with the activities of related agencies at national, state, and local levels. It is a formidable task.

The history of organizational communication studies was traced in terms of its bearing on public sector organizations. From a political science perspective, systems-level studies of the impact of information flows are most important. Karl Deutsch's pioneering work in *The Nerves of Government* was cited as a particularly rich source of concepts that have continued to attract the attention of researchers. The introduction calls attention to a number of important studies of decision making because this phase of organizational communication has benefited from a great deal of analysis.

The focus then turns to a series of studies of intraorganizational communication and the theories that have guided them. These studies have been greatly enriched by their interdisciplinary approach, with input from sociologists as well as communication specialists. Historically, studies of intraorganizational communication flows have been grounded in three types of orientations. The Scientific Management School views messages largely as a means to accomplish work-related tasks. The Human Relations School emphasizes human needs, seeing messages as contributing to the psychological welfare and work satisfaction of members of the organization. The Systems School looks at communication from a larger perspective that combines concern about the psychological welfare of members with concerns about organizational goals in general.

Most studies of organizational communication have reflected a positivist scientific perspective. However, in recent years, a number of scholars have argued that it is unsuitable for studying human interactions. From this "interpretist" perspective, what matters most is how people perceive and conceptualize relationships, so that the focus of communication studies should be on perceptual elements. Other scholars opt for "critical" approaches that examine the social flaws of existing systems and attempt to remedy them by prescribing new systems. The concluding section of this chapter reminds the reader that organizational communication, like any young field, has been approached from many perspectives without as yet developing any consensus about the relative merits of these approaches.

What lessons can be drawn from this chapter? It seems clear that communication is increasingly crucial for attaining the goals of the public sector in American society. Patterns of organizational communication influence patterns of political power. Organizational communication and information management are linked to the efficiency and effectiveness of organizational performance. When communication is flawed, major and minor disasters ensue. Despite its importance, and the fact that administrators have long paid heed to its significance, organizational communication in the public sector remains neglected by scholars of the political scene. The time is ripe for a change.

This chapter has shown that sound tools for analysis of public sector organizational communication are available, even though they need to be honed further. A variety of useful theories have been expounded that can guide scholars in selecting facets of communication for further study.

Chapter 1 also reveals the complexity of communication problems faced by public officials. Regardless of the quality of analysis of these problems and the soundness of remedies prescribed, major communication problems will always plague the public sector. When they occur, they should be used constructively to learn how best to cope with them, not destructively to bash public agencies. Obviously, there is room for improvement in public agencies in the wake of better studies of their problems, but they are far better than the impressions conveyed when communication horror stories are told.

Notes

1. Barbara S. Romzek and Melvin Dubnick, "Accountability in the Public Sector: Lessons from the Challenger Tragedy," *Public Administration Review* 47 (May/June 1987): 227, 233. The full report is available in U.S. Congress, House, Committee on Science and Technology, *Investigation of the Challenger Accident,* Report, 99th Congress, 2d session (Washington, D.C.: Government Printing Office, 1978).
2. David E. Sanger, "Communications Channels at NASA: Warnings that Faded Along the Line," *New York Times,* February 28, 1986.
3. James Fisher, "Is Safety NASA's Nemesis?" *Chicago Tribune,* February 7, 1988.
4. Daniel Katz and Robert L. Kahn, *The Social Psychology of Organizations* (New York: Wiley, 1978), 428.
5. John M. Stevens and Robert P. McGowan, *Information Systems and Public Management* (New York: Praeger, 1985), 7.
6. Katz and Kahn, *The Social Psychology of Organizations,* 431-432.
7. Harold D. Lasswell, "The Structure and Function of Communication in Society," in *Mass Communications,* eds. Wilbur Schramm and Donald F. Roberts (Urbana: University of Illinois Press, 1971), 84; Claude E. Shannon and Warren Weaver, *The Mathematical Theory of Communication* (Urbana: University of Illinois Press, 1949).
8. Everett M. Rogers and Rekha Agarwala Rogers, *Communication in Organizations* (New York: Free Press, 1976), 6-7.
9. For arguments that the differences between public and private organizations have nearly disappeared because all are public now, to a degree, see Barry Bozeman, *All Organizations Are Public: Bridging Public and Private Organizational Theories* (San Francisco: Jossey-Bass, 1987), and Michael A. Murray, "Comparing Public and Private Management: An Exploratory Essay," *Public Administration Review* 34 (July/August 1975): 364-371.
10. Romzek and Dubnick, "Accountability in the Public Sector," 233.
11. James Q. Wilson, *Bureaucracy: What Government Agencies Do and Why They Do It* (New York: Basic Books, 1989), 135.
12. William Eddy, *Public Organization Behavior* (Cambridge, Mass.: Winthrop, 1982), 4-15.
13. Herbert Kaufman, *The Administrative Behavior of Federal Bureau Chiefs* (Washington, D.C.: The Brookings Institution, 1981), 28.
14. W. Michael Blumenthal, "Candid Reflections of a Businessman in Washington," *Fortune* (January 29, 1979): 39.

15. Nathaniel C. Nash, "New Postal Chief Looks at the Really Big Picture," *New York Times,* July 27, 1988.

16. Stevens and McGowan, *Information Systems and Public Management,* 5.

17. Romzek and Dubnick, "Accountability in the Public Sector," 234.

18. John Rawls, in *A Theory of Justice* (Cambridge: Belknap Press of Harvard University Press, 1971), argues that social harmony is fostered when individuals or groups possess complementary information.

19. Washington State Commission for Efficiency and Accountability in Government, "State Mail Operations Review," *Efficiency Quarterly* (August 1990).

20. Richard F. Fenno, *Homestyle: House Members in Their Districts* (Boston: Little, Brown, 1978).

21. Representative works include: Harold D. Lasswell et al., *The Language of Politics: Studies in Quantitative Semantics* (Cambridge: MIT Press, 1965); Edward Sapir, *Culture, Language and Personality: Selected Essays,* ed. David Mandelbaum (Berkeley: University of California Press, 1962); Kenneth Burke, *Language as Symbolic Action* (Berkeley: University of California Press, 1966); Ernst Cassirer, *Language and Myth* (New York: Harper, 1946); Alfred North Whitehead, *Symbolism: Its Meaning and Effect* (New York: Macmillan, 1958); Susan Langer, *Philosophy in a New Key: A Study in the Sociology of Reason, Rite, and Art* (Cambridge: Harvard University Press, 1951); Kenneth Boulding, *The Image: Knowledge in Life and Society* (Ann Arbor: University of Michigan Press, 1956); Murray Edelman, *The Symbolic Uses of Politics* (Urbana: University of Illinois Press, 1964).

22. Karl W. Deutsch, *The Nerves of Government: Models of Political Communication and Control* (New York: Free Press, 1966).

23. Among these scholars, Lucian Pye, *Communication and Political Development* (Princeton, N.J.: Princeton University Press, 1963), Daniel Lerner, *The Human Meaning of the Social Sciences* (New York: Meridian Books, 1959), and Wilbur Schramm, *Mass Media and National Development: The Role of Information in Developing Countries* (Stanford, Calif.: Stanford University Press, 1964), studied communication patterns in governmental systems as a whole, while Richard Fagen, *Politics and Communication: An Analytic Study* (Boston: Little, Brown, 1966), and Gabriel Almond and James Coleman, eds., *The Politics of the Developing Areas* (Princeton, N.J.: Princeton University Press, 1960), focused on parts of political systems from a communications perspective. Also see David Easton, *A Systems Analysis of Political Life* (New York: John Wiley, 1965).

24. Part III of Deutsch, *Nerves of Government,* is most relevant.

25. Fagen, *Politics and Communication,* 17-33.

26. Richard Neustadt, *Presidential Power* (New York: Wiley, 1960), chap. 3.

27. Robert F. Kennedy, *Thirteen Days* (New York: W. W. Norton, 1969); Graham Allison, *Essence of Decision: Explaining the Cuban Missile Crisis* (Boston: Little, Brown, 1971); Irving L. Janis, *Groupthink: Psychological Studies of Policy Decisions and Fiascoes* (Boston: Houghton Mifflin, 1983); Irving L. Janis, *Crucial Decisions: Leadership in Policymaking and Crisis Management* (New York: Free Press, 1989).

28. Alexander L. George, *Presidential Decisionmaking in Foreign Policy: The Effective Use of Information and Advice* (Boulder, Colo.: Westview, 1980); Lloyd Etheredge, *Can Governments Learn?: American Foreign Policy and Central American Revolutions* (New York: Pergamon, 1985).

29. These studies are based on a variety of decision-making theories. See Robert P. Abelson and A. Levi, "Decision-making and Decision Theory," in Gardner

Lindzey and Elliott Aronson, eds. *Handbook of Social Psychology*, 3d ed., vol. 1 (New York: Random House, 1986), 231-310 for an overview.

30. Herbert A. Simon, *Administrative Behavior: A Study of Decision Making Processes in Administrative Organizations*, 2d ed. (New York: Macmillan, 1957); Rogers and Rogers, *Communication in Organizations* (New York: Free Press, 1976); R. Wayne Pace and Don F. Faules, *Organizational Communication*, 2d ed. (Englewood Cliffs, N.J.: Prentice-Hall, 1989); Gerald M. Goldhaber, *Organizational Communication*, 3d ed. (Dubuque, Iowa: Wm. C. Brown, 1983).

31. Katz and Kahn, *The Social Psychology of Organizations;* Jeffrey Pfeffer, *Power in Organizations* (Marshfield, Mass.: Pitman, 1981); Karl Weick, *The Social Psychology of Organizing*, 2d ed. (Reading, Mass.: Addison-Wesley, 1979).

32. Frederick C. Taylor, *Scientific Management* (New York: Harper, 1911); Chester L. Barnard, *The Functions of the Executive* (Cambridge: Harvard University Press, 1938); Elton Mayo, *The Social Problems of an Industrial Civilization* (Cambridge: Harvard University Press, 1945); Ludwig van Bertalanffy, *General Systems Theory* (New York: Braziller, 1968); Anatol Rapoport, "Modern Systems Theory—An Outlook for Coping with Change," *General Systems* 15 (1970): 15-26; Boulding, *The Image: Knowledge in Life and Society;* Talcott Parsons, *The Social System* (New York: Free Press, 1951). For a more detailed discussion of these various schools, see Rogers and Rogers, *Communication in Organizations*, 27-58.

33. Henri Fayol, *General and Industrial Management* (London: Pitman, 1949).

34. Barnard, *The Functions of the Executive*.

35. Douglas McGregor, *The Human Side of Enterprise* (New York: McGraw-Hill, 1960); Rensis Likert, *The Human Organization: Its Management and Value* (New York: McGraw-Hill, 1967); Chris Argyris, *Personality and Organization* (New York: Harper & Row, 1957).

36. E. Wight Bakke, *Bonds of Organization* (New York: Harper & Row, 1957); Argyris, *Personality and Organization*.

37. Works dealing with the organizational environment include anthropologist W. Lloyd Warner and J. O. Low's *The Social System of the Modern Factory* (New Haven: Yale University Press, 1947); also Tom Burns and G. M. Stalker, *The Management of Innovations* (London: Tavistock, 1961); and Paul Lawrence and Jay Lorsch, *Organization and Environment: Managing Differentiation and Integration* (Cambridge: Harvard University Press, 1967).

38. Charles Walcott and Karen M. Hult, "Organizing the White House: Structure, Environment, and Organizational Governance," *American Journal of Political Science* 31 (February 1987): 112-113.

39. Katz and Kahn, *The Social Psychology of Organizations*.

40. Simon, *Administrative Behavior;* Herbert A. Simon, *Models of Man: Social and Rational; Mathematical Essays on Rational Human Behavior in a Social Setting* (New York: Wiley, 1956); Richard Cyert and James March, *A Behavioral Theory of the Firm* (Englewood Cliffs, N.J.: Prentice-Hall, 1963).

41. Alvin Toffler, *Future Shock* (New York: Random House, 1970).

42. Gerald M. Goldhaber, *Organizational Communication*, 3d ed. (Dubuque, Iowa: Wm. C. Brown, 1983), 35.

43. See Michael T. Harmon and Richard T. Mayer, *Organizational Theory for Public Administration* (Boston: Little, Brown, 1986) for details.

44. Weick, *The Social Psychology of Organizing;* David Silverman, *The Theory of Organisations* (New York: Basic Books, 1971).

45. See Harmon and Mayer, *Organizational Theory for Public Administration*, 300.

46. Jürgen Habermas, *Toward a Rational Society: Student Protest, Science, and Politics* (Boston: Beacon, 1970); Max Horkheimer, *Critical Theory: Selected Essays* (New York: Herder, 1972).

47. Robert B. Denhardt, "Toward a Critical Theory of Public Organization," *Public Administration Review* 41 (1981): 628-632; Harmon and Mayer, *Organizational Theory for Public Administration*, 326.

48. Harmon and Mayer, *Organizational Theory for Public Administration*, 329.

C H A P T E R 2

Information-Gathering Problems

In the past, social scientists have been more concerned about public agencies' use and misuse of power rather than misuse of information. Yet control over information and the knowledge it produces gives power. It may enable the knowledgeable to set organizational goals, to control the performance of activities within the organization, and to make innovations. Hence, use, acquisition, and misuse of information should be major concerns.[1] In this chapter we will examine the types of information that public agencies need and the problems they face in getting high-quality information.

The Need for Technical and Political Information

In the public as well as in the private sector, organizations require a great deal of technical information to operate effectively. The Environmental Protection Agency, for example, deals with literally millions of toxic substances that threaten the soil, water, and air. It must know what these substances are and what should be done by millions of private enterprises to keep them under control. The agency must monitor its own programs and evaluate how well it is doing in its own estimation and in that of others of importance. The Department of Defense needs technical information to predict how many missiles of various types its potential enemies are likely to deploy over specified periods of time. Billions of dollars of defense expenditures, along with the security of the country, hinge on the accuracy of such forecasts.

The Department of Veterans Affairs serves 30 million former members of the armed forces and their families. Its more than 200,000 full-time employees administer a vast array of programs ranging from education and medical and disability benefits to low-interest home loans for veterans and their 50 million dependents and survivors. To run these agencies efficiently, a vast amount of technical information is needed.

This need is exceeded only by the need for political information, particularly in the public sector. Take the example of the EPA. Since the agency's mandate and funding depend on Congress, its policy-making officials must know what types of activities will please powerful congressional leaders and what will anger them to the point of retaliation against the agency. When a decision is made to attack pollution problems in a particular industry or company, the decision makers need to be aware of the political connections of that industry or company. It may be counterproductive to undertake projects to which there is powerful, politically well-connected opposition.[2]

Executives in public agencies need information about the political climate in which agencies operate and about the tactics that spell the greatest success, especially under adverse conditions. The Reagan years, for example, were billed as a period of bureaucratic contraction. A lot of political information was required to know the scope of contraction and to ascertain the not inconsiderable areas in which expansion remained possible. Executives must also discern the extent of the resource base available to them for carrying out particular policies and the potential for mobilizing political support for programs. For instance, they must know whether a certain program concerns opposing groups, such as business and labor. In that case, bureaucrats may have to steer a middle course between the interests of these groups. Bureaucrats need to know what kinds of appeals are most suitable for attracting support for a policy. They also need to know how these appeals should be framed to capture the attention and gain the support of appropriate publics and to avoid antagonizing potentially hostile groups.

Even the choice of what technical information to collect and how to use it is often a political decision. Agencies may decide to avoid technical information that promises to be politically harmful to the agency or its constituencies, or that might alienate its external support structure, such as Congress. For example, the Department of Education may be loath to collect data showing that infant education is more beneficial than nursery-school training when it is trying to gain support for an expanded nursery-school program.

Political considerations rather than analyses of technical data determine how an agency formulates goals and means of implementation. Decisions about who will collect information, and from whom, on which action will be based are also political. The choice of experts matters very much, especially when they are summoned while the problem is still being formulated. The way it is formulated determines what information will be gathered and narrows the options for dealing with the problem. For example, information needed to deal with the problem of alcoholism varies considerably depending on whether alcoholism is defined as a disease, a personal vice, or a social problem.

Information needs vary at different management levels. Table 2-1 illustrates how such divergent goals require tapping into different information pools. At the top levels, where broad organizational strategies are devised, information about the organization's external controllers may be most crucial. Mid-level administrators, responsible for implementing the strategies, must draw on information supplied by the top levels to draft operational plans. At the operational level, the official's primary task is to provide specific directives and monitor the actual operations to ascertain whether or not they are in line with organizational goals.[3]

The Information Environment

To a degree, public agencies create their own information environment by selecting information sources and deciding what to ignore and what to heed. Table 2-2 illustrates the preference for different information sources expressed by staffs of various types of congressional committees. It also demonstrates the fact that most agencies must rely on outsiders for information, including, as Edward Lauman and David Knoke point out, "the very actors upon whom they are to confer benefits or harm."[4] Staffers on eight congressional committees were asked: "How would you rank the following information sources in terms of importance for your work on this committee staff?" Response options were "very important," "somewhat important," and "not very important." The answers reflect widely varying preferences.[5]

If one assumes that preferences reflect actual choices, then all staffers relied heavily on information from executive agencies. The majority of staffers on clientele-oriented committees, such as Merchant Marine, Interior, and Public Works also relied heavily on interest-group information, while committees such as Armed Services, Budget, and Appropriations slighted these sources. Committee staffers also differed in their regard for information from congressional support agencies, from other committees, and from the staffs in their own offices. Additionally, they varied in the extent to which they used information generated during public hearings. Nearly all of the staff members of the Armed Services, Government Operations, and Appropriations committees claimed to make ample use of information from such hearings.[6] These patterns suggest differential use of sources and, since sources are unique in the information they provide, differential exposure to information. The consequences can be profound.

Changes in the knowledge industry are continually altering the patterns of information sources that public officials consult. Monitoring capacity has

Table 2-1 Information Systems Needs for Public Managers

Management level	Type of information needed	Primary sources	Decisions supported	Goals
Organizational-institutional—agency strategic level	Statutory authority, charter, long-term economic and budget resources, forecasting information on political uncertainty, social and technological trends	Executive, legislative, and judicial controllers Charter/laws Economic forecasts Technology forecasts Political environment Constituencies	Overall objectives Budgetary allocations Authority allocation Overall organization structure Level of differentiation and integration External coordination Intergovernmental relations	Acquire statutory authority Acquire budgets Achieve goals, support organizational stability and survival Ensure overall organizational independence
Management—midlevel or coordinating	Control objectives, resources available, long-term needs, operational capability, resource potential	Internal resources Top level management Operational environment Past performance Financial sources	Allocate financial and personnel resources Ensure alignment of strategy and operations Reallocation of tasks	Resolve organizational conflict Achieve organizational objectives Align goals and set standards
Operational task/supervisory	Task technology, process requirements, resource availability, performance data, financial support, standards development, service impact	Technology requirements Past performance Personnel resources Budget forecasts Clients/recipients Top-level information	Evaluate and monitor operations Task design Procedures Measures needed for evaluation Efficiency determination Cost reduction	Support objectives Efficient operations Low cost Meet standards Align top, mid, and operational level objectives

Source: John M. Stevens and Robert P. McGowan, *Information Systems and Public Management* (New York: Praeger, 1985), 16. Reprinted by permission of Greenwood Publishing Group, Inc., Westport, Conn.

Table 2-2 Percentage of Staffers Indicating Various Information Sources as Very Important, by Congressional Committee

Question: "How would you rank the following information sources in terms of importance for your work on this committee staff? (Close-ended responses provided: very important, somewhat important, not very important.)

	Merchant Marine	Budget	Interior	Armed Services	Public Works	Government Operations	Ways & Means	Appropriations
Executive agency	87%	88%	78%	100%	87%	94%	78%	94%
Interest groups	53	12	67	7	57	39	53	18
Congressional support agencies	53	83	39	36	52	39	59	23
Other committees	20	39	22	29	30	28	12	12
Personal offices	0	12	22	29	17	17	18	0
$N \doteq$	15	18	18	14	23	18	18	17

Source: Adapted from Edward I. Sidlow and Beth Henschen, "The Performance of House Committee Staff Functions: A Comparative Exploration," *Western Political Quarterly* 38 (September 1985): 486-487. Reprinted by permission of the University of Utah, copyright holder.

Note: In the spring of 1982, 305 questionnaires were mailed; 140 were returned for a response rate of 46 percent. The response rate did not vary significantly across committees.

increased by leaps and bounds. Members of Congress, for example, rely increasingly on outside specialists such as lobbyists from inside and outside government, on expert consultants, and on their own staffs for information inputs. These specialists filter information, provide facts and opinions, and often initiate proposals. Each congressional office, as well as each congressional committee and even subcommittee, tends to develop its own group of experts who determine what information needs to be considered and how it should be evaluated.

Creation of multiple clusters of experts may lead political subsystems to be isolated from each other. Each subsystem constructs and lives in its own communication ghetto and bases decisions on its information base. There is also much duplication of effort. From an efficiency perspective, one might recommend that legislators use the same information sources to assure a uniform information base for decision making and to avoid duplication. But sharing sources would also reduce diversity and impoverish the supply of information available for decisions. Moreover, major turf battles are likely to develop about control over information gathering and processing and the choice of experts. People on opposite sides of the political fence are likely to want different experts and data and are likely to arrange them differently.

Control over an agency's information environment is far from complete, however. Political considerations may force it to rely on sources that it would not freely choose. Time and money stringencies may put limits on information gathering, as may difficulties in locating desired sources. Agency personnel often become hostages to technical experts because they are not fully familiar with technological information. For example, during the early years of the space flight program, NASA deferred almost completely to the judgments and recommendations of technical experts.[7] The complexity of the enterprise made it well-nigh impossible to question the experts. Social and political concerns were slighted.

Imprisonment by technical experts is not the only information web in which government agencies may become enmeshed more or less unwittingly. Stereotypes held by members of organizations or circulating in their environment may preclude open-minded information searches. As Harold Wilensky points out, "Francis Bacon's warning that man converts his words into idols that darken his understanding is as pertinent today as it was three centuries ago." [8] For instance, once safety engineers have labeled nuclear-energy plants inherently unsafe, agency personnel may think about them exclusively in a mental framework suggesting that the plants must be shut down. Information searches related to the possibility of less drastic measures are unlikely to be encouraged. Likewise, once agency personnel have made a policy choice, information searches and interpretations will focus primarily on data supporting the choice rather than on countervailing information.[9]

Instrumental v. Tactical Information

Most of the information collected by public agencies relates to their mission. However, it may be necessary to collect information for tactical purposes as well, thereby making use of the symbolic aspects of information gathering. For instance, agencies frequently collect information from diverse publics primarily to create the impression that government is run democratically. The informational base for a particular policy or issue under consideration may already be firmly established. Nonetheless, a series of public hearings may be held to provide interested groups with an opportunity to air their views. These hearings serve the additional tactical purpose of permitting people to let off steam.

Similarly, many of the data solicited from experts are used largely as window dressing for decisions that have already been made. When decisions misfire, such as plans to inoculate the entire American population against influenza because of an epidemic, expert testimony may help save face for executives who can blame the problem on faulty information. The fact that experts supplied it absolves the lay people who presumably are unable to assess the quality of the information. Likewise, many reports prepared by study commissions are scientific window dressing. Or they may owe their creation to the need to placate pressure groups who want governmental action in areas of concern to their constituents.

Study commissions are usually carefully selected to ensure that the information they will present agrees with the views of the commissioning agency. As one wit put it, members of Congress want "vindicators" rather than "indicators." If commissioned reports advocate radical undesired changes, these are unlikely to be adopted. Members of study commissions know this and usually structure their reports with an eye to acceptability. This may amount to profound self-censorship. Similarly, reports by bureaucrats are often structured primarily to achieve political purposes, such as enhancing funding for the agency or obscuring shortcomings. Exaggerating budgetary needs in anticipation of routine budget trimming by funding bodies has become a pervasive ritual.[10]

Many study reports are commissioned merely to symbolize governmental concern about problems, with no expectation that they will lead to action of any kind. For example, to quiet concerns about U.S. military policy, the Reagan administration commissioned a study of long-term strategies, which took a year to complete and cost $1.6 million. It used a star cast of investigators, including high military brass, two former secretaries of state, and well-known scholars of defense policy. Although its recommendations were cautious, it was doomed from the start to join the huge array of similar reports gathering the dust of oblivion.

In addition to the usual reasons for burying reports, this particular one faced the handicap of being commissioned by an administration that would soon leave office. Incoming administrations, for political reasons, are rarely willing to base their operations on information packages assembled by their predecessors. Moreover, the State Department had been alienated early on when the Defense Department was instead selected as sponsor of the study. There was also resistance to the basic concepts of the report among influential Pentagon officials. Given such formidable opposition, the recommendations made in the report were predictably stillborn. Its sole value was symbolic, a value often bought at high costs that are nonetheless deemed defensible.[11]

Efforts to make government reports politically palatable to diverse constituencies often doom their usefulness. As Martha Feldman states, "Analysts representing many different interests need to combine their many points of view on the issue they are writing about. The result is seldom a forceful analysis or a strong presentation of a position. Positions and analyses are watered down. Obtaining consensus on the report often means either leaving out so many points that the paper is bland or putting in so many points that it is wishy-washy." Consequently, a large number of reports requested by legislative bodies and other oversight agencies, while placating their constituencies, are useless for decision making or problem solving.[12]

Tactical considerations frequently determine what structures will be created to collect and process information. Such structural decisions may have profound, often unexpected, consequences for information flows. For example, transacting congressional business through task-specific rather than geographically organized committees has put the focus on nationwide policy concerns rather than on policy geared to the needs of individual states or regions. Tactical maneuvers to control structures in order to shape functions are discussed more fully in the next chapter.

Whether information will be used instrumentally or tactically often depends on the phase of policy making in which a particular agency is engaged. A study of how congressional committees use information available from the Office of Technology Assessment (OTA) documents that policy makers are likely to make instrumental use of technical information when they are not yet committed to a particular solution to a problem and are groping for an acceptable policy.[13] This is most likely to occur during the early stages of deliberation. If policy makers are partially committed, they use the information to support, extend, and refine the preferred policy. If they have made a strong commitment to a well-defined position, they will make tactical use of the information to reconfirm the merits of their position and to advocate it.

The level of political conflict surrounding particular decisions is also crucial. When conflict is high, tactical use of information increases. Positions tend to be held too strongly to yield to new information on substantive grounds. The primary role of new information then is to support positions that have already been taken. When the conflict level surrounding an issue is low, information is more likely to be used instrumentally to adopt or to extend and refine a chosen policy. Overall, the use of information for all purposes increases with the concern about particular issues.[14]

Building Information Bases

Locating and Selecting Information

The explosive growth of available knowledge poses a number of difficult problems for all types of organizations. In the first place, they must decide how to locate the information that appears to be needed. Possibilities include retrieving it from recent and long-term organizational memory, generating it through reading or research, or contacting others who may have the information.

Political scientist Herbert Kaufman observed six federal bureau chiefs in action over a one-year period. They were from the Forest Service, the Social Security Administration, the Food and Drug Administration, the Internal Revenue Service, the Customs Service, and the Animal and Plant Health Inspection Service in the Department of Agriculture. He found that they used all three tactics for intelligence gathering. Conferring singly or in group meetings with knowledgeable people including consultants, lobbyists, and pollsters, took up 60 to 75 percent of their time.[15] Much of it was spent receiving and giving information over the telephone. Reading old and new reports came next, and direct observation was last. In addition, bureau chiefs gathered information through their own reflections about the situation and during special briefings prior to meetings, press conferences, and congressional inquiries.

Once access to information has been gained, organizations must determine what is essential and then ignore or discard what is not because information gathering is costly in terms of time, money, and human resources. For example, organizations must provide facilities where communication can take place, such as meeting rooms, broadcast studios, communication equipment, supplies, and labor. It takes time for agency personnel to think, compose, transcribe, and present data. It also takes time and effort to receive messages and interpret them, particularly when they are very complex. Costs are high for preparing reports and publications, even for making contact with informants or attending hearings. In fact, the high costs of gathering information may persuade agencies to retain past policies whenever possible and to prefer incremental changes to major policy revisions. Limiting new information input has the added advantage of avoiding change that may be disquieting and may disturb a carefully constructed consensus that supports the status quo.[16]

After information has been chosen, it must be encoded into messages that may or may not provide explicit interpretations of its meaning. Much paring of available information occurs at the lower organizational levels so that top executives work with extracts selected and condensed by their subordinates. If these subordinates are savvy and attuned to their chief's needs and desires, the process benefits the organization because it would be impossible for the chief to deal effectively with the copious stream of raw information. But if subordinates do a poor job, especially if they omit or distort important information, the chief's effectiveness is seriously compromised.

While it is essential to be highly selective to avoid overloading the information transmission and processing channels, it is also important for organizations to keep as fully informed as possible. Multiple sources must often be tapped for the same information to guard against depending on a single source that might be biased or otherwise flawed. To conserve resources, decisions need to be made through "satisficing"—gathering enough information to make a reasonably good choice likely—rather than "optimizing" procedures, which would entail gathering or using all the data that might possibly affect the decision. The bureau chiefs observed by Kaufman seemed to place the highest priorities on three types of information: data related to important pending decisions, information to appraise their agency's performance in relation to its goals and resources, and information needed to avoid embarrassment, should questions about it arise.[17]

The last category reflects the fact that executives in the public sector must endure innumerable interrogations by political superiors and journalists. This forces them to keep on top of a great deal of information that they might otherwise disregard because it is not directly relevant to their jobs. In particular, they believe that it is essential to be informed about incipient problems so that corrections can be made before outside agencies become alerted and give publicity to these problems.

Information related to decision making usually involves examining various options prepared by the chief's staff, along with projections of their positive and negative consequences. Chiefs appraise the agency's internal performance largely by studying the periodically required reports of its activities and by occasional spot checks through direct observation. Such observations mostly come as by-products of visits undertaken by agency executives for other reasons. Because so many decisions need to be made about general policy directions, as well as specific programs, budget, and personnel matters and the like, top-level executives must handle vast amounts of information even though data collection and initial processing have been done at lower levels.[18] How information can be reduced to manageable proportions will be discussed more fully in Chapter 4.

Intelligence gathering is usually best during the early years of an organization's life, before routines have hardened. During these years organizations tend to hire innovative leaders. Once policies are established, the emphasis is on continuity, and people are chosen and socialized accordingly. New approaches to information gathering are viewed as a threat rather than a challenge and a promise. Personnel shift from innovators and committed pioneers who cast their information nets widely to resolve the many uncertainties faced by new organizations to well-socialized professionals and bureaucrats who follow in the tracks already laid out for them.

Access Problems

Gaining access to needed information frequently poses serious difficulties for public organizations. Information storage and retrieval practices may cause major access problems for several reasons. High turnover of key personnel, which is common at the executive levels of the public service, means loss of organizational memories about important past events. So do inadequate or improper filing systems for the kind of retrieval that is needed. A study of the state of Washington's motor pool, for example, revealed that there were no adequate records of the number of state-owned vehicles. Estimates ranged from 4,000 to 10,000.[19] Similarly, when records of AIDS patients are filed according to disease symptoms to protect the individual's privacy, rather than by name and social security number, these records may be useless for retrieving information on particular patients.

Obstructing Regulatory Policies. At times, crucial information is deliberately withheld from public agencies. Such problems tend to be particularly acute for regulatory agencies such as EPA, Occupational Safety and Health Administration (OSHA), or transportation safety agencies, which need potentially incriminating information from industries subject to their control who are understandably less than eager to disclose this information. For example, in 1978 the National Highway Traffic Safety Administration (NHTSA), as part of its mission to assure vehicle safety, asked the Firestone Tire and Rubber Company to provide information about its "500" tire, which was its top-of-the-line steel-belted radial tire.[20] Consumers had complained about its safety, alleging some 14,000 instances of tire failure and hundreds of accidents caused by tire failures, which led to twenty-nine deaths and more than fifty cases of nonfatal injuries. Firestone charged that the problems were due to underinflation of tires and consumers' lack of experience in handling radials, but refused to make available its records regarding the complaints. In fact, Firestone contested NHTSA's right to ask the company to surrender information. The agency then issued an administrative order in early April 1978 compelling Firestone to answer its inquiries. Firestone refused to comply, forcing

NHTSA to institute proceedings in the Washington, D.C. district court to obtain the information.

Four months later, on August 15, 1978, a district court judge ordered Firestone to surrender all complaint letters and reports about its own investigations of complaints. The judge ruled that NHTSA could order the release of information nationwide, that its inquiries were for a legitimate purpose and not unduly burdensome, and that there was no evidence of harassment. Firestone then supplied massive amounts of information shortly before the deadline set by the court, putting a tremendous burden on NHTSA to cope with so much data. Finally, almost a year later, settlement terms were worked out and the "500" tire was recalled. NHTSA later released the documents regarding the dispute, which suggested that Firestone knew of the problems long before NHTSA entered the fray.[21]

The magnitude of information involved in such cases is illustrated by the government's attempts to secure information from General Motors about the safety of the brakes on its so-called X-cars: Chevrolet Citation, Pontiac Phoenix, Oldsmobile Omega, and Buick Skylark. There had been complaints that the brakes locked and caused skids, which had resulted in more than 1,500 accidents, 322 injuries, and 17 deaths.[22] NHTSA used its subpoena power to force a reluctant General Motors to release the required information. Ultimately, the government's case came to rest on more than 100,000 documents supporting the charge that General Motors had falsely denied having data about problems with the braking system.

The problems of getting essential information for regulatory policies are not solely due to private sector intransigence. Agency inefficiencies, many of them caused by understaffing and lack of adequate facilities, are also to blame. The EPA's pesticide-control program provides a case in point. Before pesticides can be sold, the agency must certify that pesticides are safe and effective when used properly. But EPA lacks the staff to carry out the testing program to obtain required information on the nearly 50,000 certifiable products manufactured by 10,000 firms and must therefore rely on the experimental results provided by manufacturers. If these results or the underlying tests are flawed, EPA certification about product safety and effectiveness is flawed.[23]

Obtaining needed data has been especially troublesome when pesticides are imported, forcing EPA to rely on the Bureau of Customs for the necessary documentation. In the past, information-exchange procedures between the two agencies were not properly specified so that imported pesticides had already been dispatched to their destinations and often distributed to users before EPA even became aware of their importation. When EPA discovered product flaws, it was often slow to notify consumers. For example, on one occasion EPA was so slow in recalling defective disinfectants that the Veterans Administration and the General Services

Administration were awarding contracts for these defective disinfectants while the recall was under way.

Faulty transmission and withholding of information may also be a purely intraorganizational problem. Because information is a strategic resource, it is hoarded by officials who do not wish to lose control over it.[24] For example, when internal disagreements developed in EPA about the best way to control air pollution from power-plant emissions, proponents of various approaches deliberately withheld information from each other. The office favoring scrubbing of emissions kept its proposals from the EPA planning office, which considered the procedure overly costly and wasteful. In turn, the planning office, instead of consulting internal staffs, commissioned an outside consulting firm to provide information supporting the policies it favored.[25]

Refusing Data Sharing. Information-withholding problems of a different kind arise from the frequent political tensions between the government and the academic and nonacademic science community. For example, to implement the building of the Strategic Defense Initiative, a space-based nuclear defense system proposed by the Reagan administration, the government needs scientific information already available, or likely to be generated, within the private sector science community. Increasingly, American scientists have refused to make their know-how and creative capabilities available to the government because they oppose the project for a variety of reasons. Universities that used to be willing to house government think tanks have also closed their doors to such ventures.

Several issues are involved in such refusals to make information and experience available to the government. Many scientists face the dilemma of balancing their obligation as citizens to make knowledge available to the government against their convictions that they must refuse to cooperate with a policy they oppose on moral, ethical, or rational grounds. The government faces the dilemma of needing the expertise of such citizens to carry out controversial policies but lacking means to compel their cooperation. Its only recourse lies in persuading reluctant scientists that the policy deserves support or using the government's carrot-and-stick policies of financial support for the science community to elicit cooperation.

Protecting Privacy. Privacy rights raise yet another information-gathering problem. The Privacy Act of 1974, which was adopted to protect individuals against undue invasion of privacy by disclosure of their records on file with various government agencies, has changed the nature of government information collection and use of such records. The act sets out guidelines for the disclosure of personal data files to other agencies and individuals. It outlines procedures by which individual files and records are maintained by government agencies and gives individuals the right to inspect their files and ask for corrections. Agencies are required to report annually about the character of their record system and are subject to civil remedies and criminal penalties for violations.[26] (See Appendix 1.)

Various government agencies acquire extensive dossiers about individual citizens. Welfare clients, for example, must disclose data about family composition and living arrangements, education and training, economic resources, employment history, efforts to find jobs, medical status, nationality and citizenship, and past recourse to welfare. Some of these data are germane to the work of other agencies, such as the Immigration Service, various health agencies, the Department of Education, and the Internal Revenue Service. Yet privacy considerations have long barred many of these public bodies from sharing data. For instance, state welfare agencies have found it difficult in the past to gain access to the records of the Internal Revenue Service to check whether a welfare client has concealed the fact of lucrative employment. In most jurisdictions, the records of welfare clients are deemed confidential to spare them the embarrassment of having their economic needs become public knowledge.

In May 1984 the Senate finally passed legislation requiring the Internal Revenue Service to share income data about recipients of government aid with a variety of federal and state agencies.[27] The legislation affects the financial records of vast numbers of people. In 1987, 20.6 million people were getting food stamps; 10.7 million received aid for dependent children; 21.6 million citizens were covered by Medicaid. Supplemental Security Income went to 4.4 million elderly, disabled, or blind persons, and 3.2 million people received unemployment compensation. Despite some cutbacks in programs such as food stamps, the numbers have grown steadily since then.

To skirt the Privacy Act, the 1984 law stipulated that data about aid recipients would *not* come from individual tax returns, which were deemed confidential. Instead, they would come from reports of payouts made by employers, banks, brokerage houses, and similar sources that the government uses to cross-check individual returns. The goal of the legislation, which authorized computer matching programs to detect discrepancies in information received by government agencies, was to reduce fraud in various programs providing medical care for the poor, unemployment benefits, and aid to dependent children. Aid could not be terminated under the law until the information released by the IRS for matching had been verified and until recipients had the opportunity to protest the cutoff.

Congress had previously authorized the sharing of income information in connection with state and local efforts to track down parents who were delinquent in paying child support. The benefits flowing from these efforts to discourage fraud have to be weighed against the threats to constitutionally protected privacy and due process rights of individuals. A number of agencies have been accused of acting on the basis of these matches without the safeguards of cross-checking and allowing rebuttal. Moreover in many instances the data are not entirely suitable for the purposes to which the secondary users put them, with unfortunate results. Also the costs of collecting such information may exceed the revenues available from cheaters.

Ethical dilemmas abound as well. For instance, when government agencies collect data for one purpose, such as welfare payments, should they be used for another? People may volunteer information for one purpose, such as health matters, but would not do so for another. If this information is used for an unforeseen purpose, must people be at least notified that disclosure will occur or has occurred? The Social Security Administration maintains files on most Americans, which cover their age, sex, race, yearly earnings, work and benefit history. Some files also contain information on alcoholism or drug addiction and financial resources other than earned income.[28] Is it ethical to pass such data on to other agencies without the consent of the individuals whose lives are bared to the gaze of unknown observers?

Safeguarding National Security.   Another serious access problem concerns the security of sensitive information. It has become increasingly difficult for government agencies to safeguard such information from other agencies and from the public. Technological advances have made it relatively easy to gain access to computer files, telephone conversations, and confidential documents. In addition, as discussed more fully in Chapter 7, politically inspired leaking of sensitive information has become rampant. The problem is further complicated by the often difficult and always controversial task of determining what information is genuinely sensitive and what is not. Moreover, the sensitivity label has been misused to hide information that should be open to scrutiny. Security problems become particularly difficult to handle when sensitive and nonsensitive information is intermingled so that one cannot be pursued without damaging the other. For example, the Justice Department's attempts to prosecute National Security Council staff members for illegally diverting funds from arms sales to Iran to anti-government forces in Nicaragua were partially stymied because much of the crucial information was either unavailable to the prosecution and defense or could not be disclosed in open court. Prosecutors were forced to drop a number of charges to protect the security of sensitive information.

In recent decades, government secrecy has been expanding steadily. This is dangerous in an era when public agencies collect increasingly huge amounts of information that may require checking to ascertain its accuracy. Many secret files, such as the Federal Bureau of Investigation (FBI) records, are full of unchecked information. Such secret information is likely to be defective. It is often drawn from small numbers of informants and has not had the benefit of open discussion and possible challenge. When its authors remain anonymous, checking their credibility becomes impossible. Access to secret information is usually granted only to safe, compliant people who would not be likely to challenge its accuracy. However, liberal interpretation of the Freedom of Information Act of 1966 has led to much easier access to hidden files in recent years, making corrections easier. It has also increased the danger that genuinely sensitive information will be jeopardized (see Appendix 2).

Access to guarded information is most difficult when it is controlled by various intelligence agencies or in the hands of the police. The generally cautious behavior of public agencies fosters a tendency to exaggerate security threats. Bureaucrats know that it is safer to be overzealous in labeling documents as secret than to permit access to them and be reprimanded for exposing secrets. Moreover, it is the nature of information that once the cat is out of the proverbial bag, it is irretrievable. In the past, courts have usually supported refusals to disclose information when they were based on claims that disclosure might endanger national security. The Pentagon Papers case may have changed that permanently. In that case, the court sanctioned media coverage of foreign policy documents that the Nixon administration had tried to shield.[29]

Nonetheless, when the United States has become involved in military operations, such as the Grenada intervention in 1983, the Panama intervention in 1989-1990, and the Persian Gulf War in 1991, military censors severely restrict access to information. In the Persian Gulf War, for example, reporters were allowed to observe front-line operations only as members of pools arranged and supervised by the military. Most of the time, top-level military commanders refused to answer questions that would shed light on plans and operations, claiming that responses would endanger the conduct of the war. Under such circumstances, journalists have little chance to contest such policies.

During the Reagan years, efforts were especially tight to protect scientific information that had military applications and to limit the right of foreigners to obtain research data on technological breakthroughs such as high-temperature superconductors. Numerous U.S. scientists, concerned about what they considered excessive government secrecy, were therefore leaving research jobs with the government or refusing to take such positions. They feared that military reviewers might veto publication of their findings from sensitive but unclassified research conducted by universities for the government. They were also concerned about the damaging consequences of throttling unhampered scientific interchange.[30] The presidents of Stanford University, the California Institute of Technology, and the Massachusetts Institute of Technology told the Reagan administration in 1984 that they would refuse to conduct sensitive unclassified research for the Defense Department if their findings were subject to military censorship.[31]

Promoting Therapeutic Ignorance. While secrecy is a problem, uncontrolled access to information coupled with excessive publicity can be equally damaging to the public welfare. Many institutions, such as drug firms, grocery chains, and brokers, depend on public confidence. When reports drawn from government investigations into the safety of their services and products suggest that they may have betrayed their trust, they can be ruined because the reports enjoy credibility and usually receive wide publicity. Being exonerated of the charges does not restore losses suffered or even restore confidence. Suspicions linger. This happened, for example, in 1989 in the wake of news that the Environmental Protection Agency was investigating the need for a ban on the use of Alar, a potentially cancer-causing chemical used by apple growers to enhance the quality of the fruit. Although the cancer danger was denied in short order, sales declined sharply, hurting the economies of apple-growing states. Industry representatives estimated the losses in 1989 at more than $100 million, roughly 10 percent of total sales. A portion of this loss was expected to be permanent because it came from cancellations of orders by school districts loath to take any chances with children's health.[32]

There is always a danger that certain types of knowledge may actually be harmful to organizations because it may undercut internal morale. Ignorance may indeed be bliss. Political scientist Harold Wilensky calls this "therapeutic ignorance."[33] Ignorance may be beneficial, for example, when it keeps members of organizations from knowledge that might paralyze action. For instance, a survey of top administrators of sixty-two social service agencies in central Iowa disclosed firm knowledge that budget cuts were imminent, which led to drastic, often unwarranted service curtailments.[34] By contrast, uncertainty about possible budget cuts led to creative strategies to manage with fewer resources. Similarly, when agency members were unaware of major threats facing their agency, they were less likely to be paralyzed by fear.

It may also be good for subordinates to be unaware of the foibles of their superiors so that they retain faith, respect, and high morale. This accounts for the common practice of explaining high-level personnel changes in terms of socially acceptable reasons such as illness or the executive's personal wishes rather than disclosing his or her incompetence or dishonesty. Similarly, to keep up morale, it may even be essential to maintain false stereotypes about the organization that enhance its image and that of its personnel. Finally, many organizations benefit from concealing information about salaries paid to various staff people, thereby avoiding jealousies and possible difficulties with workers, either singly or collectively.

Information may be particularly harmful at certain times. For instance, in the spring of 1984, then Speaker of the House Thomas P. O'Neill, Jr., agreed to postpone debate on a comprehensive immigration bill until after the California Democratic primary on June 5.[35] Democrats were hopeful that the postponement could be extended to prevent possibly harmful debate prior to the November elections. O'Neill's maneuver had been initiated in response to a plea by the California Democratic congressional delegation and a speech by Democratic presidential candidate Walter Mondale.

Similarly, some information may be too politically sensitive for open discussion during a particular historical period. For instance, a White House Conference on Civil Rights in June 1966 intended to focus on the problems of the black family, but the organizers discovered that it would be unwise to discuss the topic because criticism of certain groups of blacks would be construed as racism. By 1984 this sensitivity to criticism had lessened to the point that a conference called by the National Association for the Advancement of Colored People (NAACP) and the National Urban League could schedule the topic for discussion.

More recently, both the Carter and Reagan administrations shied away from discussing the emotionally explosive issue of artificial insemination of a woman willing to produce a child for adoption by a sperm donor and his wife. The two presidents avoided the debate by refusing to appoint members to an unstaffed federal ethics advisory committee.[36] Congress, equally timorous, allowed its own commission on bioethics and its fourteen-member advisory commission to remain inactive. The failure to discuss and agree on national public policies in this controversial area of human reproduction has led to a maze of conflicting state regulations and has paralyzed publicly financed fetal and embryo research. But it has allowed federal agencies to delay action in the hope that societal consensus about these matters will eventually evolve.

Rather than stopping discussion entirely when politically touchy issues are involved, agencies may opt for partial suppression of information or for slanting it in ways that reap political benefits. Several techniques have been widely used.[37] Agencies can report information selectively, omitting those parts that might harm their cause. In making reports, they can turn to favorable "experts" to support their claims and avoid unfavorable experts. They can also bury important information in low-level reports that are unlikely to arouse the attention of decision makers. Finally, agencies can submit so much information that the receivers are swamped and cannot digest it.

The latter tactic recognizes the fact that an oversupply of information creates serious problems. Too much information is as bad as and can sometimes be even worse than too little. This fact is often forgotten in American culture, where "more is better" has become the norm and the belief is common that ample information about problems permits their solution. This is false, of course. As James Q. Wilson points out, much information does not constitute "a full, accurate, and properly nuanced body of knowledge about important matters." Rather, it is "a torrent of incomplete facts, opinions, guesses, and self-serving statements about distant events." [38] The overload can overwhelm an organization's processing capacities and grind operations to a halt. Moreover, piles of data may merely reinforce what is already known about a problem. Military and police intelligence services, for example, are particularly prone to accumulating unmanageable amounts of redundant information about security problems.

Overload sometimes springs from excessive internal communication. To cope with the problem of units of an organization inundating each other with messages, restrictions on the number, length, or subject matter of interoffice memos may become necessary. Without such restrictions, officials may find that their other duties suffer. For example, President Nixon estimated that 42 million documents passed through his office and that he personally attended to some 200,000. [39] The draconian whittling still left him with an obvious overload.

Overcoming Information Barriers

Legislative Solutions

Congress has tried to address various information-gathering problems that plague the public sector. The Paperwork Reduction Act adopted on December 11, 1980, is designed to reduce excessive paperwork, which is costly in terms of money and labor and produces information overloads that delay governmental activities. [40] Sponsors of the act claimed that it could cut the public's paperwork burden by 25 percent. [41] The act mandates a federal information policy and establishes an implementing Office of Information and Regulatory Affairs (OIRA) in the Office of Management and Budget (OMB). The office reviews tests, inspection procedures, labeling, and disclosure requirements, as well as records, questionnaires, and forms used for applications, census data, and taxes. [42] While on its face this appears to be a nonpolitical office, the facts are otherwise.

Choosing messages for elimination can be highly political. For example, in 1987 OMB found itself involved in a major political battle when it proposed to eliminate thirty questions from the 1990 census. OMB claimed that the information duplicated data collected at state and local levels about the nation's housing supply, energy consumption, population fertility and migration, and participation in the labor force. Groups who had used federal data about these matters for their own benefit argued otherwise. Such conflicts have often been adjudicated in the federal courts. In 1990, in a case involving communications about hazards in the construction industry, the Supreme Court ruled that the reach of the act was far narrower than OMB had contended. OMB control extends only to information solicited by government for itself, not to information that government requires private parties to furnish to each other.[43]

Excessive paperwork, producing unneeded information, is common in government because of politically inspired caution. Check, double-check, and triple-check are the watchwords designed to guard against dishonesty and poor performance. To protect their turf, agencies may engage in numerous costly and time-consuming studies and analyses to forestall external review or scrutiny. Other contributing factors, as previously noted, are the vagueness of directives and inadequate communication among agencies, which results in duplication of work.

Another key law is the Brooks Act, passed October 30, 1965, as an amendment to the Federal Property and Administrative Act of 1949. The Brooks Act tries to reduce information-processing burdens for government and the private sector by setting standards.[44] For example, agency forms must have prior approval from a single staff agency, the Office of Management and Budget. An Office of Federal Information Policy was established in OMB to monitor and guide information practices by government agencies. The act also deals with acquisition and use of automatic data-processing equipment by federal departments and agencies. It charges three government agencies—the Office of Management and Budget, the General Services Administration, and the National Bureau of Standards—with the responsibility for improving and managing information resources in the executive branch. In a 1978 report, issued by OMB, this troika approach was criticized as "confusing, contradictory, and in many instances detrimental to the effective application of information technology" and excessively hardware oriented.[45] Staffing deficiencies at the three agencies seemed to be the main problem, along with lack of attention by leaders throughout various agencies. Frequent changes in top management were partly responsible for this lack of attention.

The Freedom of Information Act of 1966, as mentioned earlier, has eased disclosure of information.[46] It counteracts the tendency of government agencies to try to use executive-privilege arguments to retain control over information in order to increase their power. However, nine categories of information are specifically exempted from disclosure: (1) designated information on national defense or foreign policy; (2) internal personnel rules and practices; (3) information exempted by statute; (4) trade secrets and commercial or financial information obtained as privileged or confidential; (5) interagency and intra-agency memoranda or letters that would not otherwise be available by law; (6) personnel and medical files when disclosure would constitute an unwarranted invasion of personal privacy; (7) investigatory files compiled for law enforcement; (8) various reports required of financial institutions; and (9) geological and geophysical information and data about wells.

Freedom of Information laws at the state level parade under diverse names, such as Public Records, Public Information, Right to Know, Open Government, and Uniform Information Practices acts. They are similar to the federal laws, although some state laws are somewhat more restrictive. The fact that these laws exist and are drafted to make access to information easy does not necessarily mean that they are carried out according to the letter and spirit of the law. A 1991 study conducted to ascertain whether the city of Chicago had implemented a mayoral Freedom of Information executive order first promulgated in 1983 disclosed numerous compliance gaps. Moreover, several designated Freedom of Information officers refused to talk to the researchers, a stand that ultimately received official sanction from the mayor's office. The appeals officer, whose job is to monitor denials of information requests, remained elusive and did not return phone calls, making it impossible to complete the inquiry.[47] Such noncompliance has been common at all levels. When serious issues are involved, requesters of information have repeatedly taken the matter to court, usually successfully.

Freedom of Information laws are helpful in providing access to otherwise hidden information, but only when investigators know that the information exists and search it out and publicize it. A good example are the files of President Reagan's Secretary of Housing and Development, Samuel R. Pierce, Jr. Normally this treasure trove of evidence of corrupt dealings would have remained buried and untouched in storage boxes and computer files. There is no regular scrutiny of the mountains of information accumulated year by year by public agencies at all levels of government. In Pierce's case, charges of massive corruption in the office happened to surface. Newspeople then requested and received access to these files, thanks to the Freedom of Information Act.[48]

Other Remedies

As discussed earlier, government agencies often encounter resistance when they seek high-quality information. Getting at the truth is especially difficult for regulatory agencies that investigate behaviors having the potential to inflict serious harm on communities. The records of EPA, OSHA, and various traffic-safety agencies provide plentiful examples of difficulties in getting adequate information. These agencies usually have limited resources and often insufficient authority to conduct full-scale investigations on their own. Hence, they depend on the willingness of organizations in the private sector to disclose information that may reflect unfavorably on the organization. The fact that some of this information is likely to become public increases the reluctance of private agencies to allow access to their data.

Government agencies have several ways to extract information from unwilling private parties.[49] Litigation is one. The government may simply seek a court order to obtain information if private parties are obligated by law to disclose it. When that avenue is foreclosed, the government may sue the recalcitrant party, although the adversary process is not ideal for getting complete information. In a lawsuit the contending parties define the issues and determine what is relevant. That tends to be less than the full picture. Courts, eager to conclude cases speedily, prefer to decide them on the basis of a sharply limited amount of evidence. Lacking the resources for large-scale investigations, they are not usually eager to examine all aspects of the matter. In many cases it may be evident from the start that full disclosure will be elusive, so that attempting to elicit it may not even be worthwhile. When private sector agencies have near-monopoly status, as the Bell system did before its breakup, it becomes particularly difficult to get the necessary information to regulate them appropriately.

Public agencies can also try to get at the truth through expert testimony. Again, this route entails problems. Scientists often have political motivations, as seen in the conflicting testimony they provide, which frequently corresponds to their own or their employer's political orientation. In fact, the most highly regarded scientists in many technical fields are already paid consultants for industry or have received research grants from industry which may create a conflict of interest when government requests their services. The nature of the specialized knowledge brought to bear on particular situations may also color the outcome. If, for example, psychiatrists are invited as consultants in a court case involving the adequacy of safety devices, a psychiatrically based solution is far more likely than if engineers or economists are the chief consultants. Thus the nature of the expertise that is tapped shapes the nature of the truth that will be found.

Although expert testimony is not infallible, it is tempting to accept it uncritically instead of questioning experts to discover the basis for their findings. When special-interest groups, acting as experts, provide information on issues of concern to them, problems arise if no countervailing intelligence is produced. For example, transportation lobbies have often made an excellent case and received resources for highway construction. At the same time, mass transit has been starved for resources because it lacked a good lobbying organization to present its case effectively.

Legislative investigations are yet another avenue to discover information. They have the advantage of drawing on a wide array of informants who have access to more knowledge than would be available to individual experts. They also often capture wide public attention through media coverage, which may elicit input from previously untapped sources. The problem with legislative investigations is that much of the information submitted and widely publicized may be unverified and even unverifiable. The mere fact that the proceedings are publicized may affect what will and will not surface. Witnesses may try to play to the galleries rather than focus on the truth. Moreover, there is no assurance that all views that ought to be exposed are represented in public hearings.

Fact-finding commissions are a British contribution to the truth-finding devices. Although generally they do not take any kind of action, limiting themselves to investigations, they frequently have led to major social reforms. British royal commissions often explore the feasibility of policies with people who are the targets of prospective policies, allowing them input into policy formation. This makes nongovernmental elites part of the policy process. Commission findings arouse public attention, but that does not usually harden policy proposals because final decisions are far off.

A final way of finding truth consists of building countervailing information sources. President Franklin D. Roosevelt did this by overlapping the responsibilities of various agencies and individuals, and Congress has done it by duplicating presidential information sources. The information provided by the Office of Management and Budget, for example, can be checked against comparable data collected by the Congressional Budget Office. This tactic will be discussed more fully in Chapter 4.

Information Quality and Quantity

Quality

Finding needed information is not the only problem. One must also be concerned with the quality of the information collected. Harold Wilensky, in his pioneering studies on gathering organizational information (which he refers to as "intelligence"), indicates that high-quality information must have six characteristics.[50] It must be clear, timely, reliable, valid, comprehensive and diverse.

Clarity. Above all, information must be clear to those who use it. Enough information must be made available so that it can be interpreted in a meaningful context. Clarity also means that it must be encoded, either by the original source or by those who transmit it to the organization, in ways that can be readily understood by the users. It must be free from typical bureaucratic jargon, in which a simple garden spade may turn into a "weed removal facilitator," "invasions" become "incursions," and cutbacks are "resource reallocations."

Message senders must understand how potential users are likely to interpret the information and tailor it accordingly. Again, the complexity of the public business and the diversity of its clienteles are major barriers. For example, real estate agents have to be able to comprehend complex open-housing laws, tradesmen have to cope with building and zoning codes, and tax consultants have to administer constantly changing tax laws. Lack of

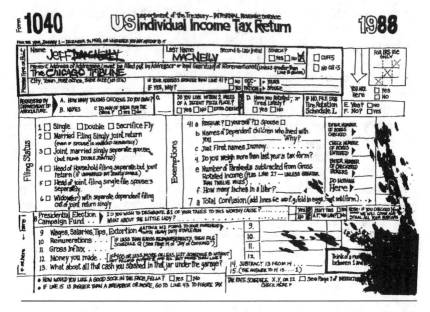

Source: Reprinted by permission: Tribune Media Services.

clarity in the directives transmitted by government to such business groups creates major problems in implementing public policies effectively.

Much important information intended for various clienteles remains unused because it is encoded in ways that are ill suited to the proclivities and capacities of the intended users. For example, the Food and Drug Administration requires warning labels to be attached to medicines to alert consumers to potentially serious problems, but these are largely disregarded because they are couched in excessively technical language. Bulletin boards at public agencies describing available services remain unread because their messages are too complicated. The directions provided by the Internal Revenue Service to its millions of clients are a prime example of government instructions that are far too complex to be useful to average citizens. No wonder that Jeff McNelly's annual cartoon, poking fun at the notorious density of the typical income-tax form, provides welcome comic relief for frustrated taxpayers.

In the public sector, achieving clarity in the transmission of information is no mean task. Given the complexity of messages and the diversity of communicators, much information is relayed imprecisely and is therefore unclear. Problems of clarity are particularly serious when they occur in communications between legislatures and public agencies. This happens often because, as Robert Cunningham and Dorothy Olshfski point out, "Differences in constituencies, power bases, tenure in office, and status encourage different perceptions and expectations, thereby complicating the relationship between administrator and legislator." [51] For example, administrators tend to take long-term views, while legislators are more oriented to short-term considerations. This makes it difficult for each side to put messages into the proper perspectives that are apt to produce shared meanings. Nonetheless, one study of twenty-seven Tennessee legislators and thirty administrators showed that each group can, if it tries, put itself into the shoes of the other and judge correctly how the other side perceives a particular political situation.[52]

Legislative directives concerning the activities of public agencies are usually exceedingly vague, which makes it difficult to discern the precise legislative intent and also easy to evade it if bureaucrats so desire, as they often do. Interest groups frequently take advantage of flexibility in interpretation to push bureaucrats to make decisions in their favor. A typical example of a vague power grant is the congressional mandate to the Federal Communications Commission in the Communications Act of 1934 to exercise its regulatory powers so as to "serve the public interest, convenience and necessity." Over the years, the meaning of the phrase has sparked countless debates whenever FCC policies have been challenged as contrary to these goals and defended as complying with them.

Besides leading to controversial actions, vague directives often produce inaction. The Law Enforcement Assistance Administration (LEAA), for instance, was authorized to make grants to cities under its Pilot Cities Program, but it failed to issue specific directives to potential applicants. Consequently, the program, which was inaugurated in March 1970 with a grant to Santa Clara County in California, languished for several years because applicants were uncertain about application procedures.[53]

The reasons for vague communications in the public sector are manifold. They include the complexity of the issues with which governmental institutions frequently deal and the unpredictability of future circumstances. When language must cover unforeseen and unforeseeable contingencies, it cannot be specific and to the point. Moreover, consensus is often lacking about the best ways to accomplish desired objectives. This is especially true when the area of government activity is new, such as environmental protection policies, and when the expertise to devise appropriate solutions is still questionable. Precise guidelines may be difficult to frame.

Legislators often choose vague language to protect their political hides by avoiding clear choices that could alienate constituents. They believe that bureaucrats can make unpopular decisions with more impunity because they do not face elections. In return for avoiding the wrath of constituents and interest groups, they are willing to pay the price of bestowing excessive discretion on bureaucrats. Vague legislative directions lead to more or less welcome second-guessing by bureaucrats about what might have been meant. These guesses, molded by the bureaucrats' own preferences, often stray far from the legislators' intentions.

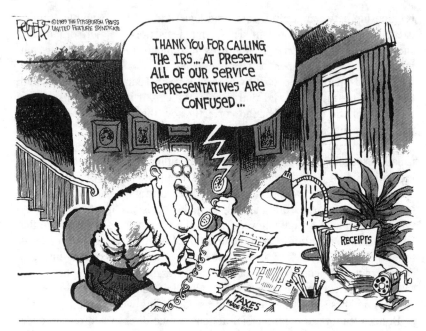

THANK YOU FOR CALLING THE IRS... AT PRESENT ALL OF OUR SERVICE REPRESENTATIVES ARE CONFUSED...

Source: Reprinted by permission of United Feature Syndicate, Inc.

Timeliness.   In addition to being clear, good messages also must be timely. This means that they must be available when needed and be kept up-to-date. For instance, the availability of an immunization program to protect vulnerable citizens from the influenza virus must be known by them many months before an epidemic strikes. Similarly, people who are trying to influence decision making in governmental agencies, including legislative bodies, must make sure that their information reaches these bodies before the decision process has hardened and narrowed down to a few options.

Reliability.   Good intelligence must also be reliable. This means that it should be correct, unambiguous, and consistent so that bureaucrats do not receive contradictory messages. For example, much consternation was aroused in 1987 when the Internal Revenue Service's field branch chief in Baltimore issued a directive instructing his agents to seize property promptly when taxpayers failed to honor a demand for payment. The branch chief indicated that promotions would be linked to the number of property seizures made by IRS agents and the amount of money they collected. These instructions ran directly counter to directives issued by IRS Commissioner Lawrence Gibbs, which prohibited linking employee rewards to the harshness of enforcement measures. The case is typical of instances when written directives from the central administration clash with verbal instructions passed on to field staffs.[54] The staffs are torn between relying on agency directives or on those issued by their immediate superiors. The latter course is usually taken.

The extremely serious problems that can be caused by contradictory directives are well illustrated by the fate of President John F. Kennedy's 1962 order to remove American missiles from Turkey.[55] The order was never carried out because it clashed with a simultaneous order to strengthen NATO defenses and to avoid irritating Turkey, which wanted the missiles to remain. Since Kennedy's dealings with the Soviet leadership during the Cuban missile crisis were based on the assumption that the United States had removed its missiles from the Soviet borders, failure to implement his order proved embarrassing and potentially highly dangerous.

An example of the disastrous consequences of ambiguous messages occurred during the Johnson presidency when the Department of Labor received vague guidelines from Congress about implementation of the Comprehensive Employment and Training Act (CETA).[56] These guidelines were transmitted to the regional and local offices where they caused endless confusion at all levels. Various interest groups used the seemingly conflicting directions to lobby for implementation in line with their preferences. For example, the U.S. Conference of Mayors, the National League of Cities, the National Association of Counties, and the National Governors' Conference, relying on one set of interpretations, claimed that the act required more local control. Liberals in Congress, labor unions, the National Urban League, and numerous community-based organizations disagreed. Relying on different interpretations, they argued that Congress had mandated more national control.

Validity.   Good information must also be valid. Concepts and measures used must be logically consistent and reflect the real world, rather than totally unrealistic conditions. Unfortunately, much of the information available from academic writings does not meet the real-world test and cannot be used by policy makers.

Validity may also be threatened by the biases of the information source. Much information flows to public agencies from interest groups that present data and analyses structured to favor particular conclusions. When agencies deal with competing interest groups, it may be possible to balance their arguments and arrive at a reasonably valid version of reality. In fact, during public hearings, government officials will frequently ask each interest group to assess the validity of arguments made by other interest groups, This produces critical analyses of interest-group data along with methodological critiques of data sources.[57]

Even information from specially commissioned research is often flawed. Thus a careful validity check of a report on a multi-city survey, commissioned in the 1970s to determine the causes of juvenile delinquency, found twenty-five common errors, omissions, and ambiguities.[58] They included inaccurate factual claims, faulty sampling procedures in selecting juveniles for study, and de-emphasis of problematic aspects of the research findings. The investigators attributed these faults to the research agency's desire to gloss over flaws in the execution of the project and to produce a politically pleasing report likely to lead to future research contracts. Some of the flaws had resulted from bureaucratic procedures mandating rigid research guidelines as part of the original contract award. Such guidelines are common in government-sponsored research. They may take the form of rigid timetables set for each phase of the research, requirements regarding the hiring of research personnel and subcontractors, and precise specification of the issues to be addressed by the final report. The result of flawed research reports is invalid information for policy making and difficulty in replicating improperly reported projects.

Depth. Wilensky's remaining two points relate to the ampleness of the information gathered. He points out that intelligence must be adequate, including all essential facts about the situation, and must also be wide-ranging so that a broad array of options are presented. By and large, feedback about an agency's activities and even about the helpfulness of its reports is what is most lacking. When the eye is on the here and now, an in-depth focus on the past and the future tends to get lost. A National Research Council report, for example, noted that the Environmental Protection Agency, despite its concern with excellence in data collection, had failed to learn from its past experiences by not developing systematic self-evaluation measures.[59] The stipulation that all essential facts must become available begs the difficult, often highly political question of which facts are essential and which are not. For instance, when prospective employees are screened for jobs in a particular agency, is it essential to know their policy preferences or party affiliation? A good case can be made for either a yes or a no answer. It may be good that they are ideologically attuned to the policies that the agency is trying to promote. Or it may be valuable that they take a critical stance, questioning the pet theories of the agency's staff.

Judgments of adequacy also hinge on the goals sought by bureaucrats and their operating styles. Many agencies are interested primarily in planning policy for the short term, which deflects their interests from data that would be important for long-term estimates. Some users of intelligence, such as lawyers and military professionals, want primarily "facts" rather than evaluated facts. They are suspicious of interpretations. Other officials deem information inadequate if it is presented out of context and fails to suggest an appropriate interpretation. Members of Congress, for example, do not want undigested, unprocessed information. Instead, they like a combination of facts, values, and suggestions for action.[60]

As Table 2-1 illustrates, the information needs of people in an organization often vary widely and are often at cross purposes for people at various levels of the hierarchy. Agency heads may want the very information that their subordinates are least willing to provide. An example might be information about a new computer program that can perform the tasks currently being done by workers whose jobs could be eliminated. Problems of adequacy may also spring from transmission difficulties. Information that is available in the system may fail to reach the parties needing it. The *Challenger* case is a good example of such a problem.

Wilensky's recommendation that information should come from a wide range of sources to present decision makers with various alternatives raises difficulties. It may lead to delays that make the information untimely. It may be hard to determine who should be consulted and what kinds of information should be solicited. Are interested or disinterested parties best? Should ordinary citizens be included? If so, to what extent are their unsupported beliefs and gut feelings likely to prevail over the advice of experts? Given democratic ideals, should they prevail? Can they, without jeopardizing public welfare? There are no easy answers.

Obviously, it is difficult to devise objective evaluation criteria that can assess the quality of information in terms of the six variables. Therefore, evaluations of the quality of information are largely subjective, which makes it difficult to determine whether available information is good enough to permit valid inferences and to serve as the basis for action. Wilensky's estimates of the quality of information are disquieting, to say the least.[61] He contends that generally only big, costly, urgent decisions activate high-quality intelligence. Such decisions tend to be made outside "channels" by top-level generalists who are advised by technical experts.

Even if messages are initially accurate, clear, timely, and relevant, they may still become distorted by intermediate receivers. As Gordon Tullock points out, when information gathered at the bottom level of the hierarchy is filtered upward through several intermediate levels, most of it is lost.[62] If, for instance, 5,000 bits of information are received at the entry level, and if one assumes that half of the information is omitted each time it is passed on to the next level, less than 80 bits will survive a trip through six levels. That is less than 2 percent. (See Figure 2-1.) Intelligence thus deteriorates routinely between initial collection and its final use in a policy decision.

Moreover, the weeding-out process is often intentionally or unintentionally biased, not random. Successive receivers along the line screen out message elements that do not fit their preconceptions or the accepted collective wisdom of the agency. James March and Herbert Simon call this "uncertainty absorption." Instead of passing on messages as received, the transmitters may pass on the inferences that they have drawn from these messages. Transmitters also screen out information that comes from sources that they deem to have low credibility. Additionally, they may change the emphasis given to various parts of the message, thereby altering its overall thrust.[63]

Figure 2-1   Tullock's Model of Hierarchical Distortion

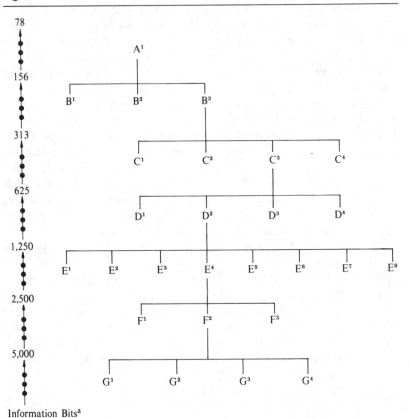

Information Bits[a]

Source: Anthony Downs, *Inside Bureaucracy* (Santa Monica, Calif.: Rand, 1967), 117. Reprinted with permission.

[a] Half of the information is lost as it passes from level to level.

Quantity

Wilensky points out that the information requirements of an organization and its need for professional help in securing and disseminating this information hinge on four factors.[64] One factor is the degree of conflict, competition, or systematic contact with the external environment. The more an agency is in conflict with or dependent on its environment, or needs to keep in constant contact, the more it requires information about this environment and about possible ways to reduce conflict and friction. For instance, if the agency's goals are closely monitored by Congress, as happens with the Environmental Protection Agency, or if it is likely to be in open conflict with Congress, as happened with the Federal Trade Commission, it needs to have more information about the interests motivating Congress at that particular time than would be necessary if relations with Congress were placid. The organization may have to hire press officers, lobbyists, legislative representatives, or legal counsel to gather and disseminate information. For example, public corporations such as the Postal Service, which interact constantly with their environment, need regular and continuous contacts with Congress, the executive branch, and the public.

The degree of dependence on internal support and unity is a second factor. When internal support and unity are needed, specialists may be required to transmit information from the leadership to members of the organization. In the military or in social service organizations, for example, it may be necessary to monitor the opinions, feelings, and morale of lower-level personnel. When people join the organization, they may have to be carefully taught about its culture. It may also be essential to train leaders so that they can attain a willing following and maintain morale in crisis situations.

The need for information and advice also varies, depending on the degree to which the organization's internal and external environments require scientific data. If internal and external relationships depend heavily on scientific data, there may be a constant need to stay ahead of rapidly moving developments. The Federal Communications Commission, for example, must cope with extremely swift major technological changes that often make rulings obsolete before they have been implemented. Vast amounts of technical information are needed for decision making within the agency and for effective communication with its clients and relevant public institutions. Scientifically targeted public relations efforts may be required to achieve the agency's goals. These may entail gathering studies of the intended target individuals so that messages can be tailored to their interests and needs. Social scientists may be required to generate facts and figures.

Finally, there is a direct correlation between the size, structure, and heterogeneity of an organization and its information needs. Increases in size, heterogeneity of personnel, tasks, and clients, and complexity of structure all generate greater communication demands. Organizations must have information about the publics they are serving, their sponsors or regulatory agencies. They must know about relevant professional associations, citizens' groups, and potential support groups such as the financial community and educational institutions who train personnel. It may also be important to get information on indirect effects of the organization's operations.

There is also a great deal of variation in the amount of information needed for particular decisions at particular times. The start-up of programs may require large amounts of new information. Conversely, when decisions must be made rapidly, time pressures limit the amount of information sought and the number of sources consulted. Wilensky points out that during crises executives are more likely to rely on trial and error and precedent than on scientific advice, except when decisions are purely technical.[65] They have learned to be skeptical of the opinions of experts, who often lack political insights. When stakes are high, more information is usually sought, although there is also a temptation to cling to the tried and true. Increased information then enhances the likelihood of overload and its attendant problems. Decisions about what is and is not needed are difficult to make and organizations tend to err in the direction of oversupply.

Intelligence Failures

Operation Urgent Fury

Given the vastness of the governmental enterprise, it is easy to find horror stories of botched communication that present multiple examples of violations of the canons set forth by Wilensky. Operation Urgent Fury ranks with the best—or perhaps one should say "worst"—of these horror stories. It heavily involved the Department of Defense and the Central Intelligence Agency, which presumably are especially geared to securing adequate intelligence.

Operation Urgent Fury was the code name for a 1983 military invasion of Grenada, a small Caribbean island that was experiencing political turmoil in the wake of a pro-Communist coup d'état. Six hundred American medical students on the island were presumed to be in danger and in need of rescue by their countrymen.

The invasion, which had been planned since the spring of 1983, started in earnest on October 24 of that year. Serious communication problems were evident almost immediately. The landing forces lacked adequate information about the location and strength of enemy positions. The information they had was unreliable and did not warn them adequately about the resistance they were likely to face. They paid in lives for that mistake.

Three branches of the military were involved in the invasion: the Navy, the Army, and the Marines. This raised numerous problems in coordinating information. For example, the three branches operated from different maps, and therefore could not coordinate their assaults. In one instance, because of unclear information, a Marine aerial attack destroyed an Army command post, killing one soldier and wounding seventeen. An air attack destroyed a local mental hospital that did not appear on the map used for the attack, killing and wounding more than a score of patients and staff.[66]

Marine and Army ground units use different radio frequencies and cannot talk directly with one another even when deployed in the same area unless they know these frequencies. When the Army needed aircraft support for ground troops from Navy and Marine units, the request had to be relayed through headquarters at Fort Bragg, North Carolina, because the naval units at the scene lacked modern communication equipment. Messages often had to be relayed through long chains, causing delays and distortions. Some were even transmitted through public telephone booths.[67] One lieutenant used his telephone credit card to request air support from his stateside commanding officer.

Even laymen know that a military operation requires good maps so that units can learn where they are going and direct fire power to the appropriate targets. Yet the soldiers involved in Operation Urgent Fury were supplied with 1978 tourist maps, published by the Grenada tourist board, which were useless for directing artillery fire. Fears that plans about the operation would be leaked had delayed an order for adequate maps until the day of the invasion. High-quality maps were delivered when the operation was nearly over, fully nine days after the initial assault, hardly a "timely" delivery of information.[68]

The mission called for rescuing the medical students. Yet the Defense Department had never bothered to find out where they were located, even though school authorities had been in touch with the State Department and CIA and presented maps showing campus locations and student distribution. The outdated tourist maps used during the actual invasion showed only one campus for the medical school. The rescue effort was therefore directed to that campus, which housed only 138 of the 600 students, leaving the rest for twenty-four to forty-eight hours in an exposed location where they could readily be taken hostage.

Moreover, the validity of the assumption that the students were endangered by the political turmoil and needed to be rescued was never adequately examined. School authorities had been in touch with the State Department, indicating that the Grenadan government was eager to keep the medical school in operation and to protect the students. Although information provided by the school's administration had proved useful on prior occasions, it was not used this time to supplement other information sources, apparently because it ran counter to preconceptions already formed in the department. Charles Modica, chancellor of the medical school, complained: "Well, the State Department didn't give much credence to what I was saying at least from my own point of view, and they intimated that they had their own sources and their sources were probably much better than mine.... I was questioning whether they were even taking any of the information I was giving them at any higher level." [69]

Years later, the reasons for the breakdowns in communication had not been made public, although investigations had been conducted. Senator Sam Nunn, chairman of the Armed Services Committee, has commented that the evidence shows that the CIA had correct information but that "there was a fundamental breakdown between the intelligence community and the customers of that intelligence, that is, the troops who had to have it to perform their mission." [70]

Similar intelligence failures have led to disaster for U.S. military forces in Lebanon and Iran and also in Asian waters when President Ford ordered the Marines in 1975 to free the freighter *Mayaguez* and its crew, which had been seized by Cambodian forces. However, such failures should not obscure the fact that many military missions have been carried out successfully, with precision and foresight. The air and ground operations conducted by the United States during the 1991 Persian Gulf War were praised for their efficiency. Communication failures did occur but were much less than might have been expected considering the complexities involved in coordinating a multinational force fighting at the behest of the United Nations organization.

Achilles' Heels

When organizations are unable to muster the information needed for the successful pursuit of their goals, one can speak of intelligence failure. This happens when essential information is not readily available from internal or external sources, or when it is inaccurate, untimely, or poorly interpreted. The Grenada situation is an excellent example. Wilensky cites six causes for most intelligence failures.[71] These are an organization's Achilles' heels that make it vulnerable to intelligence failures. One of them, *secrecy,* has already been discussed. Three others—hierarchy, specialization, and centralization—are common problems springing from the nature of complex organizations. They will be discussed more fully in Chapter 3. Here it suffices to mention that the *hierarchy* of roles often causes poor communication links between the various levels of the organization for technical as well as psychological reasons. *Specialization* of functions, such as dividing the military into Army, Navy, and Air Force components, may lead to disabling interagency rivalries that prevent proper exchange of information and resistance to accepting information gathered by other agencies. Each agency may guard its own information, believing that it must do so to protect its turf. The relationship between the branches of the military, between the Departments of State and Defense, and between the Bureau of Mines and the Army Engineers, or among the many local police departments, furnishes numerous examples. *Centralization* becomes a problem when too much information is diverted to the top levels of an organization, causing overload, while lower levels are deprived of the information needed to function efficiently. Decision making in the Carter administration often bogged down because the president insisted that information relevant to minor as well as major decisions be funneled through the White House.

Wilensky also mentions *anti-intellectualism* and *narrow empiricism* as common causes of intelligence failures.[72] People conducting the business of government often scorn theories as abstract and impractical. They fail to realize that theories help to make sense of the mass of information received in the course of carrying out the work of the organization, so that trends can be discerned and predictions made about future developments. Narrow empiricism may also lead to intellectual myopia. When agency personnel insist on collecting only verifiable, objective data, many important insights may be lost. For example, much important information is ignored when personnel officers concentrate only on objective facts about recruiting expenditures, hiring, and retention rates, without assessing subjective feelings that people have about an organization or looking at the societal benefits of hiring transient workers. Interpretist and critical theorists have called attention to these problems.

The nature of organizations and data are not the only hurdles to acquiring the information needed to function effectively. Human personality traits, information-processing capabilities, and interactions are other potential obstacles. The dynamics of individual, group, and organizational behavior are particularly likely to create problems.[73] The dynamics of individual behavior include bio-psychological factors and information-processing capabilities. The dynamics of group behavior include internal group processes, group structure, and leadership factors. These problems, as well as the dynamics of organizational behavior, will be discussed in Chapter 4.

Summary and Conclusions

Information is the lifeblood of organizations. This chapter has focused on the major challenges faced by public agencies in gathering the information needed to function properly. The interdependence of diverse strands of information needed by public agencies, ranging from the technical and political to the instrumental and symbolic, was pointed out.

Although government agencies are compulsive information collectors, it is impossible to collect all salient data. Because the choices made shape the information environment for policy decisions, political considerations are an important factor. One can predict decisions with a fair degree of accuracy by knowing who supplied the information for the decision. This does not mean that all sources are deliberately partisan, but that value differences affect judgments about what is important and why. A bird-watcher and a hunter are apt to see a duck from different perspectives.

The discussion then moved to problems encountered in gathering information. Unwilling sources in both the private and public sectors are major barriers. Reasons for withholding information range from protecting selfish interests to ethical concerns about the uses to which the information will be put. The Privacy Act of 1974 and the Paperwork Reduction Act of 1980 also constitute barriers, although other laws, such as the Freedom of Information Act of 1966 and 1974, ease the problems. However, it is sometimes necessary and wise to protect information from disclosure, which can pose major public policy problems.

The final sections of the chapter discuss factors that determine the quantity of information that an organization needs and criteria by which the quality of information can be judged. In terms of quality, it is particularly important for information to be clear, timely, reliable, and valid. It must also be adequate to meet the needs of the situation and should preferably be drawn from a wide range of sources representing a variety of perspectives. The public sector faces very serious obstacles in obtaining information that meets all these requirements.

Some of the major quality-control difficulties are illustrated by the description of a military intervention on the island of Grenada in 1983. Despite the importance that the military places on intelligence operations and its access to comparatively ample resources, major flaws plagued Operation Urgent Fury. To a degree, such flaws are endemic in bureaucracies. Secrecy, anti-intellectualism, and narrow empiricism are to blame, as are hierarchy, specialization, and centralization—the hallmarks of bureaucratic structures.

The major lessons to be drawn from Chapter 2 are threefold. Public administrators must never lose sight of the political environment in which they operate. They must gather information about politics for political reasons and disseminate it to accomplish political purposes vital to their agency's welfare. It is unfortunate that American political culture holds politics in such disdain that public officials often feel compelled to hide political motivations behind a skimpy cloak of excuses, apologies, and often outright lies.

The second lesson is that all information is not equal in value and that less can be better than more. Administrators need to scrutinize sources and learn to distinguish between the wheat and the chaff. This is extraordinarily difficult in the public sector, where vast amounts of information are needed, much unwanted information is submitted, and much needed information is withheld or controlled by self-interested outsiders.

Finally, obtaining and using information is costly. It requires more time, effort, and money than most administrators are willing to acknowledge. More resources need to be allocated to attend to this vital activity.

Notes

1. Charles E. Lindblom and David K. Cohen, *Usable Knowledge: Social Science and Social Problem Solving* (New Haven: Yale University Press, 1979).
2. Harold F. Gortner, Julianne Mahler, and Jeanne Bell Nicholson, *Organizational Theory: A Public Perspective* (Chicago: Dorsey, 1987), 301.
3. John M. Stevens and Robert P. McGowan, *Information Systems and Public Management* (New York: Praeger, 1985), 111.

4. Edward O. Lauman and David Knoke, *The Organizational State: Social Choice in National Policy Domains* (Madison: University of Wisconsin Press, 1987), 191.
5. Edward I. Sidlow and Beth Henschen, "The Performance of House Committee Staff Functions: A Comparative Exploration," *Western Political Quarterly* 38 (September 1985): 487. The committees were Appropriations, Armed Services, Budget, Government Operations, Interior and Insular Affairs, Merchant Marine and Fisheries, Public Works and Transportation, and Ways and Means. They were chosen to represent committees varying in environment and prestige.
6. Ibid., 488.
7. Barbara S. Romzek and Melvin Dubnick, "Accountability in the Public Sector: Lessons from the Challenger Tragedy," *Public Administration Review* 47 (May/June 1987): 231.
8. Harold L. Wilensky, *Organizational Intelligence: Knowledge and Policy in Government and Industry* (New York: Basic Books, 1967), 22.
9. Martha S. Feldman, *Order without Design: Information Production and Policy Making* (Stanford, Calif.: Stanford University Press, 1989), 7-9.
10. Jonathan Bendor, Serge Taylor, and Roland Van Gaalen, "Politicians, Bureaucrats, and Asymmetric Information," *American Journal of Political Science* 31 (1987): 797.
11. Bernard E. Trainor, "Another U.S. Study Down the Drain?" *New York Times,* January 13, 1988.
12. Feldman, *Order without Design,* 2-3.
13. David Whiteman, "The Fate of Policy Analysis in Congressional Decision Making: Three Types of Use in Committees," *Western Political Quarterly* 38 (June 1985): 298.
14. Ibid., 304-307.
15. Herbert Kaufman, *The Administrative Behavior of Federal Bureau Chiefs* (Washington, D.C.: Brookings Institution, 1981), 33.
16. Anthony Downs, *Inside Bureaucracy* (Boston: Little, Brown, 1967), 249-252.
17. Kaufman, *The Administrative Behavior of Federal Bureau Chiefs,* 26-33.
18. Ibid., 31.
19. "Dollars and Sense," *Washington Journal* 2 (April 16, 1990).
20. The first request for information was made on December 22, 1977. NHTSA's Defects Panel announced a formal investigation on February 28, 1978.
21. For similar problems faced by EPA in collecting data about industrial wastes, see Wesley A. Magat, Alan J. Krupnick, and Winston Harrington, *Rules in the Making: A Statistical Analysis of Regulatory Agency Behavior* (Washington, D.C.: Resources for the Future, 1986), 26-40.
22. *New York Times,* April 17, 1984.
23. Magat et al., *Rules in the Making,* 36-40.
24. Hugh Heclo, *A Government of Strangers: Executive Politics in Washington* (Washington, D.C.: Brookings Institution, 1977), 205.
25. Bruce A. Ackerman and William T. Hassler, *Clean Coal/Dirty Air* (New Haven: Yale University Press, 1981), 84.
26. The full text of the original act is reproduced in Appendix 1.
27. *New York Times,* May 3, 1984.
28. Stevens and McGowan, *Information Systems and Public Management,* 197.
29. *New York Times Co. v. United States,* 403 U.S. 713 (1971).
30. "Pentagon's Scientist Curb Hit," *Chicago Tribune,* April 27, 1984.
31. Philip M. Boffey, "Three Major Research Centers Reject Censorship," *New York Times,* April 10, 1984.

32. James Warren, "CBS-TV's Apple Scare Is Costly to Growers," *Chicago Tribune,* May 11, 1989.
33. Wilensky, *Organizational Intelligence,* ix-x.
34. Frederick O. Lorenz, Betty L. Wells, Charles L. Mulford, and Daisy Kabagarama, "How Social Service Agencies React to Uncertainty: Budget Cuts Need Not Curb Creativity," *Sociology and Social Research* 71 (October 1986): 29-30.
35. *New York Times,* May 2, 1984.
36. Timothy J. McNulty, "Ethics Run Weak 2d to Birth Technology," *Chicago Tribune,* October 18, 1987.
37. Gortner et al., *Organizational Theory,* 187-189.
38. James Q. Wilson, *Bureaucracy: What Government Agencies Do and Why They Do It* (New York: Basic Books, 1989), 228.
39. Hugh Heclo, "Issue Networks and the Executive Establishment," in *The New American Political System,* ed., Anthony King (Washington, D.C.: American Enterprise Institute, 1978), 99.
40. Public Law 96-511. The original act expired on September 30, 1989, but was subsequently renewed. Earlier laws included the Federal Reports Act of 1942 under which paperwork requests by the executive branch were scrutinized by the Bureau of the Budget to make sure that costs to the government and private sector were justifiable. Kitty Dumas, "Congress or the White House: Who Controls the Agencies?" *Congressional Quarterly Weekly Report,* April 14, 1990, 1131.
41. Ibid., 1130.
42. Ibid, 1133.
43. *Dole v. Steelworkers,* ___ U.S. ___ (1990). The case is discussed in Linda Greenhouse, "High Court Decides Budget Office Exceeded Power in Blocking Rules," *New York Times,* February 21, 1990.
44. P.L. 89-306. The act has been amended repeatedly, but the substance remains intact. Stevens and McGowan, *Information Systems and Public Management,* 199.
45. U.S. Office of Management and Budget. "Report of the General Government Team to the President's Federal Data Processing Reorganization Project, 'Information Technology: Challenges for Top Program Management in the General Government Agencies,'" *President's Reorganization Project* (Washington, D.C.: Government Printing Office, 1978), 10.
46. The act is reproduced in Appendix 2.
47. The research was conducted by the author's graduate students.
48. Philip Shenon, "The Freedom of Information Act and Its Role in Disclosing Influence Peddling," *New York Times,* August 28, 1989.
49. Wilensky, *Organizational Intelligence,* 151-171, provides additional detail.
50. Ibid., viii-ix.
51. Robert Cunningham and Dorothy Olshfski, "Interpreting State Administrator-Legislator Relationships," *Western Political Quarterly* 39 (March 1986): 104.
52. Ibid., 112.
53. William S. Pierce, *Bureaucratic Failure and Public Expenditure* (New York: Academic, 1981), 224-229.
54. Rose Gutfeld, "Employees Pressured by Managers to Seize Property, Senate Panel Told," *Wall Street Journal,* June 23, 1987.
55. George C. Edwards, III, *Implementing Public Policy* (Washington, D.C.: CQ Press, 1980), 41.
56. Ibid., 42.

57. Carol Weiss, "Congressional Committee Staffs as Problematic Users of Analysis," 1984 APSA paper, 14.
58. David R. Maines and Joseph Palenski, "Reconstructing Legitimacy in Final Reports of Contract Research," *Sociological Review* 34 (August 1986): 575-589; also see Carol H. Weiss and Michael Bucuvalas, "Truth Tests and Utility Tests: Decision-Makers' Frames of Reference for Social Science Research," *American Sociological Review* 45 (1980): 302-303.
59. National Research Council, *Decision Making in the Environmental Protection Agency,* vol. II (Washington, D.C.: National Academy of Sciences, 1977), 119-121.
60. Carol Weiss, "Congressional Committee Staffs as Problematic Users of Analysis," 1984 APSA paper, 21.
61. Wilensky, *Organizational Intelligence,* 173-191.
62. In Anthony Downs, *Inside Bureaucracy,* 117.
63. This is discussed in Charles A. O'Reilly, III, "The Intentional Distortion of Information in Organizational Communications: A Laboratory and Field Investigation," in Daniel Katz, Robert L. Kahn, and J. Stacy Adams, eds., *The Study of Organizations* (San Francisco: Jossey-Bass, 1982), 328-344.
64. Wilensky, *Organizational Intelligence,* 8-16.
65. Ibid., 80-81.
66. James G. March and Roger Weissinger-Babylon, *Ambiguity and Command* (Boston: Pitman, 1986), 295.
67. Richard Gabriel, "Scenes from an Invasion," *Washington Monthly* (February 1986): 40.
68. March and Weissinger-Babylon, *Ambiguity and Command,* 293.
69. Frontline #602 Broadcast, "Operation Urgent Fury" (Boston: WGBH Educational Foundation, 1988), 14.
70. Ibid., 22.
71. Wilensky, *Organizational Intelligence,* 41-74.
72. Ibid., 62-63.
73. Alexander L. George, *Presidential Decisionmaking in Foreign Policy: The Effective Use of Information and Advice* (Boulder, Colo.: Westview, 1980), 11-12.

The Interface of Structure and Function

General Issues

Why Structures Are Needed

This chapter deals with the problems faced by administrators who must design structures appropriate to organizational goals. *Structure,* in this context, refers to the prescribed patterns of relationships, as reflected in the formal organization chart and work manuals. For example, when the city of Chicago established a Commission on Human Relations, it was divided into offices for refugee and immigration matters, veterans' affairs, and gay and lesbian issues. The structure reflected the intent of city officials to pay particular attention to these three areas. James March and Herbert Simon contend that organizational structures are essential for regularizing behavior and decision making because human rationality is limited.[1] Without prescribed structures, the "bounded" rational capabilities of human beings would make it difficult for them to coordinate their efforts to achieve common goals. Organizational structure thus guides organizational behavior, including communication behavior.

Thanks to the nature of the structure in which they work, employees know what their particular position requires and with whom they are supposed to communicate. Chicago's administrator of immigration reform, for example, knows the boundaries of his official tasks and the administrative units with which he must interact. The official structures provide a restricted, standardized communication environment that enhances the stability and predictability of organizational behavior.[2] As Daniel Katz and Robert Kahn put it, "The very nature of a social system . . . implies a selectivity of channels and communication acts—a mandate to avoid some and utilize others." [3]

Structure affects how communication functions, just as communication behavior affects organizational structures. When messages do not move well in the existing structures, these structures may be altered to better serve the communication flow patterns. Reorganization of the Federal Aviation Administration's (FAA) terrorism warning system for airlines is an example. When a Pan-American flight exploded over Lockerbie, Scotland, in December 1988, killing 270 people, flaws in the transmission of danger messages were highlighted. The Department of Transportation, which oversees the FAA, ordered major changes in channeling warnings to endangered aircraft and to the public in the hope that the altered structures would lead to better communication in the future.[4]

What Structures Are Best?

In the public sector, basic options for designing organizational structures include emphasis on geographical divisions, functional divisions, line and staff functions, or client types. Various mixtures of these elements are also possible. Which of these structures is best, considering the functions to be performed, has remained a matter of some controversy. Some analysts contend that communication flows best if work is functionally divided, so that units are concerned with a single project or task or deal with only one problem. For example, the Illinois Public Health Department is divided into units dealing with Consumer Health Protection, Geriatrics and Long Term Care, Reduction of Infant Mortality, Parents Too Soon, and Nuclear Safety, among others. Divisions by discipline, as is common in universities, or skill, as done for work involving the building trades, or clientele, as in veterans' affairs, also work well. Dividing work by geographical unit, according to this view, is least conducive to good information flows because political boundaries become barriers to information exchange. Police departments, which are geographically organized, are examples. They often experience communication difficulties attributable to political boundary problems.

By and large, the difficulties encountered in creating effective communication systems mount with increasing size of the organization and increasing complexity of the functions to be performed. It then becomes harder to design a standardized system. More improvisation becomes necessary, guided by feedback from ongoing and past activities.[5]

Appropriate structures do not necessarily mean that information flows will be perfect. Human error is an ever-present likelihood. Executive branches, for instance, tend to have well-developed lines of communication throughout the bureaucracy. Nonetheless, even when special efforts have been made to assure flawless communication, serious information-flow lapses occur routinely, particularly when important technical information needs to be transmitted.[6] A typical incident involved the Savannah River nuclear-weapons plant near Aiken, South Carolina, which is the nation's only source of tritium, a perishable gas essential for thermonuclear warheads. The plant is owned by the Energy Department but was operated for the government for thirty-eight years by E. I. du Pont de Nemours & Company. When du Pont decided in 1987 to give up its contract to run the plant, the company's chief executive personally assured the secretary of energy and President Reagan's chief of staff that the plant was in good condition. This information was accepted without cross-checking adequately, even though the Energy Department maintained its own office at the plant to assure good communication.

After Westinghouse Electric Corporation contracted to take over operations, it became clear that the plant was in bad shape. This information had been available to the government for many years. Du Pont scientists had reported major weaknesses in the plant's equipment, and Energy Department officials in South Carolina had been notified about the problems but had failed to respond. For example, in 1985 the Energy Department office at the plant received a memorandum summarizing thirty accidents and mishaps during du Pont's stewardship. The information was not passed on to safety officials in Washington largely because of the physical separation between the South Carolina and Washington offices of the Energy Department, although this should not have been a structural hurdle.[7] Three years after the 1985 memorandum, no action had been taken. When Westinghouse Corporation was finally able to bring the message about the plant's problems to the attention of Washington officials, the government was forced to shut down the plant's three reactors in April 1988. This action threatened to compromise the readiness of the nation's nuclear arsenal because of the shortage of tritium.

Structures differ because of the varied needs of organizations dictated by their activities and essential information flows. However, in many instances, structures are not adequately adapted to the needs they must serve. This is particularly true in the public sector, where political concerns often determine structures. The structures may then be the end product of a bargaining process among political forces that are trying to maximize their particular goals. Power factors determine the outcome, often producing "organized anarchies" whose structures may look rational but are really inappropriate. Frequently they reflect outdated phases of the organization's life.[8]

Structure as a Political Tool

The drive of various minorities to gain more access to centers of political power provides many examples of politically motivated restructuring in the

1980s. Chicago's Mayor Richard Daley, for instance, was under fire in late 1989 from gay and lesbian lobby groups who criticized his failure to meet with them as often as they deemed appropriate. Other organized minorities voiced similar complaints. Since it seemed impossible to provide satisfactory direct access to all groups clamoring for the mayor's attention, he restructured communication routes. Representatives from organized minority groups were accredited as advisory councils to the city's Human Relations Commission so that future communications with the mayor would flow through this umbrella organization. Reaction to the proposal was mixed. It had the advantage of relieving the mayor of the politically explosive task of having to restrict direct access to his office on a case-by-case basis. From the standpoint of minority groups, it represented yet another bureaucratic barrier, albeit a lower one, in their struggle to gain access to the top echelon of power.

Since organizational structures have a major impact on the effectiveness of political leaders, it is not surprising that they spend considerable time and effort on creating the kinds of structures deemed best for accomplishing their purposes.[9] At the top levels of decision making, it is particularly important to structure who has access to decision makers during various phases of the process and who prepares the final reports that serve as the information base for decisions.

For example, the intelligence agencies in the State Department, Defense Department, and Central Intelligence Agency prepare the National Intelligence Estimates that are used for foreign-policy decisions. The estimates presumably represent a consensus among the contributing bodies, who often disagree substantially about facts and their implications. But the CIA director chairs the meetings and edits the joint report, which offers the opportunity to dominate the process so that it reflects his views. There is ample evidence from the Reagan administration that CIA director William Casey used his key position in the reporting structures to ensure that the National Intelligence Estimates supported his often controversial policy preferences.[10]

Decisions about structure occur at all levels of organizational life. They range from determining what new structures will be created and what additions will be made to existing structures to resolving how existing structures should be modified to alter the ways of carrying out governmental functions. All of these decisions are vulnerable to political influence. The incentive to control them is particularly strong because structures in government are usually formalized through laws or administrative regulations that have the force of law. They are difficult to modify because of their legal status and because they represent allocations of power and behavioral routines in which organizational members quickly acquire a vested interest. This is why Governor Terry E. Branstad of Iowa called speedy action a crucial element in the structural reform of administrative agencies. He was able to reduce departments from sixty-eight to twenty and to eliminate forty boards and commissions. As he explained in an address at Duke University in 1987, "[C]ompression of time allowed us to build enough momentum to reduce the drag caused by the opposing interest groups during this entire process. If we had waited longer to devise or to accomplish the plan, the interest groups would likely have simply picked it apart." [11]

At times, prospective changes in communication patterns are a key factor in arousing opposition. This happened when the Carter administration wanted to create a separate Department of Education, removed from the Department of Health, Education and Welfare. Secretary of Health, Education and Welfare Joseph A. Califano opposed the move for several reasons. He pointed out that an extra department would mean an extra voice with direct access to the president, increasing the overload of messages with which the executive office was already struggling.[12] From a departmental perspective, the separation would make it much more difficult to coordinate health and welfare matters with education because messages previously handled as internal matters would now become external communications. The proposed structural changes would also produce radical changes in the responsiveness of the educational bureaucracy to various elected officials and interest groups. In this case, Califano's arguments failed to stop the creation of the new department, which was established in 1979 in the waning years of the Carter administration. Although it was subsequently marked for extinction by the Reagan administration, like most doomed organizations, it has managed to survive.

The Impact of Legislative Structures

The legislative committee system prevalent in Congress, state legislatures, and city councils illustrates particularly well how structure shapes function. Most American legislatures are organized to perform their duties by dealing with specialized areas of concern, even though one might expect them to be geographically organized because legislators represent geographically defined districts. Patterns of communication and the resulting patterns of influence reflect the specialized tasks. For instance, congressional committees and their subordinate units do not draw information primarily from individual states or from clusters of states representing certain regions. Rather, legislators deal with concerns of agriculture or banking or air transportation predominantly on a nationwide basis, although they do remain attuned to pressing needs of the people who elected them.

In line with the old adage that "you stand where you sit," legislators' policy positions vary, depending on the committees on which they serve. For example, legislation to provide access to transportation for handicapped people is likely to be viewed from quite different perspectives when it comes before Health and Human Services committees and Transportation committees. The former are likely to stress human needs; the latter tend to be concerned with efficiency and costs in public transportation systems.[13]

Because the work clusters around specialized tasks, much current legislation emphasizes technical matters. Hence, technical concerns become a major criterion when selecting information sources, so that members of Congress may feel compelled to base their decisions on data from expert studies.[14] Since legislators usually have a choice among several technical studies that reach conflicting conclusions, they can normally tap expert opinions that support their own inclinations. The number of committees created to deal with specialized needs has escalated at all governmental levels. The work patterns of legislators accordingly have become more fragmented. As time spent on meetings increases, time for research and reflection decreases. Therefore more of the work underlying legislators' decisions has to be based on work by their staffs and by respected colleagues.[15]

Overall, because the congressional structure is decentralized and nonhierarchical, it offers numerous access points where outsiders can convey information and pressure for consideration. Appeals and information transmitted to Congress will vary depending on which of the formal or informal structural units is approached. A group of African-American citizens seeking help to combat racial discrimination in their hometown will use different arguments when contacting their senator's office, the offices of the Congressional Black Caucus, or a civil rights lobby group.

The fact that Congress is structured as a bipartisan body encourages committees to search for and select information that will lead to compromises with a good chance of winning acceptance from a majority of the congressional membership. Gathering information in support of a single policy direction would be deemed counterproductive in a bipartisan organization because it would probably hamper compromise. The bipartisan character of Congress also means that congressional staffs are hired on a partisan basis and view information gathering and processing accordingly. They scrutinize information for its political dimensions as well as its substantive qualities. This is particularly true since committee staffs lack civil service status, their jobs hinging on the reelection of the member of Congress who hired them.

In recent years money available to members of Congress for hiring information-gathering staffs has risen vastly.[16] The fact that congressional staff positions are now held by more than 20,000 people has significantly restructured information-intake patterns. The information on which decisions are based has become far more subject to congressional control than in earlier years when much of the expertise, of necessity, depended on information provided free of charge by interest groups and their lobbyists.

Research on information flows within Congress indicates that the members who are most involved in shaping legislation now rely most heavily on their personal staffs and on committee staffs for advice and information.[17] These young, well-educated professionals are intellectually and ideologically far removed from the former ranks of lobbyists and special-interest pleaders. Similar patterns prevail in many state legislatures.

This does not mean that special-interest groups and their lobbyists have lost their clout entirely. As members of political bodies, dependent on constituencies that can provide campaign resources and votes, most legislators feel compelled to consider information offered by interest groups. Moreover, despite the growth in staffs, resources for gathering information are insufficient, so that legislators must still rely to a substantial degree on data provided by outside sources. Organizations and individuals who control information that is attractive to legislators, and whose activities are structured to bring it to legislative attention, become powerful.[18] Those who do not control information or control information that is not highly prized, or who lack the structure to present it effectively, tend to be low on the power scale. As Table 2-2 in Chapter 2 shows, the extent to which various staffs rely on information submitted by interest groups differs significantly. Among the eight House committees studied by Edward Sidlow and Beth Henschen, the staffs in clientele-oriented committees such as Merchant Marine, Interior, and Public Works were more concerned with interest-group information than were committees such as Ways and Means, Budget, or Government Operations.[19]

Structuring Bureaucratic Information Flows

The congressional example points up the two main decisions that administrators face when relating structure to function: the "who" and "how" decisions. The first concerns personnel. Which individuals, with all the intellectual baggage they carry, will be major cogs in the communication process? The "how" decision relates to the rules that organizations devise to cope with their communication processes. We will first discuss "who" and "how" issues and follow this with a discussion of major structural constraints on information flows in typical organizations.

Personnel Structure

To gather needed information, organizations must set up appropriate personnel structures. These range from assigning information functions as sidelines in jobs primarily concerned with other matters to hiring part- or full-time communication specialists or setting up attached or freestanding organizational units solely devoted to information functions. To mesh the information-processing structures of a multitude of agencies and overcome excessive fragmentation, coordinating structures have also been created. Examples are the federal Office of Management and Budget, the Office of Planning and Evaluation established during the Reagan years, and the Economic Policy Board set up by the Ford Administration.[20] In addition, various structures have been created to gather information systematically. The Bureau of the Census, which collects demographic information, and the Federal Bureau of Investigation, which collects crime data, are examples.

Internal monitoring staffs may encompass personnel directors who deal with information about the organization's work force. They are primarily concerned with the important human-relations aspects of organizational communication, with the technical expertise of internal dialogue, and with the efficient transmission of work-related information throughout the organization. The work of the internal monitoring staffs may be supplemented by education and training staffs who continuously develop the organization's human resources in line with changing needs and by staffs who prepare internally circulating publications. On the whole, the quality of personnel work in public agencies lags behind the private sector, where it is easier to evaluate performance because most private organizations produce readily measurable goods and services and have profit bottom lines.[21] Advances have nonetheless been made. Public agencies have begun to draw on a much wider array of skills to satisfy their communication needs. For instance, the military now uses psychologists to guide training operations; it also uses sociologists to study internal communication and aspects of organizational climate, such as morale.

Structures are also needed for the creation of organizational memories. Information storage and retrieval have become major concerns in an age of overabundant messages. Someone has to decide what to store and what to let pass and how to store it so that it can be readily retrieved when needed. This job may be assigned to an archivist, but most public agencies lack the funds for such a position. In fact, little formal attention has been given to creating structures for preserving organizational memories aside from legal requirements that mandate retention of designated information, such as contracts, financial data, or client files that must be kept for a specified number of years. These record-keeping requirements, coupled with a fair degree of job stability in the lower civil service ranks, keep organizational memories in the public sector in better shape than might be expected. To save physical and electronic filing space, many organizations destroy information about intermediate steps in decision making and aborted transactions. It is thus often difficult to track major considerations that entered into decisions and thereby learn from past failures.

For external communication, a public relations staff may be required, along with lobbyists, legislative representatives, and supporting legal personnel. Such staffs provide information about the organization to outsiders and gather needed technical, organizational, and political information. Successful communication may also require hiring a research staff, planners, analysts who monitor internal proceedings, economists, statisticians, and management consultants, as well as lawyers who negotiate, arbitrate, and litigate. Generally, public agencies falter when it comes to scanning the external environment in order to mesh it with the agency's work. Research and development personnel tend to be technologically oriented and rarely produce the broader picture that is needed to keep the organization in balance with its environment.

Organizations increasingly need staff members who devote all or most of their time to gathering information because so much is available and so much is needed. Structures designed to handle communications therefore tend to multiply and become more complex in proportion to the increasing complexity of tasks assigned to an organization and the increasing heterogeneity of sources that need to be consulted. The Department of Agriculture's structure is a typical example of a highly complex modern organization. As Figure 3-1 shows, it has fourteen major divisions and thirty-five subdivisions. Three units deal primarily with information management: the Office of Public Affairs, the Office of Congressional Relations, and the Office of Information Resources Management. Obviously, the task of coordinating the work of all of the units and communicating across the organization's internal and external boundaries is shaped by many other officials in the Agriculture Department besides those in the three specialized units.

Concern about obtaining the general public's reactions to government programs has led to the establishment of many new liaison structures in recent decades. A number of states now appoint advocates for the public interest.[22] Wisconsin, for example, has a public intervenor, located in the attorney general's office, who has successfully represented the views of citizens on environmental issues considered by state agencies. The office also helps build and sustain public interest in environmental issues. Other states have created offices that counsel consumers and have appointed ombudsmen who funnel citizens' concerns to public agencies.[23] Public hearings prior to policy making have become common requirements, especially when regulatory and tax policies are under consideration. Similarly, the White House now has an Office of Public Liaison to provide a two-way information channel for various segments of the public. The impact of these access structures in bringing public views to bear on decision making is discussed more fully in Chapter 4.

Compared with large private enterprises, the public sector generally is not well supplied with personnel dispensing and gathering information. In fact, many public organizations are distinguished by the puny size of these staffs. The State Department is an example. American diplomats stationed abroad have always lacked sufficient personnel to gather the information

Figure 3-1 Organization Chart of the Department of Agriculture

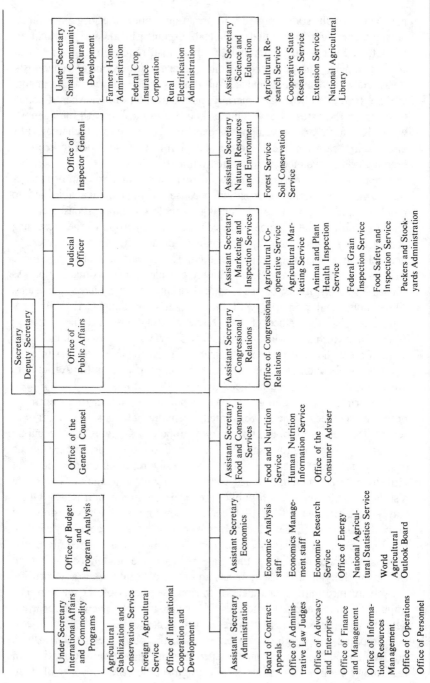

they need to function effectively. As a result, they are heavily dependent on press reports, contacts with a small number of upper-class informants, and reports volunteered by disaffected elements within the society. The difficulties of setting up appropriate liaisons in foreign countries and keeping in touch with people who belong to often vastly different cultures also militate against effective communication structures.

Personnel inadequacies are made more serious by the penchant of government agencies to collect excessive amounts of information, often in very wasteful ways. Consequently, government resources are drained needlessly, as are the resources of information providers. As described in Chapter 2, Congress passed a Paperwork Reduction Act in 1980 to improve information-collection procedures and ease the burden of handling government paperwork. At the time it was estimated that it took citizens 12.7 billion hours a year to fill out federal government forms.

All requests for reports and reporting forms issued by federal agencies must now meet standards set by OMB. For Internal Revenue Service forms, for example, OMB now requires a simplified format and a published estimate of the time it will take an average citizen to complete each form. Thus Form 1040, the standard individual income-tax return, is listed—obviously too optimistically—as requiring three hours and seven minutes for record keeping throughout the year, two hours and twenty-eight minutes to study the instructions for completing the form, three hours and seven minutes to complete the form, and thirty-five minutes to assemble the documents, copy them, and prepare them for mailing. That comes to a total of nine hours and seventeen minutes—more than a full day's work.

OMB claims that its rules have been successful in streamlining paperwork handled by federal agencies. Between 1980 and 1987, according to OMB, the new rules reduced the public's workload by 600 million hours annually. This amounted to roughly 44 percent of the time that citizens had previously spent on required reports to the government. If one figures the hourly value of a citizen's time at ten dollars or more, the savings were enormous, even without figuring the savings in the federal government's processing expenses.[24]

The Rules of the Communication Game

Turning to the "how" issue, administrators must formulate a variety of rules to guide the flow of information within their organization. These include descriptions of the duties encompassed in each job, guidelines about work procedures, descriptions of reporting structures to be followed in ordinary and extraordinary circumstances, and the like. Once established, the patterns of formal communication flows are relatively stable. The network of contacts established among members of a group becomes its structure, and the group's shared beliefs become its culture.[25] Information flows change slowly because they become hardened in custom and are buttressed by the power relationships that they create. Stabilizing these relationships fosters regularity and predictability, so that people within the organization as well as outsiders find it easy to know the routines that must be followed. If asked to funnel their requests through "channels," they know precisely what is meant.

Organizational charts usually indicate for each position who communicates with whom and who has authority over whom. The position thus furnishes a frame of reference that its occupant quickly learns to adopt. In Chicago's Economic Development Commission, the deputy commissioner for capital improvement reports to the commissioner of economic development, who reports to the entire Economic Development Commission and to the mayor. Since there is a separate commissioner for financial assistance to business, matters pertaining to financial aid are outside the realm of concern and reporting by the deputy commissioner for capital improvement.

The position held within an organizational structure serves as an extremely strong social constraint that determines how a person is likely to act. A study of business executives, for example, showed that their attitudes were better explained by their position within the organizational structure than by their self-interest or ideology.[26] Accordingly, officials who hold different jobs in different subsystems within an organization will seek out different information and respond quite differently to a given message. The chief financial officer, charged with keeping budgets low, looks for different information to make her case than the research and development chief who wants to advocate a new program.[27]

Once political power relationships have hardened as part of the established communication game, it is difficult to switch to new rules. An example from local politics in Chicago is relevant. Harold Washington, Chicago's first black mayor, faced grave difficulties during the early years of his administration in controlling city politics. Many aldermen opposed his leadership. Washington therefore decided to curb their power by rerouting communications to positions controlled by his allies. Such a change could be justified as a streamlining of communication circuits. Predictably, it died in the political battle royal that ensued.

Chicago aldermen have traditionally derived political power from their ability to secure city services for their constituents, who in turn cast their votes as instructed.[28] The heart of aldermanic operations is the ward office where people telephone their requests for services from city government, such as repairing gutters, planting trees, or installing street lights. The aldermen then relay these demands to the appropriate offices in the city and capture the plaudits when the service is rendered. Mayor Washington proposed to eliminate the aldermanic hub in the communication system, suggesting that city residents go directly to City Hall for help, bypassing aldermen and their various political helpers. A "Right to Service" campaign would instruct citizens how to get services directly from City Hall, which was controlled by the mayor and his allies. The intercession of local politicians would be unnecessary.

As typically happens in these political battles, Washington denied that his proposal was an effort to reduce the power of aldermen and increase City Hall clout, but the consequences, if not the intent, were clear to political observers familiar with Chicago politics. Similarly, the aldermen put their opposition on technical grounds, skirting the political issue that was at the heart of the move. They argued that the bypass would produce a backlog of service requests at City Hall. They pointed out that the Mayor's Office of Inquiry and Information already handled 25,000 telephone calls each month, indicating that the capacity of City Hall to handle such messages was already strained. Besides, they argued, City Hall would not know the neighborhoods well enough to render services efficiently.

Some of the serious difficulties plaguing the public sector in making rules for adequate information flows are illustrated by problems faced by the Federal Aviation Administration in structuring its external communications. The FAA is charged with monitoring airline safety and therefore receives numerous reports about terrorist threats against aircraft. Many of these reports are exceedingly vague, indicating only that some unidentified terrorist group is planning an attack on American aircraft in some imprecisely specified area of the globe. Lacking its own overseas investigation staff, the FAA must rely on military and CIA information and on warnings supplied intermittently by foreign governments. Most of the time the information is too sketchy to verify the credibility of these reports. If they contain specific information, details that could identify secret intelligence sources must be kept confidential in subsequent communications sent out by the FAA.

Even though the data may be shaky, as is true of data gathered by public agencies, the FAA must disseminate it to segments of the public that have a vital interest in the information. For the FAA, threatened airlines are the target public. They must receive the information soon enough to take precautions, but not so hastily that they respond to false alarms. The FAA finds it difficult to pinpoint the ideal time and to have its messages ready on time because communication by its sources is often slow. Moreover, airlines need far more specific data than the FAA is usually able to provide. The outcome is frustration all around. Even worse, the outcome may be major disasters such as the failed warnings about the possibility of a bomb aboard the Pan-American flight that exploded over Scotland in 1988.

The Impact of Physical Settings

Communication flows are also affected by the physical structures of offices, including locations assigned to offices and room layouts. Accordingly, German and Swedish management scientists have developed the concept of "office landscaping" to facilitate communication. For example, research shows that people whose work stations are separated by more than seventy-five feet rarely tend to communicate.[29] Hence, it is important to structure office space so that people who should communicate continuously are located close to one another, particularly at the start of their working relationship. Once communication ties become established, personal and professional attraction serve to overcome physical distance. The fact that a goodly portion of congressional committee staffs are dispersed among spatially distant offices may be detrimental to their performance.

· In recent years the importance of office landscaping has been forcefully impressed on American managers in the private sector who have compared Japanese management styles with their own. The Japanese office structure is designed to keep people as close to one another as possible to encourage communication. Up to fifty members of a department may be arranged in one big room with desks closely crowded together.[30] Such a "Burolandschaft" without walls makes supervision easy. Departmental executives share these same rooms, although their desks may be on a raised dais to provide more visibility and allow them to keep in better visual contact with their work force. There is no privacy. All transactions, whether business or personal, are readily observable by co-workers.

These office layouts reflect a distinct management philosophy. The emphasis is on teamwork and group performance. In the American system, where individual offices and privacy are much more common, the emphasis is on clearly defined specialties and job assignments. This creates "turfs" that their owners try to protect by keeping information to themselves.[31] The Japanese office design encourages gossip and idle chatter, but this waste of time is more than compensated for by high morale and team spirit. People get to know one another well, and the feeling of closeness encourages further communication and mutual helpfulness. When superiors make decisions in such a closely knit system, subordinates feel that they have had a share in the process through constant contact with the superior. If the Japanese system seems dismaying to Americans who value privacy, Japanese complain that the American system is excessively individualistic and makes workers feel lonely. It also makes it easy to hide unproductive and even illegal behavior.

The psychological impact of architectural settings is well known and implemented by using opulent interiors as organizational status symbols and erecting awe-inspiring buildings to house heads of state or high courts. But these insights are rarely given sufficient consideration in planning the offices of less-exalted public agencies. As John Crompton and Charles Lamb write,

When discussing facility development or renovation, government and social service agencies frequently think only in terms of functional considerations and minimum costs. Economies are made on such items as carpeting, drapes, furnishings, lighting and landscaping because they are considered peripheral items that can be cut from the budget without adversely impacting the basic service. In fact, however, these are often the most critical ingredients in a new facility. They are the very things that create the welcoming atmosphere necessary to encourage potential clients to use the service. . . . Even if they are added later, the initial image of the facility has been established in the minds of its potential clientele. . . . You never get a second chance to make a first impression.[32]

The physical setting of an agency communicates messages about its professionalism to employees and clients alike.

People use visual and audio cues to generalize about the entire agency. Overflowing waste baskets, filled ash trays, temporary signs, and outdated posters may lead a client to infer that (1) this is "just a job" for the staff and they do not take pride in their agency, (2) the manager is ineffective, or (3) the agency is not concerned about its clientele. If an environment is perceived as desirable, relaxing, comfortable, nonhostile and hence rewarding, it is likely that the activities that take place in that environment will also be perceived as desirable and rewarding.[33]

A welfare client interviewed in a homelike setting, with appropriately placed seating facilities, is likely to feel more relaxed, making communication easier, than when the interview takes place in a crowded office where clients have to stand in front of a counter and discuss their personal affairs across a desk and within earshot of a multitude of strangers.[34] All too often, in the public service, the physical setting of agencies is unattractive, dowdy, and even dirty and neglected, making users feel uncomfortable and degraded.

Research by a number of psychologists indicates the significant impact that physical settings can have on communication. Psychologists Abraham Maslow and Norbert Mintz, for example, found in one typical experiment that when subjects in a beautiful room were shown pictures of faces they had a more positive response to them than did subjects situated in an ugly room.[35] Overall, the subjects placed in the ugly room felt more discontented, tired, and hostile and tried to end the encounter, whereas subjects in the beautiful setting felt comfortable, energetic, and were eager to continue the interaction. Room colors, too, often affect transactions. Warm reddish colors stimulate people to interact, while cool bluish colors produce more restrained communication patterns. These facts should be considered when designing public facilities so that the physical setting enhances rather than diminishes the effectiveness of the tasks that need to be accomplished.[36]

Structural Constraints on Communication Flows

It should be clear by now that organizational structure may facilitate communication flows or it may impair them. We now turn to several problems that are endemic in organizations because they arise from the very nature of bureaucratic structure. According to Max Weber, the main characteristics of a bureaucracy include: (1) a hierarchy of formal positions that makes task performance more rational; (2) division of tasks by specialization; and (3) central direction and coordination of tasks. All of these characteristics produce major communication problems for public bureaucracies.

Hierarchy Problems

Hierarchical structures require superiors to direct the work and subordinates to carry out the directions. Superiors give commands and instructions that flow downward from top-level personnel to the lower echelons in stepwise progression. The lower echelons, who carry out these commands and instructions, in turn are told what kind of information and reports they must provide to upper-level personnel. Several problems ensue.

The number of levels through which information must pass is a problem per se. In Chapter 2 we discussed how distortions occur as messages travel upward and downward in the hierarchy. Major information loss is likely at every transmission point. The hierarchical layers through which information must pass also produce delays that are detrimental to efficiency and may lead to inaction. There is much evidence that multiple clearances and consultations stultify action in government agencies. Multiple levels may also discourage innovation because it is easier to persist in old ways requiring no further communication than to make suggestions for change. Each bureaucratic level becomes a hurdle to be cleared or to trap the innovator. People with the power to make changes may never receive proposals. Hierarchical communication also impedes the flow of information that does not fit precisely into the formally established patterns.

Political scientists Robert O'Conner and Larry Spence warn that "hierarchical communication systems may be 'rational' in some abstract sense but, according to human communication theory, they deny rules basic to the successful exchange of information." [37] People normally need to interact face to face to capture the implicit messages conveyed through voice, tone, gestures, vocabulary, and style. Yet such interactions are largely lacking in the typical bureaucratic situation. Hence, people find it difficult to discern the real intentions of message senders, which leaves them either uncomfortably uncertain or pleasantly in a position to interpret messages to fit their own predilections. According to O'Conner and Spence, "the neglect of implicit messages makes bureaucratic organizations ponderous, inefficient, and unable to learn from their mistakes."[38] However, this inability to capture all the nuances transmitted in face-to-face interactions can be advantageous when it reduces the tasks that agencies are requested to perform. It is far easier to turn down requests for help or ignore them when dealing with impersonal messages, stripped of the emotional content that face-to-face interactions supply.

The depersonalization common in hierarchical communication makes it especially difficult to know to what extent messages are meant to lead to action and to what extent they are tactical or purely symbolic. Hugh Heclo entitles his book *A Government of Strangers,* referring to communication among bureaucrats who do not know one another. He comments about the difficulty of transmitting meanings accurately under such conditions: "Those on the receiving end of messages from political executives are accustomed to applying a heavy discount factor to mere proclamations." Heclo quotes a typical comment by a line official that "over the years you see that a lot of the instructions aren't intended to be carried out. It takes extra effort to make it clear to people down the line that something is meant, not just another statement for the record or some speechwriter's inspiration." [39]

The extra effort to overcome doubts may take the form of structures and functions designed to build additional redundancy into the system. Examples are complex information-management systems, written reminders, beefed-up reporting structures, and the like. But, in Heclo's view, "none of these techniques are substitutes for personalized networks and discussions." There is, as yet, no substitute for information gained from body language and other types of nonverbal behavior not ordinarily transmitted through hierarchical channels.

Several scholars have pointed out that hierarchical structuring is conducive to concealment and misrepresentation.[40] In turn, this may encourage "whistle-blowing," where employees bypass the hierarchy and take their concerns directly to higher authorities or to the public. There are several reasons for these phenomena. Subordinates may be unable to pierce the middle layers and reach the top of the hierarchy if the information they seek to transmit does not fall within the formally prescribed upward information flow. When subordinates do manage to reach their superiors, these superiors often close their ears to lower-level information because of the difference in their status. Superiors are not likely to be receptive to information coming from lower levels, especially if it is contrary to their perception of the situation. The much-told story of the Japanese attack on Pearl Harbor in 1941 is an example. The attack planes were spotted by an army private nearly one hour before the attack. He notified his lieutenant who, "knowing" that no attack was in the offing, told him to forget it.[41]

Even when good channels exist to link various levels of the hierarchy, subordinates are often loath to use them because they feel intimidated by the trappings of hierarchy and are fearful of being perceived as meddling or as troublemakers. Subordinates are reluctant to report problems because they want to look good in order to receive favorable evaluations. Hence, bad news often does not flow upward. This depressing yet understandable yielding to self-interest occurs even when outside experts are hired. They prefer to pass on messages that please rather than disturb the top echelons of the bureaucracy. Subordinates may also be inclined to withhold potentially disturbing information because they do not want to be saddled with extra work to correct problems. If there is fierce competition for promotions, subordinates seeking to increase their own chances may restrict information to withhold it from ambitious co-workers. However, if promotion and tenure are protected by a civil service system, this concern becomes less acute.

Acculturation to the organization is yet another factor that stifles the upward flow of information within hierarchies. Organizations emphasize loyalty, adherence to rules, and enthusiastic support for the agency's mission. They indoctrinate their staffs and often the public to believe that the agency's performance is excellent. This discourages critical questions and reduces the number of fresh slants that are likely to be presented. The political culture also suggests that it is usually improper to contradict people in higher organizational ranks. Even officials in the top ranks, such as the secretary of state or the secretary of defense, hesitate to voice opposition to their superiors. An example was the reluctance of Secretary of State George Shultz and Secretary of Defense Caspar Weinberger to voice strong opposition to the illegal sale of arms to Iran during the Reagan administration. Similarly, when the press reported that appraisals of appropriate tactics made by General Norman Schwarzkopf, commander of American forces in the Persian Gulf War, conflicted with President Bush's views, Schwarzkopf promptly recanted. Top-level officials have occasionally resigned from their jobs as a precondition to feeling free to disagree with their boss. For example, President Ford's press secretary, J. F. ter Horst, resigned so that he could freely protest Ford's pardoning of former President Nixon.

Several structural and procedural changes may help to surmount the hurdles of hierarchy.[42] Among them is making lines of communication available that are outside the normal hierarchical channels. For instance, top-level administrators may seek information from education directors or auditors in the organization because these staff people are in touch with all levels of the hierarchy. They may periodically spend time in the field to observe and contact employees at all levels or they may establish direct contacts with rank-and-file employees, bypassing intermediate levels. At best, however, intermediate levels should be consulted before they are bypassed, lest both morale and efficiency suffer.

Alternatively, top bureaucrats may talk with external contact people such as reporters and researchers who may be studying the organization. It may be necessary to call on experts such as consultants or statistical analysts to investigate what is going on at remote lower levels. However, it is not clear how useful such unofficial sources are compared with more readily available inside sources. As one close observer of the Peace Corps described it:

> Unfortunately, neither the congressmen nor the press display much enthusiasm for visits to the mines. Yet this is what I found to be the key to getting the real story about the Peace Corps. I had to go to Ouagadougou and talk to the volunteers at their sites before I could really know what the Peace Corps was doing and what its problems were. I wasn't going to find out by asking the public affairs office. But that's where most reporters go and sit all day—outside Larry Speakes's office or its equivalent throughout the government.[43]

Other possibilities for reducing the ill effects of hierarchy may be the rearrangement of structures to reduce the number of bureaucratic layers through which information has to travel. Hierarchies then become flatter. This may be particularly important in bureaucracies in which lower-level employees are faced with complex nonroutine decisions. Case workers in social welfare agencies, for example, can make better decisions about an individual client's case when they directly observe the situation than is possible for higher-ups who have no contact with the client. A flat hierarchy may be the ideal configuration. Psychological barriers to superior-subordinate communication may also be easier to bridge when the hierarchy is flatter. However, as discussed previously, major restructuring is extremely difficult to accomplish in the public sector because it alters power relations and often requires cumbersome changes in the law or in official rules.

It may be somewhat easier to rearrange the organizational structure so that people can work in teams in which hierarchical levels are de-emphasized. Sometimes teams of experts representing various specialties and ranks work together to perform specific tasks. The informality of this type of organization encourages exchange of information irrespective of the bureaucratic ranks of the members. The team approach also spurs innovations. "Quality circle" programs, discussed in Chapter 4, have become popular to improve performance, bringing together individuals from a cross section of hierarchical levels to brainstorm solutions to problems.[44] It may also help to rotate experts and executives among jobs to break down barriers.

Specialization Problems

Specialization is another source of communication problems related to the structure of organizations. Agencies may be divided into numerous highly specialized units that speak in mutually unintelligible jargons. Definitions of key terms such as "unemployment" may be so incompatible that data about the same phenomenon may be useless for comparisons. Examples are furnished by the diverse bureaus of the Department of Commerce, which encompass such varied domains as the National Bureau of Standards, the Maritime Administration, the Patent and Trademark Office, and the Economic Development Administration. Each has its own language and interpretations. When research units are highly specialized and often physically remote from the organization they serve, their specialization may be a serious communication barrier. They may not fully understand what the ultimate users of their research need and how it should be packaged for greatest usefulness. Much academic research, for example, is structured and presented in ways that make potential users in public agencies shy away from it as "purely academic," which translates to "operationally useless."

Specialization often produces unhealthy competition among units to control aspects of the work that each specialty sees as primarily within its domain. An example is the conflict between the Census Bureau, eager to retain previously used housing questions in the 1990 Census, and OMB's edict that these questions must be scrapped as superfluous paperwork. Each group claims jurisdiction and pleads that its concerns must prevail. Subunits often try to bias situations in their favor by engaging in overblown rhetoric that overstates the advantages of their case and exaggerates the risks of other options. They may also pass incomplete, contradictory information to top executives to boost their particular unit at the expense of the larger organization's welfare. Competing units may not want to communicate with others to avoid betraying weakness or incurring obligations to release information they would rather keep for their own exclusive use. Substantial waste occurs when units do not share information and the analyses based on them. It is therefore not surprising that specialization often leads to parochialism and failure to reach out to other units.

Damaging rivalries among specialized units are more common in the public than in the private sector because people tend to remain affiliated with the same unit. Bureaucratic rigidities make it difficult to circulate easily among various units, thereby learning to identify with them, as is common in the private sector. The perennial tensions between the Bureau of Mines and the Army Corps of Engineers, and between the Department of State and the Department of Defense, are examples of damaging rivalries. In the past, coordination of intelligence among Foreign Service agencies, the military, and intelligence agencies has been especially poor.

Remedies for parochialism born of specialization and mutual ignorance require bringing specialists and their clients into closer contact. Techniques may involve rotating assignments to familiarize people with all branches of their organization, as has been done in the Forest Service.[45]

Conferences of various types that bring generalists and specialists together are another method. The many White House conferences organized around such problems as child welfare, pornography, or drug abuse are examples. President Franklin D. Roosevelt routinely used a large array of information sources to keep him abreast of events and then stirred up competition and rivalry among these sources. Purveyors of information were thus forced to familiarize themselves with the positions of other agencies. When special problems had to be tackled, Roosevelt created new teams to solve them, chosen from diverse organizations. Again, it was hoped that each team member would draw from a different pool of information and beliefs. The tactic worked well for Roosevelt, but it backfired for President Dwight D. Eisenhower. When he created the Joint Chiefs of Staff as a super team of diverse specialists, it turned into a logrolling operation rather than an arena where specialists pooled their expertise to reach broadly based decisions.[46]

Centralization Problems

Centralization is another structural barrier to good communication.[47] In many organizations most of the important communications are directed to top-level officials who are faced with overloads of messages beyond their capacity to handle them effectively. Undesirable, sometimes disastrous, delays occur before the information is processed and appropriate decisions made. As a result of communication overloads in the top echelons, managers often devote insufficient time to communicating with subordinates at lower levels. This may mean that the information requirements of line agencies are not properly met. Bottom levels of the organization may be deprived of information needed to conduct operations efficiently.

For example, when the head of a large agency orders all staff complaints to be funneled through his or her office, there is likely to be an unmanageable glut at the top. Lower levels, well equipped to deal with complaints, may not become aware of them in timely fashion. When information is scarce, people at the bottom may vie for it, producing unhealthy rivalries. On the other hand, if there is no centralization and information is widely dispersed, much duplication of effort may result. Many more costly experts may be needed. Cohesive planning for the entire organization may be impeded.

The crux of this problem is the difficulty in devising appropriate structures and guidelines to channel information to various levels. When it becomes physically impossible for top administrators to scan all information, how much and what kind should be diverted to other levels of the organization? How does one balance the need for central control and accountability with the need for procedural efficiency? The answers remain elusive. After studying practices at the Internal Revenue Service, the U.S. Customs Service, the Food and Drug Administration, the Social Security

Administration, the U.S. Forest Service, and the Animal and Plant Health Inspection Service over the period of a year, Herbert Kaufman reported that subordinates "could not always explain fully how they decided whether to handle things themselves or pass them on to their bosses for signature; 'you just know' was a common answer. Within a few months after a new chief took over, it seemed to be a reflex action, apparently satisfactory to the subordinates and the chiefs alike." [48]

Kaufman points out that the quality of the bureau chief's leadership hinged on avoiding excessive centralization. "If great numbers of matters were referred to them for decision, other vital parts of their jobs would have been neglected and backlogs of matters awaiting decision would have accumulated." The fear of backlogs provided "strong incentives to install fine-mesh screens around the chiefs to hold down the number of things they decided personally." [49] However, when decentralization is excessive, so that subordinates make too many important decisions, their chiefs may become figureheads. The flow of intelligence to them may dry up when informants discover that the chiefs are not handling their messages.

Decisions are likely to move to the top level when subordinates are risk-averse, when they believe that the chief has contextual information that they lack, when subordinates respect the chief's knowledge or cannot resolve differences of opinion, and when chiefs worry about the judgment and reliability of subordinates. The need to make uniform policy decisions throughout an agency or throughout the country also forces decisions upward. Decisions are likely to remain at lower levels when subordinates have special expertise, are highly committed to the outcome of particular programs, when speed is essential and subordinates are competent, and when chiefs want to encourage employee self-reliance and innovation.[50]

These various, sometimes contradictory, factors make it hard to predict which decisions will end up at top levels. Kaufman found that decisions reaching the top ranged from the trivial to the very important. To strike a balance between overload and isolation at the top, decisions affecting the internal management of the agency were often made by subordinates because they believed they knew the agency better than the chief. The chief could then concentrate more on external communication, an especially important arena in the public sector because democratic norms demand ready access to public officials. Kaufman found that in the agencies he studied access to top administrators was fairly automatic when calls came from members of Congress, the White House staff, top officers of the departments in which the agencies were housed, civic leaders or clientele or professional groups, other government agencies, and journalists.[51]

Centralization of information seems to work best in single-purpose organizations such as the Forest Service, particularly when there is good rapport throughout the organization. But when the goals are diverse, centralization may be inefficient. Top officials may not fully understand the problems faced at lower levels that deal with areas outside their competence. In that case, centralization may have to be limited sharply to the few areas that concern all levels of the organization and require uniform policy making. The results may be a hybrid organization that combines centralized with decentralized authority.

The increasing complexity of the tasks performed by public organizations and the mushrooming of information have exerted strong pressure to decentralize information intake and decision making. Emphasis on responsiveness to clients and employee participation in decisions has enhanced these trends. Decentralization makes lower-level officials feel more important and may expedite decision making, but it also creates problems of consistency and integration within organizations and may make large-scale planning more difficult. When implementation of decisions is decentralized, it may be more difficult to communicate with all the units involved in carrying out tasks.

The Direction of Communication Flows

The discussion of hierarchy, specialization, and centralization has called attention to the fact that communication flow problems vary, depending on the direction of the flow. Here we shall focus more specifically on problems related to the direction of communication flows. As Figure 3-2 indicates, flows may be directed downward, laterally, as horizontal or cross-channel messages, or upward.

Downward Communication

General Considerations.   Daniel Katz and Robert Kahn have identified five major types of downward communication in a typical public or private organization.[52] They are (1) specific task directives, which are the most common type of downward message; (2) rationales for doing the job; (3) information about organizational procedures and practices, which tends to be sketchy; (4) more or less helpful job appraisal feedback to subordinates; and (5) indoctrination about organizational goals. These communications, in addition to internal distribution in the organization, may be transmitted at the lowest level of the hierarchy across organizational boundaries to outsiders. Messages to clients of street-level bureaucrats are examples of such cross-boundary message transmission. For example, a police officer may inform an inebriated motorist that departmental policy prohibits dismissal of drunk drivers with merely a warning to avoid future offenses. By selecting the information made available to a client about the agency's policies and procedures, street-level bureaucrats are often able to control

Figure 3-2   Four Directions of Organizational Communication

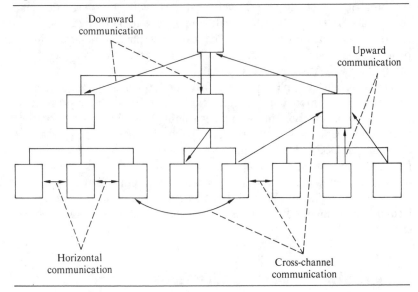

Downward
communication

Upward
communication

Horizontal
communication

Cross-channel
communication

Source: R. Wayne Pace and Don F. Faules, *Organizational Communication*, 2d ed. (Englewood Cliffs, N.J.: Prentice-Hall, 1989), 98. Reprinted with permission.

how clients will react and how they will be classified and treated by an agency such as the police department or housing office.[53] A client who is told that his request is futile is unlikely to pursue it.

Different units within organizations tend to develop idiosyncratic communication styles and vocabularies related to the functions they perform. Accordingly, messages from the top may have to be translated into these styles and vocabularies. The specific meanings of messages for various units must also be spelled out. For example, a directive from top management to improve the financial performance of the organization—a national park, for example—may have many different implications.[54] For public information offices, the directive may translate into a need to plan for more advertising. For park maintenance staffs, the directive may mean that worker productivity must be raised and costs lowered.

Superiors tend to communicate more freely and more often with subordinates than the reverse. In general, the greater the differences in status and power and the more formal the procedures in an organization, the more likely it is that downward communication will predominate and upward communication will be inhibited. This can become troublesome.[55] If subordinates receive many orders and have little opportunity for feedback, the atmosphere may become so authoritarian that it will breed resentment. Therefore, it is very important for executives to take time to establish rapport with their subordinates and create an atmosphere of mutual respect.[56] Chief executives who have brief tenures in huge agencies find this very difficult to do. Building rapport between top and bottom levels is easiest in military or quasi-military organizations where loyalty to the organization and its leaders is stressed as an important aspect of its culture. When leaders are charismatic, loyalty ties may grow extremely strong. The space program under the leadership of Wernher von Braun is an example, as are the nuclear submarine program under Admiral Hyman Rickover and the Federal Bureau of Investigation under J. Edgar Hoover.

Top-level politically appointed executives in the public sector are at times particularly maladapted to communicating with lower-echelon personnel. There are several reasons. These executives, who owe their appointment to political skills, frequently lack the necessary technical information to provide task directives. Because of the typically short tenure of political executives, they are unfamiliar with organizational procedures and practices and often with the rationales for doing certain kinds of jobs. Their short tenure and lack of familiarity with civil service rules make it difficult to become involved in personnel evaluations. The area in which politically appointed executives generally communicate most effectively is indoctrination about organizational goals. Yet this is the area where they are likely to encounter the most resistance from long-term civil service personnel who have formed their own ideas about the best goals for the agency.

In fact, there is substantial research evidence to indicate that bureaucrats at lower levels of the hierarchy are generally able to resist policy directives from higher authorities through their control over day-to-day operations and their intimate knowledge of the agency's operations. As noted earlier, this holds true even for directives coming from the legislature or the executive branch. For example, although the Reagan administration attempted to ease enforcement of clean-air legislation, lower-level bureaucrats kept established stricter policies fairly much intact.[57]

Labor-Management Relations.   When labor-management problems erupt in the public sector, inadequate downward communication is a frequent complaint. The perennial teachers' strikes in major American cities are good examples. Because teachers often believe that their superiors bestow too little praise for their achievements and fail to address problems that impede performance, they feel alienated. They also think that policies are often imposed on them by administrators who are unfamiliar with classroom realities. Many of the problems that surface during contract negotiations, when the atmosphere is heated and not conducive to settlement, could be better resolved through establishing permanent communication channels between school administrations and school boards on the one hand and teachers and teachers' unions on the other.

Table 3-1   Percentage of Workers Perceiving Specific Communication Disturbances

Disturbance	Percent reporting
Messages do not result in prompt responses	80.3
Too many messages to read or digest	76.6
Officials do not understand daily casework problems	75.6
Officials preoccupied with enforcing bureaucratic rules	63.2
Messages inconsistent	55.0
Failure to acknowledge messages	46.9
Responses frenzied and overbearing	44.5
Messages vague	44.4
Messages surprising	44.3
Records checked excessively	42.2
Instructions not meant seriously	38.3
Messages difficult to interpret	35.6
Messages repetitive	30.7

Source: Robert E. O'Conner and Larry D. Spence, "Communication Disturbances in a Welfare Bureaucracy: A Case for Self-Management," *Journal of Sociology and Social Welfare* 4 (1976): 186.

A 1981 report for the Chicago school system recommended that key administrative officials should schedule regular visits to schools, touring the facilities and then meeting with school personnel to discuss their problems and system-wide goals. The input of teachers and principals should be collected and funneled to a central office where time would be set aside by school administrators and school boards to discuss and respond to their suggestions. Through such permanent arrangements, information could be channeled properly upward as well as downward.

A study of the Pennsylvania Department of Public Welfare furnishes a good example of problems in downward communication and the difficulties they can cause.[58] The study was undertaken to discover the reasons for excessively high rates of job turnover and pervasive low morale in the agency. The rate of psychosomatic disabilities was also high. Well-educated employees, in particular, found the working situation undesirable and were most likely to leave.

The study involved 1,313 case workers who felt alienated by an inadequate communication network. A questionnaire was administered that sought information about three issues: (1) communication disturbances—the kinds of difficulties that the workers perceived; (2) remedial responses—the kinds of attitudes and actions they employed to overcome these difficulties; and (3) communication distortion—the kinds of defensive, possibly faulty, communication habits that the workers thought they had acquired.[59]

As Table 3-1 shows, case workers believed that the agency's system of communication was seriously flawed and that their superiors were preoccupied with bureaucratic rules and did not understand their problems. They felt that they were overloaded with messages from the top that were often vague and difficult to interpret. At the same time, their messages to superiors were not accorded appropriate consideration. Thirty-eight percent of the workers claimed that the instructions issued by their superiors were not intended to be carried out. This is a common complaint in public agencies where laws and rules often spell out in excessive detail what should be done, even though the superiors know that these regulations are ill adapted to the realities of field situations.

Fifty-five percent of the case workers also complained that they received inconsistent requests. Conflicting federal, state, and local regulations may be the explanation. They were also unhappy about excessive checking of their records, repetitive messages, and frenzied and overbearing responses to upward messages sent by subordinates to superiors. Seventy-one percent of the workers said that it had not been made clear to them what was expected of them. Downward messages took little account of workers' information needs or the need to validate their performance. The messages were therefore viewed as disorienting and dysfunctional.

The overall result of these difficulties was the case workers' belief that inadequate communication hurt the agency's goal of rendering humane service to the poor and disabled. Workers felt ill informed. As in many public agencies, much bureaucratic communication was ignored or circumvented because employees thought it involved unnecessary and burdensome reporting that seriously interrupted their work. Often they were hostile toward superiors, or at best indifferent. They felt that implicit messages, conveyed by superiors through styles of interaction and body language, were demeaning. They also complained about limited opportunities for lateral communication whereby workers performing the same tasks could exchange ideas and benefit from one another's experience. Two-thirds of the workers admitted that they violated explicit rules despite the risk of disciplinary action. Fifty-seven percent said that they withheld helpful information because of communication difficulties.

After studying communication patterns in the Pennsylvania Department of Public Welfare, the analysts recommended that decision making about clients should take place largely at the case-worker level rather than at upper levels. In addition to making more client-centered, nonbureaucratic solutions possible, decentralizing decision making would reduce the need for downward communication of orders, which were resented. Decentralization would also increase the need for upward communication of information and suggestions by case workers, enhancing their sense of self-worth. The study's concluding observations noted: "While all this may violate traditional ideas about hierarchical organization and the necessity of status differentiation, that only means the time has come to question and criticize those ideas." [60] The analysts recommended a "self-managed welfare delivery system" where decisions are made at the client level with substantial information input by clients.[61]

Lateral (Horizontal) Communication

Lateral (horizontal) communication occurs when individuals who are positioned at the same organizational level communicate with one another. When lateral communication involves members of functionally distinct organizations, it is often referred to as 'cross-channel' communication and usually involves specialists. Lateral flows are used mainly to coordinate the work of various units, although they may also contribute importantly to the social and emotional support of organization members. Lateral communication usually takes the form of meetings, telephone conversations, memos, and notes, even social activities. It tends to be rapid, facile, and often quite informal. It is more likely to occur in organizations with diverse structures and much task specialization. Specialists in one unit then feel the need to communicate with their counterparts in other units. A nuclear physicist can often gain more from communicating with another nuclear physicist than with an electrical engineer in his own unit. Similarly, when administrators go outside their own organizations to coordinate activities with related organizations, they often concentrate their contacts at a peer level in the belief that communication needs will be similar.

Lateral communication in the public sector is often more constrained than in the private sector because of the sheer size of the governmental enterprise and because public agencies compete more directly for the same scarce resources. An additional damper on lateral communication is the fact that members of the government work force are less likely to belong to professional associations and unions than their counterparts in the private sector. They therefore lack some of the opportunities for knowing and meeting their peers in other organizations.

Lateral communication may be troublesome when it occurs because members of an organization feel more comfortable communicating with people in other units. This is particularly true when the units are competing for resources. For this reason Henri Fayol specified in his famous Fayol's Bridge rule that cross-channel communication should occur only when authorized either by general or particular rules. Employees involved in these communications should convey the substance of their messages to supervisory personnel. However, such rules generally work only for formal communications; they fail when informal interchanges are involved. Top administrators often view lateral communication with concern because it has the potential for reducing their power. Talking with their peers gives people insights that might otherwise be available only to the top leadership, who could choose to share or withhold them. Accordingly, top administrators are tempted to restrict lateral communication, insisting that all communication pass through them.

A case in point occurred in 1979 when Patricia Harris became secretary of health, education, and welfare. Because she inherited a staff that was not of her choosing and apt to be hostile, she curbed lateral communication as a possible threat to internal efficiency.[62] To prevent the flow of potentially harmful messages from her organization to outside constituencies through lateral messages, she prohibited meetings, calls, and staff contacts on a number of subjects between her subordinates and members of Congress, congressional and White House staffs, and the Office of Management and Budget. All such messages required prior authorization by her or her assistant secretary for legislation. In this way she could be sure that only authorized representatives would present departmental views. Other cabinet secretaries have issued similar directives. For example, James Watt, as secretary of the interior in the Reagan years, barred department officials from meeting informally with staff members of congressional oversight committees in preparation for public hearings. Of course, this did not stop Congress from interrogating these officials at public hearings.

While beneficial in terms of power, restraints of lateral flow can result in lack of coordination and much duplication of intelligence-gathering efforts among public agencies performing related functions. Coordination between the State and the Defense departments, for instance, has been notoriously poor, often with dire consequences. A typical situation occurred in early 1989 when a Pentagon report listed the African National Congress, a militant anti-apartheid organization, as a dangerous terrorist group. This happened at a time when the State Department was trying to build ties to the organization and had endorsed some of the ANC's objectives while opposing its use of violence. Better lateral communication between the relevant personnel in the two departments could have avoided a great deal of embarrassment and harm to U.S. foreign-policy objectives.

Upward Communication

Upward messages are of four types: (1) self-reports by subordinates about work they have performed or about their problems (messages about problems may come as part of formalized grievance procedures); (2) reports about others and their problems; (3) messages concerning organizational practices and policies in general; (4) normative messages, suggesting how actual or potential tasks should be performed.[63]

Upward flows are mainly used to provide feedback on operations within the organization. They are important for assessing the effectiveness of internal communications. They indicate whether downward messages have reached their targets and whether intended receivers actually understood the messages and are acting appropriately in response. Given the vagueness of many directives and the wide geographic dispersion of many government offices, feedback about the accuracy of meaning and the nature of performance is essential. The information provided by upward flows may be crucial for sound decision making because it taps important internal data that may not be available from other sources. Facilitating upward flow has the added advantage of boosting morale and providing a safety valve for potentially explosive gripes. Unfortunately, as the numbers and diversity of internal and external message senders increase, structuring adequate upward feedback becomes problematic.[64]

As discussed earlier, upward communication is restrained by several concerns. One is the simple fact of hierarchy. People feel inhibited about communicating with their superiors, especially at levels above their immediate supervisors. Even if top management keeps an open door, this opportunity to communicate upward is rarely used. Such gestures of openness may foster management's sense of ready accessibility, but they accomplish little else.

Another problem hampering upward communication springs from the desire of subordinates to use it as a tool for manipulating superiors for personal or group advantage. Subordinates may tailor messages carefully to please their superiors, if possible, and avoid messages likely to discredit themselves or to elicit penalties. As Katz and Kahn state, "It is not only that they tell the boss what he or she wants to hear, but what they want the boss to know. . . . Full and objective reporting might be penalized by the supervisor or regarded as espionage by peers." [65] Hence, the messages that flow upward often provide skewed versions of reality.

Because of such inhibitions, it is essential to encourage upward communications by creating special access channels for them and generating an environment of trust. Executives must be good listeners, receptive and sensitive, and must respond to legitimate demands. Placing suggestion boxes throughout the organization or giving awards or citations for helpful suggestions may be useful. When Admiral Elmo Zumwalt assumed command of the U.S. Navy, for example, he encouraged employee correspondence by regularly publishing selected letters in the Navy newspaper, along with his response. This showed that the letters were valued and that the top commander was interested enough in their content to answer them personally.[66] To encourage the flow of accurate feedback about problems, communications scholar Everett Rogers recommends setting up special channels for negative feedback and rewarding employees who make reports about negative aspects of the organization. [67] Given the U.S. political culture's disdain for "whistle-blowers" or "stool pigeons," it is doubtful that such encouragement will be potent.

As discussed earlier, when upward flows of information are very ample, difficulties may ensue. For example, when George Romney was secretary of the Department of Housing and Urban Development (HUD), he once displayed a thirty-inch-high, fifty-six-pound stack of paper that represented a single urban-renewal application sent to him.[68] To prevent top officials from drowning in an excess of information, organizations must therefore condense upward flows. Unfortunately, the most responsive public officials are most likely to receive the greatest overloads of messages. Restriction of upward flow carries the danger that superiors may become isolated. Isolation has been a major problem for key leaders, such as presidents, governors, mayors of large cities, and their inner-circle advisers, whose scope of responsibilities is vast. While much feedback can safely be processed by lower-level employees, top-level administrators must make sure that they remain aware of operations throughout their agency.

Informal Communication Flows

Formal communication patterns, which mirror an organization's formal authority structure, are always supplemented by an informal system because people need to communicate spontaneously. In fact, every formal system has an informal structure that may parallel the formal structure or operate in quite different ways. The formal and informal structures are usually complementary. They can also serve as substitutes for each other, enabling many messages to pass through either one or the other. This gives people within the organization a choice between bypassing formal rules or going through "channels."

Informal communication—christened *grapevine* during the Civil War because of the configuration of makeshift telegraph lines—is needed for several reasons.[69] Formal structures are always somewhat out-of-date because they do not change as fast as circumstances may demand. Informal channels can arise quickly and spontaneously whenever they are needed, thereby enhancing the organization's adaptability and effectiveness.[70] Rapid diffusion of messages is assured when they operate in cluster fashion, with one receiver of the grapevine message relaying it to a cluster of associates (see Figure 3-3).

Another spur to the creation and use of informal channels is that formal structures deal mostly with routine situations, such as relaying organizational charts, policy directives, correspondence, and reports. The grapevine also carries information that would be unsuitable for formal channels, including social and personal messages. Likewise, formal structures often fail to provide the fine distinctions that must be made in specific situations. Formal rules provide general frameworks for sending messages; informal communication adapts these to specific situations. The formal network tends to be dominated by top executives, whereas control over informal communication is dispersed more widely. Moreover, grapevine communication can ignore positional roles. It can move helter-skelter, depending on the situation.

Grapevine usually travels by word of mouth. Such face-to-face communication fosters trust, social support, and rapid feedback. This trust is apparently justified. While it may not give a complete picture, researchers agree that usually 75 to 90 percent of the information traveling via grapevine channels is accurate.[71] Informal communication also encourages

Figure 3-3   Information Transmission in a Grapevine Cluster

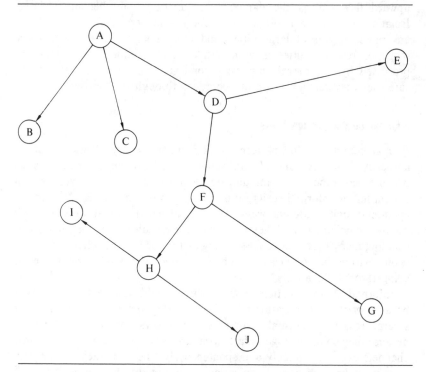

innovation because feedback is immediate and situation specific. It does not prematurely alert opposition that might try to fight innovations.[72] Moreover, it leaves few paper trails or other permanent traces and can therefore be officially denied when this is advantageous.[73]

Grapevine communication also has several drawbacks. It is unsystematic and generated and driven largely by individual self-interest. Grapevine channels are often restricted to privileged groups, leaving out the disadvantaged. When such "old boy" networks develop informally, laws against discrimination are usually powerless to force inclusion of disadvantaged groups. Grapevine may also degenerate into rumor, which involves the circulation of unsubstantiated, often erroneous information, particularly in times of crisis when information is scarce.

Summary and Conclusions

Since communication has become a complex major function in large modern organizations, specialized personnel have been trained to handle various aspects. The public sector still lags behind the private sector in deploying such expertise, but much has been accomplished.

A number of serious communication problems spring from the nature of bureaucracy. As Max Weber described it, a bureaucracy should be characterized by hierarchical structuring of authority and communication flows, by centralizing authority at the top and providing for specialization so that various functions are performed by experts rather than generalists. Yet in a hierarchy important communications usually pass through multiple layers of officials before reaching their targets, so that much information is lost and intentionally or unintentionally distorted.

Since control is centralized at the top, message overloads and the resulting delays and slipshod processing of information are almost inevitable. Organizations face difficult problems in developing workable systems for identifying messages that must go to the top to keep executives informed and those messages that can be handled at a lower level to protect executives from paralyzing overloads. Finally, specialization has turned the organizational world into a Tower of Babel where experts speak languages that their nonexpert colleagues—and occasionally even their fellow experts—cannot understand.

The chapter closes with a discussion of the nature and problems involved in communication flows, depending on whether their direction in the organization is upward, downward, or lateral to internal or external units at the same level. These issues are discussed from the perspective of formal communications, traveling along established channels. But that is only part of the story. Much communication is informal, via what has come to be known as the grapevine.

The structure of organizations is far more important in determining how they will function than is generally acknowledged. Their design deserves much more attention and careful planning than it has received thus far. The fifty American states constitute natural laboratories for experimenting with different structures to carry out common state activities. These laboratories need to be used more often and more systematically, leading the way to fruitful comparative studies and sounder organizational structures.

Similarly, the impact of physical settings on the quality of organizational communication has been unduly neglected by practitioners and scholars. Although much is known about the relationship between physical structures and organizational performance, little has been done to apply that knowledge. Short-range cost considerations and broadly shared beliefs that public services should feature a no-frills austerity have blocked physical improvements that could be extremely beneficial and cost-effective in the long run. It makes little sense to build impressive-looking public edifices whose grand exteriors give way to crowded, dowdy interior offices that offend the sensibilities of ordinary clients who must spend time in them to transact business with government officials.

Notes

1. James G. March and Herbert A. Simon, *Organizations* (New York: Wiley, 1958), 158-169.
2. Robert D. McPhee, "Formal Structure and Organizational Communication," in Robert D. McPhee and Phillip K. Tompkins, eds., *Organizational Communication: Traditional Themes and New Directions* (Beverly Hills, Calif.: Sage, 1985), 152. Also see Anselm Strauss, "The Articulation of Project Work: An Organizational Process," *The Sociological Quarterly* 29 (1988): 163-178.
3. Daniel Katz and Robert L. Kahn, *The Social Psychology of Organizations* (New York: Wiley, 1978), 430.
4. "Terrorism Alerts: The FAA's Dilemma," *Wall Street Journal*, April 3, 1989.
5. Jerald Hage, Michael Aiken, and Cora B. Marrett, "Organization Structure and Communications," in Daniel Katz, Robert L. Kahn, and J. Stacy Adams, eds., *The Study of Organizations* (San Francisco: Jossey-Bass, 1982), 304.
6. George C. Edwards, III, *Implementing Public Policy* (Washington, D.C.: CQ Press, 1980), 18-19.
7. Keith Schneider, "Bomb Flaws Known to du Pont and U.S. for Years," *New York Times*, January 16, 1989.
8. McPhee, "Formal Structure and Organizational Communication," 154.
9. Charles Walcott and Karen M. Hult, "Organizing the White House: Structure, Environment, and Organizational Governance," *American Journal of Political Science* 31 (February 1987): 122.
10. Stephen Engleberg, "Doubts on Intelligence Data: Iran Affair Renews the Issue," *New York Times*, August 31, 1987.
11. Terry E. Branstad, "Restructuring and Downsizing," in Robert D. Behn, ed., *Governors on Governing* (Washington, D.C.: National Governors' Association, 1991), 148-149.
12. David Stephens, "President Carter, the Congress, and NEA: Creating the Department of Education," *Political Science Quarterly* 98 (Winter 1983-1984): 645.
13. Robert Katzmann, *Institutional Disability* (Washington, D.C.: Brookings Institution, 1986), chaps. 2-5.
14. For examples, see Michael J. Malbin, *Unelected Representatives: Congressional Staffs and the Future of Representative Government* (New York: Basic Books, 1980), 232-233.
15. Stephen Kelman, *Making Public Policy* (New York: Basic Books, 1987), 54.
16. Edward I. Sidlow and Beth Henschen, "The Performance of House Committee Staff Functions: A Comparative Exploration," *Western Political Quarterly* 38 (September 1985): 485.
17. David Whiteman, "The Fate of Policy Analysis in Congressional Decision Making: Three Types of Use in Committees," *Western Political Quarterly* 38 (June 1985): 295-296.
18. For insights into lobbying practices of major corporations, see Conference Board, *Managing Federal Government Relations*, Research Report No. 905 (New York: Conference Board, 1988).
19. Sidlow and Henschen, "The Performance of House Committee Staff Functions," 487.
20. Walcott and Hult, "Organizing the White House," 116.
21. Katz and Kahn. *The Social Psychology of Organizations*, 455.
22. William T. Gormley, Jr., "The Representation Revolution: Reforming State Regulation through Public Representation," *Administration and Society* 18

(August 1986): 181.

23. William T. Gormley, Jr., "Intergovernmental Conflict on Environmental Policy: The Attitudinal Connection," *Western Political Quarterly* 40 (June 1987): 300.

24. "Public May Have a Say on Paperwork Burden," *Insight*, August 17, 1987, 28.

25. Everett M. Rogers and Rekha Agarwala Rogers, *Communication in Organizations* (New York: Free Press, 1976), 78.

26. Raymond A. Bauer, Ithiel de Sola Pool, and Lewis A. Dexter, *American Business and Public Policy* (New York: Atherton, 1963).

27. Rogers and Rogers, *Communication in Organizations*, 78-80.

28. David Axelrod, "New City Services Plan Threatens Political Truce," *Chicago Tribune*, May 3, 1984.

29. Rogers and Rogers, *Communication in Organizations*, 102.

30. Terence R. Mitchell and James R. Larson, Jr., *People in Organizations: An Introduction to Organizational Behavior*, 3d ed. (New York: McGraw-Hill, 1987), 237.

31. Sherry Devereaux Ferguson and Stewart Ferguson, "The Physical Environment and Communication," in Sherry Devereaux Ferguson and Stewart Ferguson, eds., *Organizational Communications*, 2d ed. (New Brunswick, N.J.: Transaction Books, 1988), 183-187.

32. John L. Crompton and Charles W. Lamb, Jr., *Marketing Government and Social Services* (New York: John Wiley, 1986), 212.

33. Ibid., 211.

34. Gerald M. Goldhaber, *Organizational Communication,* 3d ed. (Dubuque, Iowa: Wm. C. Brown, 1983), 200.

35. Abraham H. Maslow and Norbert L. Mintz, "Effects of Esthetic Surroundings: Initial Effects of Three Esthetic Conditions upon Perceiving 'Energy' and 'Well-Being' in Faces," *Journal of Psychology* 41 (1956): 253. Also see Ferguson and Ferguson, "The Physical Environment and Communication," 197.

36. The impact of physical settings is discussed fully in Charles T. Goodsell, *The Social Meaning of Civic Space* (Lawrence: University Press of Kansas, 1988); Fred I. Steele, *Physical Settings and Organizational Development* (Reading, Mass: Addison-Wesley, 1973); and Ferguson and Ferguson, "The Physical Environment and Communication."

37. Robert E. O'Conner and Larry D. Spence, "Communication Disturbances in a Welfare Bureaucracy: A Case for Self-Management," *Journal of Sociology and Social Welfare* 4 (1976): 182.

38. Ibid., 183.

39. Hugh Heclo, *A Government of Strangers: Executive Politics in Washington* (Washington, D.C.: Brookings Institution, 1977), 207.

40. Harold L. Wilensky, *Organizational Intelligence: Knowledge and Policy in Government and Industry* (New York: Basic Books, 1967), 42-48; Janet Fulk and Sirish Mani, "Distortion of Communication in Hierarchical Relationships," in *Communication Yearbook 9*, Margaret L. McLaughlin, ed (Beverly Hills, Calif.: Sage, 1986), 483-510.

41. Quoted in Harold F. Gortner, Julianne Mahler, and Jeanne Bell Nicholson, *Organizational Theory: A Public Perspective* (Chicago: Dorsey, 1987), 165.

42. Harold L. Wilensky, *Organizational Intelligence*, 42-48; Alexander L. George, *Presidential Decisionmaking in Foreign Policy: The Effective Use of Information and Advice* (Boulder, Colo.: Westview, 1980), 148-159.

43. Charles Peters, "From Ouagadougou to Cape Canaveral: Why the Bad News

Doesn't Travel Up," *Washington Monthly* 18 (April 1986): 31.
44. Terrance L. Albrecht and Vickie A. Ropp, "Communicating about Innovation in Networks of Three U.S. Organizations," *Journal of Communication* 34 (Summer 1984): 79-80 and sources cited in the article.
45. Herbert Kaufman, *The Forest Ranger: A Study in Administrative Behavior* (Baltimore: Johns Hopkins Press, 1967).
46. Wilensky, *Organizational Intelligence*, 54.
47. Ibid., 58-62.
48. Herbert Kaufman, *The Administrative Behavior of Federal Bureau Chiefs* (Washington, D.C.: Brookings Institution, 1981), 21-22.
49. Ibid., 21.
50. Ibid., 21-22.
51. Ibid., 35.
52. Katz and Kahn, *The Social Psychology of Organizations*, 440.
53. Jeffrey Manditch Prottas, *People-Processing: The Street-Level Bureaucrat in Public Service Bureaucracies* (Lexington, Mass.: D. C. Heath, 1979), 137.
54. Mitchell and Larson, *People in Organizations,* 297.
55. Gortner et al., *Organizational Theory: A Public Perspective*, 160.
56. Ibid., 162.
57. B. Dan Wood, "Principals, Bureaucrats, and Responsiveness in Clean Air Enforcements," *American Political Science Review* 82 (March 1988): 213-234.
58. O'Conner and Spence, "Communication Disturbances in a Welfare Bureaucracy."
59. Ibid., 181-182.
60. Ibid., 198.
61. Client issues are discussed in chap. 8.
62. Kaufman, *The Administrative Behavior of Federal Bureau Chiefs*, 167.
63. Katz and Kahn, *The Social Psychology of Organizations*, 446.
64. Ibid., 432.
65. Ibid., 447.
66. Goldhaber, *Organizational Communication*, 159.
67. Rogers and Rogers, *Communication in Organizations*, 99.
68. Gortner et al., *Organizational Theory: A Public Perspective*, 47-48.
69. Goldhaber, *Organizational Communication*, 164.
70. Katz and Kahn, *The Social Psychology of Organizations*, 449.
71. Goldhaber, *Organizational Communication*, 164 and sources cited there. Also see R. Wayne Pace, *Organizational Communication: Foundations for Human Resource Development* (Englewood Cliffs, N.J.: Prentice-Hall, 1983), 58.
72. Albrecht and Ropp, "Communicating about Innovation in Networks of Three U.S. Organizations."
73. Lori A. Fidler and J. David Johnson, "Communication and Innovation Implementation," *Academy of Management Review* 9 (1984): 704-711.

Information Management in Organizational Decision Making

Information Needs

Organizational life involves a constant round of decisions about what to do and what to refrain from doing. All administrators must therefore be able to identify issues that affect them and make decisions that will enable them to take appropriate actions. Many of these decisions are quite routine, involving day-to-day operations, and many have minor consequences, such as the purchase of office supplies. Others, such as the development of major new policies or coping with important events in areas of concern to agencies, are likely to have significant consequences. Irrespective of their significance, all decisions involve gathering information and evaluating it in order to choose courses of action. Figure 4-1, adapted from John Stevens and Robert McGowan's study of *Information Systems and Public Management*, identifies the multitude of interacting information streams that impinge on the decision-making process.[1]

Overall, Figure 4-1 indicates that decisions must be made in light of information about the environment at the agency's operational level, its broader general setting, and its remote environment. Environmental information includes knowledge about current national economic conditions affecting the agency, social and cultural values impinging on it, and concerns about future developments in the various environments. Decisions also require knowledge about applicable professional standards, budget controls, interest-group pressures, and the like. Decision makers must also consider information available within the agency. This includes data concerning various staff and line functions, such as planning and research, human-resource management, financial operations, and operational tasks. The most important feature illustrated by Figure 4-1 is the

Figure 4-1   Systems and Contingency Perspective on Public Sector Organizations

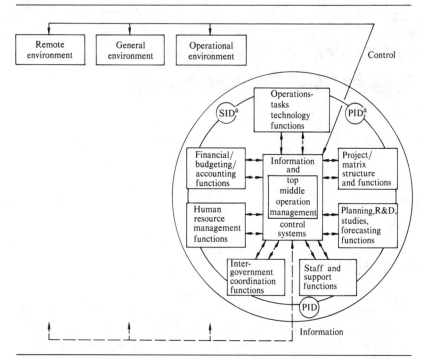

Source: John M. Stevens and Robert P. McGowan, *Information Systems and Public Management* (New York: Praeger, 1985), 25. Reprinted by permission of Greenwood Publishing Group, Inc., Westport, Conn.

[a] PID's and SID's are processual and structural integrating devices, respectively.

great dependence on a diverse array of external and internal data and the commensurate difficulty in creating structures for producing and gathering information necessary for sound decision making. Moreover, as the problems become more complex, ambiguous, and unstable, more information will be required to resolve uncertainties.

Since information is costly to produce, store, disseminate, and use—presently roughly one-third of the Gross National Product (GNP) goes for knowledge production and distribution—organizations need to determine how many resources should be allocated to these functions. As Figure 4-2 indicates, they must also consider that the marginal utility of new information often decreases progressively, especially when situations are highly uncertain. Thus, it is unwise to extend information gathering indefinitely.[2]

The vertical axis in the graph measures the cost and value of additional units of information, while the horizontal axis measures the increasing perfection of information on a scale from zero to 100 percent. Because initial information about problems requiring governmental action

Figure 4-2   **Cost of Additional Information**

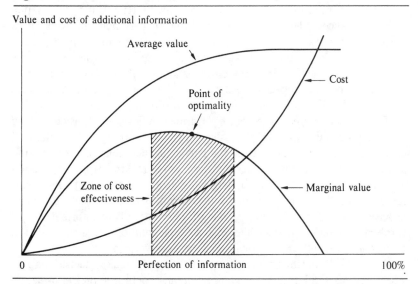

Value and cost of additional information

Source: E. Frank Harrison, *The Managerial Decision-Making Process*, 3d ed. (Boston: Houghton Mifflin, 1987). Used with permission.

is easy to obtain, the cost curve remains low initially. For example, it is easy to establish that two airliners have collided, leaving 100 people dead or injured and damaging both aircraft. But costs rise as it becomes increasingly difficult to locate new data to establish the cause of the disaster. The average-value curve, unlike the cost curve, begins with a sharp rise in value of information at the start of an investigation when little is known and new information is cheap. It levels off as the value of additional units of information decreases in the face of rising costs. The marginal-value curve, which reflects the value of the next unit of information rather than the average cumulative value of all units, levels off and declines much earlier and more sharply. The zone of cost effectiveness reflects the area where it becomes prudent to terminate the information search because benefits are no longer commensurate with costs. The zone falls far short of 100 percent perfection of information. However, one cannot ever be certain that the most important piece of evidence will not be the last to surface. Hence, there is considerable risk in premature termination of information searches.

Under what circumstances are administrators likely to make the greatest effort to gather information for decision making? There are several contingencies. First, when decisions are very important, they prompt above-average efforts to gather adequate information. The same is true when decisions are irreversible and resources are ample, with no time or money constraints. Finally, greater vigor in the information search is common when the administrator who makes the decision is personally accountable.

Although there is a presumption that information is always good and that more information is better, this is not always true. When information lacks relevance, when it contributes little that is new, or when it is misleading or erroneous, it becomes undesirable noise that is a hindrance to decision makers. Likewise, not all decisions require information streams from multiple sources.[3] In many circumstances, only a limited number of interests and their spokespersons need to be heard so that it becomes counterproductive to widen the circle of informants.

The structures created to control information flows for decision making and the procedures used in processing information strongly affect the pool of information brought to bear on particular decisions. Structures and procedures determine who takes part in decision making, what information will be considered, and which options will become viable. The public sector faces especially serious problems in making structural and functional provisions for gathering and analyzing various strands of information and combining them to produce the best possible solutions because goals are often controversial, and political concerns receive priority.

When the Department of Defense, for example, makes decisions about adopting a particular nuclear defense system, should it gather information about the impact of various options on the economy? How much information should it collect about the nuclear defense systems of other countries? To what extent can and should it assess the chances that the international community will outlaw nuclear weapons, making defense systems unnecessary? What weight should be placed on concerns about the political popularity of such a system in Congress and in the country at large?

The amount of information to be gathered for decision making also hinges on the availability of time in an environment of many conflicting demands on that precious resource. For instance, members of Congress make many important decisions. Yet they allow themselves little time to weigh all the information because they choose to serve on multiple committees that enhance their power base. Furthermore, as Carol Weiss observes, "analysis is alien to the traditional style of the Congress' collection and processing of information."[4] Members of Congress gather information primarily through oral communication, such as meetings with constituents and interest groups, public hearings, and talking to their staffs and fellow members. "They take pride in their ability to 'read people' rather than read reports," notes Richard Fenno.[5] They filter information intuitively to reach judgments, buttressed by their past experience. They want scientific analysis largely to support the judgments they have already reached.[6]

The discussion that follows deals primarily with information needs for major decisions. These have one or several of the following characteristics. They affect large numbers of people in important ways, or smaller numbers in more profound ways. They involve high economic or political stakes, the survival of a government agency, or are of great concern to influential people.[7] Compared with the millions of less significant decisions made daily throughout all levels of public bureaucracies, the number of major decisions that occur in government are infinitesimal. We therefore will also discuss the major characteristics and problems involved in routine decision making, most of them occurring at lower organizational levels.

The Four Phases of Decision Making

To illustrate the decision-making process in public agencies more concretely, we shall use as a hypothetical example EPA decisions about the steps required to clean up an oil spill.[8] Decision-making entails four major phases, each requiring gathering and processing different strands of information. During the first phase the problem is analyzed. During the second phase various options to cope with the problem are explored. The third phase involves the selection of a particular option and its implementation. The fourth phase entails monitoring the consequences of the decision and feedback to the agency about changes that might be needed.

The Problem-Analysis Phase

First of all, EPA officials would need sufficient information about the situation—a coastal oil spill in this case and the problems caused by the event—to provide a basis for determining which options seem reasonable. The precise definition of the problem may not be easy. Should the focus be on reversing environmental damage, on preventive measures to forestall future oil spills, or on ways to compensate for the lost fuel? Should the incident be treated as an act of negligence leading to civil or criminal liability or as an unavoidable accident? Should the costs be borne locally or from national resources?

Depending on the definition of the problem, information requirements will vary. This does not mean that everything about the situation can or must be known. The concept of "satisficing" as contrasted with "optimizing," is useful. Since the complexity of situations and time pressures usually make it too costly or even impossible to assemble all of the facts, "satisficing" allows fact-finding to stop when a reasonably satisfactory solution has come into view. Accumulating all of the available facts and options and weighing them against one another before deciding would be an "optimizing" approach.[9]

Frequently, the facts of a particular situation are unclear. Administrators cope with this problem in a variety of ways. They may delay appraisals until more information becomes available, or they may decide to take no action at all. Alternatively, they may draw on institutional memories for analogous events in the past—such as previous oil spills—and the insights gained in coping with them. Past appraisals by staff members steeped in the organization's history form part of the organizational culture that strongly influences subsequent appraisals. Such insights can be invaluable for dealing with current problems.

But reliance on analogies with the past also poses dangers. It is easy to overlook contextual changes that make the analogies false, or to put too much faith in lessons from events that occurred only once or twice before, making it unclear whether they represent a particular type of event. Depending on the extent of new elements in the situation, additional relevant information and suggestions must be sought from as broad a spectrum of informants as time and resources will allow.

Input can be solicited formally or informally from sources outside the agency, or it can be generated internally during brainstorming sessions. Many public agencies are constrained by authorizing legislation, internal inflexibility, or political considerations from freely choosing informants, analysts, and policy options. Bureaucrats often feel compelled to tap only sources that are likely to support the goals of the agency's leadership and the authorities on which the agency depends.[10] This poses serious problems because the established procedures may prevent a full and accurate appraisal of the situation. At best, such constraints are apt to severely discourage innovative approaches to various situations. Decision making does not always begin with the delineation of a particular problem requiring solution. Often it begins with a series of proposed measures. Congressional bills for expensive projects in certain districts, for example, are often introduced for political reasons and then require discovering appropriate problems to justify passage.

The Option-Exploration Phase

Once the dimensions of the problem have been defined, the range of feasible policy options needs to be explored. To assess feasibility, EPA decision makers must have enough information about the agency's internal environment to be able to judge the kinds of decisions it can implement. The powers legally available to the agency and its budget and personnel authorizations are among important internal factors that need to be explored. If, for example, the agency is already overextended or lacks personnel knowledgeable about oil spills, the range of options is reduced. The predispositions and operational codes of decision makers within the agency also need to be known. For instance, if top decision makers are averse to using chemicals to control spills, that option becomes excluded.

EPA would also need relevant information about the external environment in which the situation is developing. The activities of other public and private actors must be considered. It might make a significant difference, for example, if authorities in adjacent states were already taking measures to cope with the problem. Coordination of various approaches to the problem would then become a major task.

Certain aspects of American political culture must also be considered. Decisions to retain the status quo or those favoring small incremental change are generally preferred over decisions involving major or radical changes of direction. There are several reasons. Small changes are less likely to arouse opposition by those who dislike the direction in which the agency is moving. Hence, decisions entailing relatively minor changes are politically safer. Similarly, if a decision involving change turns out to be wrong, it is easier to reverse it if the change has been minor. If the decision proves correct, subsequent decisions can push policies further in the successful direction. Finally, most Americans are inherently averse to change. They prefer the status quo rather than some unfamiliar situation with which they have not yet learned to cope.

In the public sector, most major decisions are going to be publicly scrutinized. In fact, when the federal government makes rules involving regulatory agencies, the proposed rules must be published in the *Federal Register* at least thirty days prior to adoption to solicit public reactions. In addition, many agencies publish an Advance Notice of Proposed Rulemaking to invite comments. Various interest groups then get busy and write to the agency, commenting on the proposed rules. These comments usually do not include many substantive suggestions, but they do indicate the climate of opinion in which the proposed rules will have to operate.

The publicity requirement makes it essential to be aware of how acceptable the various options are likely to be to interested external groups, particularly vocal ones, and how the decisions might possibly be justified to overcome opposition by these groups, Congress, and the executive branch. Solutions that run counter to major ideological predispositions or political goals will have to be excluded. The need to consider the preferences and dislikes of various segments of the public may severely limit the available options. On the positive side, this is a powerful check on the danger that internal idiosyncrasies and operational codes will dominate decision making. To gain support for policy choices, agencies often resort to justifying them in terms of widely accepted goals that lack identifiable dimensions by which the policy can be judged and condemned. Such nonoperational goals include the "national interest," the "public interest," and "the general welfare."

The chief problem during the pre-decision phase is making certain that an adequate range of options has been presented for evaluation and comparison. Costs and benefits need to be weighed. Modern computers have made it easier to consider a variety of options, but machines are only as smart as their users. Options must be programmed into computers, and human ingenuity must determine what combination of factors ought to be considered.

The uncertainties that affect calculations used in comparing options must also be identified. Calculating the utility of alternative choices requires knowledge about causes and effects so that the consequences of each option can be projected with a reasonable degree of accuracy. The uncertainties involved in this process may lead to controversies among decision makers that can threaten consensus within the organization. Disappointed groups must be mollified by acceptable explanations or appeased in other ways. Attempts to put a gloss on a disputed policy may ultimately backfire by hiding faults that might otherwise become obvious.

The Decision-Making Phase

Numerous typologies have been developed to describe what happens at the third stage when decisions are made to adopt particular options. Each of these typologies represents a different slicing of the same cake. Here we shall use a fairly simple set of models that draw on the work of a number of public administration experts, including Herbert Simon, James March, Johan Olsen, and Charles Lindblom. Four basic approaches to decision making can be readily identified. Depending on the circumstances, they are used singly or in combination.[11]

The Rational-Choice Model constitutes an optimizing approach to decision making. Information about all options is rigorously explored and compared in terms of cost-benefit ratios to arrive at the decision that provides the greatest return to the agency at an acceptable cost. The model is based on the idea that decisions should be grounded in scientific principles of management. As Figure 4-3 indicates, the model postulates a sequence that begins with delineating the problem and then developing alternative solutions based on a comprehensive search of all available information. Sophisticated methods are used to make sure that all relevant information has been considered and to analyze the data on which the ultimate decision is based. Finally, measures are taken to win adoption of the rationally derived decision.

Many people consider this an ideal model because they believe that human reason is the most desirable and effective guide for human action. Hence, decisions based on selected rationales are often mandated by law. Regulatory agencies may be required by statute or directive to use cost-benefit analyses and related devices to identify, quantify, and compare policy effects in the hope of encouraging rational decision making. For example, the Consumer Products Safety Act stipulates that decisions about safety rules must consider the risks of injury, the number of products subject to the safety rules, the public's need for the products involved, the probable effect of the rule on the utility, cost, and availability of the regulated products, and the possibilities for minimizing adverse effects on

Challenge:
Threat or opportunity (crisis posing threat to vital interests)

Step 1
Formulating the problem: What requirements should be met:
- Dangers to be averted?
- Gains to be attained?
- Costs to be kept to tolerable levels?

What seems to be the best direction of solution? (top-of-the-head survey of alternatives)

Step 2
Using information resources: What prior information can be recalled or retrieved?

What new information should be obtained:
- Expert's forecasts
- Intelligence reports

Step 3
Analyzing and reformulating: Any additions to or changes in the requirements?

Any additional alternatives?

What additional information might reduce uncertainties?

Step 4
Evaluating and selecting: What are the pros and cons for each alternative?

Which alternative appears to be best?

Any requirements unmet? (If so, can they be relaxed or changed? If not, would modification be better?)

How can potential costs and risks be minimized?

What additional plans are needed for implementation, monitoring, and contingencies?

Deciding after adequate search, appraisal, and planning—manifested by absence of the following defects in decision-making procedures:
1. Gross omissions in survey of objectives.
2. Gross omissions in survey of alternatives.
3. Poor information search.
4. Selective bias in processing information at hand.
5. Failure to reconsider originally rejected alternatives.
6. Failure to examine some major costs and risks of preferred choice.
7. Failure to work out detailed implementation, monitoring, and contingency plans.

Closure
Internal consolidation of the choice:
- Bolstering it by playing up the advantages and playing down the disadvantages.
- Soliciting supportive information
- Refuting unwelcome information about drawbacks.

+

Social commitment to the choice:
- Announcing it to interested parties
- Promoting it, especially among implementers and policy evaluators who are unenthusiastic

Source: Reprinted with permission of The Free Press, a division of Macmillan, Inc., from *Crucial Decisions: Leadership in Policymaking and Crisis Management* page 91 by Irving L. Janis. © 1989 by The Free Press.

competition and manufacturing. The standards mandated for public agencies rarely include political concerns such as the democratic mandate that governmental decisions should be responsive to the desires of the citizenry.[12]

Despite the emphasis on rational-choice approaches, studies of actual decision making indicate that scientific research findings generally fail to have a major impact on the nature and quality of policy decisions, even though they are often cited.[13] Analysis of decisions made by various congressional committees showed that research findings by Congress's own research agency, the Office of Technology Assessment (OTA), increased the sophistication of policy debates but had little measurable effect on final decisions. The reasons lie in the complexity of the political environment, which denies a dominant role to scientific findings. They are just one among many important factors to be considered.

Although examples of fairly rational decision making abound, even at best the process is usually not as orderly as the model suggests.[14] Information searches are never complete, and the full range of options rarely surfaces, even in the age of the computer. Much information is withheld for technical and political reasons. Computers have made it possible to consider much broader ranges of options, but they also have increased limitations on information use. Managers who base their decisions on computerized models may avoid factors that cannot be quantified readily and included in computer calculations.

As Figure 4-2 suggests, complete exploration of all facts and options may be so costly and time-consuming that the potential gains are not commensurate with the costs. Public bodies are usually inundated with information, much of it contradictory, making it extremely difficult to digest everything. Congress, for example, is overloaded with information generated by several internal information-gathering bodies, including the Congressional Research Service and the Office of Technology Assessment, as well as data supplied by diverse executive-branch agencies and a multitude of lobbies. In determining which information to examine and which to ignore, it is difficult to establish choice criteria and priorities. To do so adequately requires a great deal of political wisdom.

Because public agencies operate in a complex political environment, a much larger array of considerations must enter into the decision-making process than is normally the case in the private sector. Final decisions result from the interaction of a series of decisions made by various players whose roles differ somewhat depending on the agency's structure, clienteles, and funding sources. For example, decisions made at the National Labor Relations Board, a comparatively small and functionally simple body, nonetheless reflect the combined influence of a great many political forces. These include the president and presidential appointees to the board, congressional committee members, and the constraining role of the courts, which always loom in the background in public agencies whose decisions are ultimately subject to judicial scrutiny. Other factors that impinge on the board's decision making include a broad array of economic conditions, particularly unemployment and inflation rates, internal agency procedures and goals, and the nature of complaints brought by business and labor.[15] The problems encountered in measuring all of these factors simultaneously make it difficult to accurately trace decision-making influences in the public sector.

Even when a broad range of options is recognized, they may not be seriously considered. Prior events, predispositions, and decisions may have foreclosed many. For example, when President Kennedy and his advisers discussed diverse options to cope with communism in Cuba, he ruled out numerous possibilities largely because he believed that plans to dispatch military forces to Cuba to displace the country's government had already achieved momentum. The CIA strongly supported these military options.[16]

Rational choices are also hampered because costs and benefits, which include economic, social, and psychological factors, cannot be appraised accurately. Known "facts" become questionable when situations change in unpredictable ways. It is difficult to compare alternatives because value considerations enter into determining which alternatives satisfy the multi-plicity of goals generally sought through a public policy. Political consider-ations may run counter to technical considerations, yet are likely to prevail. When political considerations enter the information-selection process, decision makers with varying political concerns are likely to differ about information choices and the merits of various options.

The Incremental-Bargaining Model involves negotiations about policy directions among representatives of conflicting interests. They may be officials within an agency who represent different political persuasions, or they may represent internal constituencies as well as those outside the agency whose concerns must be taken into account. The main job for decision makers is to ascertain the preferences of interested groups and to calculate how the various alternatives developed during the option-exploration phase will benefit or harm the groups that have a stake in the decision. The final decision represents a balancing of diverse political interests. It generally involves only small deviations from existing policies because it is easier to agree on small rather than large changes. A decision is "good" if all groups involved are willing to agree to it.

As mentioned earlier, incrementalism suits most bureaucrats well because it saves them from major rules changes that might require reorganizing their thoughts and activities. It is a lot easier to stay with tried-and-true procedures and steer clear of innovations. A series of small changes may ultimately amount to a major change without arousing the opposition that could be anticipated from moving quickly. For example, if job qualifications are raised marginally every time a new hiring decision is made, ultimately the standards of the organization may rise substantially. But incrementalism is slow and does not lend itself to long-range planning; it generally encompasses the concerns of only a limited array of interest groups and discourages innovation.

Communication in incremental decision making is far different from rational-choice decision making.[17] Cost-benefit analysis is concentrated on in terms of individual or group interests rather than in terms of the ultimate goal. As a result, the emphasis is on persuasion, debate, and bargaining, *not* on disinterested analysis. Proposals are formulated and exchanged to achieve consensus. The fact that there are usually many interested parties means that ample diverse information is introduced, even though the search for information is not systematic, as happens in rational-choice deliberations.

The Incremental-Bargaining Model is also called the Governmental or Bureaucratic Politics Model because bureaucrats often control most of the information and are able to present their evidence to decision-making executives in ways that make outcomes favoring their points of view highly likely. For example, President Kennedy's decision to undertake the Bay of Pigs invasion against Cuba was largely determined by the manner in which the CIA presented the relevant information. The final decision, according to Lucien Vandenbrouke, resulted from "a process of 'pulling and hauling' among different players with different interests and power resources."[18] Who these players were and how they communicated or miscommunicated became extremely important.

The CIA was in a particularly strong position to structure its advice because secrecy constraints about the planning of the operation gave it a near-monopoly on information. It could define the options and provide the information needed to evaluate them. Only a handful of White House advisers and top-level bureaucrats knew of the plan, and they were generalists. Secrecy constraints cut them off from Cuban specialists in the State Department who might have provided counterbalancing information.[19] Pentagon officials consulted about the plan examined it only cursorily because it did not affect them directly and they did not wish to antagonize another powerful organization. As General Lyman Lemnitzer put it, "You couldn't expect us . . . to say this plan is no damn good, you ought to call it off; that's not the way you do things in government. . . . The CIA were doing their best in the planning, and we were accepting it. The responsibility was not ours."[20]

Severe misunderstandings may develop among the participants in a negotiated decision when the ultimate goals are fuzzy or change repeatedly as bargaining proceeds. In the Bay of Pigs case, for example, tight deadlines, the pace of events, and the need to accommodate many diverse political pressures all contributed to obscuring the situation.[21] When its initial plan was rejected, the CIA quickly devised several alternatives. These plans were changed constantly up to the last minute in response to objections from various quarters. Changes were made one by one, without keeping the operation as a whole in sight. In the end, President Kennedy thought he had ordered a large but quiet infiltration of anti-Castro forces into Cuba. Meanwhile, the CIA was staging a miniature Normandy landing. Crucial air support was canceled at the last minute when the pilots were already prepared for takeoff.

At times, attempts to reach mutually acceptable decisions go astray because, states political scientist Paul Schulman, "members of a set of decisions interact progressively to circumscribe one another—distorting processes of search and calculation, and narrowing the scope of available options." [22] This happens often in the wake of attempts to sway a decision by submitting false data or covering it up. The initial deception, which seems to serve the beneficial role of a "white lie," then requires a string of subsequent deceptions to conceal it. Each step is dysfunctional and may finally lead to a disastrous outcome.

Schulman calls such dysfunctional decision-making behavior "the logic of organizational irrationality." "Under these circumstances," he observes, "decisions cannot be described as rational in a value-maximizing sense because they act to undermine the very values they are directed to secure." [23] Yet the pressure to protect the organization forces its members to progress from an initial error to serious decision-making pathologies.

The Aggregative Model involves decision making utilizing a combination of information, advice, and options drawn from many internal groups and outside agencies. Outsiders may include expert consultants. These groups are called together for brainstorming sessions at which various options are developed. The participants may then vote for the option they prefer. The final choice represents an aggregation of individual preferences, indicating which option has the most support, rather than a negotiated decision, as in incremental decision making.

Brainstorming has the advantage of introducing a wide array of options and reducing the political tensions that inevitably creep into negotiated settlements. However, it discourages in-depth discussion of these options because it is geared toward suppressing attempts to sway the choices of participants. Overall, the process is good for generating ideas but may be unrealistic because it ignores political interests and power relationships among the participants. In the end, political considerations will have to be factored into agency decisions. Various brainstorming techniques, such as the Delphi approach and Nominal Group procedures, are discussed later in this chapter.[24]

The Garbage-Can Model as described by James March and Johan Olsen, involves drifting into decisions without a well-planned search for relevant information and without making explicit choices.[25] Various options are discussed, but more as a way to air goals than to reach a decision. March and Olsen contend that the more deliberative decision-making models are unrealistic. In most decisions, problems are not fully understood, goals are not clear, and interpersonal relations are unpredictable. Debates reflect personal and social needs of the participants as much as an attempt to solve problems rationally. Solutions are generated haphazardly and final decisions emerge from the interplay of this "garbage-can" collection of disparate ideas, decisions, and nondecisions. Retrospectively, the decision may then be attributed to initial goals that were never expressed initially. Viewed in this way, attempts to gather relevant information to bring to bear on the decision would be mostly window dressing. If sincere, they would be futile.[26]

Decision making during the Cuban missile crisis illustrates the garbage-can model.[27] No comparisons were made between alternative choices in an attempt to reach the best overall decision. Rather, the final decision emerged from a series of yes-no decisions on specific proposals. Once a proposal had been rejected in a single context, it was not reconsidered. For this reason, the sequence in which various proposals came to the fore was extremely important. The overall goals of the policy emerged haphazardly as decisions on specifics proceeded. Given the severe danger presented by the crisis, the blandest alternatives, with the most predictable consequences, were preferred.

Decision making at the National Labor Relations Board provides other examples of the importance of the initial decision and the sequence it generates in a decision chain. The board begins its deliberations by deciding whether claims filed with it justify investigation of a particular situation. A negative decision usually means that the case will not proceed further. Even before this initial decision, prior decisions by potential parties to a case on whether or not to file a complaint constrain the ultimate decisions made by the board. Regardless of the importance of an issue and the board's eagerness to handle it, it cannot act until a claim has been filed. Its decisions are also partly shaped by its previous decisions, which are weighed by potential complainants when they assess chances of making a successful appeal. As political scientist Terry Moe points out, "[T]he implication is one of reciprocal causality: constituent filing behavior is a basic determinant of staff and Board decision outcomes, but these outcomes have feedback effects that shape subsequent constituent decisions to file charges." [28] Moreover, the various staff members of the board are guided in their initial decisions by a knowledge of its past policies and goals. Relying on precedent therefore develops its own logic of consistency. But it is an unpredictable logic, since even precedents vary. What will be decided and how thus hinge on an intricate interdependent web of decisions made by different players in the organizational process rather than on deliberate, rational choices based on the most relevant current information.

Even seemingly orderly, rational procedures can still lead to garbage-can style decision making. Lawrence Pinfield's experience as a participant/observer in a senior Canadian government task force is illustrative. The task force was charged with developing personnel policies for recruiting senior government executives. The decision process began with four background papers prepared by the task force that provided information about various existing practices. These papers then inspired a pre-policy proposal drafted by the task force that outlined various options. The pre-policy proposal was then circulated to interested parties for their suggestions. Just as the composition and attendance patterns of the task force had an impact on its work, so the list of critics and their attention to the project, in the face of many competing demands on their time, had an unpredictable, nonrational impact on the pool of ideas on which the final decision was based.[29]

Nonrational decision making was encouraged because there was no agreement among the participants about appropriate goals and technologies, making the nature of the decision highly fluid. Moreover, the political context for the decision changed over the two-year period of its gestation, as did the identity of the participants in the deliberations. All these circumstances fostered a garbage-can approach to decision making. Pinfield concluded that decision making involved a mixture of rational and anarchic processes. Whenever goals and procedures were clear and uncontested, decision making moved in rational steps from problem recognition to resolution. When these conditions were not met, the process was anarchic. The critical factor in determining which process would prevail thus was clarity and acceptability of goals and the steps to reach them.[30]

The Feedback Phase

The fourth and final decision-making phase—monitoring the consequences of decisions so that adjustments can be made—has become common practice in public agencies. In fact, since accountability is a political and legal necessity in public organizations, internal feedback systems tend to be more complex than in the private sector.[31] Positive feedback tells agency personnel that current policies are working; negative feedback indicates the need for change. There is also "feedforward," which means that information or guesses about the future state of the organization are used to prepare for these changes.[32] A cybernetic system, in the strictest sense, would automatically correct itself in line with the nature of the feedback. But self-correcting systems have remained a dream. Automatic adjustments are well-nigh impossible to devise because there are too many chances for error in information intake and interpretation. The built-in rigidities of public agencies deter changes. Thus the large amounts of feedback data collected by many organizations are largely wasted.

In addition to internal feedback monitoring, public agencies are subject to external monitoring of their decisions, operations, and feedback. This includes both legally mandated and politically inspired feedback, as well as monitoring by government agencies and private institutions. Lobby groups, for example, may insist on being privy to the feedback. For instance, environmental lobbies want to make sure that decisions about pollution standards and other regulatory efforts are carried out to the full extent required by law. Anti-nuclear groups closely follow nuclear licensing decisions and implementation of safety rules.

The various investigations of the CIA and its decisions and operations are good examples of external monitoring by other governmental bodies. Concerned about possibly undesirable decisions and behavior by the agency, Senate and House committees undertook extensive investigations of CIA covert operations abroad and in the United States in the mid-1970s. The upshot was legislation designed to curb the freewheeling performance of the agency's covert missions. External monitoring by congressional committees—the congressional oversight function—may be particularly strict during tense political periods or during elections.

Even when investigations are not common, agencies must always be prepared for them. The need to prepare for investigations and lawsuits vastly increases the phenomenon commonly known as red tape, which entails excessive record-keeping requirements. Agencies must also anticipate the political fallout of the type of feedback they are accumulating. Therefore, they choose data likely to be advantageous and avoid data likely to be embarrassing. Unemployment agencies, for example, are much more likely to accumulate date indicating that their decisions have been procedurally fair than data about how well they have served the unemployed. They fear lawsuits about procedural fairness, which have been common in the past, rather than the less-common suits about effectiveness of performance.[33]

Similarly, the Navy adopted a sophisticated management-information system, called Project Evaluation and Review Technique—PERT, for short—largely to quiet the critics of its Polaris submarine project.[34] The feedback data elicited by this system shed little light on the progress and problems of the Polaris project, but did provide a reassuring aura of administrative competence and concern with monitoring decision outcomes. Many other types of Management Information Systems (MIS) have been developed to provide upper-level administrators with qualitative and quantitative data about performance, either out of genuine concern about feedback or as window dressing. Usually Management Information Systems rely more heavily on formal than on informal lines of communication to collect information and channel it to the proper people.

Monitoring performance by drawing inferences from feedback is especially difficult in the public sector because the value of the services provided by government is hard to measure. The goals of many public policies are expressed as ill-defined, broad concepts without explaining what terms such as "national interest" mean in relation to specific policies. Other policies are aimed at such diffuse goals as improvement of the economy, better economic security, or higher employment throughout the nation, or a combination of all of these. It is difficult to judge from feedback data whether these goals have been achieved. Even statistics are hard to interpret. For example, unemployment statistics may exclude an undetermined number of people who have abandoned job searches that have proved fruitless.

It is equally difficult in the early stages of the decision process to compare the utility of various policy options in order to determine which is more or less in the public interest or conducive to the general welfare. Moreover, people disagree about what should be considered good or bad results. Some, for example, deem it good when a governmental agency cuts back on its activities, while others prefer to see expansion. Response to feedback is made extraordinarily difficult and often costly because so many clashing goals have to be met. Additionally, national, state, and local laws often conflict so that compliance with the laws of one governmental level means violation of the laws of another.

Ideally, decision making in general and feedback in particular are learning processes through which governments gain knowledge of the world in which they operate as well as the ability to make sound decisions. The special difficulties that make most public officials slow learners prompted political scientist Lloyd Etheredge to write a book entitled *Can Governments Learn?* [35] His conclusions about the ability of governments to learn from past experiences are pessimistic.

Several major factors contribute to the inability to gain insight from past experiences that can be utilized to improve subsequent decisions and practices. Most importantly, these factors involve personnel issues, such as frequent turnover of high-level personnel, recruitment for political rather than professional and administrative skills, a passion to dominate decision making, compromise plans that relieve all parties of assuming full responsibility, and failure to foster learning. The fact that personal goals of advancement and maintaining rapport with colleagues often make it disadvantageous to express criticism of prevailing thinking is also an important deterrent to creating and using sound feedback.[36]

Barriers to Sound Decision Making

Students of decision making in the public sector, drawing on a variety of theoretical orientations from personality theory, have tried to identify the main factors that lead to faulty use of information. Based on such studies and on his own investigations, political scientist Alexander George, in a book dealing with the effective use of information and advice, identifies individual, group, and organizational psychological predispositions and pressures that hamper decision making.[37] George used foreign-policy decisions by the executive branch as his primary examples, but his findings and recommendations, which form the basis of our discussion, apply to decision making at other levels and in other policy contexts.

Individual-Level Communication Problems

The human mind is an information-processing system that acquires, stores, appraises, and utilizes information about the physical and social environment. To cope with the vast amounts of information they receive, people simplify it and organize it into sets of beliefs and personal constructs, often called schemata. These schemata are then used as the basic framework into which subsequent information is fitted. They also guide what information will be noted or ignored. Once established, this basic framework for acquiring and processing information tends to be stable and hard to disconfirm. This is particularly true in bureaucracies where judging the future by past performance carries the fewest risks of censure and where the chances for rewards for innovative decisions are small. Discrepant information is downgraded or rejected. While this framework is useful for handling large amounts of information, it leads to stereotyped reasoning that may be dysfunctional.[38]

Many people find schema formation and decision making arduous, often painful and potentially dangerous to their own careers. Therefore they avoid making decisions whenever possible, or they delay them unreasonably or make them hastily, ignoring relevant information sources, so that they can quickly turn to other matters. Avoiding tough decisions is particularly tempting in the public sector because nondecisions, despite their frequently serious consequences, are less likely to draw fire than decisions. Accordingly, public officials may ignore problems for long periods of time, failing to accumulate needed information. If information has been accumulated, they may procrastinate in putting it to use. If a decision is unavoidable, they may decide in favor of small incremental changes even when their information indicates that bold new policy directions are required. Problems of indecision are also common in the private sector, but they are more pronounced in the public sector because of the career-damaging criticism that officials are more apt to encounter from the press or from hostile colleagues.

When careful scrutiny of the available options seems particularly agonizing because every choice has serious drawbacks, bureaucrats may reach closure prematurely to end the stress. Practicing what has been called defensive avoidance, they may ignore or insufficiently explore important evidence, including reasonable options, and fail to examine thoroughly data about costs and risks. To simplify the process, decisions may be based on information from a single readily available source, such as the CIA or FBI. Once a decision has been reached, countervailing information may be ignored. For example, in 1961, once CIA planners had decided that the Bay of Pigs invasion was advisable, they ignored all evidence to the contrary.[39] Similarly, President Kennedy wanted to believe that the invaders could infiltrate Cuba without being detected. He ignored data clearly indicating that a force of 1,400 men with tanks and artillery, supported by an invasion fleet and air cover, could hardly escape detection, particularly since the American press had publicized the prospective invasion on the eve of the troop landing.

Cognitive inflexibility was also evident during the invasion of Grenada in 1983. President Reagan and his advisers were convinced that the Soviet Union and Cuba intended to use a new airport under construction in Grenada for military purposes. Therefore, no thorough investigations were undertaken, and contrary information available from the American ambassador to Grenada and the Grenadan government was ignored. When reporter Seymour Hersh, in a subsequent investigation, asked Ambassador Francis McNeil, then senior deputy in the State Department's Bureau of Intelligence and Research, about information gathering, McNeil said that little effort had been made to ascertain the facts. "We did not, so far as I know, make an effort, we didn't have the diplomatic presence on the island and I think we pretty much lived by the descriptions in our own rhetoric rather than seeking the reality of the situation on the island." [40]

When choices are difficult, decision makers may engage in "bolstering," which entails exaggerating the attractiveness of one option and deflating the rest so that choice becomes easier. Analogies may be used inappropriately to rationalize replicating past decisions. The motives and action styles of other people may be deliberately misconstrued to justify what the decision maker wishes to do. When individuals encounter information that calls into question their established beliefs and established modes of behavior, they feel uncomfortable. As a result, they are prone to misconstrue facts to reconcile them with previous beliefs and thereby avoid cognitive dissonance—the realization that one's own cherished beliefs are clashing.

Alternatively, decisions may be based on an existing consensus rather than on the objective criteria that ought to be considered. The rationale behind the firm consensus may not be explored to discern whether it deserves to prevail. During the *Mayaguez* crisis of 1975, for example, the four key decision makers—President Gerald Ford, Secretary of State Henry Kissinger, Secretary of Defense James Schlesinger, and General Brent Scowcroft, the deputy of national security affairs—all favored the use of force to retrieve the merchant ship *Mayaguez* and its crew, which had been captured by a Cambodian gunboat. In retrospect, it is clear that the Cambodians would have released the ship and crew without the military action by American Marines, which cost many lives, including forty-one Americans. An examination of the records of the policy deliberations, subsequent memoirs, and observation of the behavior of the four key decision makers made their uncontested disastrous decision to order a Marine invasion readily predictable.[41]

The desire to control the decision process may lead to distorting or otherwise manipulating information. In the *Mayaguez* crisis, for instance, the secretary of defense disagreed with the president's decision regarding air strikes. To abort the decision, he deliberately couched the presidential commands in ambiguous language likely to be misconstrued, covering his behavior with ambiguous reports. Similarly, the secretary of state concealed information from the National Security Council that would have informed it of options that he deemed undesirable.[42]

Another psychological weakness that impairs decision making is the desire to curry favor with powerful individuals. Decision makers may pander to the preferences of influential people within the organization and ignore unpopular options or deliberately cast them in an unfavorable light. Information searches and the ensuing decisions may also be warped by overly heavy reliance on partisanship, ideology, or general principles to guide actions. Established beliefs about correct strategies and tactics may be applied without retesting the applicability of these "operational codes" to the new situation. Accepted theories rather than data may drive information processing.

To ease and speed decision making, bureaucrats often use various flawed common sense heuristics rather than scientific reasoning.[43] For instance, they draw on readily available examples even when these constitute purely anecdotal evidence that is statistically unsound. When situations are uncertain, they are more likely to guess favorable rather than unfavorable outcomes without exploring the real odds. When gains seem likely, they tend to be risk-averse; when faced with losses, they tend to choose high-risk strategies.[44] Such psychologically based flaws have long plagued decision making. Historian Barbara Tuchman's book *The March of Folly* documents how decision makers throughout history have persisted in foolish courses of action well beyond the bounds of rationality.[45] A better understanding of these pathologies and ways to overcome them could lead to better use of decision-making information.

Group-Dynamics Problems

Most decisions in public organizations are made by small groups. Group contributions to decisions broaden the information base and often ease the implementation of decisions. Team members who have participated in making a decision are usually better able and more inclined to carry out the plans. The fact that a group participated in reaching the decision enhances its legitimacy. If it misfires, the burden of blame rests on multiple shoulders.

But the group process presents hazards to formulating sound decisions. Regular communication among its members increases consensus and blurs many individual differences of interpretation and opinion that would enrich the group's thinking.[46] Even reports from research groups often lack incisiveness because conflicting views have been unduly blended.[47] Group members settle comfortably into small communication ghettos where, secure in their shared knowledge, they resist unsettling information. Members also develop personal friendships that they are loath to strain by expressing unpopular views. The public sector is particularly prone to these pathologies because protected tenure allows groups to work together over long periods of time.

An experiment conducted with small decision-making groups illustrates the point. Sociologist Ralph Katz investigated the performance of fifty small Research and Development project groups in a large American corporation. He discovered that the groups whose membership did not change became increasingly isolated from key internal and external information sources the longer they worked together. "With increasing group longevity, the effects of behavioral stability, selective exposure, and group homogeneity combine to reduce the group's willingness to search out and actively internalize new or conflicting knowledge and developments."[48] Isolation from communication channels, which did not necessarily mean a drop in overall communication, was accompanied by a drop in quality of work performance. Whether or not outside input is needed and how much is needed depend, of course, on the projects in which particular groups are involved.

Group size and composition are important factors in decision-making effectiveness. Ideally, all interested parties should be included in complex governmental decisions. Yet this would make the size of these groups unwieldy, so they are usually kept deliberately small. This means that important options and concerns may fail to be considered because they lack an advocate. The smallness of the decision-making group may make it difficult for lone dissenting members to speak up. These constraints are particularly damaging to the free flow of diverse information if the group becomes dominated by higher-ups and power-wielders during the early stages of deliberations.[49]

If the groups are limited to officials at the top of the hierarchy, as is often the case, they may lack crucial information that is available only at lower levels. They may also be unable to detect whether lower-level bureaucrats have screened out information that casts doubts on prevailing assessments of the situation or seems otherwise undesirable to the receiver.

Such uncertainty absorption is common. To make superiors happy and earn the praise that comes to bearers of good tidings, subordinates often pass on only pleasing interpretations and data. Thus it is highly unlikely that disfavored options will be considered. Once top-level policy makers have agreed on the nature of the prospective decision, it becomes very difficult for lower-level personnel to challenge their deliberations and decisions.

Another very dangerous pathology of group decision making is the phenomenon of "groupthink." It plagues highly cohesive groups, especially in times of crisis when the perception of external dangers heightens feelings of solidarity. Members of the group who have reservations about its decisions keep silent, lest they destroy the treasured image of consensus. The chief symptoms of "groupthink" are a feeling of euphoria and of overconfidence by members who feel that their shared opinions must be correct because no serious objections have been aired. Overconfidence may then lead to undue risk taking and even aggressive behavior. For example, sociologist Irving Janis claims that crisis decision making by the Kennedy and Johnson administrations was plagued by groupthink.[50] During the planning of the disastrous Bay of Pigs invasion of Cuba, the small decision-making group seemed to feel invincible and on morally unassailable ground. All twinges of doubt were suppressed in the wake of feelings that the group was in total agreement about the steps to be taken and that conformity was essential. Criticism and questions by outsiders were given short shrift.

Working with subsequently disclosed evidence, political scientist Lloyd Etheredge casts doubts on the groupthink diagnosis. He claims that group cohesiveness was assured when Kennedy, like other chief executives, appointed like-minded people to his cabinet. In Etheredge's view, overconfidence is the hallmark of every new administration rather than a unique groupthink phenomenon.[51]

Organizational-Dynamics Problems

Organizational dynamics can also lead to difficulties in reaching sound decisions. The hallmarks of bureaucracy—hierarchy, specialization, and centralization—cause major information-flow problems during decision making, such as message overload and message distortion. These problems have been discussed extensively in Chapter 3.

Reducing Malfunctions

Enriching the Information Stream

Malfunctions in decision making can be addressed through structural or functional reforms. In the past, structural reorganization of agencies was often the answer to improve information flows and narrow or broaden the number of people whose views were elicited. By and large, purely structural reforms have failed. Now emphasis has shifted to a combination of structural and functional reforms involving the design of structures for better management of information flows and information processing.

Alexander George, for example, recommends various remedies to enhance the diversity of information flows in decision making. To make sure that disfavored options are explored rather than automatically rejected, a decision-making group may select one of its members to play the role of *devil's advocate*. This tactic acquaints the group with dissenting views and may pacify real dissidents who feel that their views have at least received an airing. It also allows the group to develop formal rebuttal arguments that may be useful if the decision is later challenged. However, the process suffers from being artificial. The devil's advocate, taking a position to which he or she is not fully committed, may be unaware of important arguments. In many instances, the devil's advocate may emphasize features that a real dissident, aware of strategic considerations, might choose to slight. Viewpoints pleaded by a real dissident, which might be fully or partially acceptable to the group, thus may never receive exposure.[52]

A second approach discussed by George is called a *Formal Options System*. The problem of considering too few options is alleviated by creating interdepartmental committees composed of a diverse group of individuals drawn from various departments within an agency. To provide central direction and coordination, these committees are generally chaired by the top executive's chief of staff. They then prepare options to be considered by various departments. The approach combines lateral coordination among departments with hierarchical direction. The system can also be used when several agencies are involved in a decision.[53]

The major drawbacks of this approach are that new structures have to be created and that options development and adoption occur at different levels. Departments may reject the options if they do not reflect departmental concerns adequately. If options are rejected, a second round of research and options development may be needed. Overall, the process tends to be slow and is therefore not particularly useful during crises.

Another approach—the one favored by George—is a *Multiple-Advocacy Strategy*. It is based on the assumption that advocates of various points of view cannot make an effective case if they lack resources that are available to others, or if political concerns, rather than the substantive issues, color their advocacy. To ensure that all viable options have an equal chance during deliberations and that distortions are exposed, regardless of the power and influence of the perpetrators, the resources of various advocates must be equalized. Hence, disadvantaged groups must receive support in gathering and analyzing information and in selecting skilled advocates. If possible, the status and power of their representatives should match that of other groups involved in the decision. Interdepartment or interagency task forces may be appointed when necessary to bridge parochialism. Sufficient time is set aside for adequate presentation of information, appraisals, and debate. The deliberations, which are guided by the chief executive, strive for dispassionate analysis of issues and avoid bargaining for adoption of a particular decision. The drawback of the multiple-advocacy strategy lies in the comprehensiveness of the process, which is costly and time-consuming. Because of the slow pace, it is unsuitable for situations that require rapid decisions.

Some of the barriers to expressing ideas that arise in group settings can be overcome through *brainstorming* techniques. Typically, brainstorming has three main features intended to spur spontaneous creation of ideas in the group.[54] First of all, participants are asked to generate ideas without concern about their quality or practicality. Anything goes. Secondly, evaluation takes place only after all ideas have been presented. The delay avoids discouraging participants from voicing their ideas because prior submissions seem to have wide approval or because they sense group hostility to particular suggestions. Finally, members are encouraged to elaborate on the ideas of others as well as their own. This allows for refinements that the originator of the idea may not have envisaged.

To aid decision making and problem solving, two other techniques have also been used. In *Nominal Group Techniques* (NGT), selected persons who are assembled as a group are asked individually to generate ideas in writing about a task or problem. Each person, irrespective of status in the group, presents his or her idea, which is recorded. All of the ideas are then discussed for clarification and evaluation. Finally, the group casts secret votes ranking the acceptability of the ideas.

The *Delphi Technique* works similarly, often without actually assembling a group. Advisers are polled separately about their ideas and recommendations for future needs and policies. The results are then circulated to the actual decision-making group, which clarifies and judges them. Ultimately, after repeated rounds of discussions and revisions, the advisory Delphi group votes on the acceptability of final options. A prime advantage of NGT and Delphi techniques is that they encourage participation by all group members without the intimidation often faced in ordinary groups where certain personalities are dominant.

Quality Circles (QC) is the term for another problem-solving and decision-making technique designed to broaden the flow of information. Groups of employees meet regularly for several hours per month on company time to talk about solving job-related problems. Viewpoints from the perspectives of people at the bottom of the hierarchy are thus aired. The groups consist of five to ten volunteers who have been trained in group process and problem solving. The effectiveness of such groups initially and over time has varied. Many have started out well but declined afterward.[55]

For technical problems that might benefit from computer technology and other aids, automated decision conferencing (ADC) has been a useful technique. It involves executive teams assisted by staff members trained in decision sciences and computer techniques who test divergent views with data during two- or three-day sessions. The objective is to reach solutions that have been scientifically tested and found workable and advantageous.

Achieving Policy Coherence

The multiplicity of voices that must be heard because of their legitimate interest in particular public policy decisions raises the problem of achieving policy coherence. A number of structural arrangements have been proposed to cope with the problem at the presidential level, where it is especially acute. The principles involved in these recommendations are applicable for executives at all levels of government. For example, economic policy decisions generally cut across the interests of several departments and involve both macro- and microeconomic concerns. Integrating these diverse concerns and reconciling conflicting messages become major problems.

Coordinating Structures.   To mesh macro- and microeconomic concerns in economic policy decision making and relieve the president of responsibility for making major department-bridging decisions, the creation of a *superdepartment* has been suggested. For instance, the Commerce, Labor, Agriculture, and Transportation departments might be combined into a Department of Economic Affairs, which would find it easier to resist the claims of particular constituencies and special interests and to focus on policies of widest national benefit. Experience with existing superdepartments that integrate multiple services, such as the Department of Defense or the Department of Health, Education and Welfare, does not indicate that this is a particularly effective solution. Alternatively, arrangements can be made for *regular information exchange by departments.* For example, the Office of Technology Assessment (OTA) coordinates its work with other congressional research agencies, such as the Congressional Budget Office and the Congressional Research Service at the Library of Congress, through an interagency Research Notification System that brings agency representatives together. It also publishes a directory of congressional research activity. Despite these comparatively elaborate arrangements, interagency coordination remains difficult.

Another possibility is appointing an *economic policy assistant* to help the president, governor, or mayor integrate information and policies, or designating a supersecretary as coordinator. John Connally, President Nixon's secretary of the treasury, served in a supersecretary capacity and dominated economic policy decision making. The approach concentrates ultimate responsibility and therefore increases accountability.[56] It works well when executives are willing to delegate responsibility in particular areas, but it is difficult for one individual to tie all of the threads together. Moreover, operating responsibility remains scattered. Use of an economic policy assistant may require a specialized staff to support the assistant's activities in preparing policy alternatives for the chief executive to consider. Advocates of this approach recommend that such an assistant should be a facilitator and coordinator rather than a policy creator.

A *National Economic Council* resembling the National Security Council has been proposed as a third option at the federal level. It might consist of forty to fifty professionals appointed to manage the flow of communications between the president and the departments dealing with economic policies. Council members would be under the president's control and presumably in touch and in tune with his preferences rather than departmental viewpoints. They would therefore serve as a counterweight to departmental parochialism and inertia. The council would coordinate the diverse policy strands and make policy recommendations. The council setup encourages careful, systematic examination of economic policy questions from a national perspective. A possible disadvantage of such a council is that it might cling too closely to presidential preferences. Its existence might also undermine morale in cabinet departments that deal with economic policy and must carry out recommendations.

A fifth possibility—the one favored by Alexander George—is creation of a *cabinet-level council* designed as a forum for *multiple advocacy*. It would bring the administration's leading economic policy officials together on a regular basis to advise the president on these issues. The group's function would be to provide a broader setting for appraising departmental concerns and developing coordinated economic policies. Designing such a council to overcome typical group-interaction problems would be difficult. The more talented advisers are likely to dominate the dialogue, even when their claims do not have the greatest merit. Group norms may emerge, stifling creativity. Such deficiencies can be minimized if the president insists on genuine collegiality, or if a manager for the council serves as an honest broker to make sure that all viewpoints emerge.

Cross-level Coordination. Another difficult task arising from the extraordinary complexity of decision making in the public sector involves the coordination of economic policy decisions at various governmental levels ranging from the local to the international. In the latter sphere, the National Security Council or specially created councils or committees have performed the coordinating function. However, the existing structures have often artificially separated foreign from domestic issues, which has led to a neglect of foreign issues when presidents have been oriented toward domestic economic interests.

Coordination among national, state, and local levels has posed similar problems. Political scientist William Gormley surveyed 780 federal environmental regulators from the midwestern offices of the Environmental Protection Agency and their state-level counterparts in Ohio and Wisconsin. He found that state regulators in Ohio sharply disagreed with federal regulators about air-pollution policies, and Wisconsin regulators disagreed with federal regulators over waste-management policies. Ohio officials, for instance, were willing to sacrifice clean air to foster employment and economic development, whereas federal officials gave far greater weight to environmental safety.[57] Such fundamental differences do not bode well for carrying out unified policies. Since the major decisions implementing environmental policy are made at the state level, producing consensus between state and federal regulators is especially crucial.

Gormley suggests four strategies that might ease these difficulties and achieve greater policy coherence. All are designed to change the attitudes of state regulators by exposing them to new information. The federal government could encourage more citizen participation in environmental hearings. Gormley believes that citizen views would be a counterweight to the strongly protective views voiced by special-interest groups, to which state regulators often respond. A related tactic designed to give greater exposure to environmentalist viewpoints is the establishment of a *public intervenor*. Such a state official would represent the general public when environmental issues are discussed in various public offices and would also serve as a rallying point for environmental groups. In Wisconsin, a public intervenor's office has helped to build and sustain public support for environmental protection.[58] A third tactic, designed to arouse the public to voice its support for stricter environmental rules, is the creation and airing of public service announcements on radio and television. Finally, greater exchange of information between regulators at various governmental levels, with the aim of achieving consensus, could be promoted through programs such as the 1970 Intergovernmental Personnel Act, which permits officials in federal regulatory agencies to spend several years in state agencies and vice versa.

The success of policy-coordination efforts depends on more than the procedures used. The personalities of the individuals involved in decision making and the organizational culture are important factors. Successful coordination requires parties who are willing to introduce and fairly discuss all reasonable options brought to their attention.[59] They must also be willing to supplement one another's information and to admit errors in their thinking or practices. Finally, decision makers must be willing to accept conclusions that run counter to their established preferences. As discussed, such flexibility is the exception rather than the rule.[60]

Organizational cultures that encourage collaboration produce exceptionally free information flows and lead to decisions encompassing the views of all participants.[61] The term "clan" has been used to characterize such organizations, which are usually small and involve frequent face-to-face encounters. In part, cohesiveness results from selecting members with shared values and socializing them to reinforce common attitudes.[62] The Reagan White House was an example. When values are shared by the group, and only means of execution are uncertain, decision making takes place in a collegial setting. Innovations are readily accepted and implemented. Decisions mainly revolve around the choice of experts and insiders who will be called to present their views to the group. By contrast, when values are in conflict and goals are uncertain, decision making shifts toward bargaining or consensus building to agree upon acceptable goals. Decision-making systems resemble markets where competing visions are thrashed out by the participants, or arbitrated or adjudicated by the leadership.

Coping with Crises

Malfunctions are particularly common during crises because quick decisions must be made under extraordinary emotional and physical stress. This may lead to impaired attention to information and flawed perception. Because of the time pressures and anxieties, periods of crisis may enhance cognitive rigidity among decision makers. Their receptivity to information that contradicts existing beliefs may be reduced because there is less tolerance for ambiguity. Creativity may be impaired. Stereotypical thinking increases. Past experiences may dominate because there is little time to consider new alternatives. Decisions are made more hastily. Communication channels may be overloaded. There is less attention to long-range consequences and less attention to the side effects of various options. Perspectives have thus become shortened and narrowed. If decision makers are aware of these pitfalls, they can guard against their consequences or take preventive steps.

For example, President Eisenhower, among others, directed his staff to engage in continuous planning so that crisis decision making could benefit from broad-based, long-range studies.[63] During a crisis he could then draw on a small number of staffers for advice without sacrificing expertise and breadth of perspective. Eisenhower also made it a point during crises to listen to dissenters from prevailing policies and to explore fully the reasons for their dissent. He kept his own public statements about policies deliberately ambiguous to allow himself greater flexibility to change his position.

Modern technologies carry the potential for producing many major crises that public agencies are expected to avert. Preventing nuclear power plant catastrophes, forestalling damaging environmental pollution, or diminishing cancer-causing substances in foods are examples. Studies of decision making to limit these risks indicate that it is well-nigh impossible to use rational-choice approaches in such situations because they are rife with major uncertainties and value conflicts. Instead, decision makers must rely on variations of trial-and-error strategies, along with precautions designed to forestall the worst calamities. The precautions buy them the freedom to experiment with various policy options and then use feedback to correct mistakes.[64]

For example, the probability of nuclear-reactor failures cannot be estimated at present. No one even knows the scope of the consequences of a reactor-core meltdown, such as the amount of radioactive-fission products that would actually escape from the reactor. To protect the public from a worst-case scenario, the Nuclear Regulatory Commission has opted for increasing safety installations at nuclear-reactor sites. Beyond this initial decision, it has generated numerous proposals to cope with meltdown risks and has revised them as more technical and political information becomes available. Some of the cost-benefit issues that enter decision making about ill-defined, grave risks seem almost beyond resolution. If the zero-risk option is unavailable, as is usually the case, how safe is safe enough? What price is American society willing to pay to save a relatively small number of lives? What does "relatively small" mean? These are political and ethical issues that administrative agencies, in their search for viable decisions, find it difficult to raise, let alone resolve.

Structuring Information Flows

Structural arrangements in organizations impinge on the issues discussed thus far. They determine the information flow patterns, which, in turn, affect decision agendas and outcomes. The direction of the flow of communication through the hierarchy determines which options surface first and may thereby influence which are accepted or rejected. The direction of information flow also determines which individuals make the preliminary decisions that so strongly affect final outcomes.

For example, when information and advice originate at the bottom and flow upward, top-level decision makers may make their choices from the predigested, limited options brought to their attention.[65] As mentioned, uncertainty absorption is common when information is screened at lower levels of the hierarchy. Employees pass familiar and acceptable cues upward and ignore unfamiliar information that does not fit into the beliefs held by members of the organization. Superiors do not ordinarily reexamine information screened out at lower levels. Structural arrangements can also be used to determine the specific role that executives will play in decision making. Depending on these arrangements, executives may either participate in the initial problem analysis and option exploration or they may become involved only at the option-selection stage. In fact, the executive may leave even final option selection to a group of trusted advisers, reserving the right to approve or reverse their choice.

When agencies are structured so that important decisions are made at the bottom, these decisions may never come to the attention of upper-level officials. Therefore they tend to reflect the preferences of individuals in low-level positions. By and large, decisions are relegated to the bottom level when they are of minor importance, when they require expertise that abounds at that level, when speed is essential, when lower-level officials are trusted by their superiors, and when upper levels are already clogged with decision-making activities.[66] Effective control from the top is unlikely when a large number of decisions are made at the bottom of the hierarchy.

Top-Level Decision Structures

Alexander George described five types of arrangements used by recent presidents to gather and process decision-making information. The five models encompass three basic types: the formalistic arrangements used by Presidents Harry S. Truman, Dwight D. Eisenhower, and Richard M. Nixon (Figure 4-4); the competitive model used by President Franklin D. Roosevelt (Figure 4-5); and the collegial model used by President John F. Kennedy (Figure 4-6).[67] All of these models are also suitable for decision making at state and local levels.

The Formalistic Model.   This model represents the typical hierarchy in which information travels upward from lower-level to upper-level agencies and personnel. Truman, Eisenhower, and Nixon, as well as other executives who have used this very common model, created structures of varying complexity, but the basic principle of clear division of labor and hierarchical flow of information is the same. Lower-level units screen and pre-process incoming data and then select the information that will be reported to mid-level decision makers. They, in turn, further screen and condense the flow to be passed on, eliminating many options that they consider undesirable. There is relatively little communication among units at the lower levels and hence little controversy about information choices and little interpersonal and intergroup bargaining.

In Truman's case, information traveled from agencies within the executive departments to advisers and cabinet heads and thence to the president, providing him with information and recommendations from multiple advisers, each drawing on different information sources. In Eisenhower's case, a chief of staff was interposed between the president and high-level administrators to act as a gatekeeper. The gatekeeper limited the president's exposure to information prepared at lower levels, allowing him to concentrate on the most important decisions only. The price paid for conserving presidential energies was further loss of control over the

Figure 4-4 **Formalistic Models of Decision Making Used by Presidents Harry S. Truman, Dwight D. Eisenhower, and Richard M. Nixon**

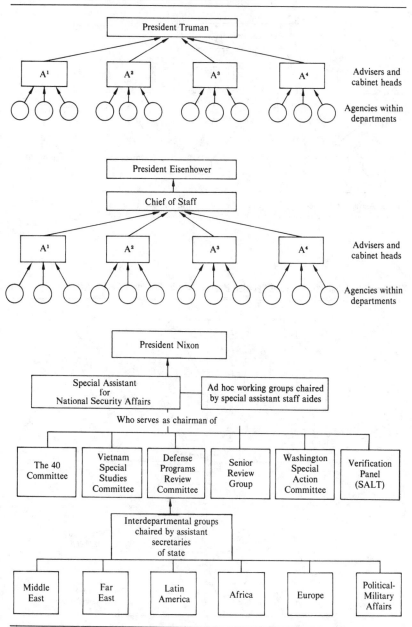

Source: Alexander L. George, *Presidential Decisionmaking in Foreign Policy: The Effective Use of Information and Advice* (Boulder, Colo.: Westview, 1980), 152, 154, 156. Reprinted with permission.

Figure 4-5   Competitive Model of Decision Making Used by President Franklin D. Roosevelt

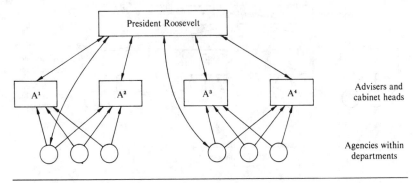

Source: Alexander L. George, *Presidential Decisionmaking in Foreign Policy: The Effective Use of Information and Advice* (Boulder, Colo.: Westview, 1980), 150. Reprinted with permission.

Figure 4-6   Collegial Model of Decision Making Used by President John F. Kennedy

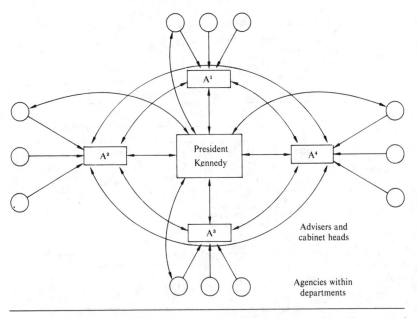

Source: Alexander L. George, *Presidential Decisionmaking in Foreign Policy: The Effective Use of Information and Advice* (Boulder, Colo.: Westview, 1980), 158. Reprinted with permission.

decision agenda. With ever-increasing complexity of decision making in the Nixon years, top-level gatekeeping positions became more specialized, and a number of specialized advisory committees were added as well. Many of these committees drew on the expertise of lower-level units so that information from various bodies could be integrated at these intermediate levels.

The Nixon version of the formalistic model shows the specialized structures for foreign-policy decision making. The special assistant for national security affairs was the key gatekeeper, providing the president with a condensed, centralized information flow. The assistant kept in touch with many sources, gathering information through a series of permanent task-oriented committees chaired by the assistant and through a series of ad hoc working groups chaired by the assistant's aides. At lower levels, information flowing from various sections of the State Department was integrated through merging structures, which then passed information upward to the committees that supplied information to the president's special assistant. Ultimately, the merged and filtered information reached the president in the form of heavily preprocessed decision-making data.

The formalistic model has the advantage of representing an orderly policy-making structure in which each unit performs well-specified tasks. Turf battles and intergroup bargaining are kept to a minimum. Since final decision making is concentrated at the upper levels of the organization and problematic options are screened out along the way, the choice of final options is relatively easy.[68] When lower-level units report to the chief executive through a chief of staff, the executive has the benefit—or disadvantage—of exposure to an even more tightly prescreened information flow, stripped of most data that may be extraneous. Even though the rigidity of transmission channels may deprive top-level executives of important data that have been screened out when information passes through a many-layered hierarchy, it remains possible to use informal grapevine communications to supplement the formal information flows and cut across structural barriers.

The Competitive Model. In this model, favored by Franklin Roosevelt, lines of communication crisscross because lower-level agencies report upward to more than one department head. With jurisdiction over policy areas overlapping, policies are scrutinized from different perspectives and benefit from diverse information inputs. Presumably this cross-fertilization of ideas leads to more broadly informed decisions. The price paid for this wealth of information sources and analytical perspectives may be tensions among competing departments, minimal cooperation, and often serious infighting. The multiplicity of interests involved in making recommendations may make it difficult to agree on policies and procedures.

Roosevelt thought that infighting spawned by the competitive approach would unearth deficiencies in policies that might otherwise remain hidden. He was willing to pay a high price for this benefit. Roosevelt also made it a practice to bypass hierarchical layers by keeping in intermittent contact with units at the bottom level. Such contacts served as a corrective to distortions of information that inevitably result when it is transmitted through hierarchical layers. On the negative side, additional contacts strained the energies of an already overburdened chief executive. To relieve strain at the top, the competitive model also provides for making some decisions at mid-level. It does not provide for horizontal communication or collaboration among units.

The Collegial Model.   Favored by President Kennedy, this model has interconnected units so that information flows freely back and forth through the system horizontally as well as vertically, enabling units to solve problems jointly. If they work as a team, competition and infighting are reduced, while the entry of new and diverse information is made easy. Kennedy liked to create special task forces drawn from various units to deal with particular problems. These groups were presumably task-oriented so that members would ignore loyalties to their respective units. The informal procedures made possible through the task-force approach blurred status and power differences. Task forces were encouraged to act as generalists rather than specialists so that they would consider problems as a whole rather than focusing on a special area.

The tone and quality of information flows and decision making in collegial groups hinge on a number of factors. The most important is the choice of the individual group members. Each brings a distinct information base and style and contributes to the interpersonal chemistry of the group. As discussed, willingness to make compromises and to reconsider past decisions and policies is crucial. Group dynamics may produce constraints on expressing disagreements. In fact, significant problems may be slighted in an effort to maintain group consensus. The methods used by the group to collect, synthesize, and analyze information and to achieve consensus are important, as are the methods of identifying, discussing, and evaluating policy alternatives. The tone of the proceedings will vary depending on whether individual members are asked to contribute specialized or general information. If technical expertise is emphasized, it may become the chief determinant of the ultimate decision.

The Roles of Top-Level Administrators.   Irrespective of the model used to structure information flows, the extent to which the executive dominates the decision-making process is vital. Even when the collegiate model is used, which blurs status and power differences, subordinates nonetheless tend to follow the chief executive's lead. This is especially true when major decisions are at stake and in times of crisis, when deference to the chief executive's wishes recognizes the fact that the chief bears ultimate responsibility for the decision.

Whether or not other high positions will translate into great influence on decisions hinges on the chief executive's views of the office, policy goals, management style, willingness to listen, and the openness of the decision-making system. It also hinges on the type of policy at stake. An adviser may carry a lot of influence in one issue area but not in another; influence may ebb and flow over time. Occupying a strategically advantageous position in the decision-making structure does not assure influence. For example, Nelson Rockefeller, vice president in the Ford administration, and Walter Mondale, who held that office in the Carter administration, both had ample access to a chief executive willing to listen to their advice. But only Mondale had influence.[69]

Four resources appear to be essential for influencing decisions: possession of relevant information, persuasive expertise, internal capital, and a top executive who can be persuaded. Possessing information is particularly important when others are unprepared or underprepared. In the Carter White House, for example, officials who knew the Washington scene, which Carter did not, held a distinct advantage. Their advice was heeded because they controlled vital information that Carter and his cohorts lacked. Willingness to use persuasive skills and opportunities for access to the chief executive are also important. Access is best when the chief executive favors a collegial style and the advisers' goals and style mesh with those of their chief. Internal capital involves respect and support from the chief executive's staff. Rockefeller's influence on White House decisions was impaired because the White House staff never trusted him and therefore often withheld important information from him.[70]

As voices multiply, individual advisers may lose influence, particularly when the competition for the chief executive's attention is heated. Vice President Rockefeller's influence was seriously damaged because he became enmeshed in an internal power struggle involving Chief of Staff Donald Rumsfeld. Rumsfeld wanted all information to flow through him rather than sharing it with Rockefeller because he considered the vice president a political and an administrative threat to his power. Rumsfeld also had ambitions to be vice president during a second Ford term, so that it was to his advantage to deprive Rockefeller of influence. Influence is also closely connected to the electoral cycle. When elections are imminent, executives often become more willing to listen and heed new voices. Alternatively, election campaigns may also take the president and some of his advisers out of the decision-making cycle while they are away on campaign errands.

Advisers to chief executives are most likely to succeed if they carefully plan their strategies. These include setting priorities so that resources are used for the most important and most promising issues where success seems probable and opposition is weak. It is also important to build policy coalitions among the people likely to be involved in the decision-making process. Mondale did this readily in the Carter years because he already had many inside friends and because a lot of people thought that he could provide them with a line to Carter in exchange.[71]

Tapping Fresh Information Sources

Expert Advisers. For decisions that require a high level of expert judgment, the pool of decision makers may be enlarged by creating advisory boards, as illustrated in the Nixon model in Figure 4-4. For example, several expert advisory boards have provided economic information and advice to presidents. One is the Council of Economic Advisers, created in 1946 as a three-member body assisted by a small professional staff largely drawn from academia.[72] The council was charged with forecasting future patterns of overall economic activity, in addition to providing presidents with an economic analysis of various issues and preparing an annual report to Congress. The council was detached from the regular departmental structures and was given no operational responsibilities so that its advice to the president would be guided by purely professional economic concerns.

Other economic advice has come from an ever-changing constellation of councils and formal and informal groups, such as the Council on International Economic Policy, the Cabinet Committee on Small Business, and the Advisory Board on Economic Growth and Stability. Each president has created his own patterns, favoring more or less structured approaches and including various types of governmental insiders and outsiders in these advisory organizations.[73] An often unintended consequence of soliciting advice from prestigious leaders with expertise in various areas is that such consultations allow leading institutions to shape decisions and thereby perpetuate their already great influence.[74]

The creation of advisory bodies also serves political and symbolic purposes. In addition to demonstrating the chief executive's concern about particular issues, they may assuage the bruised feelings of particular constituencies who have felt left out of the decision-making circuit.[75] For example, in March 1976 President Ford created an advisory Agricultural Policy Committee to improve his sagging popularity among farmers. The influence of such bodies depends on their liaison with existing structures. When they operate quite independently with little direction and coordination, as many do, much of their advice does not reach the chief executive, who tends to rely most heavily on internal sources and well-established advisory boards.[76]

Some government bodies specialize in brokering information, collecting, analyzing, using, and dispensing it.[77] The Office of Management and Budget performs these services for the federal executive branch, as the

Office of Technology Assessment (OTA) does for Congress. Such bodies are structured quite differently from the more traditional bureaus responsible for running the government's business or providing specific services to various segments of the public. The Office of Technology Assessment, for example, in addition to its professional staff and board composed of members of Congress, also has an advisory council of ten eminent physical and social scientists. When OTA investigates complex issues involving science and technology, it appoints panels of experts on a particular subject who are drawn from various walks of life. It also uses expert contractors and consultants drawn from industry, universities, private research organizations, and public interest groups. The goal is to supply Congress with a wide range of options representative of the best thinking in a particular problem area.

The advisory teams also include representatives from groups likely to be affected by prospective congressional action or generally interested in the issues at hand. These groups assist in defining the scope of the research as it progresses and in reviewing OTA reports prior to their submission to Congress.[78] Given the settings in which major political decisions must be made in the 1990s, it is important to include input from interested parties for substantive as well as political reasons. Substantively, all available expertise ought to be tapped regardless of whether it exists inside or outside the agency that is making the relevant decision. Politically, people are more likely to accept and cooperate with decisions in which they have had a hand. They need to be assured that public agencies are eager to have their input and have made provisions to elicit it.

Lay Advisers. Many administrative decisions, particularly when they involve innovations, now require open hearings or other forms of consultation preceding adoption of new policies. Since the mid-1960s, enabling laws for regulatory agencies have routinely mandated consultation with advisory committees and funding for lay advisers who wish to participate in agency proceedings. Special efforts have been made to solicit opinions from groups who have lagged in political influence in the past, such as ethnic populations, the elderly, and women. Courts have encouraged broadening the circle of citizen advisers by allowing a steadily wider group of clients to ask for review of administrative decisions.[79] Agencies that fail to provide for such input when it is not mandated by law may be accused of being unresponsive to their clients' needs. In fact, the *process* of decision making often may be more important in the public sector than the nature of the decision. This explains why the substance of citizens' advice is often ignored by public agencies while their requests about issues to be discussed by policy makers are heeded.[80] Agenda responsiveness may be largely symbolic, but it is important nonetheless.

Citizen advisory boards have been used at all levels of government since the 1960s, particularly at the local level. Public input into decisions by regulatory agencies has become especially common. Representatives of citizen groups regularly air their views at public utility commission hearings, during environmental-protection proceedings, on occupational licensing boards, and in hearings pertaining to nursing-home regulations.[81] Cable television has made the deliberations of various public bodies more readily available, and this openness has further facilitated and encouraged lay input.

The War on Poverty program during the Johnson administration is an example of structured efforts to incorporate the concerns of clients into decisions. The enabling legislation urged their "maximum feasible partici- pation." Local programs were then designed so that likely clients had a chance to influence how and where money was being spent. "Obviously, this changed the power relationships within the bureaucracy as well as between the bureaucracy and those it served." [82]

The case of the Occupational Safety and Health Administration (OSHA) provides another example of mandated input by interested parties into important agency decisions. When OSHA considers new regulations to make the workplace safer, it generally appoints ad hoc committees to formulate and recommend a safety standard. These committees must represent the views of workers, employers, and state health and safety organizations.[83] OSHA is also required to solicit written comments and hold hearings to encourage participation in rule making by outside parties. These requirements allow affected parties to put their concerns on record. Lay advisers can challenge agency premises through cross-examination and submission of competing testimony. Agencies must respond to such challenges. Similar procedures are followed by other agencies, such as the Consumer Product Safety Commission.

Agencies frequently create a special office to deal with citizen advisory boards to ensure that their input will be transmitted to the appropriate people within the agency. Lay advisory boards can be quite influential because, unlike review boards, they become involved at the earliest stages of the decision-making process.[84] Their influence appears to be inverse to the power of the agencies they advise. To maintain full control over decisions, strong agencies avoid catering to advisory boards. Weak agen- cies, on the other hand, view these boards as constituencies that can lend them prestige and support.[85]

The use of lay advisory boards, which has faced a few setbacks in recent years, amounts to institutionalizing pluralism in the administrative process. Its main drawbacks are dilution of responsibility for decision making and undue slowing, or even paralysis, of the decision process. There is also some evidence that public input, like that from prestigious experts, often comes from groups and individuals whose views are not broadly representative of their communities.

Critics claim that excessive openness requirements have prevented agencies from developing or pursuing coherent policy agendas.[86] They point out that agencies such as the Consumer Product Safety Commission spend a major part of their time analyzing and responding to outside grievances and proposed standards. Pluralistic policy making is most likely to lead to damaging delays when various legitimate interests see value in different aspects of a decision. Agencies may spend years preparing arguments to cope with a controversy. Massive dossiers are prepared by all parties and followed by rebuttals. Costs skyrocket. An example is the effort of the city of Chicago to select a site for a third airport. Claims and counterclaims by proponents of three different sites have delayed the decision for many years while real estate and construction costs have escalated. Thus, when pluralism becomes excessive, it defeats the purposes of rationality and responsiveness in the decision process.

Table 4-1 compares various forms of public representation on decision-making bodies in terms of resources they bring to bear, the strategies used to achieve goals, and their effectiveness. The types of agencies most likely to use a particular form of representation are noted. In the cases on which the table is based, ombudsmen were most likely to be effective in reaching their goals; lay members of otherwise expert boards enjoyed the least influence.[87]

Routine Decision Making

Most studies of decision making have focused on crucial policy decisions at the top, ignoring the decisions required at lower levels of the hierarchy to implement these policies.[88] The rationale has been that lower-level decisions lack importance.[89] This is not necessarily the case. Many lower-level decisions are very important and involve a great deal of discretion. This certainly holds true for street-level bureaucrats who make the operational decisions by which policy is carried out and who often shape policy in the process.[90] In fact, the shaping may be quite contrary to what top-level decision makers have intended. The situation is similar when legislative mandates are vague because legislators cannot or will not indicate a specific course of action. Lower-level decision makers then determine what the policy will be in practice. When decisions at lower levels resemble the crucial, nonroutine policy-making decisions discussed thus far, they should be made with the same care, irrespective of the level of the hierarchy where they occur. This is rarely the case.

Conversely, major top-level decisions that recur regularly are often routinized like minor decisions so that little new information is sought. For example, the same simple approach is often used by government agencies for annual budget decisions. The existing budget becomes a baseline for

Table 4-1 A Comparison of Public Representation Options

Form of public representation	Policy arena	Resources	Strategies	Goals	Effectiveness
Public hearing	Environmental regulation	Community support, strong statutes	Political pressure	Policy responsiveness (environmental protection)	Low to high
Ombudsman	Nursing-home regulation	Technical expertise	Jawboning	Service responsiveness (eldercare)	High
Proxy advocacy	Utility regulation	Technical and legal expertise	Formal intervention	Policy responsiveness (consumer protection)	Moderate to high
Public membership	Occupational licensing	Decision-making authority	Discussion	Policy responsiveness (consumer protection)	Low

Source: William T. Gormley, Jr., "The Representation Revolution: Reforming State Regulations Through Public Representation," *Administration and Society* 18 (August 1986): 191. Reprinted with permission of Sage Publications, Inc.

requesting relatively small raises. In one study of federal agencies and subagencies, better than 90 percent of decisions about budget requests apparently resulted from such routine formulations.[91] The pattern was the same for budgetary decisions in Detroit, Cleveland, and Pittsburgh.[92] The use of such simple formulations is politically sound because it produces changes that are small enough to escape the ire of pressure groups. Major changes are likely to stir battles over reallocations of resources.[93]

Elaborate procedures are unnecessary for routine bureaucratic decisions that involve applying previously agreed-upon criteria in particular cases. Such routine decisions constitute the bulk of decision making at the lower levels of the hierarchy. For example, when a mother applies for welfare support payments for her child, the criteria for granting such aid are well established and can be applied routinely to her case. In fact, the criteria may be so clear-cut that questions and answers have been programmed into computers. When enabling legislation sets forth clear goals, even the process of devising appropriate classification criteria becomes routine. This is why classification procedures can be left to local operational units without fear that there will be excessive deviation. The discretion exercised by operating agencies is hedged further by budgetary constraints that set limits to activities.[94] For example, the extent to which the validity of a welfare client's claims of need can be investigated hinges on the funds allotted for hiring investigators.

The major concerns in routine decision making are to determine what information should and reasonably can be considered as a basis for dealing with a problem and to make arrangements for securing this information. The overall goal is standardization so that decisions involve a minimum of personal discretion. The agency's performance can then be judged by the rationality of its standard operating procedures, the consistency with which they are applied, and the conformance of the results to the agency's policy goals.[95]

While bureaucracies, by definition, are routinized information-processing systems, bureaucrats as well as the public often resent the degree of depersonalization that this notion suggests. However, on balance, studies indicate that routinized procedures, particularly when they are standardized via computerization, are fairer than discretionary tactics used by individuals, who often yield to personal and political pressures. If steps to a decision are properly programmed into a computer, the end result differs little from decisions made in less regimented ways. For instance, when students were tested for admission to graduate psychology programs, outcomes were almost identical regardless of whether testing was exclusively by computer or by procedures that included a lengthy personal interview.[96] As political scientist Michael Inbar points out, "Relying more heavily (or exclusively) on either man or machine for decision-making merely represents a different choice of trade-offs, and a different partition of possible pay-offs; *in either case a continuous process of review and monitoring is an unavoidable necessity."* [97]

Not all bureaucratic decisions at lower levels lend themselves to routinization, including computerization. Bureaucratic jobs that involve physical actions or sequences of actions, such as the jobs of police and public health physicians, cannot be totally or even largely routinized. It may even be hard to set automatic criteria for repetitive work that involves mostly documents or information-gathering in a standardized environment, such as screening applicants for employment or registering patients at a health facility. For instance, it may be difficult to specify precisely how much education and experience are essential for a particular job. In prison systems, where parole procedures have been standardized to a great extent, it may be difficult to use routine criteria to assess a prisoner's attitude toward society. Because of the difficulty of fitting every decision into the same information norms, agencies frequently choose to forego standardization even when there are ample models for routinized decision making.[98]

Summary and Conclusions

Officials charged with making weighty decisions face a multitude of perplexing considerations. What information should be considered? From whom? How should it be weighted in terms of various policy goals? By what criteria should the merits of these goals be judged? While the answers are elusive, the procedures used for decision making and the structures created to guide the process lend themselves to description and evaluation.

Chapter 4 details information needs during the various phases of decision making: the initial problem analysis phase, the option exploration phase, the actual decision making phase, and the post-decision feedback phase that permits, but does not ensure, improvement of the original decision. Discussion of actual decision making calls attention to four common approaches that are used singly or in combination. They include the *rational-choice* approach, in which decision makers attempt to base decisions on carefully calculated cost and benefit criteria, and the *incremental bargaining* model, in which information searches focus on selecting data likely to lead to consensus among the members of decision-making groups. Decisions can also be reached through assembling knowledgeable persons who express their individual recommendations, which are then combined in an *aggregative model*. Finally, and probably most realistically, most decisions wholly or in part take the form of the *garbage-can model*—a motley assortment of opinions and recommendations that are accumulated more or less haphazardly in stepwise fashion. Though the collection is driven more by circumstances than logic, it may retrospectively lend itself to being proclaimed the offspring of logical processes.

The complexity of public sector decision making taxes human capabilities so that numerous problems may develop at the individual, small group, and larger organizational levels. The most common problems are stereotypical thinking, succumbing to group pressures, or excluding important data from consideration for a variety of extraneous reasons. The chapter discusses ways in which the information stream reaching decision makers can be enriched, ways to ease the difficulties of coordinating information and decisions, and ways to cope with decision making during crises when haste and physical and psychological stresses can wreak havoc with normal procedures.

Structural arrangements shape information flows for decision making and determine the sequences in which information will be processed. They also lay the groundwork for making preliminary decisions on which final decisions rest. Therefore, the chapter analyzes a series of common structural arrangements used for top-level decision making. They include formalistic, competitive, and collegial models. Top-level decision makers often supplement the information resources available from their staffs by relying on specially created expert and lay advisory bodies. Their advantages and drawbacks are analyzed.

The chapter concludes with a brief discussion of various features of routine decision making. While routine procedures are often attacked as dehumanizing, these charges appear to be ill founded when the procedures are carefully designed. Given the huge number of routine decisions required to run the American governmental establishment, standardization is essential. More, rather than less, seems to be required.

It should be clear from the discussion in Chapter 4 that decision making is an eclectic mixture of searching for rationally sound criteria while accommodating conflicting interests and perceptions to arrive at an unplanned, often unforeseen acceptable compromise. This compromise must avoid poisoning the decision making climate so that future sound decisions about the same or other issues remain possible.

Although numerous analysts of decision making have made these points, the public has been reluctant to accept them because they run counter to widely shared ideal images of what decision making ought to be—but rarely is. The capacity of average Americans for self-delusion seems almost endless when political idealism confronts a less than perfect reality.

Theories of public sector decision making remain incomplete. Most ignore the fact that the political context of decisions affects information flows. Theorists have failed to differentiate decision making under ordinary conditions from decision making in crisis situations. As the Eisenhower administration demonstrated, it is possible to make preparations for crisis decisions. Agencies charged with handling physical disasters have pioneered along these lines. Why not institutionalize the equivalent of crisis decision-making fire drills?

Notes

1. John M. Stevens and Robert P. McGowan, *Information Systems and Public Management* (New York: Praeger, 1985), 25.
2. E. Frank Harrison, *The Managerial Decision-Making Process* (Boston: Houghton Mifflin, 1975), 30; Terence R. Mitchell and James R. Larson, Jr., *People in Organizations: An Introduction to Organizational Behavior,* 3d ed. (New York: McGraw-Hill, 1987), 336.
3. Charles Walcott and Karen M. Hult, "Organizing the White House: Structure, Environment, and Organizational Governance," *American Journal of Political Science* 31 (February 1987): 117-119.
4. Carol Weiss, "Congressional Committee Staffs as Problematic Users of Analysis," 1984 American Political Science Association paper.
5. Richard F. Fenno, *Homestyle: House Members in Their Districts* (Boston: Little, Brown, 1978).
6. G. R. Boynton, "When Senators and Publics Meet at the Environmental Protection Subcommittee," *Discourse and Society* 2 (April 1991): 131-155.
7. Herbert Kaufman, *The Administrative Behavior of Federal Bureau Chiefs* (Washington, D.C.: Brookings Institution, 1981), 19-24.
8. For some actual examples, consult Marc K. Landy, Marc J. Roberts, and Stephen R. Thomas, *The Environmental Protection Agency: Asking the Wrong Questions* (New York: Oxford University Press, 1990).
9. James March and Herbert Simon are credited with initiating the "satisficing" concept as part of the notion of "bounded rationality." They pointed out that limits to human attention and finite resources set bounds to the amounts of information that can be processed. James G. March and Herbert A. Simon, *Organizations* (New York: Wiley, 1958), 141. Also see Harold F. Gortner, Julianne Mahler, and Jeanne Bell Nicholson, *Organizational Theory: A Public Perspective* (Chicago: Dorsey, 1987), 258.
10. Martha S. Feldman, *Order without Design: Information Production and Policy Making* (Stanford, Calif.: Stanford University Press, 1989), 24.
11. The various approaches are outlined in Gortner et al., *Organizational Theory,* 247-274; also see Irving L. Janis, *Crucial Decisions: Leadership in Policymaking and Crisis Management* (New York: Free Press, 1989), 114.
12. William F. West, "Structuring Administrative Discretion: The Pursuit of Rationality and Responsiveness," *American Journal of Political Science* 28 (May 1984): 343, 350.
13. David Whiteman, "The Fate of Policy Analysis in Congressional Decision Making: Three Types of Use in Committees," *Western Political Quarterly* 38 (June 1985): 307-308.
14. Janis, *Crucial Decisions,* 125-129; Lawrence T. Pinfield, "A Field Evaluation of Perspectives on Organizational Decision Making," *Administrative Science Quarterly* 31 (1986): 365-388, and sources cited there; Lucien S. Vandenbrouke, "Anatomy of a Failure: The Decision to Land at the Bay of Pigs," *Political Science Quarterly* 99 (Fall 1984): 471-491, and sources cited there.
15. Terry M. Moe, "Control and Feedback in Economic Regulation: The Case of the NLRB," *American Journal of Political Science* 79 (December 1985): 1095. For a comparable discussion of decision making at the state level, see Jeffrey L. Brudney and F. Ted Hebert, "State Agencies and Their Environments: Examining the Influence of Important External Actors," *Journal of Politics* 49 (February 1987): 186-206.

16. Vandenbrouke, "Anatomy of a Failure," 473.
17. Gortner et al., *Organizational Theory,* 254.
18. Vandenbrouke, "Anatomy of a Failure," 480-490.
19. Ibid., 475.
20. Ibid., 477. Vandenbrouke describes the decision in detail.
21. Ibid., 486.
22. Paul R. Schulman, "The 'Logic' of Organizational Irrationality," *Administration and Society* 21 (May 1989): 32.
23. Ibid., 36.
24. See page 138.
25. James G. March and Johan P. Olsen, eds., *Ambiguity and Choice in Organizations,* 2d ed. (Bergen, Norway: Universitetsforlaget, 1979), 26.
26. March and Olsen, as cited above, present case studies to support their views. For an excellent comparison of decision making in structured and unstructured situations, see Pinfield, "A Field Evaluation of Perspectives on Organizational Decision Making," 365-388.
27. Paul Anderson, "Decision Making by Objection and the Cuban Missile Crisis," *Administrative Science Quarterly* 28 (1983): 201-222.
28. Terry M. Moe, "Control and Feedback in Economic Regulation," 1098.
29. Pinfield, "A Field Evaluation," as cited.
30. Ibid., 382.
31. Gortner et al., *Organizational Theory,* 204.
32. Ibid., 207.
33. Ibid., 208.
34. Ibid.; the PERT approach breaks projects into discrete tasks and allots various types of resources to each phase.
35. Lloyd Etheredge, *Can Governments Learn? American Foreign Policy and Central American Revolutions* (New York: Pergamon, 1985).
36. Ibid., 95-107.
37. Alexander L. George, *Presidential Decisionmaking in Foreign Policy: The Effective Use of Information and Advice* (Boulder, Colo.: Westview, 1980), chaps. 2-5. Also see Etheredge, *Can Governments Learn?;* Janis, *Crucial Decisions;* Philip E. Tetlock, "Policy-Makers' Images of International Conflict," *Journal of Social Issues* 39 (1983): 67-86. Also see Barbara Farnham, "Political Cognition and Decision-Making," *Political Psychology* 11 (1990): 83-111.
38. Doris A. Graber, *Processing the News: How People Tame the Information Tide,* 2d ed. (New York: Longman, 1988), chaps 8-9.
39. Vandenbrouke, "Anatomy of a Failure," 488.
40. Frontline #602 Broadcast, "Operation Urgent Fury," Boston: WGBH Educational Foundation, 1988, 6.
41. Chris Lamb, "Belief Systems and Decision Making in the Mayaguez Crisis," *Political Science Quarterly* 99 (Winter 1984-1985): 683.
42. Ibid., 690-692.
43. Richard E. Nisbett and Lee Ross, *Human Inference: Strategies and Shortcomings of Social Judgment* (Englewood Cliffs, N.J.: Prentice-Hall, 1980).
44. Terence R. Mitchell and James R. Larson, Jr., *People in Organizations: An Introduction to Organizational Behavior,* 3d ed. (New York: McGraw-Hill, 1987), 358.
45. Barbara Tuchman, *The March of Folly: From Troy to Vietnam* (New York: Knopf, 1984).
46. Ralph Katz, "The Effects of Group Longevity on Project Communication and

Performance," *Administrative Science Quarterly* 27 (1982): 101.

47. Feldman, *Order without Design,* 2.
48. Katz, "The Effects of Group Longevity," 85.
49. For a discussion of ways to assess how group members are interacting, see Doris A. Graber, *Verbal Behavior and Politics* (Urbana: University of Illinois Press, 1976), 226-229, 261-265; also see George, *Presidential Decisionmaking,* 109-119. Common analysis methods include Bales's Interaction analysis, Sign Process analyses, Sociometric techniques, and Psychiatric Gaming.
50. Janis, *Crucial Decisions,* 56-60.
51. Etheredge, *Can Governments Learn?* 112-116.
52. George, *Presidential Decisionmaking,* 124-126, 169-174.
53. Ibid., 126-127, 242-244.
54. Mitchell and Larson, *People in Organizations,* 382.
55. Ibid., 586.
56. Roger B. Porter, "Economic Advice to the President: From Eisenhower to Reagan," *Political Science Quarterly* 98 (Fall 1983): 420.
57. William T. Gormley, Jr., "Intergovernmental Conflict on Environmental Policy: The Attitudinal Connection," *Western Political Quarterly* 40 (June 1987): 291.
58. Ibid., 300.
59. John P. Burke, "Responsibilities of Presidents and Advisers: A Theory and a Case Study of Vietnam Decision Making," *Journal of Politics* 46 (August 1984): 827.
60. Ibid., 838-842.
61. Terrance L. Albrecht and Vickie A. Ropp, "Communicating about Innovation in Networks of Three U.S. Organizations," *Journal of Communication* 34 (Summer 1984): 80.
62. Charles Walcott and Karen M. Hult, "Organizing the White House: Structure, Environment, and Organizational Governance," *American Journal of Political Science* 31 (February 1987): 117-119.
63. Richard M. Saunders, "Military Force in the Foreign Policy of the Eisenhower Presidency," *Political Science Quarterly* 100 (Spring 1985), 111-112.
64. Joseph G. Morone and Edward J. Woodhouse, *Averting Catastrophe: Strategies for Regulating Risky Technologies* (Berkeley: University of California Press, 1986), 138-161.
65. Thomas Hammond, "Agenda Control, Organizational Structure, and Bureaucratic Politics," *American Journal of Political Science* 30 (May 1986): 384.
66. Kaufman, *The Administrative Behavior of Federal Bureau Chiefs,* 21-22.
67. George, *Presidential Decisionmaking in Foreign Policy,* 150-158.
68. Gortner et al., *Organizational Theory,* 268.
69. Paul Light, "Vice-Presidential Influence under Rockefeller and Mondale," *Political Science Quarterly* 98 (Winter 1983-1984): 617.
70. Ibid., 629-632.
71. Ibid., 636-639.
72. Porter, "Economic Advice to the President," 404-406.
73. Ibid., 408.
74. Gregory A. Caldeira, "The Transmission of Legal Precedent: A Study of State Supreme Courts," *American Political Science Review* 79 (1985): 191.
75. Porter, "Economic Advice to the President," 413.
76. Ibid., 415.
77. Gortner et al., *Organizational Theory,* 413.
78. Office of Technology Assessment, PC-104, revised March 1986.

79. West, "Structuring Administrative Discretion," 346.
80. William Gormley, John Hoadley, and Charles Williams, "Potential Responsiveness in the Bureaucracy: Views of Public Utility Regulation," *American Political Science Review* 77 (September 1983): 704-717.
81. William T. Gormley, Jr., "The Representation Revolution: Reforming State Regulation through Public Representation," *Administration and Society* 18 (August 1986): 179-196.
82. Gortner et al., *Organizational Theory*, 404.
83. West, "Structuring Administrative Discretion," 347.
84. For evidence that citizen input is influential, see Paul A. Sabatier and Neil Pelkey, "Incorporating Multiple Actors and Guidance Instruments into Models of Regulatory Policymaking," *Administration and Society* 19 (August 1987): 236-263.
85. Ray H. MacNair, Russell Caldwell, and Leonard Pollane, "Citizen Participants in Public Bureaucracies: Foul-Weather Friends," *Administration and Society* 14 (February 1983): 507-524.
86. West, "Structuring Administrative Discretion," 356; Feldman, *Order without Design*, 2.
87. Gormley, "The Representation Revolution," 190-195.
88. Michael Inbar, *Routine Decision-Making: The Future of Bureaucracy* (Beverly Hills, Calif.: Sage, 1979), 15-16.
89. E. Frank Harrison, *The Managerial Decision-Making Process* (Boston: Houghton Mifflin, 1975), 15-17.
90. Michael Lipsky, *Street-Level Bureaucracy: Dilemmas of the Individual in Public Services* (New York: Russell Sage Foundation, 1980), makes the point throughout.
91. Inbar, *Routine Decision-Making*, 152.
92. Ibid., 158.
93. Ibid., 165.
94. Ibid., 160.
95. Walcott and Hult, "Organizing the White House," 220.
96. Inbar, *Routine Decision-Making*, 121-122.
97. Ibid., 136. Italics are in the original.
98. Walcott and Hult, "Organizing the White House," 222.

Information Network Patterns

The Nature and Importance of Network Patterns

Network Origins and Types

Networks can be formally defined as relatively stable patterns of information flow that develop within organizations among individuals and groups of people who generate and exchange information on a regular basis.[1] Network analysis focuses on these patterns in an effort to identify communication links and assess their impact on the performance of the organization as well as on individuals within it. Unlike survey research, which concentrates on individual-level variables, network analysis examines relationships. It is more realistic than survey research because it pays attention to the social contexts that limit options and behavior wherever communication takes place.[2]

Since people live and work in groups, networks are common throughout society. They are, as Ithiel de Sola Pool observes, "the thread that holds any social organization together."[3] Social psychologist William Schutz contends that people construct communication networks for three interpersonal needs: the desire to be included in a group to permit interaction with others, the quest for affection through warm interpersonal relations, and the wish to control their environment through acquiring power and influence. His theory of the motivations that drive network constructions is called FIRO—fundamental interpersonal relations orientation.[4]

The suitability of the network for the tasks to be performed is important. If networks are larger than needed, people are burdened unnecessarily with information; if they are too small, organizations may be unable to gather and process all that is needed for sound operations. Once established, networks tend to maintain their patterns over long periods of time. This can be troublesome when the organization is changing rapidly. In times of flux, it is essential to keep network structures open enough so that new information can be readily encountered.

When organizational components become too unwieldy or functionally diverse to allow inclusion of all members in a single communication circuit, networks linking selected individuals only tend to develop spontaneously. Most public agencies operate through multiple networks because they carry out many diverse functions and employ large numbers of people who do not need to be in touch on a regular basis with everyone else in the organization.

Analysis of typical information flow patterns within most organizations clearly shows that information does not circulate freely to everyone. Some groups are regularly privy to the most important information. Widely known as "old boy" networks, these insiders often develop shared values and expectations. People who do not regularly belong to insider networks are usually part of other communication networks that share in less politically significant information. Outsiders often differ substantially in outlook from the in-group. A few of them may be loners who do not communicate regularly with any network. Since messages are interpreted differently as they move from one network to another within the organization or beyond it, they may require explanatory commentary geared to particular needs.

Participation in the insider network, besides providing crucial information, also gives access to key decision makers. Insiders are likely to be influential, particularly when they carry out key network functions, such as controlling the flow of information reaching the network or connecting internal networks with each other or with those outside the organization's boundaries. Deliberate or inadvertent exclusion from insider networks reduces opportunities for influence. Network configurations thus determine and reflect the power structure, which explains why the study of networks is a prerequisite for understanding organizational power and functioning.

Information flow problems are often diminished or corrected through deliberate network restructuring. According to William Eddy, this "involves regrouping and sometimes redefining the functions to be carried out by various government agencies in such a way that responsibilities, reporting lines, communication channels, and other structural characteristics are changed. The assumption is that such structural changes will eventually bring about changes in the performance of individuals and an improvement in the efficiency or effectiveness of work."[5]

Events in Dayton, Ohio, are a case in point.[6] Like many city governments in the 1960s, Dayton could not cope with its many social problems. To break away from the established networking molds, a series of task forces were set up, drawn from all city departments, to focus on specific problems and develop goals and work plans. Because all departments were represented and also were kept informed about activities, resistance to task-force proposals was minimized. The task force had tapped into a variety of communication networks, giving its members a broad view of the city's needs and possibilities for reforms. This approach, Eddy points out, thus stimulated "new ways of communicating among the various city departments and a considerably greater degree of involvement of employees at all levels in goal setting and problem solving." [7]

Adding new people to a network sometimes produces major changes because they introduce perspectives drawn from other networks. For example, when environmental analysts were added to the staffs of the Army Corps of Engineers and the Forest Service to help them in preparing mandatory environmental-impact statements, environmental considerations became part of the deliberations of these agencies. Since these concerns were introduced during the very early stages of planning, they could be highly influential.[8]

Networks may reflect the formal structure of the organization or they may be dictated by functional needs and interpersonal chemistry. The latter is more common. Most network patterns, although influenced by formal structures, differ from formal lines of communication. They are less structured and often cut in unpredictable ways across hierarchical levels and interorganizational barriers.[9] Networks may also be deliberately created because political leaders like to decide who the insiders and outsiders will be.

Friendship Networks

Presidential cabinets are good examples of the many networks that reflect friendship patterns. Structural arrangements determine the formal cabinet membership, with occupants of specified offices automatically becoming cabinet members. But it is not uncommon for presidents to add personally chosen informal networks of advisers. These have been known as "kitchen cabinets." [10] Networks based on friendship have both advantages and disadvantages. On the positive side, they permit executives to tap into congenial information networks that they might not otherwise reach through formal organizational networks. On the negative side, tapping into groups of soul mates decreases opportunities for detached criticism and diversity of thought.

The 1961 decision to invade Cuba's Bay of Pigs shows the disastrous consequences that may follow when friends talk only to friends. Friendship was the basis on which CIA officials created supportive networks for their ill-fated invasion plans.[11] For example, CIA Director Allen Dulles and Deputy CIA Director Richard Bissell had many friends in high places. Dulles had met President Kennedy in Palm Beach, Florida, and the two had become friends through common acquaintances. Membership in this network made it easy for Dulles to gain access to the president and get a sympathetic hearing for his views. McGeorge Bundy, who was the president's special assistant for national security affairs, knew Bissell through friendship networks formed as an undergraduate at Yale University. He admired Bissell's intellect. White House aide Arthur Schlesinger, Jr., had known Dulles in the Office of Strategic Services during World War II and had become Bissell's friend when Bissell worked for the Marshall Plan for European recovery in the post-World War II years. Assistant Secretary of State for Latin American Affairs Thomas Mann was a personal friend of both Dulles and Bissell. Given such personal friendships, it was easy for the CIA leadership to get its views across to top-level White House decision makers and to have these views accepted.

Opponents of the invasion plans, such as the Joint Chiefs of Staff, were unlikely to voice their reservations, knowing how well connected the CIA leadership was. The friendship ties do more than ease access and lend weight to the voice of the friend. They also discourage other voices from expressing contrary views. Nonetheless, friendship networks remain common because drawbacks are balanced by major advantages. Interaction is easy because it is based on shared experiences, values, and mutual trust and understanding.

Issue Networks

Just as friendships can become the magnet that draws people together into networks, so shared interests in particular issues may generate network structures. Political scientist Hugh Heclo has pointed out that communications among governmental agencies frequently spring from joint involvement in issues. In fact, overlapping jurisdictions over various issues have become the rule in policy areas such as occupational health and safety, air and water pollution, consumer protection, and energy production. The nature of the issue, rather than the more formal ordinary relations among agencies, then determines what shape this network will take. In many instances, issue networks are composed of a combination of public agencies and selected private groups, technical experts, and policy activists concerned about the issue.[12] Since the members may disagree about the appropriate policies for dealing with the issue, they may subdivide into coalitions that share information to foster their preferred goals.[13] Once formed, these networks tend to grow whenever issues move onto the public policy agenda and new groups decide to join. This has happened in areas such as health and energy policy.

In the case of energy policy, the initial proposal of the Carter administration was worked out by a network of conservation-minded experts who pictured it as a fight between the big oil companies and consumer interests.[14] Other interested parties then joined the network, such as tax reformers, nuclear-power specialists, and civil rights groups eager for energy-related jobs. Each new group contributed fresh information and perspectives. In many respects, this diversity of interests and information made it more difficult to construct policy coalitions within the network. In other respects, the proliferation of players eased coalition building because it offered new opportunities, as Heclo writes, "to split and recombine the many sources of support and opposition that exist on policy issues." [15] Public hearings often serve as a way to recruit new groups into coalitions. Since the life of these networks is limited to the life of particular issues, their construction has become a perennial task for political leaders.

When issue networks involve complex technical problems, as often happens, information contributed by technical experts with political savvy tends to become dominant. Heclo refers to such experts as "technopols." They are activists with specialized knowledge, which includes knowing people who share an interest in the particular issue. Because they serve as experts in a variety of different networks, they are extremely influential. In time, they become so well known that they are repeatedly consulted, which gives them entry to an exceptionally wide array of issue networks. As Heclo puts it, "More than ever, policy making is becoming an intramural activity among expert issue-watchers, their networks, and their networks of networks. In this situation any neat distinction between the governmental structure and its environment tends to break down." [16]

The prevalence of issue networks has several adverse consequences for American political life. Technopols tend to ignore average people who lack expertise in the issue under discussion. Accordingly, public influence on policy outcomes diminishes because of the deference accorded technical expertise. When various groups of technopols do compete for the support of average citizens and each group emphasizes its own perception of "truth," people can become totally confused and often cynical about the possibilities of knowing where the truth lies. Disagreements among experts also hamper consensus within an issue network, particularly when political considerations run at cross purposes with scientific "truth." Technocrats cannot usually be bought off with the kinds of material rewards that have been the coin of the realm in politics.

When issue debates become battles over the merits of scientific findings, it becomes difficult to reach closure of the debate so that action can take place. There is always just one more study that needs to be done or one more player who needs to be heard. Afterward, the additional information must be fully considered, reopening many previously reached decisions. Political executives who try to push for urgently required action may find it hard to oppose the delays recommended by the "experts." They manage to do it occasionally by appealing to nonpolitical values such as efficiency and the need for the service, but more often than not, action is delayed and important goals are frustrated.

Despite their drawbacks, issue networks are an important and needed political development.[17] They serve as bridges between the various branches and levels of government and fill the void left by the weakening of party-based networks. "For example, on energy policy," writes Heclo, "regardless of one's position on gas deregulation or incentives to producers, the policy technocracy has established a common language for discussing the issues, a shared grammar for identifying the major points of contention, a mutually familiar rhetoric of argumentation. . . . Like experienced party politicians of earlier times, policy politicians in the knowledge networks may not agree; but they understand each other's way of looking at the world and arguing about policy choices."[18] The new focus on issue networks dominated by technical experts has led all branches and levels of government to hire issue experts for their staffs. The public and pressure groups, too, have become more oriented to joining issue networks.

Network Analysis Payoffs

To fathom who enjoys power and influence and what kinds of information are likely to be transmitted or excluded, one needs to know who is part of a particular network and who is not. Political scientist John Kessel, for example, studied communication networks at the top levels of the Carter and Reagan White House to assess who was in close touch with the president and how information traveled among top White House advisers and to more remote parts of the executive branch.[19] Kessel's findings, which are reported later in this chapter, demonstrate that even relatively minor variations in communication structures can produce substantial differences in information flow patterns and in the distribution of political influence. The two White House staffs varied considerably in the number of people included in the network, the quality of their interpersonal relations, the frequency of their internal and external communication, and the substance of their interactions. Network analysis helped to identify dominant members whose views were likely to prevail. It thus provided a tool for studying the effectiveness of network structures available to Presidents Carter and Reagan.

Knowledge about an organization's network structure is also essential for outsiders who want to deal with it. This includes lobbyists eager to influence governmental action as well as legislators and ordinary citizens concerned about governmental activities. All of them need to understand where the key points are for introducing certain types of information and which networks should be avoided as unproductive for particular transactions. In fact, knowledge of how various government networks are structured and operate is the chief asset of ex-officials turned lobbyists. (On the negative side, they have often been accused of influence peddling when they profit from former insider status.) Former Reagan aide Michael Deaver worked on the acid-rain problem during his government days. Knowing the network for this issue helped him become a consultant on acid rain for the Canadian government.[20] Understanding network structure thus serves practical needs in addition to its importance in abstract and theoretical terms.

Understanding network structures may be the key to unraveling how citizens develop their political views in mutual discussions and how they gain access to decision makers. Thus, a team of researchers conducted an innovative investigation, the Redwood Project, in the San Francisco Bay Area in the 1980s.[21] It was based on the assumption that citizen influence on policy arises largely through participation in groups that are in direct or indirect contact with power structures. The researchers questioned a sampling of citizens about their normal conversational networks and also those whose help they would seek about problems such as crime, undesired industrial development, book censorship, and excessive taxation at the federal level. It was found that some citizens participated in tightly structured networks whose members communicated almost exclusively with each other. These citizens reinforced each other's opinions but lacked contacts with people with access to public officials. Other citizens had loosely structured communication networks through which they were able to reach public officials directly or through an intermediary. Citizens with connections to the right networks had the opportunity for genuine participation in governmental decisions. Citizens without these connections lacked this opportunity.

The power configurations created through interorganizational network patterns at the local level can be illustrated by the hypothetical city health network shown in Figure 5-1.[22] Besides the five hospitals designated by blackened circles, the network contains a supporting academic network cluster shown as circles with horizontal crossbars. The academic group encompasses a state university, a medical school, a nursing school, and a government research agency as well as a private research foundation. There is also a cluster of regulatory and special interest groups, identified by circles with vertical bars. This cluster includes a state regulatory agency, a labor union to which employees of the municipal hospital belong, a hospital council, a labor council, and the Welfare Department and the Community Chest. Finally, two political bodies, identified by blank circles—City Hall and the dominant political party—are involved in the network.

The figure includes strong ties only, omitting unimportant connections that convey routine and symbolic messages. This concentration suggests that communication networks must be judged by crucial connections, which represent the organization's influence structure. As proponents of exchange theories and power dependence theories have long argued, social relations can be best understood by tracing the networks through which valued items are exchanged, such as information or advice, or goods and

Figure 5-1 **Hypothetical City Health Network**

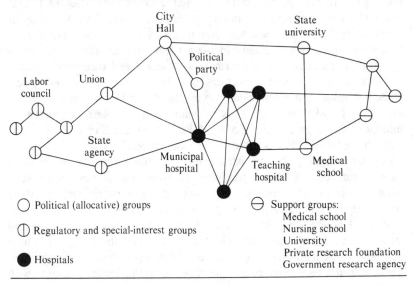

Source: Charles Perrow, *Complex Organizations: A Critical Essay*, 2d ed. (Glenview Ill.: Scott, Foresman, 1979), 222. Reprinted with permission of McGraw-Hill, Inc.

services, or by focusing on the communicators' respective power and dependence on each other.[23] Communications among units may be ample, but it matters little unless the message exchange is significant in terms of the power relationships among the units.

Figure 5-1 illustrates how the density of communication links can vary considerably in different parts of an interorganizational network. Some units are tightly coupled, others loosely, and still others are barely connected at all even though they are part of the network. The influence of each unit depends in part on its location in the network. Two identically organized units may vary greatly in influence if they occupy different positions in their respective network structures. The kinds of network relationships shown in Figure 5-1 may vary over time. Hence, understanding the significance of networks requires studying them not only comparatively but also repeatedly at different points in time.[24]

In Figure 5-1, the five hospitals are tightly coupled, as shown by the dense pattern of interconnecting communication channels that links each unit directly to all others within the hospital cluster. The hospitals obviously interact with one another regularly and in important ways. By contrast, the five support groups, all dealing with training and research, are loosely coupled. Some communicate; others do not. Hence, they are only partially interactive. Only one of the support units, the medical school, is in direct contact with the teaching hospital, and there is only one additional direct link between the hospital cluster and the support units.

The scarcity of ties across the boundaries of various organizations that are part of the network may suggest a lack of sufficient interunit connections. It may also indicate where new links are needed to correct current deficiencies. For example, the state university lacks strong direct ties to the municipal hospital. If it wants to influence the level of care at that hospital, as it might, it must go through City Hall and the political party, both of whom control funding and positions for the municipal hospital. The state university could also ask the medical school to use its ties with the teaching hospital to bring influence to bear on the municipal hospital, which has strong contacts with the teaching hospital.

The regulatory and special interest groups are hardly coupled at all, suggesting that they do not collaborate despite their often complementary interests. Moreover, most of them have no direct lines into the hospital system. Only the union and the state regulatory agency are linked to the hospital cluster, and then through only one of its units, the municipal hospital. When the state regulatory agency makes rules for the municipal hospital, such as requiring the use of generic drugs to reduce the cost of health care, these rules may spill over to other hospitals because of their tight linkage to the municipal hospital network. Tightly coupled networks are prone to fast, often unpredictable interactions and changes in response to shared information. It is doubtful, however, that a third-step flow would also occur whereby a rule regarding the use of generic drugs would be transmitted from one of the second-step hospitals to the support groups, such as the medical school. Again, if wide adoption is desired, the state regulatory agency may have to establish direct ties with the other hospitals and with the supporting organizations.

City Hall has the greatest reach and centrality of all the organizations in the health network. It can dip directly into the municipal hospital network, or it can reach that network through the political party, which controls employee patronage. Alternatively, it can approach the hospital cluster indirectly through its contacts among the interest groups or its ties to the supporting agencies that flow through the state university. The teaching hospital and medical school are well insulated from the interest groups and the state regulatory agency. If the medical school wishes to influence care at the municipal hospital, it can go either through the teaching hospital or through City Hall via the state university. To increase its influence, it would probably seek to gain direct ties to City Hall, lessening its dependence on the state university.

While this is a hypothetical city health network system, the relationships described are very real and common. They are the gist of most activities that fall under the heading of "organizational politics." Much of the time, effort, and scheming of successful administrators is directed toward structuring appropriate networks, placing supporters in key positions, or wooing key network figures who are already in place. Knowing which are

Figure 5-2   Hypothetical Network Interactions

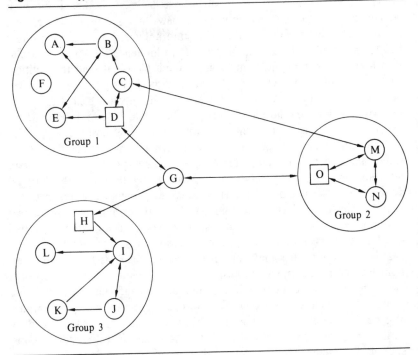

Source: Adapted from Terence R. Mitchell and James R. Larson, Jr., *People in Organizations: An Introduction to Organizational Behavior,* 3d ed. (New York: McGraw-Hill, 1987), 305. Reprinted with permission.

the right networks to join, gaining entry to them, and using these connections to the organization's advantage are hard work, but can be extraordinarily rewarding.

Individual Network Roles—An Overview

The network diagrammed in Figure 5-2 illustrates typical network interactions, though on a smaller scale than would be true for most public sector agencies. Information flows are shown inside three small groups—often called "cliques"—of three- to six-person networks and the communication links that tie the groups together. The more groups a system has, the more differentiated it is. A large number of groups makes it easier for individual groups to engage in specialized activities and to experiment.[25] However, the complexity and specialization that facilitate innovations may make it more

Figure 5-3   Small-Group Interaction Patterns

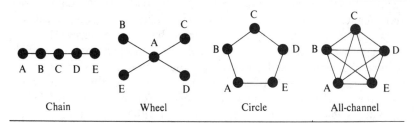

| Chain | Wheel | Circle | All-channel |

difficult to implement them. The gains from specialization and expertise may be outweighed by the losses from fractionalizing organizational activities and the problems of interclique coordination.

One-headed arrows in Figure 5-2 show predominantly one-way flows, while two-headed arrows show two-way communications. Arrows are plentiful within each unit, indicating ample internal communication. However, patterns vary. Although Figure 5-2 does not illustrate this, lab experiments have identified four patterns of interaction among network members when groups are small.[26] They are the chain, the wheel, the circle, and all-channel interrelationships in Figure 5-3. In the *circle* pattern, information travels round-robin style, with each person passing messages to the next person. The final person completes the circle by contacting the message originator, either to acknowledge that the message was circulated or to report various types of response or feedback by network members who are reacting to the substance of the message.

When this last step is missing, the pattern is called a *chain,* which reaches from the first to the last link. If the message has become distorted in its passage through the chain, the last person, who may be the individual charged with taking message-related actions, is apt to receive the most tainted information. For this reason, circle patterns are preferred whenever accuracy is essential and distortions during message passage are common.

In the *wheel* pattern, all communication passes through one centrally located node, which may be one individual or a cluster of individuals. When individuals within the wheel-type network interact with each other in addition, the wheel becomes an *interlocking* network; otherwise it is *radial.* Most networks are a mixture, but interlocking ones are more common. Because the wheel configuration centralizes information flows, the center may become overloaded and inefficient, and people at the periphery may feel dominated and dissatisfied.

In the *all-channel* pattern, messages circulate freely among all members. The pattern is ideal from the standpoint of openness because information is shared by all. However, in complex organizations, the price of openness may be debilitating communication overloads for all network members. As Daniel Katz and Robert Kahn write, "Experimental work has generally supported the hypothesis that the smaller the number of communication links in a group, the greater the efficiency of the group in task performance." [27] When the organizational climate is friendly, wheel patterns appear to be most efficient, followed by circle patterns. However, once groups learn how to communicate, all of the patterns can produce good results. Unfortunately, most of the studies on which such findings rest have been done under artificial laboratory conditions, where researchers have worked with groups of strangers who are asked to perform unfamiliar, often meaningless tasks. They have not worked with groups whose members know each other and have learned to cooperate. [28]

As Figure 5-2 indicates, some groups show more internal two-way communication and hence greater cohesiveness than others. Such variations are commonly related to the functions performed by a group and the characteristics of its members. The physical environment can be an important factor as well. Individuals whose offices are in close proximity are more likely to communicate. Comparison of actual with possible message flows permits construction of indexes of group connectedness. Besides indicating the degree to which network capacity is used, such indexes also reveal how information reaching the network is likely to travel. Analysts can then recommend appropriate channeling of information to reach particular group members most expeditiously, particularly when they are beyond direct reach. The relationship between group connectedness and other types of organizational behavior can also be examined. For example, investigators have studied how the flow of communication increases or decreases worker productivity.

In Group 1 in Figure 5-2, individual F is not connected to the other members of the network, which makes him or her an *isolate*. It means that this individual, by virtue of his or her role in the organization, would ordinarily be expected to be included in the Group 1 network. For some reason, this is not happening. Possible reasons include personality-interaction barriers, deliberate discrimination, or lack of shared interests with the group. When individuals are members of several networks, they often play an isolate role in at least some of them either because other ties occupy them fully or because these ties make them seem like outsiders in some of the networks with which they are linked.

In many organizations, the existence of isolates is a matter of concern because it may reflect major problems in structure and functioning. Additionally, isolates may perform poorly because they may not be privy to information that is important for doing their assigned tasks. Studies of communication patterns within large American corporations indicate that groups that are isolates perform less effectively than those that are well-integrated into their networks. Isolates may lack the benefit of exposure to diverse information and to external criticism. They may also exhibit many of the undesirable characteristics of groupthink discussed in Chapter 4. [29]

The sociogram in Figure 5-2 also shows one individual, G, who is in touch with all the groups but is not part of them. In network-analysis jargon, G is called a *liaison,* who links groups. Liaison among groups could be G's main function; alternatively, G may be the boss who controls all three units. If G performed the liaison function while also part of a network, she or he would be called a *bridge.* C and M are bridges between groups 1 and 2. Liaisons and bridges are also referred to as *boundary spanners* or *cosmopolites* when their communication reaches beyond the boundaries of their own network. Some boundary spanners may even be members of several networks, which would then be depicted as overlapping circles.

Within each group in Figure 5-2, the official head is identified by a square box, and other members are encased in circles. All heads contact other groups through liaison G. In Group 3, H is the only individual connected to the other networks via the liaison. Therefore, all information flowing into the network from the outside must pass through the head. That makes H a *gatekeeper* with complete control over the information entering or leaving the network. However, H seems peripheral to intra-unit communication, being in regular touch only with I, the central figure within the unit. This suggests that H, although the formal unit leader and the contact person to outside groups, has been replaced by I as the actual leader of intragroup communication.

In groups 1 and 2, the head's gatekeeping control is weaker because it is shared with the boundary spanners, who are in touch with each other. The boundary spanners, in this case, each have direct access to one group, compared with the heads who are connected to two other groups, but only indirectly through the liaison. Whether direct access to one group conveys more gatekeeping control than indirect access to two groups depends on the circumstances involved in each case.

The individual whose control is most diverse, thanks to being in touch with all three groups, is the liaison, G. In the past, such a position of centrality was automatically equated with power because of its ready access to information. More recent research has called this power equation into question. Proponents of exchange network theory argue that control over information resources that are valuable because they are desired by others, rather than central location in a communications network, is the major source of power. Individuals in the network who hold the most coveted information are dominant because others depend on them.[30] Their ability to influence other network members with some regularity may cast such individuals into the informal role of *opinion leader.*

Some opinion leaders function only in certain topic areas, while others play more diverse roles. For example, an official in a city's police department may be the opinion leader when it comes to treatment of juvenile offenders. Alternatively, the same official may be considered the leader in devising approaches to coping with many other crimes as well. Opinion leaders are usually experts whose knowledge and experience give them high credibility and status. Their reputation allows them superior access to internal as well as external information sources, even when they are not members of the top hierarchy. If opinion leaders conform to organizational norms, they are valuable to the system, enhancing organizational coordination and control by motivating others to behave in approved ways. When they do not conform to norms, the organization may be in trouble because the opinion leader may carry it in directions that are not approved by the organization's leadership.

Central location within a communication network has been linked to the ability to innovate. For example, well-connected groups produce more desirable innovations than their poorly connected counterparts. Similarly, exceptionally innovative individuals are often centrally located in organizations, which exposes them to most of the information entering the network, including information coming from people beyond their own immediate network.[31] However, it is not clear which is cause and which is effect. Individuals and groups may be innovative because they are centrally located, or they may be centrally positioned in such networks because they are innovative.

What is clear is that people eager to exercise power strive to control positions within communication networks that are perceived as power bases.[32] Key positions, providing access to information and resources, exist at all organizational levels. A prominent physician in a small specialized hospital unit, for example, who has control over key pieces of information may thereby become a key player in the overall communication network of the organization. Whether or not a potentially powerful network position will actually convey power hinges on the personal attributes of the incumbent, such as intelligence, interpersonal skills, prestige, and professional qualifications. Network positions provide opportunities, but no guarantees of automatic success.

Individual Network Roles—A Closer Look

We are now ready to take a closer look at individual positions within networks to assess their significance for organizations.[33]

Gatekeepers

As the name suggests, gatekeepers control the flow of information into communication networks. Strictly speaking, every individual who agrees to transmit a message is a gatekeeper, but the term is generally reserved for individuals who routinely perform gatekeeping functions within a particular network. Executive secretaries who scan incoming information and determine whether it should be passed on to network members, sent elsewhere, or ignored are good examples. Often their greatest value lies in protecting network members from information overloads. Organizations may also assign the information-control function to designated specialists or groups of specialists. For instance, at the Department of Defense, specialists in aircraft procurement or nuclear-submarine deployment serve as gatekeepers who screen information in their respective areas of expertise.

Gatekeepers make four types of potentially crucial decisions. They relate to (1) admitting the message to the network; (2) routing it to specified or unspecified receivers; (3) editing it; and (4) determining the timeliness of transmission. When messages or messengers seek entry to their network's communication channels, gatekeepers may grant or refuse entry. Unless there are multiple gatekeepers, refusal usually shields network members from the excluded message. Depending on its importance to the network, and to the political system in general, this may be helpful or harmful. Besides its significance for an agency's technical operations, gatekeeping also involves the sensitive issue of responsiveness to the public. If gatekeepers lack the interpersonal skills to convey openness, if they shield top personnel too much, public agencies may appear to be or may actually be unduly unresponsive. The problem of overcoming undue barriers posed by gatekeepers has been only marginally improved by structural remedies, such as creating ombudsman offices or appointing inspectors general to fight against overly zealous or inefficient gatekeeping procedures.

Once messages have been admitted, gatekeepers often have the option to route them to particular individuals or networks. Again, this is a crucial decision. Messages routed to inappropriate or unsympathetic targets may be doomed. In legislative bodies, when gatekeepers route messages to particular committees, they thereby determine what aspects of the message will receive attention. For instance, reports about the need for tax rebates for gasoline used in farm machinery will likely lead to different outcomes depending on whether they are referred to an agriculture committee or to one concerned primarily with highway traffic. The former will be favorable; the latter is likely to be hostile because slow farm vehicles obstruct traffic. Environmentalists, whose concerns are now handled by sympathetic committees, have avoided proposing pollution taxes because they fear that congressional gatekeepers might then shift the legislation to hostile tax-writing committees.[34]

Gatekeepers also have the power to decide whether to pass messages in the form submitted by the sender or to edit them. If they decide the latter, they usually have control over how this is done. They can rephrase the message, interpret it, shift its focus, abbreviate it, or even lengthen it. In the process they can frame the message in ways that affect how it will be perceived. Editing, as discussed in Chapter 2, frequently distorts the meaning intended by message senders and often results in fatal omissions.

A story from Illinois illustrates how gatekeeping routines can lead to catastrophe when a message requiring expeditious handling and well-chosen routing is poorly handled.[35] A mine explosion at Mine No. 5 in Centralia, Illinois, could have been prevented if miners' complaints had been promptly transmitted to the appropriate officials. The miners had written to the governor complaining about coal-dust problems and requesting that he order the Department of Mines and Minerals to enforce neglected safety laws.

The gatekeeper who initially received the message was one of the governor's three secretaries. After delaying two days, the secretary decided that the letter should go first to the Department of Mines and Minerals, rather than directly to the governor, because mine safety was that department's responsibility. Transmission through "channels" took another two days, even though the Department of Mines was located within sixty feet of the secretary's desk. Predictably, since the letter called into question the efficiency of that department, its director rejected the claim as exaggerated. Nonetheless, he suggested that it should be brought to the attention of the state mining board at its next meeting. The miners were informed that this would happen, but there is no record that it did. Subsequent pleas for relief also failed to pass gatekeeping hurdles and did not reach the governor until after the mine had exploded, killing 111 miners. Only then did the message get through to its intended target.

As discussed more fully in Chapter 2, the most recalcitrant problems encountered in gatekeeping relate to suitable methods for gauging the importance of messages and channeling them appropriately. How can gatekeepers judge the significance of incoming messages, label them accordingly, and route them to the appropriate parties inside or outside the communications network? These problems are particularly acute because the bulk of gatekeeping decisions are made by people with clerical rather than professional training. Political scientist Terry Moe, who encountered problems with low-level gatekeepers at the National Labor Relations Board, calls placing gatekeeping responsibilities at that level a regrettable "information asymmetry." [36] At the National Labor Relations Board low-level officials make crucial initial decisions as to whether a case should be accepted for adjudication. These decisions often do not reflect the views of upper-level personnel in the NLRB's hierarchy. Efforts to monitor or control decisions made by nonprofessional gatekeeping staffs have generally been only moderately successful. Yet switching this function to individuals in the network holding higher-level jobs is also undesirable because of the burdens it places on them when many gatekeeping decisions are indeed routine.

Bridges and Liaisons

While networks make communication more manageable and efficient in large organizations, they also tend to balkanize information flows. It is therefore essential to link various networks horizontally and vertically through personnel acting as bridges or liaisons. Like other gatekeepers, liaisons usually constitute two-way channels, receiving as well as transmitting information. In Figure 5-2, for example, liaison G both receives and sends information to all three groups. Bridges C and M are also two-way channels between groups 1 and 2. In the absence of such linkages, organizations disintegrate into uncoordinated subsystems.[37]

Unlike ordinary gatekeepers, employees involved in bridging and liaison functions are more likely to be drawn from the higher professional levels. In fact, most individuals at higher levels act as liaisons or bridges occasionally. In the average organization, five to twenty percent of the personnel are likely to be involved in liaison work.[38] Upper level personnel are used as liaisons and bridges because decisions about disseminating information to and from other agencies or departments usually are difficult to routinize.

Since bridges and liaisons function like gatekeepers, they suffer from similar problems. They are especially prone to becoming bottlenecks, particularly when they link multiple units, as liaison G does in Figure 5-2. When incumbents of communication hubs become deluged with messages, they are often forced to ignore most of them, including urgent phone calls and computer and fax messages.[39] Bottleneck problems are most serious when agencies are faced with major crises. It is almost impossible to plan adequate reserve transmission capacity when the nature and extent of such crises are unforeseeable. For example, when the United States became involved in the Persian Gulf military operations in 1990, the Defense Department was swamped with inquiries by reserve personnel and National Guard units who were anxious to know their status. It was impossible to provide rapid, individualized responses under these unexpected circumstances.

On many occasions, overwhelming bottleneck problems result from the requirement for openness which forces public agencies to comply with often excessive and unwarranted demands for information. A false rumor that contracts awarded by a municipality have excluded minority enterprises may spark a flood of requests to inspect the lists of successful merchants. Compared with overload problems, information underloads are a fairly uncommon problem for bridges and liaisons, but they do occur. When that happens, it may require additional effort on the part of network members to obtain the information that is not coming in through bridges and liaisons.

Formal leaders within a given agency or department often become part of a network of leaders at the next higher level. For example, participants in advisory networks such as cabinets or task forces are frequently drawn from

Figure 5-4   Linking Pin Model of Organization

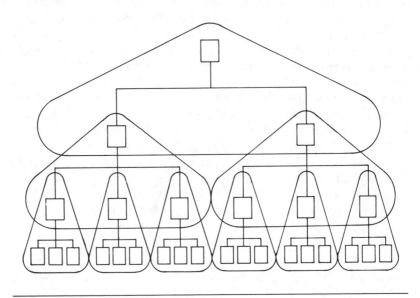

Source: R. Wayne Pace and Don F. Faules, *Organizational Communication*, 2d ed. (Englewood Cliffs, N.J.: Prentice-Hall, 1989), 43. Reprinted with permission.

Note: Each square represents an organizational unit within a network. The rounded triangles represent networks linked through overlapping memberships.

the leadership of various established agencies. Their dual roles make these individuals the *linking pins* that knit the various parts of the hierarchy together. Figure 5-4 shows a "linking pin" organizational structure. The linking pins commonly represent group-to-group relationships rather than person-to-person ties.[40]

Public agencies often do not make formal assignments to bridging or liaison roles because the mission of the organization is defined largely in terms of separate group tasks. Agency executives then assume bridging and liaison roles informally. Given the importance of these roles, public administration experts recommend making formal assignments. Gortner, for example, notes "In some instances, liaison roles may need to be created formally if they do not exist informally. Even where a liaison role is informally filled, it may be advisable to make the position formal if that is necessary to coordinate important organizational activities."[41] Providing for adequate liaison activities is particularly critical in public bodies because these important functions may be inadvertently neglected when there is rapid turnover among top personnel. To avoid turnover-related gaps, it may be wise to select career officials rather than political appointees as liaisons.

A White House Case Study

A look at White House staffs during several presidencies provides insights into the nature of liaison functions. Political scientist John Kessel has outlined the tasks that need to be accomplished.

> If the presidency is to be responsive to the political environment, then the White House staff should be scanning the environment constantly to pick up cues from congressmen, bureaucrats, interest group leaders, and other relevant actors. If several organizational units—for example, the Domestic Policy Staff, the Office of Public Liaison, and OMB—are all concerned with a decision, there must be some means of consultation between them. If the decision is sufficiently important to go to the president, there must be a flow of information from staff units to the Oval Office. Once a decision has been made, it must be communicated to those within and without the White House who have to implement it.[42]

In other words, there are four important functions that a liaison staff at the executive level must fulfill: (1) it must constantly pick up cues from the political environment to keep abreast of ongoing developments; (2) if it finds that disparate units are concerned with the same issues, it must provide the necessary liaison to coordinate their work; (3) if the information reaching the staff seems important enough to warrant presidential attention, there must be liaison to the president; (4) once decisions have been reached, they must be communicated to units in and out of the White House that are charged with implementing the decisions.

How these intelligence-gathering, transmission, and liaison functions are performed hinges very much on the types of networks established among White House staff members. To assess and compare the flow of communication during the Carter and Reagan administrations, Kessel asked White House aides: "Which persons do you spend the most time with getting your own work done?" Their answers, which named persons in various units, shed light on the formal and informal interpersonal contacts of each White House staff member.[43] From the responses, Kessel constructed communications matrices tracing direct contacts between people as well as indirect communication through transceivers. Tables 5-1 and 5-2 illustrate the nature of such matrices during the Carter administration. The analysis covered liaison among personnel from six organizations: members of the National Security Council, major economic policy advisers, the domestic policy staff, heads of miscellaneous executive units, members of the Office of Congressional Liaison, and the presidential press secretary's office.

Row totals in both tables indicate the number of message contacts initiated by each unit, while column totals indicate the number of message

Table 5-1 First-stage Communication Matrix, Reduced Form (Carter White House)

Staff unit sending messages	Staff unit receiving messages						
	National Security Council	Economists	Domestic policy staff	Unit heads	Press secretary's office	Office of Congressional Liaison	Total
National Security Council	**1.00**	0	.18	.20	.25	0	1.63
Economists	.22	**2.60**	1.33	.36	0	1.00	5.51
Domestic policy staff	0	.67	**2.28**	.46	.67	1.60	5.68
Unit heads	.20	0	1.38	**.33**	.40	.22	2.53
Press secretary's office	.25	0	.55	.20	**1.75**	0	2.75
Office of Congressional Liaison	.29	0	.80	.67	0	**1.00**	2.76
Total	1.96	3.27	6.52	2.22	3.07	3.82	20.86

Source: John H. Kessel, "The Structure of the Carter White House," *American Journal of Political Science* 27 (August 1983): 443. Reprinted by permission of the author and the University of Texas Press.

Table 5-2 Second-stage Communication Matrix, Reduced Form (Carter White House)

Staff unit sending messages	Staff unit receiving messages						
	National Security Council	Economists	Domestic policy staff	Unit heads	Press secretary's office	Office of Congressional Liaison	Total
National Security Council	**1.00**	.44	1.45	.60	0	.67	4.16
Economists	1.56	**8.60**	10.50	3.09	.89	7.25	31.89
Domestic policy staff	1.33	3.50	**10.86**	2.92	2.54	7.20	28.35
Unit heads	1.00	1.45	6.62	**6.50**	3.80	5.33	24.70
Press secretary's office	1.00	.89	3.63	1.00	**4.25**	2.00	12.77
Office of Congressional Liaison	.57	0	3.80	2.22	1.71	**5.33**	13.63
Total	6.46	14.88	36.86	16.33	13.19	27.78	115.50

Source: John H. Kessel, "The Structure of the Carter White House," *American Journal of Political Science* 27 (August 1983): 445. Reprinted by permission of the author and the University of Texas Press.

contacts received by the unit. Table 5-1 is a one-stage communication matrix that shows direct liaison among various units. The table is presented in "reduced form" because it does not show communication behavior of individual members but instead represents an average for persons in these units. For example, on average each economist initiated 3.27 contacts and received 5.51 messages. The most striking finding illustrated by the table is that members of four of the six units communicated more internally than externally. Their largest row entries lie on the main diagonal. Unit heads contacted the domestic policy staff more than one another and were contacted most by the legislative liaison staff. That staff sent most messages internally but received most contacts from the domestic policy staff. Most heads of units had stand-ins who could attend meetings for them and could be reached when they were too busy. These alternates were important auxiliary information links, sharing information with their bosses and vice versa.

Table 5-2 represents a two-stage matrix that shows which people are in contact directly as well as indirectly through a third party. Like Table 5-1, the column total in this table shows that Carter's domestic policy staff received the largest number of message contacts by far, followed by the legislative liaison staff. The row total reveals that the economists and the domestic policy staff were the most prolific message senders. Reciprocal message flows were uneven, indicating that traffic is not necessarily balanced even though liaison channels are two-way passages. Table 5-2, for example, shows that the economists had a 10.5 score for sending messages to the domestic policy staff, thus keeping it well informed about economic policy concerns. But the score for the message flow received by the economists from the domestic policy staff was only 3.5.[44] The economists transmitted an average of 7.25 messages to the legislative liaison staff, but reported no contact at all initiated by that staff.

Kessel found that staff members fell into two distinct groups—an inner network that maintained regular liaison with the president, mostly about domestic legislation, and an outer circle that maintained only sporadic contact. Members of the inner network were more likely to be generalists and communicated mostly with members of their own unit. Staff in the outer circle were usually handling specialized assignments and maintained liaison with networks that had the same substantive concerns.[45] Outer-circle staff were relatively isolated from the internal network because they were kept busy communicating with outsiders. In the Carter White House, the National Security Council staff and the press office constituted the outer circle.

A comparison of the Carter and Reagan White House staffs revealed much greater liaison activity in the Reagan administration. There were 55 percent more contacts with other units than had been the case for Carter's staff. The chief reason, as Table 5-3 indicates, was that the Reagan White

Table 5-3 Second-stage Communication Matrix, Reduced Form (Reagan White House)

Staff unit sending messages	Staff unit receiving messages							
	National Security Council	Economists	Office of Policy Development	Staff coordinators	Press secretary's office	Legislative liaison staff	Unit heads	Total
National Security Council	**1.25**	1.33	2.00	4.50	2.00	2.57	1.11	14.76
Economists	0	**6.00**	4.33	10.75	2.86	2.29	2.22	28.45
Office of Policy Development	1.00	8.67	**9.75**	14.00	4.55	3.36	3.69	45.30
Staff coordinators	0	2.00	2.50	**13.50**	3.71	3.14	2.22	27.07
Press secretary's office	0	0.57	1.27	8.57	**3.67**	1.67	1.50	17.25
Legislative liaison staff	0	2.00	3.09	6.29	.67	**1.33**	1.25	14.63
Unit heads	.22	3.78	4.00	14.22	3.50	4.00	**2.40**	32.12
Total	2.47	24.35	26.94	71.83	20.96	18.64	14.39	179.58

Source: John H. Kessel, "The Structure of the Reagan White House," *American Journal of Political Science* 28 (May 1984): 238. Reprinted by permission of the author and the University of Texas Press.

House added four senior staffers to coordinate communication: James Baker, Edwin Meese, Michael Deaver, and Craig Fuller.[46] Message contacts, which had gone directly to the White House in the Carter years, now went to these coordinators. Besides receiving a flood of messages, the coordinators were also in constant contact with each other because they held each other in high regard. However, the coordinators ranked only fourth in sending messages to the other units. The Office of Policy Development ranked first.[47] Placing the coordinators between himself and the various White House units shielded Reagan from much of the kind of information that had reached Carter directly in his less centralized network structure. It made Reagan's coordinators extremely powerful because they monopolized access to the top level of the hierarchy.

In the initial years of the Carter presidency, information from various units flowed directly to the president. When it became clear that Carter lacked the inclination to absorb and structure all the information reaching him into a coordinated policy, Hamilton Jordan moved first informally and later formally into what became a chief-of-staff position. This role enabled him to coordinate the various strands of information reaching the White House and to serve as a liaison among the various units. Nonetheless, compared with the Reagan White House, the system that emerged still allowed greater direct contacts between the president and various staff units. As problems arose, Carter would select different advisers to help him digest the information, choosing them from the units involved in particular situations.[48]

There were other significant differences as well as similarities in the communication patterns of the two presidencies. The Carter White House kept in much more frequent contact with the legislative liaison staff about the content of the president's legislative program. In the Reagan White House, this staff was rarely consulted because there was a separate legislative strategy group that made these decisions. The legislative liaison staff was thus free to devote its time to making contacts with Congress.[49] Overall, in both administrations the domestic staffs were tied most closely to the White House communication network, while the National Security Council staff was most isolated. Nonetheless, the National Security Council staff was highly influential in White House decision making, indicating that a central position in the communication network, while helpful, is neither a prerequisite for nor a guarantee of influence. Kessel concluded that influence within the White House hinged on a combination of factors including position within the hierarchy, seniority, and personal attributes.

The magnitude of the liaison function at the presidential level emerges from data collected about Lyndon Johnson's administration, for which exceptionally complete records of presidential communications are available. The picture is similar, though on a smaller scale, for other top

Figure 5-5   **Interactions of President Lyndon Johnson with His Staff (by month)**

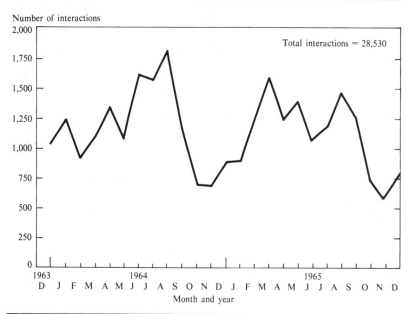

Number of interactions

Total interactions = 28,530

Month and year

Source: Adapted from James J. Best, "Who Talked to the President When? A Study of Lyndon B. Johnson," *Political Science Quarterly* 103 (Fall 1988): 536-537. Reprinted with permission.

executives. During the first twenty-five months of his administration, Johnson was directly involved in more than 28,530 interactions with over 2,000 different people. Figure 5-5 provides monthly scores.[50] The 158 people whose face-to-face and telephone interactions with the president are recorded in Table 5-4 were fairly regular contacts, speaking with him at least five times during a given month. The president kept in closest touch by far with the twenty-nine members of the White House staff, composed of Kennedy holdovers and Johnson appointees. However, 73 percent of his staff interactions were with his own rather than Kennedy's appointees, many of them close personal friends, notably Bill Moyers, Jack Valenti, George Reedy, and Walter Jenkins. Obviously, influence of individual network members shifted when the new chief executive entered the picture. This is partly explained by the president's personal likes and dislikes and partly by his own competencies and the need to deal with particular events. Overall, 75 percent of Johnson's contacts were with people characterized as political elites rather than ordinary citizens. As time progressed and the president became disenchanted with many of his advisers, this circle narrowed sharply.

Johnson maintained liaison with the most important departments and executive agencies through a fifteen-member cabinet. Over three-fourths of

Table 5-4   Total Number of "Elite" Interactions, by Group, During Johnson Administration

Group	Number of staffers	Number of interactions	% of all interactions	% of elite interactions
Congress	22	1,832	6.4	8.6
White House staff	29	11,319	39.7	53.2
Kennedy appointments	15	2,985		
Johnson appointments	14	8,334		
Executive Office of the President	17	1,269	4.4	6.0
Executive branch	18	1,120	3.9	5.3
Cabinet	15	2,532	9.9	11.9
Inner cabinet	6	1,949		
Other	57	3,205	11.2	15.1
Total elite	158	21,277	74.6	100.1
Total interactions		28,530		

Source: James J. Best, "Who Talked to the President When? A Study of Lyndon B. Johnson," *Political Science Quarterly* 103 (Fall 1988): 536-537. Reprinted with permission.

the cabinet interactions involved a powerful inner cabinet that included the secretaries of state, treasury, and defense and the attorney general.[51] Within this group, 76 percent of the interactions were with Secretary of State Dean Rusk and Secretary of Defense Robert McNamara. Johnson drew heavily on their advice and that of National Security Adviser McGeorge Bundy because the president felt comparatively unfamiliar with foreign policy issues. Contacts with his economic policy advisers were far less frequent. Compared with contacts with foreign policy advisers, the ratio was 6.5 to 1. Attorney General Robert Kennedy, a powerful figure in the Kennedy cabinet, was among the least consulted figures in the Johnson administration. Consultations with Vice President Hubert Humphrey dropped sharply after Humphrey declared his opposition to further escalation of the Vietnam War.[52]

Direct contacts with Congress were comparatively sparse but included the leadership of both houses, important committee chairmen, and Johnson's longtime Senate friends. The few individuals from the executive office of the president and the sub-cabinet executive branch who were in frequent touch with the president included the heads of the CIA and FBI, the Bureau of the Budget, and the chairman of the Council of Economic Advisers. The "other" list included the Johnson family and a half dozen longtime personal friends, notably Supreme Court Justice Abe Fortas and Texas Governor John Connally.[53]

Boundary Spanners

The Incidence of Boundary Spanning.   Boundary spanning occurs when duties of various individuals cut across organizational barriers. For example, in Table 5-4 Johnson's contacts with Congress and with personal friends who were not part of the executive branch were boundary spanning rather than liaisons because they reached into the environment surrounding the executive branch. The primary reason for boundary spanning, writes Mark Kessler, seems to be "exchange for mutual benefit when there is basic agreement on policy." [54] Boundary spanning also occurs when power-dependence relationships exist, with the stronger unit controlling material and symbolic resources desired by the weaker unit. Finally, the personal beliefs of agency members are an important motivating force for boundary spanning.

Designating contacts as boundary spanning raises tricky issues about defining the level of analysis. If the entire government is considered one unit, then contacts between the executive and Congress, for example, are internal liaisons rather than external boundary spanning. Alternatively, one could consider the cabinet or the White House staff or the executive office of the president as the unit of analysis and relations among them as boundary spanning. Choices of analysis levels are quite arbitrary. [55]

Boundary spanning through external communication is a daily event in the life of bureaucrats. The federal government alone spends $6 billion a year to disseminate information. That figure does not include the costs of collecting information, nor does it include comparable expenditures at state and local levels. [56] Bureaucrats must communicate with numerous external units and individuals such as sister agencies, clients, and legislatures. As political scientist Herbert Kaufman noted, after studying federal bureaucracies, "Programs intersect at innumerable points, and staff functions cut across each other and all line operations in comparable profusion. Hardly anything can be done anywhere that does not quickly involve other agencies, committees, and interest groups in sister triadic clusters...." Government business is "much more interdepartmental than departmental," giving rise to innumerable interagency committees that nobody really wants. [57]

Many decisions on education, for example, involve activities in nine separate departments and twenty independent agencies. [58] Cross-cutting issues include child health concerns, job training activities, and the use of animals and humans in scientific experiments. Similarly, a study of enforcement of OSHA regulations in fifty states over a seven-year period documented that most tasks required cooperation across agency boundaries. The quality of incoming and outgoing external communications therefore constituted a major factor in the agency's performance. [59] Just how effectively boundary-spanning networks operate varies depending on how well various organizations understand each other's problems and communication practices. For instance, the U.S. Department of State, which has contacts of varying credibility throughout the world, cannot be expected to control its external networks as well as the U.S. Postal Service, which operates primarily inside the United States.

Boundary-Spanning Problems.   Much remains to be done to work out problems of interagency communication in situations that cut across federal and state agencies and also involve the private sector. An example is the situation at Love Canal, a toxic waste site in New York State that began to leak noxious vapors twenty years after the last dumping ceased. In the most active stages of investigating the problem, nineteen independent agencies were involved. At the state level they included the departments of Health, Environmental Conservation, Transportation, Housing, Social Services, Banking, Insurance, the Office of Disaster Preparedness, and the Division of Equalization and Assessment. Joining these nine were the federal Environmental Protection Agency, the Niagara County Health Department, the local civil defense unit, the police and fire departments, the city of Niagara Falls, and the Niagara Falls school board. There also were three private sector agencies: the Red Cross, the United Way, and the Love Canal Homeowners' Association. John Worthley and Richard Torkelson comment, "No wonder that, although by 1976 government authorities were aware of the toxic infiltration at Love Canal, the problem was tossed among agencies like a hot potato. No one agency was in charge, no agency had responsibility for coordination." [60]

Nobody had kept track of waste disposal sites; nobody had studied medical reports about miscarriages and birth defects that could have triggered an earlier investigation. "The lack of a working information system was a key ingredient of the Love Canal catastrophe," state Worthley and Torkelson.[61] "The toxic waste problem defies existing organizational structures. The problem has health, environmental, commercial, social and political aspects beyond the operational capacities of any single government agency. Organizational research is needed to generate holistic organizational designs for administratively dealing with the problem." [62] The problem of public sector/private sector collaboration is particularly acute. "Without private sector industrial cooperation and financial involvement, environmental protection from chemical pollution is elusive if not altogether impossible." [63]

Gaps in boundary-spanning networks are sometimes filled informally and almost spontaneously by networks that develop in response to a particular problem. This often occurs in police departments and various disaster services when a disaster cuts across geographic jurisdictions or functional lines or becomes too large to be handled locally. At other times, failure to develop networks may cripple the performance of agencies that are thrust into unplanned working relationships.

The 1982 Air Florida jet crash into the Potomac River in Washington, D.C., exemplifies a disaster where rescue efforts by agencies from various localities were hampered because interagency networks did not arise informally.[64] Although the crash had demonstrated the need for interagency coordination in disasters, it took many months before effective communication channels were instituted because of disagreements about power sharing. This is not surprising because network analyses of such informally created networks remain rare. It is therefore unclear what roles various participants in interagency networks ought to play.[65]

Differences in the goals of various agencies sometimes prevent communication. Relations between the Agricultural Marketing Service (AMS) and the Food and Drug Administration (FDA) provide an example.[66] According to a 1973 report by the General Accounting Office (GAO), the AMS, which grades fruits and vegetables, did not wish to alert the FDA to food adulteration discovered during the grading process. At the time the FDA lacked the resources to monitor fruit and vegetable processing on its own. AMS inspectors, on the other hand, who monitored food processing as part of the grading process, had the needed information readily available.

The main reason for the interagency communication problems was the difference in goals. The FDA's objective was to prevent the distribution of adulterated foods, while the AMS's chief objective was the improvement of marketing and distribution of agricultural products. AMS feared that fruit and vegetable processors, who pay for its grading services, would be unhappy if the information collected for grading were used to disqualify their products from the market. They might cancel grading services, thereby reducing job opportunities for AMS personnel. Similar sweetheart relationships may prevail even when inspection is paid for by the government, as it is for poultry plants. The temptation to bribe inspectors is great when they can close plants immediately upon finding violations.[67] AMS graders, who know that their jobs depend on good relations with their clients, are inclined to protect this relationship. The intrinsic conflict of interests seems unbridgeable, yet the need to economize on government personnel makes it inadvisable to provide the FDA with its own inspectors.

The array of interconnections among government agencies is, indeed, confusing. At the federal level alone, more than 850 interagency committees have been created in an attempt to coordinate matters affecting more than one agency. In some parts of government, the creation and use of boundary-spanning offices—usually called liaison offices—have become routine. Their primary function is intelligence gathering and dissemination. For example, the National Security Council gathers information from the State and Defense departments, multinational corporations, and foreign governments and transmits it to various agencies concerned with foreign policy so that they can operate from a common information base when dealing with shared problems.

In a government that depends heavily on public support and prizes the principle of public accountability, boundary-spanning ties with various publics are deemed particularly important and deserving of special attention. As a result, the executive branch, for example, has set up numerous agencies for this purpose. Examples are the Office of Public Liaison, established during the Ford administration, which provides linkage to interest groups, and the Office of Intergovernmental Relations, which provides ties to governors and mayors and liaison with minority groups such as Hispanic and African Americans. The importance placed on contacts with some of these groups is demonstrated by the fact that Carter's Office of Hispanic Affairs employed six liaisons, compared with only two working on contacts with the Senate.[68]

Establishment of boundary-spanning offices can serve symbolic as well as instrumental purposes, signifying the chief executive's interest in the concerns of particular groups. The persons appointed to fill the outreach positions become symbols of that serious concern. On the instrumental side, a good boundary spanner may be able to explain an agency's goals so that the demands generated by various networks can be moderated and fitted more readily into overall programs. When administrators must resolve competing claims among powerful interest groups, when they must mollify irate minorities, when they must have wide public support for burdensome policies, good boundary-spanning message contacts are crucial.[69]

Overall, formal links remain inadequate to coordinate the manifold overlapping functions of federal agencies. Despite the growth of interagency committees, most boundary-spanning networking is done by individual agencies in a decentralized fashion. Likewise, most federal agencies communicate with their counterparts at state and local levels. Nonetheless, it has proved virtually impossible to achieve adequate coordination of information disseminated at these various levels.

Boundary-Spanning Patterns.   Agencies differ in terms of the complexity of their external communication networks and the volume and types of messages carried.[70] A federal agency dealing with various types of welfare payments operates in a macroenvironmental context that includes interest groups and clients and politico-economic forces. It has considerable leeway in determining procedures for carrying out its mandate. By contrast, state or county welfare departments enjoy little discretion because their policies and programs are closely tied to state and federal regulations. Their information exchange with external units is therefore far more limited. Information systems have to be designed to reflect such differences.

Figures 5-6 and 5-7 diagram the kinds of interorganizational networks that are usually depicted as boundary spanning between the executive branch, administrative agencies, and client publics. Such networks can be simple or complex, formal or informal. The simple power channel in Figure

Figure 5-6   Models of Interorganization Channels

Simple power channel

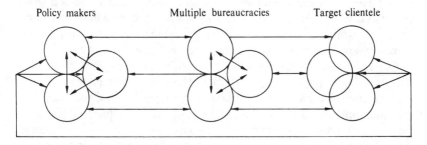

Complex power channel

Policy makers   Multiple bureaucracies   Target clientele

Source: Steven Thomas Seitz, *Bureaucracy, Policy, and the Public* (St. Louis: C. V. Mosby, 1978), 91.
Reprinted with permission.

Figure 5-7   Models of Interagency Channels

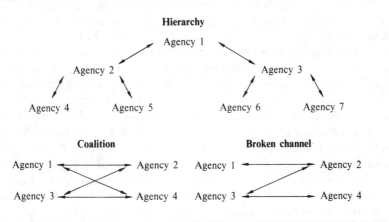

Source: Steven Thomas Seitz, *Bureaucracy, Policy, and the Public* (St. Louis: C. V. Mosby, 1978), 93.
Reprinted with permission.

5-6 traces three interrelated network clusters representing policy makers, bureaucracies, and target clienteles respectively. They show communication flows between policy makers and bureaucracies and between bureaucracies and target clienteles. This model is a simplified version, while the complex power channel comes closer to depicting the complexities encountered in real life. This figure also shows internal communication connections and multiple external connections. Figure 5-7 diagrams typical boundary spanning among seven agencies when analysis is done at the agency level. Typically, the pattern of communication flows is hierarchical so that agencies 4 and 5 communicate with agency 2, and agencies 6 and 7 communicate with agency 3. In turn, agencies 2 and 3 communicate with agency 1, which appears to be at the top of the hierarchy. In practice, however, flows are rarely as systematic as the figure suggests.

Compared with internal communication, where information transmission follows the paths indicated by the formal structure of the hierarchy, there is less evidence of a hierarchical structure in external communication. It is instead propelled more by the requirements of the situation. Channels develop and grow more informally because there are fewer structured flows. This also means that there is less centralization of the flows because centralization is closely related to hierarchical structure. Since the requirements of a particular situation are the primary criteria for determining whether or not communication takes place, external flows are more likely than internal flows to involve specialized information. They are also apt to be less plentiful than internal flows because agencies compete for resources and clienteles and therefore may be less willing to share their information.

Figure 5-7 also shows nonhierarchical relationships that may develop among agencies. When their interests coincide, they may form coalitions. Assuming that four agencies are a part of a coalition, the ties among them can be more or less direct, as pictured in the coalition and broken channel versions respectively. The coalition features two direct linkages for each unit; the broken channel has just one. In broken channel some members of this agency network are linked very indirectly. For instance, agency 1 must use agencies 2 and 3 as intermediaries to reach agency 4 and vice versa.

Boundary-spanning roles exist at both ends of the hierarchy. At the bottom levels boundary spanners cross organizational boundaries to deal with the general public or with individual clients served by public agencies or with outsiders who perform services for the agency. Examples are clerks who deal directly with the public, research analysts who study external organizations, or public relations personnel entrusted by agency heads with disseminating information to various segments of the public. This includes information on agency services offered, actions required or prohibited, and ways to claim benefits. Agencies usually publish pamphlets and leaflets describing these matters in nontechnical terms. Field staffs may give talks in communities. Sometimes there are television or radio messages.

Boundary spanners at the higher bureaucratic levels are apt to be concerned with broad policies that link their agency's activities to those of other agencies and to the larger system. They tend to accumulate information about the "big" picture, such as the general political and economic climate and the implications of major sociopolitical and economic trends on their agency. External institutions prefer to deal with top-level officials about major policy issues, rather than with lower-level communication experts, because the official's position lends authority to the message. Moreover, top-level officials are likely to perform exceptionally well in such matters because they can draw on expert staffs to monitor external relations, prepare messages, and give them advice. However, it is a common complaint that top administrators all too often function as official spokespersons for their agency without consulting their communication staffs. They are much more likely to confer with these staffs about damage control after miscommunication has occurred.

Boundary-spanning roles are most often played by people holding staff rather than line positions in the agency. Line personnel, whose expertise lies in administering the agency's programs, often lack the skills to communicate across organizational boundaries.[71] Personnel involved in important boundary-spanning activities, such as those with the press and Congress, often receive special training. They are also included routinely in policy planning sessions. For example, legislative relations experts are often members of task forces that plan legislative programs before the chief executive pushes them in the legislature. They may also sit in on cabinet meetings, daily senior staff meetings, and similar gatherings where information is exchanged and decisions are made that may be important for relations with the legislature.

Many boundary spanners are professional analysts who travel and read widely and belong to professional organizations that keep them in touch with advances in their field of expertise. When the professional values of boundary spanners clash with organizational goals, usually because of political concerns, agencies may face major problems. Having ties outside the organization often permits boundary spanners to move readily from job to job. While such moves are advantageous for the individual, they pose stability problems for the agency.

Boundary spanners usually operate as two-way relays. This is why William Cable, who was in charge of congressional relations in the Carter White House, put a large sign on his office wall that read "Pennsylvania Avenue, two way street." [72] The reminder indicated that boundary spanners must spend as much time enlightening their chiefs about outside organizations as the reverse. Executives may also schedule some direct meetings with outside organizations to avoid transacting everything through their appointed staffs. At critical times, executives routinely bypass liaison staffs and concentrate their personal efforts on communicating with key individuals with whom satisfactory contacts are essential. If these efforts are poorly coordinated with the work done by regular boundary-spanning staffs, trouble may ensue.

In fact, coordination of boundary-spanning activities is a major problem in the White House and elsewhere. For example, in addition to legislative liaison staffs in the White House, executive departments also have their separate legislative liaison staffs. The Defense Department, for instance, has had over 200 people on its legislative liaison staff.[73] Overall, estimates made during the Carter years put the number of persons involved in congressional boundary spanning as high as 1,500. The White House staff attempted to coordinate departmental boundary-spanning activities with mixed success.

Since boundary spanning produces better-integrated information environments and often encourages the spread of innovative ideas, Congress has tried to foster it through passage of the 1970 Intergovernmental Personnel Act.[74] This act, which permits federal and state agencies to exchange personnel for up to a year, has not been widely used.[75]

The Boundary-Spanning Role of the Press.   When contacts are neither mandated nor established by custom, formal or informal boundary-spanning arrangements may fail to develop. In that case, the press may partially fill the void. American court systems have been particularly deficient in interagency communications. As George Edwards observes, "In most instances, judges of higher level courts have no institutionalized means of communicating with lower courts. The U.S. Supreme Court sends its decisions only to the lower court from which the case originated." [76] Whether other judges learn about these decisions depends on their own efforts and professional contacts and the diligence of the press in transmitting these decisions. Unfortunately, coverage of court decisions, even at the Supreme Court level, is spotty and often inaccurate.[77]

Insufficient boundary spanning also plagues other governmental units. For example, local government agencies such as police departments and school boards are often totally ignorant of decisions that undoubtedly affect their operations. There simply are no regular, reliable network structures to transmit these decisions. Edwards reports that "only a few police departments have legal advisers or officers assigned to transmitting information from the courts to the police. For these reasons, police administrators have had to rely primarily upon newspapers for information on judicial decisions, when they involve officers in their own departments." [78]

To increase the opportunities for effective as well as favorable boundary spanning by the media, most government agencies now assign specially trained personnel to handle media contacts. Expert press secretaries are employed by presidents, governors, mayors, as well as major departments and agencies. To collect the necessary information for use by the media, press secretaries must be able to tap into large numbers of governmental networks. During the Carter administration, for example, press secretary Jody Powell kept in close touch with the president and with important White House staffers. He often attended meetings of the Joint Chiefs of Staff so he could ask questions and be better prepared to answer press queries.[79]

Reagan's communications director David Gergen participated in senior staff meetings. He learned a great deal about pending domestic and foreign developments through regular contacts with the Legislative Strategy Group, the Office of Policy Development, the National Security Council, the State and Defense departments, and the U.S. Information Agency. Gergen aide Michael Baroody headed a separate research staff that coordinated administration news by staying in touch with departmental public affairs directors. Press office personnel also monitor the media to be fully aware of what governmental news is covered and how it is being appraised. Press relations are discussed more fully in Chapter 7.

The dependence of many governmental units, as well as the general public, on the media's monitoring and publicizing of governmental actions makes the media important boundary spanners. Unfortunately, they do not do the job very well. Mass media channels do not cover governmental events systematically. Instead, they select stories based on their newsworthiness. Exciting and appealing stories get published while duller ones do not. For instance, it is quite likely that news stories would fail to inform gasoline station operators that a new federal regulation requires them to post gasoline prices, although this is important information needed by stations and their customers. Similarly, realtors would probably be kept in the dark about open-housing laws; merchants would not be alerted to complex consumer credit laws. When the mass media cover such information, the stories are rarely comprehensive and adequately detailed. They often contain substantial errors. What George Edwards criticized about coverage of court decisions holds true for most public policy areas: "Network television and most newspapers and magazines give very limited coverage ... [and where coverage is given] it is usually distorted, oversimplified, or exaggerated." [80]

Summary and Conclusions

The English poet John Donne reminded us many centuries ago that "No man is an Iland, intire of itselfe; every man is a peece of the Continent, a part of the maine." This chapter explores the many ways in which members of organizations and their collectivities are linked into a web of important interconnections. The chapter begins with a general discussion of the origin and nature of networks and the organizational needs that they fill. A multitude of shared concerns may lead to their formation, among them friendship networks and networks clustered around specific policy issues.

The discussion then focuses on the nature of individual network roles and their configurations in general, followed by a closer examination of important individual roles, including gatekeepers, bridges, liaisons, and boundary spanners. These role players were described in terms of the functions they perform, the influence they are likely to wield, and the problems they most often face.

Boundary-spanning activities are often the Achilles' heels of network information flows, as several disasters described in the chapter illustrate graphically. Because boundary spanning is extremely important in a complex modern society, the chapter highlights the kinds of arrangements that can lead to success. The many formal and informal channels that link organizations include the mass media, whose boundary-spanning activities are discussed briefly.

Network analysis may seem like a new approach to studying organizational communication, especially since many technical details remain to be worked out. But, in fact, it is a case of pouring old wine into new bottles. Laymen and experts alike have long recognized the importance of networks and networking, calling it by many different names, such as "making contacts," "sharing office gossip," "being an insider," "entering the charmed inner circle," and "reaching out." Wherever human beings congregate and need to cooperate, they must create channels to convey the messages that lead to coordinated behavior. Powerful individuals or groups have always influenced how the channels will be laid out and interconnected, thereby determining who will be bypassed and who will be on the main line.

The study of networking highlights the substantial powers held by the millions of gatekeepers who open or bar the entry of information into organizational communication channels. Gatekeeping is an extremely sensitive role because wrong decisions—whether excessive lenience or undue strictness—can lead to major malfunctions. Yet, of necessity, most gatekeeping roles are played out at low levels in the organizational hierarchy by people who lack complete information about current organizational policies and developments, which is essential for effective gatekeeping. No remedies are currently in sight for this major, potentially disastrous organizational weakness.

Major communication challenges are also presented by boundary spanning among networks that need to keep in touch regularly or when emergencies arise. Effective linkage among disparate networks must be made so that messages flow smoothly despite differences in organizational cultures. Communication overloads must also be overcome. When internal networks absorb a great deal of energy and resources, how far can organizations afford to reach into their environments? To what extent can scarce resources be diverted from less expensive internal networking to more costly external communications? The right answers are tough to find. Administrators and scholars alike must search for viable solutions.

Notes

1. For various other definitions of networks, see Rolf T. Wigand, "Communication Network Analysis: History and Overview," in *Handbook of Organizational Communication,* Gerald M. Goldhaber and George A. Barnett, eds. (Norwood, N.J.: Ablex, 1988), 321; Everett M. Rogers and Rekha Agarwala Rogers, *Communication in Organizations* (New York: Free Press, 1976), 109; and Robert D. McPhee and Phillip K. Tompkins, eds., *Organizational Communication: Traditional Themes and New Directions* (Beverly Hills, Calif.: Sage, 1985), 60 and sources cited there.

2. To reflect social realities, surveys should at the very least contain sociometric questions. Even when individuals are the unit of response, they need not be the unit of analysis.

3. Ithiel de Sola Pool and Wilbur Schramm et al., eds., *Handbook of Communications* (Chicago: Rand-McNally, 1973), 3. For the argument that networks are the key to understanding individual political preferences, see Robert Huckfeldt and John Sprague, "Networks in Context: The Social Flow of Political Information," *American Political Science Review* 81 (1987): 1197-1216.

4. R. Wayne Pace, *Organizational Communication: Foundations for Human Resource Development* (Englewood Cliffs, N.J.: Prentice-Hall, 1983), 136-137.

5. William Eddy, *Public Organization Behavior* (Cambridge, Mass.: Winthrop, 1982), 179.

6. Ibid., 175-176.

7. Ibid., 176.

8. Serge Taylor, *Making Bureaucracies Think: The Environmental Statement Strategy of Administrative Reform* (Stanford, Calif.: Stanford University Press, 1984).

9. Rogers and Rogers, *Communication in Organizations,* 110-111.

10. James E. Anderson, "A Revised View of the Johnson Cabinet," *Journal of Politics* 48 (February 1986): 534.

11. Lucien S. Vandenbrouke, "Anatomy of a Failure: The Decision to Land at the Bay of Pigs," *Political Science Quarterly* 99 (Fall 1984): 482.

12. Hugh Heclo, "Issue Networks and the Executive Establishment," in *The New American Political System,* Anthony King, ed. (Washington, D.C.: American Enterprise Institute, 1978), 103.

13. Paul A. Sabatier and Neil Pelkey, "Incorporating Multiple Actors and Guidance Instruments into Models of Regulatory Policymaking," *Administration and Society* 19 (August 1987): 236-263.

14. Heclo, "Issue Networks and the Executive Establishment," 104; for other examples, see Sabatier and Pelkey, "Incorporating Multiple Actors and Guidance Instruments into Models of Regulatory Policymaking," 248.

15. Heclo, "Issue Networks and the Executive Establishment," 117.

16. Ibid., 105-106.

17. Ibid., 116.

18. Ibid., 117.

19. John H. Kessel, "The Structure of the Carter White House," *American*

Journal of Political Science 27 (August 1983): 431-463; John H. Kessel, "The Structure of the Reagan White House," *American Journal of Political Science* 28 (May 1984): 231-258.

20. Phil Gailey, "Deaver Stirs a Hornet's Nest," *New York Times,* April 5, 1986.
21. Heinz Eulau, "The Redwood Network Project: Small-Scale Research at the Local Level," *ICPSR Bulletin* (January 1984): 4, Appendix A. Also see Robert Huckfeldt and John Sprague, "Networks in Context: The Social Flow of Political Information," *American Political Science Review* 81 (1987): 1197-1216.
22. Charles Perrow, *Complex Organizations: A Critical Essay,* 2d ed. (Glenview, Ill.: Scott, Foresman, 1979), 222.
23. Karen S. Cook, Richard M. Emerson, Mary R. Gillmore, and Toshio Yamagishi, "The Distribution of Power in Exchange Networks: Theory and Experimental Results," *American Journal of Sociology* 89 (1983): 276-279.
24. Perrow, *Complex Organizations,* 224-225.
25. Rogers and Rogers, *Communication in Organizations,* 144.
26. Ibid., 120.
27. Daniel Katz and Robert L. Kahn, *The Social Psychology of Organizations* (New York: Wiley, 1978), 436.
28. Rogers and Rogers, *Communication in Organizations,* 122-123.
29. Ralph Katz, "The Effects of Group Longevity on Project Communication and Performance," *Administrative Science Quarterly* 27 (1982): 81-104.
30. Toshio Yamagishi, Mary R. Gillmore, and Karen S. Cook, "Network Connections and the Distribution of Power in Exchange Networks," *American Journal of Sociology* 93 (1988): 833-851; Phillip Bonacich, "Power and Centrality: A Family of Measures," *American Journal of Sociology* 92 (1987): 1170-1182; Karen S. Cook, Richard M. Emerson, Mary R. Gillmore, and Toshio Yamagishi, "The Distribution of Power in Exchange Networks," 275-305.
31. Terence R. Mitchell and James R. Larson, Jr., *People in Organizations: An Introduction to Organizational Behavior,* 3d ed. (New York: McGraw-Hill, 1987), 306, and sources cited there.
32. Judith R. Blau, "Prominence in a Network of Communication: Work Relations in a Children's Psychiatric Hospital," *Sociological Quarterly* 23 (1982): 236.
33. Rogers and Rogers, *Communication in Organizations,* 132-140. This presents a good discussion of individual network roles.
34. Steven Kelman, *Making Public Policy* (New York: Basic Books, 1987), 48.
35. Michael Murray, *Decisions: A Comparative Critique* (Marshfield, Mass.: Pitman, 1986), 134-151; Harold F. Gortner, Julianne Mahler, and Jeanne Bell Nicholson, *Organizational Theory: A Public Perspective* (Chicago: Dorsey, 1987), 187.
36. Terry M. Moe, "Control and Feedback in Economic Regulation: The Case of the NLRB," *American Journal of Political Science* 79 (December 1985): 1094-1116.
37. Rogers and Rogers, *Communication in Organizations,* 136, and sources cited there.
38. Ibid., 137.
39. Katz and Kahn, *The Social Psychology of Organizations,* 450.
40. Pace, *Organizational Communication: Foundations for Human Resource Development,* 24, and sources cited there.
41. Gortner et al., *Organizational Theory: A Public Perspective,* 175.
42. John H. Kessel, *Presidential Parties* (Homewood, Ill.: Dorsey, 1984), 90.
43. Ibid., 90-108. Some sample answers are provided there.

44. Kessel, "The Structure of the Carter White House," 445.
45. Kessel, *Presidential Parties,* 93.
46. Richard Darman and William Clark were also members of the group at times.
47. Kessel, "The Structure of the Reagan White House," 238.
48. Kessel, "The Structure of the Carter White House," 460-461.
49. Kessel, *Presidential Parties,* 97.
50. James J. Best, "Who Talked to the President When? A Study of Lyndon B. Johnson," *Political Science Quarterly* 103 (Fall 1988): 531-545.
51. Ibid., 538.
52. Ibid., 542.
53. Ibid., 538.
54. Mark Kessler, "Interorganizational Environments, Attitudes, and the Policy Outputs of Public Agencies: A Comparative Case Study of Legal Services Agencies," *Administration and Society* 19 (1987): 63-65. For a model of interorganizational networks, see Rolf T. Wigand, "A Model of Interorganizational Communication among Complex Organizations," *Communication and Control in Society,* Klaus Krippendorff, ed. (New York: Gordon and Breach, 1982).
55. Relevant theories that attempt to explain why organizations engage in boundary spanning and how they interact have dealt primarily with the private sector. For an attempt to expand them to public sector organizations, see Mark Kessler, "Interorganizational Environments, Attitudes, and the Policy Outputs of Public Agencies," 48-73.
56. Office of Technology Assessment, *Informing the Nation: Federal Information Dissemination in an Electronic Age* (Washington, D.C.: Government Printing Office, 1988), 27.
57. Herbert Kaufman, *The Administrative Behavior of Federal Bureau Chiefs* (Washington, D.C.: Brookings Institution, 1981), 190.
58. Gortner et al., *Organizational Theory: A Public Perspective,* 47.
59. John T. Scholz and Feng Heng Wei, "Regulatory Enforcement in a Federalist System," *American Political Science Review* 80 (December 1986): 1264.
60. John A. Worthley and Richard Torkelson, "Managing the Toxic Waste Problem: Lessons from the Love Canal," *Administration and Society* 13 (1981): 152.
61. Ibid., 155.
62. Ibid., 157.
63. Ibid., 158.
64. Gortner et al., *Organizational Theory: A Public Perspective,* 169.
65. Ibid., 170. Also see David M. Boje and David A. Whetter, "Effects of Organizational Strategies and Contextual Constraints on Centrality and Attributions of Influence in Interorganizational Networks," *Administrative Science Quarterly* 26 (1981): 378-395.
66. William S. Pierce, *Bureaucratic Failure and Public Expenditure* (New York: Academic, 1981), 161-171.
67. Ibid., 169.
68. Kessel, *Presidential Parties,* 97.
69. Joseph A. Pika, "Interest Groups and the White House under Roosevelt and Truman," *Political Science Quarterly* 102 (Winter 1987-1988): 647-648.
70. John M. Stevens and Robert P. McGowan, *Information Systems and Public Management* (New York: Praeger, 1985), 28.
71. Katz, "The Effects of Group Longevity on Project Communication and Performance," 82.

72. Kessel, *Presidential Parties,* 137.
73. Ibid., 138.
74. Public Law 91-648, January 5, 1971.
75. William T. Gormley, Jr., "Intergovernmental Conflict on Environmental Policy: The Attitudinal Connection," *Western Political Quarterly* 40 (June 1987): 301.
76. George C. Edwards III, *Implementing Public Policy* (Washington, D.C.: CQ Press, 1980), 22.
77. Doris A. Graber, *Mass Media and American Politics,* 3d ed. (Washington, D.C.: CQ Press, 1989), 266-268, and sources cited there.
78. Edwards, *Implementing Public Policy,* 23; also see Stephen L. Wasby, *Small Town Police and the Supreme Court: Hearing the Word* (Lexington, Mass.: Lexington Books, 1976), 35-50.
79. Kessel, *Presidential Parties,* 145.
80. Edwards, *Implementing Public Policy,* 25.

Communication Climates and Cultures

Information management entails more than coping with problems of gathering information and channeling it in ways that best accomplish the purposes of the organization. It also involves creating and maintaining an appropriate organizational climate through explicit and implicit messages that are conveyed in many ways. These include connotational meanings embedded in verbal messages as well as messages conveyed through the behaviors of organization members, through the political culture in which the organization operates, or through various combinations of these methods.

We shall begin by discussing how messages generate the internal and external climates in which organizations operate. Because of their size and rigidity, public sector agencies find it especially difficult to engage in practices designed to create productive organizational climates. We shall then turn to an analysis of the larger organizational culture in which agencies operate. This cultural context is expressed through formal and informal rules that dictate the behavior of organization members. We shall focus on two important aspects of bureaucratic culture in the public sector. They are the use of bureaucratic symbols to convey an aura of importance to bureaucratic activities and the major intended and unintended cultural changes produced by evolving communication technologies, particularly computers.

Organizational Climates

Climate Factors

Psychological Aspects.   Organizational climate is a psychological construct. It is assessed by human minds but, since it leaves few physical traces, it eludes measurement through physical gauges. Climate has been defined as a message transmitted through a combination of interacting stimuli about the state of a system's internal nature as perceived by the members of that system.[1] More simply, it can be called the psychological atmosphere that is perceived by members of an organization. Climate refers to the properties of an entire system whose boundaries may extend to the whole organization or may be limited to an organizational subunit, or even a specific organizational activity. A variety of different climates may prevail in an organization at different times, depending on the nature and pace of its activities and on personnel factors. For example, calm may prevail at an Internal Revenue branch office following a hectic, high-pressure climate during the spring when most tax returns are filed. Some supervisors may be able to maintain islands of calm in a subunit, surrounded by a sea of turmoil, while others heighten the sense of pressure. When climates are friendly and supportive or hostile and tense, trusting or mistrusting, these qualities are diffused throughout particular units largely through verbal and nonverbal communication. The end product involves shared perceptions, not just one individual's reactions to the unit or its activities.

Questionnaires directed to members of an organization are the usual way to ascertain that these perceptions are shared. Because they focus on the *experienced* rather than the actual environment, perceptual measures are subjective, for which they have been criticized. Yet since climate is a subjective construct, it seems appropriate to measure it subjectively, even though this may reveal that the same organizational climate will elicit different appraisals. It can be measured as the aggregate of individuals' perceptions of the climate, or as their overall evaluations of climate conditions. Alternatively, employees may be asked to judge how others in the organization are experiencing the climate. An organization may receive high ratings on all aspects of climate but still receive poor overall evaluations when employees rate it in terms of their expectations or compare it with other organizations. This suggests that the determination of the character of a particular climate may be distinct from its overall evaluation.

Perceived climate may differ from objective assessments. For example, employees may feel deprived, viewing themselves as underpaid when measured against comparable workers or when they consider their non-monetary benefits as substandard. In fact, their pay and benefits may be above established norms, but their attitude toward the organization will reflect their perceptions rather than actual conditions. Idiosyncratic cues are commonly used by members to develop their own interpretations of the nature of organizational reality. Some may gauge their superior's interest in their views by the time it takes to receive a response and its degree of formality. Others may judge interest by the number of employee suggestions that have been implemented. Still others may use promotions and budget allocations to judge the organization's goals and preferences. The criteria chosen by organization members to assess the organizational climate determine, as Jeffrey Pfeffer observes, "how the outcomes of organizational politics are perceived and what various actors feel about the justice, as well as the legitimacy of the decision results." [2]

Since many factors contribute to the overall climate in an organization it can be assessed in general or broken down into distinct components. For example, one can make separate assessments of the communication and motivational climates or the climate for innovation. However, in making separate assessments, one must keep in mind that the various aspects usually interact. For example, the climate for innovation is affected by whether there is a good communication climate.

Six aspects of organizational life appear to be crucial when members assess the climates in which they work.[3] They are the importance placed on human relations, the incentive structure through which the organization motivates performance, the degree of influence accorded to lower-level employees by upper levels of the hierarchy, the adequacy of information flows within the organization, the comprehensiveness of decision-making procedures, and the availability of resources to accomplish the agency's mission.

The degree of individual recognition and autonomy and the sense of importance conveyed by an agency must be satisfying to employees. Superiors must be supportive and warm when employees perform well, and co-workers must inspire trust and liking. Employees must be imbued with the management's philosophy so that they feel in tune with the goals of the organization. Reinforcement for appropriate behavior must be communicated, just as inappropriate behavior must be discouraged.

Communication systems are appraised favorably if they are ample, comprehensive and comprehensible, and flow through channels that are perceived as efficient and attractive. In many organizations, oral communication followed by written seems to work best. The method chosen hinges on availability and cost factors as well as the skills of the communicants. It is important for employees to believe that they are well informed and that they can communicate adequately with superiors and fellow workers.[4] The organizational climate also benefits when subordinates become involved in making decisions about how their work is conducted.

Nonverbal cues transmitted through everyday interactions constitute a significant aspect of climate. They are important in establishing relationships among members of an organization within and across levels of the hierarchy. As revealed in the communication analysis of the Pennsylvania social welfare bureaucracy discussed in Chapter 3, implicit communication of dysfunctional messages through the tone of voice and through gestures, facial expressions, and other forms of body language produced problems even when explicit communications were correctly handled.

Nonverbal cues can indicate the degree of respect and concern that organization members have for each other. They also indicate the seriousness with which various situations and demands for performance are viewed. A suggestion that the agency should discontinue a service that has become troublesome may have little or no follow-through if it is given in an informal memo that suggests trivial significance or is accompanied by disconfirming body language. The receiver may even confirm intent by an equivocal remark such as "You didn't really mean that, did you?"

When the culture demands respect and equal treatment, lack of esteem is commonly communicated nonverbally or inferentially rather than explicitly. This often happens to women and minorities in organizations. Low esteem can be communicated by assigning them to tasks in occupational backwaters, by excluding them from the top levels of management, or by barring them from field assignments involving a lot of travel or from technologically demanding jobs. Women and minorities can also be stigmatized as sideliners by excluding them from the all-important social channels, such as lunchtime get-togethers and after-work social stops. During organizational meetings, women are recognized less frequently and are often given less time to present their ideas than their male counterparts.[5] Men interrupt them more readily and talk to them in patronizing fashion. Women also are more often the butt of jokes than men, signaling their lower power status.

African-American officials in the State and Labor departments have complained about being snubbed during organizational meetings and not included in planning sessions about programs for which they were responsible. Consequently, blacks serving in the public sector have felt "tolerated but not necessarily welcomed," according to Robert Pear.[6] It is difficult to cope with climates of discrimination created through such indirect messages.

Structural Aspects.   Climate is often related to structural variables, such as the number of employees under a single manager's jurisdiction, the division of labor, or provisions for on-the-job social interactions. Such factors can be assessed objectively by investigating their presence or absence. It is also fruitful to employ combinations of objective and subjective measures, although that additional effort may be wasted because these measurements tend to coincide.

As we have seen, the hierarchical structures that are most common in public agencies in the United States inhibit the flow of communication and make it difficult to create productive internal climates. Usually the span of control of managers is wide. With each responsible for many employees, interpersonal contacts are minimized. Extensive division of labor gives individuals an atomized view of the organization's work. On-the-job social interactions are rare because they cannot easily be included in organizational budgets. However, hierarchical barriers due to differences in rank are partly overcome in U.S. agencies because the mechanisms for keeping social distance are weak. Subordinates are more likely in this country than in other societies to feel that they are the equals of their bosses.

The overall size of an organization affects its climate. Larger ones are usually more bureaucratic, which encourages inflexibility, deference, and alienation. Smaller organizations are often warmer, more supportive, and encourage more risk-taking. Although these distinctions are not absolute, the stereotype persists that all government organizations, because of their size, display all the climate pathologies that go along with large, strictly bureaucratized organizations.

Performance evaluations and appraisals for promotion are areas in which formal communications are frequently mishandled in public agencies, with destructive consequences for organizational climate. Lloyd Etheredge cites many reports of undercurrents of "envy, fear, and hostility" on the part of subordinates who typically feel "insecure, powerless, vulnerable and dependent" in hierarchical settings where rewards are uncertain. Consequently, there is a "pervasive lack of enthusiasm, boredom, low productivity, red tape, and officious compensatory behavior to achieve recognition and respect." [7]

Neither managers nor employees like doing personal evaluations, even when they are part of formal organizational procedures. This is especially true when feedback about job performance has to be negative. When employees are doing well, managers are eager to praise and often give employees more credit than is due. In an attempt to maintain morale, managers may overstate chances for promotion. Such lack of candor inevitably results in disillusionment and a climate of distrust.

External Settings. An organization's external climates may also be shaped through its messages and activities directed at the individuals and institutions with whom it routinely interacts. For example, much of the working environment of the State Department has been created through publicizing slogans, such as referring to U.S.-Soviet relations as a "cold war" or as a "thaw." Cold-war rhetoric, which created a climate of distrust for Soviet-bloc countries, proved inimical to reaching any kind of disarmament agreement with these countries. Similarly, the United States described its 1990 invasion of Panama as an effort to stop drug dealing, so that it would be viewed as part of the Bush administration's well-publicized war on drugs. This reduced the level of anxiety that might have been created by characterizing the action as a war.

Efforts to control the climate of interrelationships are common in various types of negotiations and bargaining encounters. Attractive physical surroundings may be chosen and language may be deliberately restrained, even friendly, to create a climate that encourages agreement. Alternatively, threatening language and austere physical surroundings, along with timely hostile incidents, may be used to coerce an opponent into accepting terms.[8]

The negotiating agenda may also be structured with climate concerns in mind. Items on which agreement seems most likely may be placed at the beginning to create a favorable momentum for solving problems. Difficult items may be scheduled when the prevailing mood is likely to be most receptive to reaching a settlement. Accurate timing is essential, requiring such maneuvers as stalling through lengthy speeches and delays in opening sessions or rearranging meeting agendas to speed things up.

Climate Impact

Organizational climate, according to Marshall Scott Poole, "represents the linkage between the organizational situation and members' cognitions, feelings, and behaviors." [9] That makes it important for many aspects of organizational life. Most importantly, it affects job satisfaction and performance. Employees work harder or less hard, and better or less well, depending on what they perceive the climate requires.[10] Improvements in climate may have a spiral effect. The satisfactions flowing from these improvements may further enhance the quality of the climate.

It is particularly important for public agencies to use their limited personnel resources to create climates that motivate employees to high performance because the penalty and reward structures that are powerful motivators in the private sector are weak in the public sector. Terence Mitchell and James Larson discuss the plight of a police captain in a large metropolitan department who complained about his inability to motivate young police officers to prepare adequate arrest reports. The task was clearly boring, but it was essential for obtaining convictions in court proceedings. Severe budget constraints kept the captain from offering financial rewards or offering job retention or promotion as incentives. Creating team competitions also failed because there were no prizes. "No one was getting any type of reward for winning the competition, and they figured why should they bust a gut when there was no payoff." [11]

The public sector's civil service system makes it exceptionally difficult to penalize unsatisfactory performance through pay reduction, lack of promotion, demotion, or dismissal. Similarly, it is almost impossible to reward excellence through increased benefits and pay or promotion unless there are open positions that have not been claimed by aspirants under seniority rules. Motivation through creating a stimulating, challenging working environment is one of the few options to overcome these hurdles.

Loyalty, morale, and a sense of mission are important aspects of organizational climate that have a strong impact on work performance and employee retention. Agencies can develop these sentiments among their employees through personal ties between superiors and subordinates or through charismatic leadership. Examples include the U.S. Forest Service under Gifford Pinchot and his successors, the Federal Bureau of Investigation under J. Edgar Hoover, and the Social Security Administration under the guidance of Arthur J. Altmeyers and John G. Winant.[12]

As mentioned earlier, when top executives are replaced, as happens frequently in the public sector, dramatic changes in organizational climate may follow. Herbert Kaufman cites the example of the Food and Drug Administration following the accession of Donald Kennedy in 1977. The "agency's drug unit had been rent by internal conflict and division, assailed by both the industrial and the consumer wings of its clientele, afflicted with demoralization, and at war with the commissioner at the time. Some employees denounced it in congressional testimony." [13]

When Kennedy accepted the post of commissioner, some of his friends warned him that he had agreed to become the captain of the ill-fated *Titanic*. However, with the help of recommendations from a study commission, combined with excellent leadership skills, Kennedy was able to turn the agency around. Two years later, there was no evidence of internal warfare in the agency or in publicity about it. "At meetings, the atmosphere was businesslike, cordial, open, and relaxed, and at informal gatherings there was obvious camaraderie." [14] Kennedy's management style, which contributed to this change, was described as follows by Kaufman: "He treated his colleagues with respect, was receptive to their ideas, encouraged inventiveness, and did his homework assiduously when they put proposals before him. He helped create a collegial environment." [15] Reliance on personal relationships may backfire when mentors or leaders leave an organization. For instance, when Wernher von Braun, the charismatic leader of NASA's Marshall Space Flight Center in Huntsville, Alabama, left the agency, the legendary communications climate that he had created deteriorated sharply.[16]

Climate can foster a high moral tone in an agency, but it can also do the reverse. When there is a pervasive sense that flouting the rules is condoned or even encouraged, many members succumb, pushing aside personal scruples. Hence, it is no surprise that Jeb Magruder, a Nixon official involved in the illegal activities connected with the Watergate scandal, testified that his actions were inspired by the organizational climate in which he worked. As Magruder phrased it, "Because of a certain atmosphere that had developed in my working at the White House, I was not as concerned about its illegality as I should have been." [17] Pervasive corruption in police departments and even court systems has often been linked to a climate of "everybody does it, why shouldn't I?"

However, acclimatization is never complete or uniform in unsound as well as in sound climates. Some officials are inner-directed and yield only partly or not at all to the social pressures of the prevailing organizational climate.[18] *Whistle-blowing* provides a graphic example in situations where it represents the victory of personal visions of moral organizational behavior over corrupt institutional practices condoned by the prevailing climate.

Whistle-blowers who reveal their agency's transgressions are motivated by varying combinations of altruistic and selfish concerns. Irrespective of motivations, they risk severe retaliation such as censure, dismissal, and public scorn for tattling and disloyalty. Moreover, the chances are slim that their complaints will lead to major reforms.

Whistle-blowing is important because it discloses otherwise unavailable information needed to correct serious deficiencies in the public service. In 1989 Congress passed the Whistle-Blower Protection Bill to encourage this behavior by diminishing its risks. The bill establishes a review process designed to make it faster and easier for whistle-blowers to fight against dismissal. A 1983 government poll had shown that 70 percent of federal employees who knew that their agency's climate condoned waste, fraud, and other abuses were unwilling to blow the whistle because they feared the consequences.[19] These include the wrath of the wrongdoers who might be identified as well as the scorn that American political culture heaps on stool pigeons.

Faulty communication often produces faulty expectations, which, in turn, lead to climates of disappointment and even hostility. EPA's program designed to involve citizens' advisory committees in planning for improved water quality in their communities provides a good illustration.[20] Participants in the water-quality improvement programs became disenchanted with their role and many resigned because EPA descriptions of the job had led them to expect a major role in planning. Instead, they felt that they were merely completing meaningless paperwork to satisfy the legislative requirement that citizens should be consulted. They also interpreted the long delays in implementing water improvement programs as symbolic of EPA's lack of genuine concern about the issue.

EPA officials had a different perception of the role assigned to citizens' boards, viewing it as largely symbolic. Citizens were merely supposed to listen to what the experts had to say. Their questions would then reveal to the experts how well average people understood the program and the likely degree of support for it. EPA officials regarded the long delays in the implementation of programs as standard, given the constraints that Congress had written into the legislation. They felt that citizens misinterpreted the symbolic significance of the delays.

In-depth interviews of board members made it clear that EPA had failed to communicate its goals and constraints, which led to the climate of distrust and disenchantment about the role to be played by citizens in the program.[21] It became clear that much better communication between EPA and citizen boards was essential to foster an understanding of the goals and perceptions of both groups so that more mutually satisfying relationships could be established. Developing a good communication climate is particularly crucial when membership in organizations is informal, allowing people to quit easily without making major sacrifices. This is generally the case for citizens' advisory boards.

Socialization Devices

In large multifaceted organizations, it is well-nigh impossible for managerial personnel to keep in close touch with most of their work force. Loyalty, morale and sense of mission must therefore be developed through professional socialization or experientially through working in a climate where those qualities are pervasive. Indoctrination about the organization's mission generally must be circulated throughout the organization. However, various message translations may be required to convey the information effectively at different levels. When indoctrination is successful, employees are able to see their job from the perspective of the entire organization.

Indoctrination messages may be conveyed through handbooks, training sessions, internal rotations and apprenticeships, briefings, office newsletters, and the like. They may also be disseminated at the informal, word-of-mouth level. In many organizations this informal approach constitutes the most important introduction to the organizational climate. Loyalty and morale can also grow from ideological commitment to the organization's policies.

The Department of State, the Environmental Protection Agency, and the Central Intelligence Agency have been able to attract ideologically committed individuals to their ranks. This accomplishment is made possible because they are allowed to be highly selective in choosing applicants and testing them for technical proficiency and appropriate value structures. For many other agencies, ideological commitment to the organization's goals is unlikely. In fact, it runs counter to the ideal of bureaucratic culture that public servants, while loyal to their agency, must be politically neutral technicians who carry out whatever mandate is given to them by a changing cast of partisan superiors.

Climate Classifications

Climate can be described in terms of various typologies, or the focus can be on specific components, such as job performance or interactions among employees. At the typology level, one can distinguish between democratic and authoritarian climates. A democratic climate would presumably be supportive of individual employees, open in communication, and reward-oriented.[22] Leaders would care about the opinions and preferences of the rank and file to whom they would feel accountable. By contrast, an authoritarian climate would be dominated by the leader and would presumably create distrust between subordinates and superiors and even between fellow workers. It would be penalty-oriented. For these reasons, the temptation to conceal and distort might be great. Since few data are made available in authoritarian settings, a lot of guessing and spying would be likely.

Stress levels can be used as a criterion for classifying organizational climates and comparing agencies or various levels within the same agency.

At the top of the hierarchy, public agency climates are typically character-ized by high stress levels. These often reach danger points at which they harm individuals and impair work performance. Burnout is common, leading to physical and psychological distress and high job turnover.[23] High stress climates in the public sector have been attributed to executives' feelings of inadequacy about solving complex problems, fear that policy outcomes cannot be successfully controlled, and apprehension about media and public criticism. Tension at the top tends to radiate downward to mid- and lower-level officials.

When attitude toward job performance is the focus, climate has been assessed in terms of such factors as morale, crispness of task performance, and policy consensus. According to Kaufman, "Morale is the level of unity, pride, confidence, dedication, enthusiasm, conscientiousness, and industry displayed by an organization's members. Crispness is a comprehensive term for the speed, accuracy, efficiency, and competence with which members do their jobs. Policy consensus means the absence of sharp divisions among the members about the values emphasized in the organization's operations." [24]

Climate can also be characterized in terms of the perceived qualities of interaction among organization members. Six styles of interaction have been identified. When organization members are intensely *competitive* with each other, the climate may become tense. Members may become uncooperative or even hostile. Friction may spring from divergent political, policy, or personal goals or from interpersonal incompatibilities. The reverse is a *collaborative* climate, in which members believe that they share goals and are personally compatible. Collaborative behavior can be encour-aged through rotating the roles of various people and keeping them well informed about organizational goals and their relation to those goals.

Some organizations emphasize teamwork. Teams are more likely to thrive when hierarchies are flat, with line and staff distinctions blurred—an uncommon condition in public sector agencies. Other characteristics favoring teamwork include extensive face-to-face interaction among mem-bers of the organization about nonroutine decisions and fairly close consensus about values. It also helps if members have a deep appreciation of the organization's mission and goals.[25] Research and Development laboratories often have such a *concertive* climate, as do highly professional agencies like the Corps of Engineers or the CIA. When members have internalized the values of the organization, no other control mechanism is needed. Concertive climates are difficult to achieve because the personal values of organization members or the values of unions and other interest groups with whom they identify often conflict at least partially with the values of the organization.

When members differ in their goals and perceptions of organizational policies but are willing to compromise, relationships become *conciliatory*.

The ability to develop a compromise position often hinges on the leadership skills of dominant individuals within a particular communication network. Some organizations may have several leaders, each with a group of followers willing to support them in the positions they take. In such cases, a *supportive* relationship exists between each leader and his or her followers, although the overall climate of the organization may be competitive. Finally, intergroup relations may foster a climate that can be characterized as *detached*. Members of the organization accept whatever is decided and feel little or no personal involvement. Such a neutral climate is hardly conducive to enthusiastic job performance, but it comes closest to the Weberian notion of appropriately detached bureaucratic attitudes.

Over time, organizational climates often change. Different stages have been identified, as organizations move through typical life cycles. Organizational life begins with a *forming,* or developmental stage during which there is likely to be a great deal of cooperation as members learn what their tasks are and how to perform them. The climate is either collaborative, conciliatory, or supportive. A *storming* stage follows, during which open conflict is common about structural concerns such as operating rules, the arrangement of the organizational agenda, and leadership roles. A competitive organizational climate prevails. During the third phase, called *norming,* the organization returns to a more collaborative and conciliatory climate. The group tends to reach consensus about rules and procedures, and members identify more closely with group norms. During the final phase, called *performing,* the organization functions smoothly because rules and routines have become second nature. The climate is predominantly collaborative.[26] In the public sector, a post-final phase, *adjourning,* is rare. It involves the disintegration of the organization after its tasks have been completed and the agency shuts down fully or partially.

Producing a Climate for Innovation

Although anxiety about major changes in tasks and their execution is universal, changes are made fairly readily in the private sector. This is not so in the public sector, where maintaining consensus or an established policy is preferable to risking its breakdown to accomplish needed changes. The varied constituencies with vested interests in public policies almost ensure that there will be sharp conflicts over the goals of innovation and the means to reach these goals.[27] Conflicts of interests between administrators and legislators often become major obstacles to innovation, especially when action requires formal authorization by multiple layers of officialdom.[28] Would-be innovators find it exceedingly frustrating to appear at hearing after hearing to justify their proposals to defenders of the status quo or to rivals who want to capture resources available for innovations. It is far easier to remain with established procedures. When rules and procedures are based on legislative mandates, amendments or new legislation may be required to produce changes, widening the circle of interested parties who must be appeased.

Even when changes are within the power of a single agency, the mere fact of large size, entailing retraining of many employees, is a major obstacle, as is the tendency of job classifications to be too detailed to allow for major reallocations of duties. When innovations interfere with employees' lifestyles, resistance is usually high. For instance, when New York City tried to change police officers' assignments so that more of them would be on duty during peak crime periods, the plan misfired. Officers perceived it as an invasion of their rights because it shifted them from familiar beats and separated them from accustomed partners.[29] It also required adjustments in their personal lives such as changing their bowling leagues or the time spent on moonlighting jobs. Given such disturbances of their routines, a climate of resentment was unavoidable without careful steps to make the innovations palatable. The need for innovations and the advantages of new routines were successfully communicated to sanitation workers who were then willing to accept shifts in assignments designed to improve New York City's garbage collection.

Making minimal changes to adapt established procedures to a changing environment or to correct serious deficiencies in performance is the easiest and the preferred way to cope with the need for innovations. Earlier we noted the tendency of bureaucrats to adhere strictly to established rules because of their vulnerability to media criticism, political pressures, complaints, and threats of litigation about inequities. This is the hallowed rule that one should never do anything for the first time. It is part of what is indelicately known as a CYA (cover-your-ass) maneuver. Such sentiments are not conducive to creating a climate that encourages innovations, particularly since employees earn few material rewards for them in the public sector.[30]

When agency personnel perceive a gap between their expected and actual performance, they may be motivated to become more innovative. Raising performance goals is therefore a way to stimulate a climate for innovation. Again, this is more difficult in the public than in the private sector. Other measures for enhancing the climate for innovation are often unavailable to public agencies. They include structuring the reward system to foster innovation, selecting leaders committed to innovation and removing opponents, providing needed financial and psychological resources for retraining and restructuring or for new ventures and personnel, and improving communication so that information about innovations and their relevance to the agency's mission is widely circulated.[31] Alternatively, the legal base of some agencies can be changed to transform them into government corporations with increased control over making and altering their own rules and procedures. Creating incentives for innovation is particularly difficult for small agencies that lack sufficient resources to undertake such risks.

Nonetheless, many governmental units do make concerted efforts to innovate or to encourage innovations in the public sector and in private sector activities that affect the public welfare. The Commonwealth of Massachusetts, for example, in the 1975-1986 period, supported job-producing innovations in the private sector to improve the climate for business.[32] Other states have created incentives to stimulate economic development and to encourage economic ties with other states and foreign countries. Many states and cities, as well as the federal government, have set up long-range projects to identify goals and innovations to achieve them.[33]

Even when innovations have been approved or mandated, adoption is problematic in public sector agencies because of the difficulty in controlling personnel, communicating with far-flung branches, and other structural and attitudinal obstacles.[34] To overcome this problem, the state of Washington's Efficiency and Accountability Commission developed an effective mechanism to ensure compliance, which includes making specific suggestions for implementing changes, projecting costs and timetables, and asking for quarterly progress reports. The approach seems to work well.[35] Innovations backed by political clout tend to diffuse quickly, while others lag. Changes come most readily through new personnel who have learned new ways during their training. They are resisted most by older employees loath to change their ways.

Many innovations are suggested by communication with people from outside the organization. Such external contacts are usually less frequent than internal contacts and are therefore labeled as weaker. Because such occasional contacts can be extraordinarily stimulating, they have been dubbed *the strength of weak ties*. System openness to the external environment is thus important for creating a climate favoring innovation. In fact, organizations that wish to avoid innovation, as do some religious communities and educational institutions, frequently shun communication with their environments. Openness is often reduced in the public sector because there is less boundary-spanning networking and less internal networking than in the private sector, and because joint ventures cutting across agencies are relatively uncommon.[36] Political appointees in the top echelons who might provide fresh insights rarely spend enough time with an agency to understand its innovation needs. Even when they do, and come prepared with plans for major changes, they face resistance from the permanent staffs who often regard them as ill-informed outsiders. Although their innovativeness may win them plaudits from external audiences, they are likely to leave the agency without achieving most of their goals.[37]

Within organizations, information about innovations is most likely to be exchanged by people who are familiar with each other and have the same status.[38] One reason may be the fact that many people are apt to ridicule new ideas. Hence, it is safer to communicate them to friends. When the climate for circulating innovative ideas is restrictive because of fears of criticism and ridicule, innovations may not circulate widely enough to gain legitimacy. They may also fail to benefit from discussion and scrutiny. By conˈrast, total strangers, unfamiliar with the politics of particular organizations, do not hesitate to discuss innovations. In fact, they may not even realize that they are passing on an innovation, which may be old hat to them.

Organizational Culture

The Elements of Culture

Organizational culture refers to the written and unwritten, explicit and implicit rules of behavior that each organization develops and to the unique myths and symbols that guide the behavior of individuals within the organization. Organizational culture is thus, as Dennis Mumby states, "a complex web of socially constructed experiences which embodies various and heterogeneous organizational meaning structures." [39] Or, as James Wilson defines it, is a "persistent, patterned way of thinking about the central tasks of and human relationships within an organization." [40] It develops in response to the organization's need to perform its mission in a particular environment. Organizational leaders determine how that mission is interpreted and what approaches should be used to achieve organizational goals. In the process, they shape or implement organizational cultures. There is interaction between the organizational climates of particular organizations, the culture or cultures that they harbor, and the general political cultures.[41]

A shared organizational culture does not mean that members must share all meanings. They are able to take organized action even when they assign very different meanings to their common experiences. In that case, one encounters "equifinal" meanings—dissimilar interpretations that have similar behavior implications.[42] Organization members may have different reasons for acting and may interpret potential outcomes differently, but they can agree on the action. Postal workers, for example, may share in a culture that believes that mail must be delivered as fast as technology permits. For some, this may be a matter of professional pride and tradition, while others see it as a chance to collect overtime bonuses which they view as a perquisite of postal jobs.

Rules of organizational culture may be thematic, relating to the basic belief structure and values—the ethos—of the organization, or they may be tactical, designed to ease life within the organization. For example, a thematic rule that hierarchy distinctions are to be respected can be accompanied by the purely tactical command "Don't argue with your boss!" [43] At times, thematic and tactical rules may be contradictory. For example, a general thematic rule is that public agencies must keep their dealings open to public scrutiny. However, within agencies such as the CIA and the FBI there are numerous tactical rules that prescribe exceptions to the culture of openness. When such exceptions become pervasive, it may indicate a change from a culture of openness to one of secrecy and possibly deception.

Cultural rules apply to the types of goals that agencies may seek and also to the types of behavior that will achieve them. For example, the political culture of the United States is oriented toward the preservation of biological families. A child care agency would run counter to cultural constraints if it advocated the large-scale removal of children from their biological families in order to raise them in government-controlled public institutions. Given the culturally sanctioned inviolability of the home, it would probably be impossible to authorize an agency to make routine checks of parenting behavior inside private residences over parental objections. Theorists who espouse a critical interpretive perspective have claimed that political elites who control an organization's material resources also control the symbol system that creates and maintains organizational culture.[44] These elites design cultural rules to maintain existing power structures for their own benefit.

Acculturation Techniques

Because the myths, symbols, rules, and values constituting the organizational culture or cultures are unique to particular contexts, they must be communicated verbally and behaviorally so that members can learn and share them. Learning is easiest and the impact strongest when these cultures correspond to the personnel's existing values and ethics.[45] Even then complete acculturation may take a long time, and it may always remain incomplete even for long-term workers. The problems arising from incomplete acculturation may impair the effectiveness of the agency and lead to numerous personnel problems, including high turnover rates.

One can learn cultural rules through observing behavior and social interaction within the organization—what is done and not done and the likely social consequences. Michael Thompson and Aaron Wildavsky write, "The key question is 'In what way would which people, sharing which values, legitimating what practices, act to strengthen their own organization and/or to weaken their adversaries?' How do they select data so as to convert it into information that will support the mode of organization they prefer?" [46] Finding answers to these questions may be a difficult, tedious route. One can rely on word-of-mouth instructions from people in the organization who have been socialized to its cultures, usually over a lengthy period of time. Or one can glean a number of cultural rules from publications that may have been prepared specifically by personnel departments for the indoctrination of employees. In general, these publications, while helpful, cover only a fraction of the rules, symbols, myths, values, and perspectives that make up an organization's culture. Full acculturation is left to on-the-job experience.

Small-scale organizations with clear missions generally find it easiest to convey their organizational culture. For example, studies of the Forest Service indicate that its personnel could be easily indoctrinated because the values, perspectives, and rules governing work performance were clear and unvarying throughout the agency.[47] The fact that personnel wore distinctive uniforms helped to convey a sense of identity among widely dispersed officials. Most government agencies are too large and diversified to have a single culture likely to win near-universal acclaim. Clashes between internal cultures may produce serious intraorganizational conflicts. The greatest difficulties in conveying understanding of a culture arise in external communications involving culturally different countries. As difficult as it is to take climates and cultures into account in framing communication on the domestic scene, it is infinitely harder to do when national and ethnic barriers must be breached. The American preference for concluding business quickly and communicating disagreements frankly, for instance, may be resented in cultures where people believe that important matters require lengthy dealings and strict adherence to rules of politeness and decorum.

Culture Impact

The importance of organizational culture in shaping the character and performance of various public agencies becomes clear when one looks at a number of examples. For instance, the FBI's culture calls for calm and deliberate procedures because there is usually a gap between the commission of a crime and an FBI investigation. Agents know that painstaking collection and analysis of evidence are more important than speed. By contrast, the culture of local police departments usually prizes speedy action. Calming community fears by announcements that offenders have been apprehended or at least identified is considered an important goal. Depending on the particular culture of a department, police may be instructed to treat suspected offenders sternly or to try to resolve law infractions with a minimum of confrontation.[48]

On a more mundane level, some organizational cultures may dictate that executives refrain from using computerized communication to contact their peers. By contrast, other cultures may indicate that computer contacts are the most appropriate way to reach lower levels of the hierarchy. An organizational culture may use computers for simple messages but depend on interpersonal communication for more complex messages. Organizational culture generally dictates that superiors support mid-level executives against claims from bottom-level personnel, regardless of the merit of the claim. Hence, it is a tactical rule for employees at the bottom of the hierarchy to avoid complaining about mid-level managers. The penalty for ignoring the rule may be dismissal of the subordinate.

The organizational culture may be quite influential in determining how communication flows between dissimilar parties such as superiors and subordinates, service providers and clients, males and females, and people belonging to different ethnic groups and races. This becomes particularly evident in a comparison of radically different cultures such as the Japanese and the American. In a Japanese organization, the basic unit is the work group rather than the individual.[49] Discussing the structure of Japanese organizations, Tom Carney writes, "Superior and subordinate are a linked unit, not individuals in opposition in regard to their career chances." Individuals are recruited with an eye toward keeping the organization homogeneous. When they are asked to join the organization, they are explicitly indoctrinated into its culture, which calls for nurturing the ego of members. Outright negative feedback is avoided as damaging to the member's self concept. Assertiveness and confrontations are frowned upon.

Cultural rules are important in defining the nature of political and economic conflicts and the appropriate methods for seeking solutions. Appeals strategies and tactics must be constructed with these rules in mind. A labor dispute argued before a panel of adjudicators between October 1983 and May 1984 provides examples. Presenting the unions' grievances were the American Federation of State, County and Municipal Employees and the Fraternal Order of Police on one side, pitted against the labor relations section of a county government of a mid-Atlantic state.[50] Each side tried to present its case in a way designed to win a favorable ruling from the three adjudicators, who were county residents appointed by the county government.

The appeals to the adjudicators were geared to the presumed cultural expectations of the parties to the dispute. For instance, the parties referred to shared moral and rational standards and standards of responsibility, as defined in the "Content Level Coding System" on page 220. The expectation was that the adjudicators would uphold the positions that had been framed to reflect their cultural standards, such as the importance of treating people equally.[51] The opponent's perspectives were depicted as irrational or unwarranted when judged by the prevailing perspectives of what constitutes rational and appropriate behavior. The attempts at persuasion made during the hearings were impersonal, appealing to a standard to be observed by all, rather than to a personal relationship between the feuding parties and the adjudicators. This conformed to

Content Level Coding System

Moral standards—A standard or principle of morality is invoked in support of the sender's position.
Debt: People should pay their debts.
Equality: People should be treated equally/consistently.
Empathy: People should treat others as they would like to be treated themselves.
Equity: People should be treated fairly/justly.[a]

Rational standards—A standard or principle of reason is invoked in support of the sender's position.
Law: People should obey the law/rules/contract.
Authority: People should obey authority/courts/arbitrators.
Efficiency: People should behave efficiently/practically.
Logic: People should behave logically/sensibly.[a]

Standards of responsibility—A standard of responsibility is invoked in support of the sender's position.
Blaming: People who are at fault should be punished.
Second chance: People who admit they have done wrong should be given a second chance.
Mistake: People should not be punished for honest mistakes and misunderstandings.

Credibility comparison—The credibility of the opponent is called into question while the sender's credibility is assured.
Truth: They are not being honest, we are.
Motivation: They have hidden motives, we do not.
Knowledge: They do not know what they are talking about, we do.
Competence: They have not done their job, we have.

Perspective manipulation—The adjudicator is directed to view the conflict from a perspective that supports the sender's position.
Issue definition: The issue or question before the adjudicator is framed in a way that favors the sender's position or detracts from the opponent's position.
Minimization: The strength of the opponent's position is minimized by the sender.

Source: Elizabeth A. Martin and Louis P. Cusella, "Persuading the Adjudicator: Conflict Tactics in the Grievance Procedure," in *Communication Yearbook 9*, Margaret L. McLaughlin, ed. (Beverly Hills, Calif.: Sage, © 1986), 541. Reprinted with permission.
[a] Tactic was identified during coding of data.

cultural constraints that inhibit personal favors and partisan rulings by judicial bodies.

The "Content Level Coding System" on this page provides an outline of the various types of appeals that were used. For instance, within our prevailing cultural context, few would argue with the moral command that people should be treated fairly or with the rational imperative that people should behave logically. Few would contest a standard of responsibility that prescribes that people who are at fault should be punished. Other arguments called the credibility of the opponent into question and confirmed the credibility of the claimant because it is culturally customary to assess the relative credibility of the parties in legal proceedings. By presenting their pleas in such well-accepted frameworks, the contestants hoped to make them irrefutable.

Bureaucratic Symbolism

Organizational culture commonly requires that bureaucrats communicate in ponderous, often incomprehensible styles.[52] This is done to satisfy the requirements of equally ponderous legislative and judicial language and to lend an air of authority to bureaucratic transactions. Simple "yes" or "no" responses are shunned. A spade is not a spade when it can be called a soil-rotation facilitator. When then Congressman Jack Kemp asked former Budget Director Bert Lance whether the Carter administration could terminate a missile project without prior permission from Congress, the simple answer would have been "yes." Instead, Lance responded in classic bureaucratic style:

> As you know, the Impoundment Control Act of 1976 does not contain any provision governing the obligation or deobligation of funds proposed for recision during the forty-five-day period. A recision message is awaiting congressional action. There is no prohibition on terminating existing contracts, thereby deobligating funds, during this period.
>
> In the absence of express requirements with respect to obligation or deobligation of funds and in view of the recognition by Congress that funds could be withheld, there is no legal basis for precluding the Department of Defense from either refraining from obligating additional funds or terminating existing contracts during the forty-five-day period the related recision message is pending in the Congress.[53]

Bureaucratic culture mandates that announcements of organizational changes be structured to maintain the appearance of an intact and functioning power structure. As R. Richard Ritti points out, "No, it will not do to admit that your top executives have been performing inadequately. And it certainly will not do to point out that an effective executive has been removed because he lost out in political infighting." [54] When changes result from conditions that the culture deems inappropriate or embarrassing, official explanations usually hide the real facts. Instead, they "save face" by presenting socially acceptable explanations that sustain the legitimacy of the organization and its goals. Most changes are depicted as progress that will enhance the efficiency and effectiveness of the agency. Insiders who breach the etiquette of maintaining the appropriate organizational image by openly discussing the organization's shortcomings are likely to find themselves ostracized by their colleagues and often dismissed from their jobs. Destroying an image is treated as a major transgression. Indeed it is, because it is likely to undermine morale internally and cause external difficulties for the agency.

Image is also maintained through organizational rituals. For example, decision-making meetings are often closed to lower-level personnel. The usual rationale is that information intended for higher-level executives must be restricted to a small corps of especially trustworthy people. Quite aside from this justification, which may or may not be valid, the restrictions serve to set upper-level officials apart as more knowledgeable and hence more competent. Their status and treatment signify that they possess special qualifications. The symbolism suggests that they know what they are doing or they would not be in their exalted positions. This is what Ritti calls "the Creation of Awe." [55] The mystery of what goes on in high-level meetings creates awe for the participants, which then facilitates maintenance of the existing authority structure.

The Whys and Wherefores of Red Tape

The cultures of government bureaucracies mandate that procedures follow explicit rules whenever possible. Organizations therefore develop detailed guidelines for their various activities, from decision making to keeping organizational records. The term "red tape" is used to refer to the sum total of these guidelines, procedures, and forms, which political folklore stigmatizes as excessive and wasteful. The name commemorates the fact that official documents were tied with red tape during the nineteenth century.

Sometimes red tape takes the form of an excessive number of procedural steps and checkpoints that must be passed before action can be taken. When the Chicago Transit Authority wanted to sign contracts exceeding $5,000 during the late 1980s, fifty-four separate steps were required, including final approval by the agency's governing board.[56] Consequently, processing a contract took more than six months. In the wake of public complaints, nineteen steps were eliminated, thereby reducing processing time to three months.

How many of these rules and procedures are necessary safeguards to keep administrators accountable and honest and how many are excessive often becomes a matter of individual perspectives. Political scientist Raymond A. Rosenfeld therefore defines red tape in subjective terms as "guidelines, procedures, forms, and government intervention that are perceived as excessive, unwieldy, or pointless in relationship to decision-making or implementation of decisions." [57] Although the term "red tape" carries pejorative connotations, not everyone dislikes red tape. Bureaucrats prize it because it protects them. Strict guidelines absolve them from using their own discretion in making decisions and thereby risking censure. Red tape also makes bureaucracies more powerful in the eyes of the public. The bureaucrat is the all-powerful professional who knows the magic formulas that will unlock the agency's resources.

A news account of the red tape enveloping congressional activities illustrates how it can have negative as well as positive consequences. By law, Congress is required to keep a published record covering every penny paid to the 37,000 congressional staff workers—"from majority leader and administrative assistant to venetian blind technician and laborer." Expenditures as trivial as reimbursement for subway fare or lemons for tea for visiting constituents have to be included. The hefty House spending record is published quarterly, the Senate record semiannually.[58] It would seem that whatever economies may be attributed to the publication requirements are more than offset by the cost of keeping records and publishing them.

As often happens, there is also another side to the picture that makes the situation far less clear-cut. The expenditure records are valuable for members of Congress and others as a means of keeping tabs on the kinds of staffs that each congressional office has hired and the salaries that are paid. Records of expenditures for constituent services or communications, for example, provide important clues to priorities of various offices. Representative Lynn Martin, Republican of Illinois, used the records to show that two-thirds of the female staff members of twenty-five House committees earned less than $40,000 a year. By contrast, three-quarters of the male staffers earned more than that. Martin subsequently introduced a bill designed to end sex discrimination in salaries. Efforts to curtail the publishing requirements would probably arouse opposition from current users of the data and would raise the traditional cry that the legislature is trying to hide information. However, as discussed in Chapter 2, legislation such as the 1980 Paperwork Reduction Act, which was designed to eliminate unnecessary record keeping, might be used to curtail nonessential reports to Congress.

In his book *Red Tape: Its Origins, Uses, and Abuses,* Herbert Kaufman maintains that red tape is an essential part of government derived from American political culture.[59] Citizens distrust government and therefore want protective procedures. American culture mandates that these demands be heeded. Red tape provides desired assurances that government will be compassionate and representative. All these safeguards greatly complicate government, causing delays, preventing innovation, curbing needed discretion in decisions, and increasing expense. They also prevent hasty and ill-considered actions and guard against fraud and other illegalities.

The federal system makes American government particularly prone to red tape because its multiple levels lead to multiple rules for various shared activities. When various legislatures pass laws, they rarely consider the impact of the many layers of red tape that may be necessary to comply with their collective mandates. The requirements of reporting to Congress and state legislatures to meet criteria of accountability force agencies to collect and keep very extensive records. The Administrative Procedure Act and the Freedom of Information Act and their state-level counterparts have also resulted in massive amounts of red tape.[60]

The Nixon administration proposed the Community Development Block Grant Program in part to reduce federal red tape and return more responsibilities to states and localities. The Housing and Community Development Act, signed by President Ford in 1974, put the program into effect.[61] The new Housing and Urban Development regulations were only twenty-five pages long, compared with the 2,600 pages of regulations previously required when more specifically defined categorical grants were made. First-year applications under the new system averaged fifty pages compared with 1,400 pages earlier. Community Development Block Grant applications were processed within seventy-five days, and most were accepted. Application preparation time averaged eight months compared with thirty-one months before. Despite the speedups and substantial reductions in red tape, much remained because of extensive reporting requirements. The House and Senate requested different types of information.[62] HUD also had to issue reams of clarifying instructions in response to local inquiries. As programs age, red tape mounts because new regulations are added to the existing old ones. This happens even in administrations eager to reduce red tape.

The Impact of New Communication Technologies

Satellites, computers, videotapes, fax machines, and similar twentieth-century technologies are new means of communication that have a strong bearing on organizational climates. Some of the changes brought about by these technologies are inherent in their nature; others flow largely from organizational cultures that influence how the new tools are used.[63] As with any new technology, new ways to send messages are not merely additions to established practices. Rather they generate significant changes in established cultures. This does not mean that they are totally or even predominantly replacing the old order, but that established practices must be revised and new norms created to guide behavior in the new environment. These changes have improved the organizational climate in many respects, but there have also been major drawbacks.

The new technologies, especially computers, are widely available. Computers are used mostly for word processing, spread-sheet analysis, and building data bases. Congress's Office of Technology Assessment reported in 1985 that over 90 percent of federal agencies had spread-sheet software. A 1985 study of all U.S. cities with populations of over 50,000 showed that computers were used for an average of eighty-four tasks performed by city officials. They increased efficiency and were particularly helpful in fiscal control and in contacts with the public.[64]

The wide dispersion of computing facilities has created coordination problems because the diverse needs of government agencies for suitable information technologies have to be amalgamated. Because data-sharing requirements necessitate a high degree of compatibility among systems, there has been increased emphasis on solving coordination problems by planning for information technology. The Johnson Space Center, to use just one example, set up a permanent planning committee, composed of designers, users of the system, and upper-management representatives, to develop policy guidelines for the entire organization. Operational control remained decentralized in line with preferences of the majority of users of the system.

Major Advantages

On the plus side, for the most part, the new technologies create more open communication climates. They make it easier to contact people, including many organization members who are unknown to message senders. Everyone who gains entry to a particular electronic communication network, for example, has access to all the messages available from it. Given the large number of employees in public sector agencies, widespread ready access to information is a distinct advantage, making it easier to avoid creating isolates and to integrate those that do exist into organizational networks. However, the new tools may spawn new types of isolates who cannot or choose not to overcome the hurdles posed by the new technology. The gap between the information poor and rich always increases when complex new communication technologies emerge. Older workers are likely to be the most isolated and disadvantaged.

The new technologies make it simple to send and receive lengthy messages at any time in a variety of locations beyond the traditional office setting. When the intended receivers are not at the point of reception, messages can be stored for later retrieval. This flexibility allows agencies with far-flung branch offices or staffs whose work requires travel away from their offices to stay in much closer touch than was previously possible. Interconnected computers can disseminate messages with extreme rapidity and precision, making it possible to take action more quickly. Faster action increases the perception of responsiveness to client needs. When time and distance constraints become less formidable, organizational effectiveness tends to increase.

When messages are intended for a variety of receivers whose needs and comprehension levels may vary, they can be easily restructured. The adaptability of electronic messages is also useful in letters to agency constituencies, which can now be personalized even for mass mailings. A seemingly personalized message presumably enhances the quality of the relationship between the agency and its clients.

The electronic revolution has also had a major impact on the climate for organizational decision making.[65] Thanks to computer data storage capabilities, a much broader information base, including ample data from external sources, is available for decision making. The additional information makes sound decisions and actions more likely. Computer links permit large numbers of users to gain access to these data bases without requiring the intervention of computer experts. Fewer relay points lessen the chance for distortion. There is also the benefit of an instantaneous, readily accessible, accurate record stored in the computer's memory. By disseminating knowledge more widely, computers facilitate more input from lower levels of the organization. In many instances, decision making can move from higher to lower levels so that it is closer to field operations and customers.[66]

In practice, however, most computer-assisted decisions involve comparatively routine and repetitive situations. Important decisions that are novel and require discretion are still handled primarily by individual decision makers. A computer analysis can tell a city manager that one-person police patrol cars are more cost effective than those with two persons. But the costs in officer safety and union demands are difficult to quantify for computer models. As a recent study concludes, "Political judgment and insight are still key to good management decisions and cannot be supplanted by computerization." [67]

The precise nature of the data base made available for decisions is determined by information specialists within organizations who determine what will be entered into the system and how it will be packaged. Given the high prestige accorded to readily measured data, their inclusion is favored by these specialists in preference to less quantitative human relations-oriented information. This may present problems, particularly for agencies that deal primarily in social services. Discussing this issue, Richard Caputo writes, "Information systems exacerbate the all-too-common bureaucratic tendency to convert political and ethical issues to administrative or technical problems, to translate values into technical tasks. Rationality rules. . . . Technology carries with it high hopes for improvement, lulling into dormancy the critical and judgmental skills in society in general and in administrative and clinical practice in particular." [68]

Computers can be particularly helpful in making innovations because of the more ready availability of external data bases that may contain stimulating ideas. Thus they serve as boundary spanners par excellence. New ideas can be disseminated quickly to more people, who can provide feedback via computer. Computers transcend the barriers often created through hierarchies and friendship circles. When members of these widened networks communicate frequently, new friendships may develop. Collaborations across organizational boundaries may become more common and lead to beneficial innovations for all the organizations whose networks are electronically linked. Adaptations of new ideas, which often amount to reinventions, can also be more readily communicated.

Major Problems and Disadvantages

On the negative side of the technological revolution, when machine communication takes the place of face-to-face or even telephone contacts, important nonverbal message cues are lost. These include personal information revealed through the message sender's appearance and paralinguistic cues to the seriousness with which the message should be treated.[69] The absence of nonverbal cues impairs the ability to judge when meanings have been misunderstood and when clarifications and corrections are required.[70] Lack of direct interpersonal contact may also impair morale and the sense of belonging.

The table below ranks various organizational activities in terms of the importance of direct interpersonal contacts. The rankings are based on averages computed from the relevant literature. Rankings at the top indicate little need for face-to-face encounters and hence greater suitability for electronic communication. Exchanging information, asking questions, and exchanging opinions are listed as benefiting little from live interaction. Conversely, getting to know someone, bargaining, and persuading can all be done best in face-to-face settings.

1. Exchanging information	8. Exchanging confidential information
2. Asking questions	9. Solving problems
3. Exchanging opinions	10. Resolving disagreements
4. Staying in touch	11. Persuading
5. Generating ideas	12. Bargaining
6. Exchanging timely information	13. Getting to know someone[71]
7. Making decisions	

Because computers broaden the intended and unintended audiences for messages, including people unknown to message senders, it is more difficult to construct understandable messages. Data do not become "information" until collections of raw facts and figures have been put into a conceptual framework that is understandable to a particular audience.[72] These frameworks can vary substantially for different audiences, making it difficult to find a common ground. However, the fact that computer messages can be easily restructured and edited ameliorates the problem.

The sheer volume of new information available through computerized data and messages may lead to serious information overloads. Since electronic mail arrives throughout the day, it tends to interrupt work schedules because of the cultural pressure to give it immediate attention. The ease of sending electronic mail to large numbers of people simultaneously also fosters a culture where communication is excessive. As noted in an essay on "Office Automation and Bureaucracy," "Computers seem almost to serve as a pernicious nutrient for bureaucracies, allowing their structures and their flaws to grow gigantic." Instead of generating thirty useless pieces of paper, the computerized bureaucracy may generate three hundred. In sum: "Automating a mess yields an automated mess." [73]

The increased ability to communicate may actually reduce the time available for work. It also makes bureaucratic communication systems more vulnerable. The possibilities for communication breakdowns mount with the greater need for sharing information and manipulating data. Many government agencies currently use incompatible systems, leading to isolated work stations and failure of communication networks. Various technical options are available to cope with such problems, but choices are difficult because each has different technical and political consequences. The blessings of ease of access to more information may thus turn out to be a disabling curse as well.

New cultural rules are required to deal with issues of citizen access to public information stored in computerized formats. As yet, according to the Office of Technology Assessment, "there is no common information dissemination policy within the executive branch and Congress which specifies how government information is to be disseminated in other than hard copy or microfiche format." [74] Who should have access at what cost and at what price? Many government files are now available only at great cost from commercial firms. Who will be excluded from access to classified information such as personnel data or payroll accounts? If citizens have access to government files, how can privacy and sensitive data be protected? Will most citizens be able to master the technical skills required to process information held in government files?

New text-searching capabilities may have to be created. For example, tapes of the *Congressional Record* could not be searched efficiently until full text-searching capabilities were developed. Does a climate of openness require that all government documents be made available in formats that will permit computer searches? The implications could be enormous in light of the access to documents permitted under the Freedom of Information Act.[75] It will be very difficult to devise an effective, culturally acceptable system that allows citizens to monitor government activities while still protecting security and privacy interests.

If access to computer files is made easy, agencies may feel compelled to shield themselves from fishbowl effects. At this point it is uncertain what computerization will do to the reliance on informal communication flows that have been so important in the past. If members of the organization feel secure, some informal communication can continue through bulletin boards and electronic methods open to large numbers of people. But if people worry about exposure to unfriendly eyes, the informal flow may dry up or it may continue as before, through grapevine channels, despite the availability of computers.

Agencies may also try to exclude sensitive information from the system, fearing that it may fall into the wrong hands. For example, agencies may not wish to include damaging information in data bases to which members of Congress and the public will have access. As discussed more fully in the next chapter, public officials are quite conscious of the need to maintain the government's good reputation with the public and with its employees. This includes the ability to remain fuzzy about their activities in many controversial situations and even to deny that sensitive information is available. It may therefore be unwise to store all information in computer systems where it can be retrieved easily. While agencies have to provide data so that their performance can be accurately evaluated, they also need to preserve public ignorance about actions that might destroy the agency's credibility. Policy options that have not been adopted may have to be concealed. Such issues raise important ethical questions about the emerging communication culture.

Management information systems that automate communication processes in public bureaucracies tend to ignore the fact that human interaction may be the most important source of difficulties. Increased automation is likely to make these difficulties more acute because nonverbal cues that ease human relations are omitted, as are elements of instant reciprocity that can clear up misunderstandings and lead discussions into productive paths. Brief electronic messages may seem curt, and the ruffled feelings are unlikely to be soothed by subsequent face-to-face interaction.

A field study by political scientist Stephen Wasby illustrates some of the problems. Wasby examined communications among judges in the Ninth Circuit who used computerized electronic mail to send inquiries and circulate decision drafts. The pace of work was speeded up but, in Wasby's view, "use of electronic mail rather than the telephone may produce greater social isolation of the judges, dealing with each other only at the end of a terminal. The judges' lessened knowledge of each other may make it far more difficult for them to communicate informally—or to be able to pick up the phone to resolve matters for which a memorandum is inappropriate." [76] Although electronic communication disrupted work schedules less than telephone calls, it had the disadvantage of preventing the judges from learning each other's foibles readily. Hence, they did not interact as well.

Mixed Consequences

Many consequences of the new technologies cannot be easily classified as primarily positive or negative. Basically they are neither, possessing advantages as well as disadvantages. Changes in organizational networks belong in that category. We have already mentioned that computers make it easier to integrate isolates into existing networks, although there is a danger that new types of isolates may be created. Overall, networking has become simpler through electronic mail, computer program sharing, and the like. Electronic mail distribution lists have created new networks and cliques and have changed existing networks. External boundaries can be crossed more readily. Computers also encourage decentralized communication. Some scholars have documented a proportional decrease of intraorganizational messages in comparison with interorganizational ones. There is less need for formally designated bridges and liaisons.

In the process, the new technologies have the potential to change the roles and hence the possibilities for influence of large numbers of public officials. The implications for morale and other climate factors are vast. When information circulates freely throughout the organization, filtering operations diminish. This spells a loss of power for previous gatekeepers. It also becomes more difficult to ascertain who introduced certain information into the system, how this information was processed, and who is responsible for taking action. Computerization may thus increase problems of accountability.

Formal distinctions among levels may diminish when electronic mail provides subordinates with access to all levels of the hierarchy.[77] Status blurring has advantages as well as disadvantages. Greater social interaction through computerized communication may lead to greater social integration, but may also lead to more social disintegration as organizational boundaries become more indistinct and crumble.[78] Dominant leaders are less likely to emerge. Status, power, personal appearance, charisma, past achievements, and ability to communicate mean much less than before. This frees network members from possible intimidation by higher-status members of the organization. However, because computer messages often fail to identify their information sources, anxieties may develop about the status of the message sender. This happens because reactions to messages are conditioned in part by the sender's status.

How often the new communication technologies produce profound changes in organizations remains uncertain. Several studies of the impact of computers on local governments have concluded that they did not lead to major power shifts. Instead, they tended to reinforce existing power relationships. David Bollier concludes that "there is no decentralization of decision making going on. People are essentially doing what they did before, but do it easier, faster, or more convincingly. . . . Computerization tends to follow the dominant interests of power and resources." [79] If these interests seem threatened by technological changes, the changes are apt to be scuttled. This happened, for example, when the Department of Health, Education and Welfare wanted to use computers to centralize decision making and otherwise streamline overlapping services. Local agencies, fearing loss of power and control, withdrew from the program.[80]

The establishment and development of new technologies inevitably give rise to a number of serious turf battles, especially when an important power resource such as control over information is involved. Such problems can be dismissed with the adage "No pain, no gain," but one cannot ignore the fact that they may make the organizational climate tense, hostile, and excessively competitive. Many of the problems stem from conflicting motives and values. For example, managers at the operational level want information systems geared to supporting their activities. Higher-ups are more interested in gearing data toward planning and control issues. Compromises may be difficult. There are also concerns about technicians exercising control over the system, as well as concerns by technicians about oversight by nonexperts. How much control and oversight is needed? Who should have the final word when major decisions about computer policies need to be made?[81] Tensions between high-level line officials and data-processing personnel often arise because they do not speak the same language.[82] These tensions are serious because line officials are increasingly dependent on the information generated by computer technicians.

Obstacles to Change

Among the many obstacles to using the new electronic technologies to best advantage in the public sector are lack of resources, rapid turnover of top executives before cohesive policies can be formulated, political sensitivities, and turf protection by managers.[83] Older employees in particular resist the new technologies, which may threaten their authority, possibly even their jobs, and which they may perceive as undesirable pressures to change their established methods of operation. Fears have been expressed that use of computerized data depersonalizes the public service even beyond current levels and that cross-matching of computer files will lead to undue invasions of privacy when citizens are under scrutiny.[84] Many administrators still prefer basing decisions on soft data, in the belief that public policy decisions should be driven by social concerns that are hard to incorporate into computerized models. There is fear that rapidly changing technologies may make existing data bases not only obsolete but unusable. The National Archives already have scores of unreadable computer files, including Vietnam War data collected by the Pentagon, NASA's early scientific observations of the earth and planets, and voluminous public health records.[85]

Controversies about computerization policies are well illustrated by experiences at the Johnson Space Center in Clear Lake, Texas.[86] At the time of the study, the center was the leading agency in project and program management for space flight operations, particularly the space station and space shuttle programs. When officials decided to use computers for making operational and management decisions, the center's many constituencies pressured for the adoption of various systems. Managers wanted user-friendly systems that they could dominate, as well as decision support systems and well-designed data bases. End-users had their own specialized interests. Computer vendors pushed for the purchase of particular systems. Additionally, more than twenty principal contractors and a host of subcontractors, as well as consultants who worked regularly with the computer and aerospace industry, favored particular systems.

A variety of issues, each with its own network, were driving computerization decisions. During the early stages of development, pressures had been directed toward making information technology more accessible and decentralized. Subsequently, it became clear that strong communication networks had to be built because data needed to be shared. Despite the strong pressures to build networks that could interface with centralized data bases, there was also strong support for keeping data-processing capabilities decentralized.

Issues raised by conflicting demands of decentralization and integration appear to be endemic to all large government organizations. Will computer-driven organizational planning shift the balance of political power to technocrats, or will it perpetuate the status quo? Empirical research suggests that reinforcement of the status quo is the most common outcome. Computerized information systems promote either centralization or decentralization, depending on the prevailing organizational trend.[87]

Summary and Conclusions

This chapter deals with several important psychological aspects of organizational communication. Among them is organizational *climate,* which evolves from the verbal and nonverbal messages circulating within an organization. Just as weather phenomena impact human behavior, so organizational climate affects what organizations produce, how they produce it, and how comfortable or uncomfortable employees feel in their jobs.

The chapter describes major psychological and structural factors that are important in shaping organizational climates, including interpersonal relations among workers and between workers and supervisory personnel, incentive structures, and the overall size of organizational units. By and large, the public service is ill designed to score well on these factors. Given the importance of these factors to organizational morale, work motivation, and innovation, the flaws in public sector climate control are serious. The chapter outlines various dimensions for assessing the quality of climates and gauging changes linked to various stages in the organization's development.

Organizational climates depend heavily on the cultures in which they operate. Cultures are created through formal and informal rules, symbols, and myths that are developed to guide the activities of members toward organizational goals. A discussion of the development and general significance of organizational cultures is followed by an examination of several discrete aspects. These include use of bureaucratic symbolism to enhance the image of the organization and use of "red tape" to protect the integrity of bureaucratic processes and lend importance to officialdom.

The chapter ends with a lengthy examination of the impact of new communication technologies on the culture of modern American bureaucracies. The changes are potentially revolutionary. However, thus far the forces of resistance that typically are generated by pressures for disruptive changes have held the communication revolution in check. The discussion focuses on the actual and potential impact of high-speed communications, massive storage facilities, ever-expanding message audiences, resistance to technological changes, obsolescence, privacy and secrecy issues, and many more old and new problems that have emerged. Because the political ramifications of these issues are potentially vast, they remain highly controversial.

Climates and cultures have been deemphasized by public officials and scholars alike for several reasons, notably the difficulty in measuring them because they hinge so greatly on subjective perceptions. In the public sector, the ability to document phenomena scientifically is especially crucial because claims are frequently challenged. Elusive phenomena, irrespective of their significance, do not sustain challenges well.

The reluctance to deal with value conflicts is a second major reason for neglecting climate and culture factors. Evaluations of climates and cultures are controversial. Should the military, for example, encourage a culture of unquestioning obedience or one that scrutinizes the orders of superiors? Should the cultural choice be supported by the climate created through the drill sergeant's interactions with recruits? These are debatable issues and constitute the kinds of dilemmas that administrators would rather not tackle head-on.

Regardless of the desire to shy away from sensitive issues, new message transmission technologies are forcing administrators to make decisions that have the potential to produce major changes in cultures and climates. However, their long-range consequences for organizational welfare may not be apparent for many years. These decisions are currently plagued by tremendous uncertainties because they lack precedents. With typical caution, administrators have been patterning decisions more on the past than on visions of the future.

Given the troubling uncertainties, it now seems best to opt for much greater diversity in research and decisions to adapt bureaucracies to the new communication age. Only when many different approaches are tried will it be possible to discover the combinations of cultures and climates that promise the most effective results for the future. In an age when social conditions and ideologies are changing faster than ever before, bureaucracies must add flexibility and a zeal for innovation to their cultural repertoires.

Notes

1. Everett M. Rogers and Rekha Agarwala Rogers, *Communication in Organizations* (New York: Free Press, 1976), 73-74.
2. Jeffrey Pfeffer, *Power in Organizations* (Marshfield, Mass.: Pitman, 1981), 186; for some examples, see 191.
3. R. Wayne Pace and Don F. Faules, *Organizational Communication,* 2d ed. (Englewood Cliffs, N.J.: Prentice-Hall, 1989), 121-122.
4. Ibid., 125-126.
5. Martha Glenn Cox, "Enter the Stranger: Unanticipated Effects of Communication on the Success of an Organizational Newcomer," in *Organization—Communication: Emerging Perspectives I,* Lee Thayer, ed. (Norwood, N.J.: Ablex, 1986), 41.
6. Robert Pear, "Blacks and the Elitist Stereotype," *New York Times,* September 29, 1987.
7. Lloyd Etheredge, "Government Learning: An Overview," in *The Handbook of Political Behavior,* vol. 2, Samuel L. Long, ed. (New York: Plenum, 1981), 111-112.
8. Doris A. Graber, *Verbal Behavior and Politics* (Urbana: University of Illinois Press, 1976), 258-269.
9. Marshall Scott Poole, "Communication and Organizational Climates: Review, Critique, and a New Perspective," in *Organizational Communication: Traditional Themes and New Directions,* Robert D. McPhee and Phillip K. Tompkins, eds. (Beverly Hills, Calif.: Sage, 1985), 86-91.
10. For evidence that climate affects performance when other factors are held constant, see David M. Hedge, Donald C. Menzel, and George H. Williams, "Regulatory Attitudes and Behavior: The Case of Surface Mining Regulations," *Western Political Quarterly* 41 (June 1988): 323-340.
11. Terence R. Mitchell and James R. Larson, Jr., *People in Organizations: An Introduction to Organizational Behavior,* 3d ed. (New York: McGraw-Hill, 1987), 184.
12. James Q. Wilson, *Bureaucracy: What Government Agencies Do and Why They Do It* (New York: Basic Books, 1989), 95-101. The Forest Service story is detailed in Herbert Kaufman, *The Forest Ranger: A Study in Administrative Behavior* (Baltimore: Johns Hopkins Press, 1967); the FBI story is told by Thomas Gid Powers, *Secrecy and Power: The Life of J. Edgar Hoover* (New York: Free Press, 1987); and the story of the Social Security Administration can be found in Martha Derthick, *Agency under Stress: The Social Security Administration and American Government* (Washington, D.C.: Brookings Institution, 1991) and Derthick, *Policymaking for Social Security* (Washing-

ton, D.C.: Brookings Institution, 1979).

13. Herbert Kaufman, *The Administrative Behavior of Federal Bureau Chiefs* (Washington, D.C.: Brookings Institution, 1981), 139-141.

14. Ibid., 142.

15. Ibid., 143.

16. Phillip K. Tompkins, "Management Qua Communication in Rocket Research and Development," *Communication Monographs* 44 (March 1977): 1-26.

17. Poole, "Communication and Organizational Climates," 79.

18. Philip H. Jos, Mark E. Tompkins, and Steven W. Hays, "In Praise of Difficult People: A Portrait of the Committed Whistleblower," *Public Administration Review* 49 (November/December 1989): 555-558.

19. "Congress Sends Bush Bill to Protect Whistle Blowers," *Chicago Tribune,* March 22, 1989.

20. John P. Plumlee, Jay D. Starling, with Kenneth W. Kramer, "Citizen Participation in Water Quality Planning: A Case Study of Perceived Failure," *Administration and Society* 16 (February 1985): 455-473.

21. Ibid., 462.

22. Poole, "Communication and Organizational Climates," 86-91.

23. Etheredge, "Government Learning: An Overview," 110-113.

24. Kaufman, *The Administrative Behavior of Federal Bureau Chiefs,* 139-141.

25. Phillip K. Tompkins and George Cheney, "Communication and Unobtrusive Control in Contemporary Organizations," in *Organizational Communication: Traditional Themes and New Directions,* 184.

26. Raymond S. Ross and Jean Ricky Ross, *Small Groups in Organizational Settings* (Englewood Cliffs, N.J.: Prentice-Hall, 1989), 64-65.

27. Robert T. Golembiewski, *Humanizing Public Organizations* (Mount Airy, Md.: Lomond, 1985), 14-17.

28. Ibid., 24.

29. Steven Kelman, *Making Public Policy* (New York: Basic Books, 1987), 169-170.

30. Wilson, *Bureaucracy,* 221.

31. Jerald Hage, Michael Aiken, and Cora B. Marrett, "Organization Structure and Communications," in *The Study of Organizations,* Daniel Katz, Robert L. Kahn, and J. Stacy Adams, eds. (San Francisco: Jossey-Bass, 1982), 302-315.

32. Rosabeth M. Kanter, "Three Tiers for Innovation Research," *Communication Research* 15 (October 1988): 509-523; for other examples, see Golembiewski, *Humanizing Public Organizations,* chaps. 2 and 3.

33. Keon S. Chi, *State Futures Commissions: A Survey of Long-Range Planning Experiences* (Lexington, Ky.: Council of State Governments, 1983).

34. Rogers and Rogers reports an interesting study of the spotty adoption of mandated changes in schools in Thailand. Rogers and Rogers, *Communication in Organizations,* 166-171.

35. Washington Efficiency and Accountability Commission, "Dollars and Sense," *Washington Journal* 2 (April 16, 1990): 1, 4-5.

36. See Chapter 5.

37. Wilson, *Bureaucracy,* 229-230.

38. Terrance L. Albrecht and Vickie A. Ropp, "Communicating about Innovation in Networks of Three U.S. Organizations," *Journal of Communication* 34 (Summer 1984): 78-91.

39. Dennis K. Mumby, *Communication and Power in Organizations: Discourse, Ideology and Domination* (Norwood, N.J.: Ablex, 1988), 8.

40. Wilson, *Bureaucracy,* 91.

41. Maryan S. Schall, "A Communication Rules Approach to Organizational Culture," *Administrative Science Quarterly* 28 (1983): 557. The importance of the macroculture is discussed in Virginia Hill Ingersoll and Guy B. Adams, "Beyond Organizational Boundaries: Exploring the Managerial Myth," *Administration and Society* 18 (November 1986): 360-381.

42. Ann Donnellon, Barbara Gray, and Michel G. Bougon, "Communication, Meaning, and Organized Action," *Administrative Science Quarterly* 31 (1986): 44.

43. Schall, "A Communication Rules Approach to Organizational Culture," 562.

44. Mumby, *Communication and Power in Organizations,* 95-125.

45. Schall, "A Communication Rules Approach to Organizational Culture," 575.

46. Michael Thompson and Aaron Wildavsky, "A Cultural Theory of Information Bias in Organizations," *Journal of Management Studies* 23 (May 1986): 277.

47. Kaufman, *The Forest Ranger.*

48. Kelman, *Making Public Policy,* 152-153.

49. Tom F. Carney, "Organizational Communication: Emerging Trends, Problems, and Opportunities," in *Organization—Communication: Emerging Perspectives I,* 9.

50. Elizabeth A. Martin and Louis P. Cusella, "Persuading the Adjudicator: Conflict Tactics in the Grievance Procedure," in *Communication Yearbook 9,* Margaret L. McLaughlin, ed. (Beverly Hills, Calif.: Sage, 1986), 533; for a similar analysis, see Elihu Katz, Michael Gurevitch, Brenda Danet, and Tsiyona Peled, "Petitions and Prayers: A Method for the Content Analysis of Persuasive Appeals," *Social Forces* 47 (1969): 447-463.

51. Martin and Cusella, "Persuading the Adjudicator," 540.

52. Murray Edelman, *The Symbolic Uses of Politics* (Urbana: University of Illinois Press, 1964), 134-146.

53. Quoted in Gerald M. Goldhaber, *Organizational Communication,* 3d ed. (Dubuque, Iowa: Wm. C. Brown, 1983), 133.

54. R. Richard Ritti, "The Social Bases of Organizational Knowledge," in *Organization—Communication: Emerging Perspectives I,* 108.

55. Ibid., 112.

56. Gary Washburn, "Red Tape Bogs Down CTA, Report Says," *Chicago Tribune,* August 17, 1988.

57. Raymond A. Rosenfeld, "An Expansion and Application of Kaufman's Model of Red Tape: The Case of Community Development Block Grants," *Western Political Quarterly* 37 (December 1984): 603.

58. Robert D. Hershey, Jr., "Where Personal Finances Are in the Public Eye," *New York Times,* August 22, 1988.

59. Herbert Kaufman, *Red Tape: Its Origins, Uses, and Abuses* (Washington, D.C.: Brookings Institution, 1977), 29; also see Kaufman, *The Administrative Behavior of Federal Bureau Chiefs,* 42.

60. Rosenfeld, "An Expansion and Application of Kaufman's Model of Red Tape," 604-605.

61. Ibid., 606.

62. Ibid., 605.

63. Stephen Frantzich, "Legislatures and the Revolution in Communications and Information Processing: Untangling the Linkage Between Technology and Politics," American Political Science Association paper, 1990.

64. Alana Northrop, Kenneth L. Kraemer, Debora Dunkle, and John Leslie King, "Payoffs from Computerization: Lessons over Time," *Public Administration Review* 50 (September/October 1990): 508-511.

65. Sharon L. Caudle, "Information Technology and Managing Public Management Choices," American Political Science Association paper, Chicago, 1987.
66. Richard K. Caputo, *Management and Information Systems in Human Services* (New York: Haworth, 1988), 6.
67. Northrop et al., "Payoffs from Computerization," 512.
68. Caputo, *Management and Information Systems in Human Services,* 131-132.
69. Benjamin D. Singer, "Organizational Communication and Social Disassembly: An Essay on Electronic Anomie," in *Organization—Communication: Emerging Perspectives I,* 226.
70. Mitchell and Larson, *People in Organizations,* 315.
71. Adapted from Ronald Rice, "Computer-Mediated Communication and Organizational Innovation," *Journal of Communication* 37 (Autumn 1987): 77.
72. Stephen Frantzich, *Computers in Congress: The Politics of Information* (Beverly Hills, Calif.: Sage, 1982), 16.
73. James L. Gibson, John M. Ivancevich, and James H. Donnelly, Jr., eds., *Organizations Close-up: A Book of Readings,* 5th ed. (Plano, Texas: Business Publications, 1985), 263.
74. Office of Technology Assessment, *Informing the Nation: Federal Information Dissemination in an Electronic Age* (Washington, D.C.: Government Printing Office, 1988), 201.
75. Ibid., 207. These and related access problems are discussed on pp. 183-203.
76. Stephen L. Wasby, "Technology and Communication in a Federal Court: The Ninth Circuit," Midwest Political Science Association paper, Chicago, 1987, 27.
77. Sara Kiesler, "The Hidden Messages in Computer Networks," *Harvard Business Review* 64 (1986): 46-60.
78. Singer, "Organizational Communication and Social Disassembly," 223.
79. David Bollier, "The Social Impact of Widespread Computer Use: Implications for East-West Relations," *Communications and Society Forum Report* (Truro, Mass.: Aspen Institute, 1989), 9-14. Also see James M. Danziger, William H. Dutton, Rob Kling, and Kenneth L. Kraemer, *Computers and Politics* (New York: Columbia University Press, 1982).
80. Bollier, "The Social Impact of Widespread Computer Use," 9-10.
81. Caudle, "Information Technology and Managing Public Management Choices," 13.
82. Caputo, *Management and Information Systems in Human Services,* 106.
83. Caudle, "Information Technology and Managing Public Management Choices," 6.
84. Oscar H. Gandy, Jr., "The Surveillance Society: Information Technology and Bureaucratic Social Control," *Journal of Communication* 39 (Summer 1989): 61-76.
85. "Years of Computer Data May Be Lost in Old Tapes," *Chicago Tribune,* January 2, 1991.
86. E. Sam Overman and Don F. Simanton, "Iron Triangles and Issues Networks of Information Policy," *Public Administration Review* 46 (November 1986): 585.
87. Kenneth L. Kraemer and J. L. King, *Municipal Information Systems: Evaluation and Policy Related Research,* vol. 1 (Washington, D.C.: National Technical Information Service, 1975), 492.

External Communication: The Public Relations Face

The Jekyll and Hyde Faces of External Communication

The Positive Face

In their book *Leadership and Innovation: A Biographical Perspective on Entrepreneurs in Government,* political scientists Jameson Doig and Erwin Hargrove analyzed the careers of thirteen successful top-level administrative officials. One characteristic was crucial to success in all cases: the ability to generate support from key external constituencies such as Congress, the president, interest groups, and the general public.[1] As James Webb, administrator of the National Aeronautics and Space Administration, put it: "The environment is not something apart from the endeavor; it is not just something in which the endeavor operates and to which it needs to adjust; it is an integral part of the endeavor itself.... The total (executive) job encompasses external as well as internal elements, and success is as dependent on effectiveness in the one as in the other."[2]

James Q. Wilson reached a similar conclusion: "The principal source of power is a constituency ... the real work of the government executive *is* to curry favor and placate critics."[3] These and similar analyses point to the significance of external communications. Of course, their significance reaches far beyond the power games played by public officials to support the goals of their agencies and their own personal goals. As discussed in Chapter 5, transmitting information across organizational boundaries is intrinsically important. The nation's social, political, and economic health hinges on the accurate and timely transmission by public agencies of crucial information such as economic indexes and forecasts, health and disease data, crime information, and census data. Similarly, boundary-spanning communication among government agencies performing related tasks is essential to avoid undue overlap and policy incoherence. It is also important to inform the public about available services as well as the financial and service contributions and behavior expected from citizens. Communication with various publics is particularly crucial when governmental effectiveness hinges on their behavior. The Internal Revenue Service commissioner, for example, has testified before Congress that the public's perception of the efficiency of the IRS is a crucial element in maintaining voluntary compliance.[4]

The dividing line is fuzzy between public information activities, discussed as boundary-spanning communication in Chapter 5, and public relations activities, which are the focus of this chapter. Both involve dispensing information. Usually the distinction is based on the fact that public relations places more emphasis on creating a favorable image for an agency so that its personnel and activities may be viewed positively by constituencies that are deemed important to the agency. However, since image-building concerns play some part in most communications, it is often difficult to differentiate between primarily informative messages and those that are mostly image-oriented.

The Negative Face

In the United States, normative reservations about persuasive messages— often called propaganda—are deeply ingrained because to most people propaganda means slanted information. Allowing public officials to disseminate such information, and even paying them to do so, seems contrary to the ethical requirement that public officials owe the truth, the whole truth, and nothing but the truth to the American people. Citizens in a democracy, it is argued, must be well informed, but the information should be value-neutral so that it does not prejudice their judgments.

In actual fact, despite fears about distorted information, most of what is dispensed by public agencies is reasonably accurate. It may not be the whole truth, but it is unlikely to be deliberately false. The late Senator J. William Fulbright's well-founded concerns about misleading information tactics used by the Pentagon to promote support for particular weapons systems and for the Vietnam War were news precisely because the tactics were exceptional.[5] Disdain for persuasive messages also ignores the widely acknowledged political requirement that leaders in a democratic society must communicate persuasively with citizens whom they are expected to lead.

Because of the irreconcilability of the democratic ideal of totally open choice with the requirements of effective government, restraints on government public relations activities have remained predominantly informal. Numerous attempts to impose legal restraints have proved ineffective.[6] Among the few formal restraints are the prohibitions barring the U.S.

Information Agency from distributing its propaganda materials inside the United States and some restrictions on government purchasing of advertisements.[7] The United States Code, Title 18, Section 1913, makes lobbying by government officials a crime.[8] However, this anti-lobbying act has been loosely construed so that it does not apply to information disseminated by government agencies in the routine performance of their activities. Such messages are presumably impartial and geared to inform rather than persuade. The act does prevent officials from contributing money to political campaigns.

Public relations efforts have remained organizationally decentralized and haphazard because of the reluctance to undertake them. The United States, unlike many democratic as well as authoritarian countries, has no major departments of information or communication at either the federal or state levels. Efforts within various agencies to centralize control over external information flows by requiring officials to clear their speeches through agency heads, or even through the White House, have also floundered because of the ingrained reluctance to restrain free speech. Similarly, pressures exerted on the agency heads by various administrations to tout the president's programs have met with meager success.

The lack of centralized control over external communications explains why public officials in the United States often do not speak with one voice about major issues. When authoritative pronouncements are contradictory, audiences become confused, annoyed, and often cynical. For example, when the State Department announces that the United States will not release a Soviet spy suspect in trade for an American spy suspect, while the White House press office announces that "all options are open," more than embarrassment of individual officials is at stake.[9] Important messages by one agency are often weakened or totally neutralized by contrary messages from another. Moreover, as pointed out in Chapter 2, the inability to shield particularly damaging information also undermines the ability to engage in effective public relations activities.

Communication Strategies

The Uses of Political Rhetoric

Creating favorable political images is often largely a matter of rhetoric rather than substance. For example, when President Reagan wanted a new missile program, he talked about "closing the window of vulnerability" in order to make the missiles acceptable to a Congress and public eager to protect the United States from foreign aggressors. When the phrase did not persuade enough members of Congress that the missiles were needed for defense, the weapon was labeled "the peacekeeper" to dampen congressional opposition. Members of Congress, it was hoped, would not want to be seen as opponents of peacekeeping. Calling a program for the mentally retarded a school for "exceptional children" or a birth control clinic a "family planning center" creates a positive image for activities that might otherwise arouse negative reactions. In this way, Jeffrey Pfeffer points out, "Language, symbols, rituals and ceremonies are used to manage the process by which actions and events are given meaning." [10] The common government practice of using meaningless names like "Department of Human Services" or acronyms that baffle the uninitiated suggests that top-level decision makers are often unaware of the importance of images linked to an agency's name. Besides lacking meaning, acronyms are also impractical because they are difficult to locate in telephone directories. [11]

There is little quarrel with the notion that it is appropriate for public officials to convey their interpretation of a situation by framing messages that express these meanings. Obviously, the opportunity to guide people's beliefs through such messages is politically important. "The critical element in political maneuver for advantage is the creation of meaning: the construction of beliefs about events, policies, leaders, and crises," states political scientist Murray Edelman." [12] Since message framing can shape opinions and guide actions, these effects must be considered by public officials. As Edelman sees it, "The strategic need is to immobilize opposition and mobilize support. . . . The key tactic must always be the evocation of interpretations that legitimize favored courses of action and threaten or reassure people so as to encourage them to be supportive or to remain quiescent." [13] Given that the power to define issues in each society is held and used by established elites, it is also clear to most observers of the political scene, as Pfeffer states, that "the task of political language and symbolic activity is to rationalize and justify decisions that are largely the result of power and influence" and that "without this legitimation and rationalization, the exercise of power is hindered." [14]

Since it is difficult to express complex ideas clearly, charges that messages are deceptive or biased are common. A number of scholars who have examined the meanings conveyed through political language contend that all messages inevitably reflect a particular point of view. They also contend that meanings are always sufficiently unclear to leave room for diverse interpretations. In their view, conflicts over the meaning of political messages are the essence of politics. [15] Whenever message framers wrestle with the problem of trying to avoid misinterpretation, whatever the proclivities of the audience, they become acutely aware that ambiguity is endemic in political language.

Despite strong temptations to bend the truth, most agencies stress the importance of honesty and the avoidance of outright lies, which are deemed unethical and unprofessional. Tactically, lies are also undesirable because they are not only hard to construct and maintain successfully but also risky in terms of a potential loss of credibility. The excerpts in "Ground Rules for Press Relations at the Department of State" on pages 244-245, drawn from a 1982 State Department memorandum to its public affairs officers, illustrate this emphasis. The memorandum was issued to clarify the ground rules for conversations with the press as well as communications between public affairs officials and their internal information sources.[16] Interviews with public affairs officers show strong support for obeying these rules, along with realization that circumstances may compel them to skirt the truth at times or even tell an outright lie when the truth would harm important public interests.[17]

While outright lying is shunned most of the time, it is far more common to withhold information and overemphasize desirable news or slight undesirable matters. Good news is shouted and bad news is whispered. For example, announcements of new programs rarely stress their cost or how the public will have to pay for them. To prevent unfavorable publicity, hospitals, for example, often shy away from publishing morbidity and mortality figures, and employment agencies focus attention on successful placements rather than the hard-core unemployed. The Corps of Engineers may call attention to its most successful construction projects while keeping silent about its failures. To avoid unfavorable publicity, organizations may also prohibit informal communication between their employees and the media on selected topics. They may designate special spokespersons to make it more likely that the organization will speak with one voice and that no harmful information will be leaked. Given the media's penchant for trying to ferret out negative stories, avoidance of negative publicity may be a primary concern of public relations efforts.

As Martha Derthick concluded after studying the Social Security Administration,

> Organizational leaders in any milieu, public or private, tend to emphasize the strengths and obfuscate the weaknesses of their organizations in order to sustain morale internally and elicit confidence externally. Candor is not intrinsic to the role; a certain amount of calculated delusion is. In a political setting, which is to say in a public agency, incentives to present the *appearance* of success are especially powerful, because such organizations are so heavily dependent on others' confidence. Agency leaders therefore do not ordinarily testify to Congress or to presidential officials that things are going badly in their agencies unless events have given them no choice.[18]

Other Image-Building Maneuvers

As Figure 7-1 on page 246 indicates, officials have four basic strategies for using information to enhance the agency's image. When policy consider-

Ground Rules for Press Relations at the Department of State

Some Do's and Don'ts. For most officers, the following points are so commonsensical as not to bear repeating. But enough officers have asked our guidance that they may be helpful.

The first and most important is to be *honest;* we don't have to divulge everything we know, but what we do say must be accurate. And where we have to hold some facts back, the sum of what we say should not give a misleading impression.

If an officer doesn't know the facts, he shouldn't talk about the problem. The most difficult stories to clean up afterward are those which result from uninformed guesswork. Reporters are astute people; they generally know when they're talking to a spongy source, and they have no more respect for idle speculation than we do in our own reporting abroad. But in some cases they may *think* the man knows what he's talking about and go with a story. If an officer doesn't want to admit he doesn't know the facts, he can always say he's "not in a position to talk about it."

Don't talk about somebody else's problem. Let the person in charge handle it his way.

A surprising number of officers have asked what they should do when a reporter asks questions about a particularly sensitive policy problem. The answer is quite simple: tell him you just can't talk about it for the moment. The reporter won't necessarily sympathize, but he will respect your forthrightness—and will certainly prefer it to a "no comment" or to wordy evasions (which always run the risk of being misleading).

Always take or return reporters' telephone calls, even when you know you won't be able to satisfy their questions. It's a small courtesy, but courtesy oils this relationship as much as others. And you may be able to spike a story that is just plain wrong—they can be damaging, too.

Don't forget to set the ground rules *at the beginning* of a conversation with a reporter.

---

ations seem to require it, they can *withhold* information. This may be done by deliberately failing to gather information, by ignoring information that is tendered to the agency, or by keeping it secret and discussing it off the record. However, there must be legal justification for refusing to disclose information, such as claiming that secrecy is essential to protect national security or privacy rights, or that withholding is permitted under certain exceptions granted by the Freedom of Information Act.[19]

Withholding tactics, or even denying the existence of information, may be important when secrecy is essential. The need to conceal a planned raid on an illegal establishment, such as a crack house or a studio where child pornography is being created, is an example. At a time of economic difficulties it may even be wise to withhold bad economic news in order to forestall panic selling on the stock exchange. Whether

Continued

Dealing with S/PRS. We take a lot of officers' time, day-in and day-out. Interestingly, those who are most ungrudging of their time are also those who most clearly understand the impact the press can have on the department's business at home and abroad. The secretary of state and his principal deputies are *always* available to us when we need them urgently.

Apart from time, we need four things from officers in the department:

—We need *the facts* without varnish, even when (or particularly when!) they add up to a skeleton in the closet. S/PRS has a pretty good track record of discretion with sensitive information.

—We need *your guidance,* formal and informal. In tricky or sensitive situations, it's almost always better to sit down and talk the matter through, since the average written guidance is generally pretty well exhausted after the third question at the noon briefing.

—We need *absolute honesty.* The department's credibility is a matter of proud record over a long period of time, but it is tested anew every day of the year. As tempting as it may be in any given situation to shave the facts a bit, there is always another office which benefits on the same day in an equally tricky situation from the fact that the newsmen believe the department's spokesman.

—Finally, we need *ideas.* There are a lot of things going on which not only can—but ought—to be talked about if the department is to have the kind of informed support it needs from public opinion. Your offices are closer to these "discussable issues" and we would welcome your suggestions.

In closing, S/PRS would welcome an opportunity to sit down with your officers, talk all of this through, and answer their questions. If you think it helpful to do so, please let us know.

Source: Extracted from a State Department memorandum to all public affairs officers found in Stephen Hess, *The Government/Press Connection* (Washington, D.C.: Brookings Institution, 1984), 120-121.

such tactics are ethical, even when they are legal, is controversial. It is also questionable whether withholding information is wise for practical reasons because credibility is undermined if the lack of candor is discovered.

A second strategy involves the formal release of information, either through direct communication with other agencies and clients or through press releases or briefings to the mass media or disseminated through media more directly controlled by the agency. *Releasing information* through the press may have the advantage of giving it greater credibility because the media, rather than an agency suspected of being self-serving, are viewed as the source. Moreover, this strategy, particularly dissemination through the electronic media, is apt to reach a much larger audience than direct contact by the agency.

Figure 7-1   **Model of the Government Communication Process**

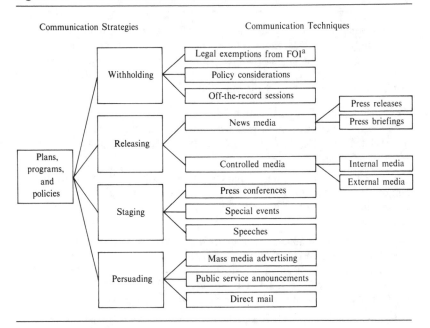

Source: Ray Eldon Hiebert, "A Model of the Government Communication Process," *Informing the People*, Lewis M. Helm, Ray Eldon Hiebert, Michael R. Naver, and Kenneth Rabin, eds. (New York: Longman, 1981), 9. Reprinted with permission.

[a] Freedom of Information Act

The disadvantage of working through the mass media is the loss of control over messages. Decisions about framing the information to present the agency in a favorable light, timing its release to the most opportune moment, and giving prominence through such factors as size of headline and placement in the newspaper or broadcast are controlled by the media. By contrast, when agencies compose and release their own media, they have full control over these matters. Examples of agency-controlled media are newsletters or information booklets and reports mailed out directly to interested parties.

A third strategy commonly used by public agencies to reach targeted audiences involves *staging special events*. These may range from declaring an Earth Day or Recycling Month to specially called press conferences, public addresses, and celebrations inaugurating a service or commemorating a historical event. Public hearings can occasionally be turned into grandstand performances that provide an opportunity for agency heads to make a reputation for themselves as well as for their agencies. In addition to the people who actually attend such events, there are potentially vast exterior audiences if the event attracts ample media coverage. The potential for reaching a mass media audience may indeed be the primary reason for staging the event.

Finally, various marketing techniques are used to disseminate *persuasive messages*. They are discussed more fully in the next section.

While favorable publicity can be highly beneficial in promoting an agency's goals, it may also be harmful. By emphasizing the positive and shrouding the negative aspects of programs and situations, public relations efforts may create false desires and expectations, often lulling observers into believing that all is well when it is not. For example, when people are falsely reassured that aircraft safety regulations meet minimum standards or that water supplies are adequate in case of fire, they may relax the watchfulness that is needed to maintain appropriate standards.[20] The National Aeronautics and Space Administration has been accused of ignoring warnings about problems with the *Challenger* space craft in its eagerness to launch the ill-fated mission to capture a public relations opportunity of stunning magnitude.[21] Similarly, as Charles Peters points out, it has been alleged that "the minutes of the Nuclear Regulatory Commission show that when the reactor was about to melt down at Three Mile Island, the commissioners were worried less about what to do to fix the reactor than they were about what they were going to say to the press." [22]

The need to engage in public relations efforts may divert an agency's energies from important substantive tasks. Publicity about new programs may generate a flood of inquiries that strain the agency's resources. This happens frequently when agencies publicize giveaways such as surplus food or mulch created from recycled organic matter. When agencies call attention to themselves through public relations activities, their visibility may make them the target of more messages than they would like from the outside, including interest-group messages. When agencies dispense or receive too much information, communication channels become clogged. Overwhelmed receivers may then ignore all messages, the essential along with the nonessential.

Targets of External Communication

External communication is a two-way street, with messages emanating from the environment reaching the agency and vice versa. Messages may travel horizontally or vertically. Horizontal messages are intended for sister agencies at similar levels of the administrative hierarchy. Generally speaking, because few formal channels exist for horizontal communications, they are usually irregular and comparatively sparse. Communications can also be vertical. Examples are messages sent upward by administrative agencies to their legislatures or downward to their clients and suppliers.

At the federal level, upward vertical messages are particularly significant. Administrative agencies need to keep in constant touch with Congress, which exercises important controls over them. As a result, all federal departments now have their own congressional liaisons.[23] Departments usually bear the brunt of the burden for promoting the concerns of agencies under their jurisdiction. They receive only occasional help from the White House. At the state and local levels, various organized political bodies represent the collective interests of the membership. Examples are the National Conference of State Legislatures, the National Governors' Association, and the U.S. Conference of Mayors.[24]

Having personal connections to congressional targets is invaluable for successful external communication. Connections to units directly involved in funding decisions affect an agency's scope of activities and even its survival. During his many trips to Washington to solicit funds for Chicago, the city's mayor, Richard Daley, was fortunate to have Dan Rostenkowski, a fellow Democrat and Illinois citizen, in control of the purse strings as chairman of the House Ways and Means Committee. The most frequent links between federal agencies and Congress, in person or through written reports, are congressional committees and subcommittees involved with the agency and congressional staffs that gather most of the information. The secretary of defense, for instance, is apt to court the leaders of the Armed Services committees in both houses; the treasury secretary will woo the Ways and Means Committee chairman, and the secretary of agriculture will consult with the appropriate Agriculture committees.

Since many different committees and subcommittees in both the Senate and the House are usually involved with the work of major agencies, maintaining adequate contacts with all of them on a regular basis can be quite arduous. In fact, government executives devote much more time than their private sector counterparts to wooing external constituencies. Typical business executives of large companies ordinarily meet with their board of directors less than ten times a year. Government executives with a comparable scope of responsibilities meet with congressional committees—counterparts of a board of directors—more than twice as often. Moreover, while board of director meetings are generally harmonious, meetings with congressional committees are often acrimonious, with the executives' requests frequently being denied. The costs of these often wasted efforts are high in that they drain valuable time from other agency activities. As James Q. Wilson has noted: "Government executives must spend so much time coping with their agencies' external environment that they have relatively little time to shape its internal life."[25]

Top administrators are usually briefed for encounters with external constituencies by their expert staffs. These people may be trained in public relations principles and techniques and devote all their time to communication tasks or they may also have other responsibilities. Briefing books are frequently prepared. Briefings are particularly thorough for encounters with appropriations and oversight committees. When committees ask questions for which top administrators are not prepared, the missing information may have to be gathered for subsequent insertion into the official records.

Report writing has become a finely honed art because agencies that are able to produce and transmit ample and convincing data about their achievements and needs are more likely to survive and flourish. Expertise in creating bureaucratic propaganda is particularly important for organizations that cannot appeal to large constituencies for grass-roots support. The preparation of reports requires excellent writing skills and familiarity with the technical and political aspects of the issues under discussion. It also involves knowing the mind-set and idiosyncrasies of those receiving the reports as well as the current political setting in both the receiver's and the sender's agency.[26]

Government reports have been dubbed "bureaucratic propaganda" by scholars, who point out their image-building potential. Official reports accomplish this mission by muffling differences of opinion and interests within agencies and painting a glowing best-case scenario of an agency's prospects and achievements.[27] The goals, as enumerated by David Altheide and John Johnson, are "to obtain further funding, promote organizational careers, assign responsibility for a particular act to an 'enemy,' and in general 'cover your ass' from revelation before a sanctioning body." [28]

Federal agencies must also keep in touch with other parts of the executive branch. Contact with the president and the presidential staff is made largely through the heads of the respective departments. For bureau chiefs and other officials below the top administrative levels, contact is rarely direct. When Herbert Kaufman examined the activities of federal bureau chiefs, he found that they mostly contacted the executive branch through the Office of Management and Budget, which exercises budgetary controls. Otherwise, their external messages went largely to other offices in the department in which the bureau was located. Many of these contacts occurred during staff meetings. Other contacts were lateral, to other federal agencies outside the department whose work intertwined with their bureau's activities. Kaufman estimates that "taking stock of both lateral and hierarchical links, the chiefs probably spent as much time with elements of the executive branch as they did with components of the legislative branch." [29]

External communications also address a variety of nongovernmental publics. The messages may be designed to instruct the agency's clients or to gain support for its goals or to placate its opposition. Constructing persuasive messages to gain support for controversial governmental programs can be extraordinarily difficult. The Tennessee Valley Authority, established in 1933 to produce electric power in the Tennessee River region and control floods and navigation, is a good example of the challenges that must be met when painful, disruptive changes are initiated.[30] Citizen support had to be mobilized for economic development plans that would be very costly for the affected communities.

Convincing farmers that they must move off their lands to make room for dams and reservoirs was especially difficult. Because the issues to be explained were so complex, the agency felt that adequate communication required face-to-face encounters in public meetings. However, the farmers who needed to be addressed were not eager to come, so the agency used the tactic of promising that attendees could apply at the meeting for free fertilizer. The tactic worked, bringing the target audience to the meeting and suggesting to them that the TVA project might carry at least some benefits for them. Still, it remained difficult to convince the farmers that the costs to them were tolerable.

To make transmission of difficult messages easier, they are often directed to opinion leaders to whom others in the community turn for information and advice. This two-step flow approach is based on the fact that advice from a known and trusted source is more persuasive than advice from strangers. Moreover, the opinion leader usually knows how to tailor messages to the needs of particular audiences. For example, local public health physicians may find it easier to transmit information about an influenza epidemic and a preventive vaccination program to neighborhoods they know well than would the U.S. Surgeon General appearing on television from Washington. Hence, messages are more likely to be effective for a target audience when they are routed by federal public health authorities via local opinion leaders in a multiple-step approach that may involve several levels of opinion leaders. The trick, of course, is to identify appropriate opinion leaders for various types of messages. Who, for instance, could effectively carry the anti-alcoholism message of the National Institute on Alcohol Abuse and Alcoholism to pre-teens and their parents and teachers? The Children's Television Workshop, producers of the alcoholism prevention campaign, recommended a music video that featured the Jets, a performing group who were popular with pre-teens.[31]

Contact with legislators and the executive branch, as well as with average citizens and various interest groups, can be very time-consuming. The federal bureau chiefs studied by Kaufman "probably averaged about as much time with a host of nongovernmental interests as with either branch of government." Most of these contacts were with various types of organized interest groups. To keep these lobbies favorable or at least neutral, all bureaus "had programs to explain their policies to the outside world, to discover the views and concerns of external groups and the media," and to enlist the support of favorable groups, especially when unfavorable ones were on the prowl.[32] Successful communication with various interest groups is often essential in sustaining existing programs and launching new ones. For example, until agencies concerned with the problem of homelessness were able to alert various political elites and the general public to the problem, discussion of programs for the homeless was absent from the public agenda.

Public relations activities may also be essential to appease disaffected external publics whose complaints to the legislature or other influential bodies might harm the agency. To counteract such criticism, it may be necessary to mobilize agency supporters or counter-constituencies or solicit mass media backing so that legislative support is not lost. Maintaining support in the face of opposition may require regular contacts in meetings, speeches to professional groups, responses to requests, and the like. Advisory commissions may have to be set up. If retrenchment or major changes in services or eligibility rules are in the offing, they need to be carefully explained and justified to publics who may feel that they are adversely affected.

Public Information Offices

Structural Arrangements

There is little agreement about how agencies should be structured to carry out public relations activities. Preferences depend on the goals to be maximized. For example, in order to prevent the Federal Energy Administration (FEA) from casting itself in an unduly rosy light, Congress decreed that public information and relations functions should be kept separate from other operations. Therefore, when Congress extended the mandate of the agency in 1976, Senators Floyd Haskel (D-Colorado) and Henry Jackson (D-Washington) proposed an Office of Energy Information and Analysis within FEA that was to be explicitly separated from other parts of the agency. The senators believed that this was the only way to ensure that data received from the agency would be free from any taint of advocacy. Their proposal became part of the final legislation.[33] In most other agencies, public affairs offices are more closely integrated to assure coordination of efforts with the agency whose needs they serve.

Internal and external public relations efforts may be viewed as distinct enterprises, pursuing different strategies, and therefore may be assigned to different offices within the agency. Alternatively, the strategies for maintaining internal morale and gaining external support may be deemed basically similar, warranting a combination of these activities in one office. Questions have also arisen about appropriate structures to facilitate coordination of public relations activities when agencies have many local branches. What is the most desirable degree of centralization? If public relations activities are handled locally, they can be geared to local concerns,

Figure 7-2   Organizational Chart of the Office of Public Affairs in the Department of Agriculture

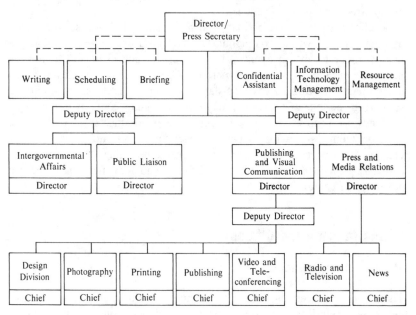

but this may lead to fragmentation and inconsistencies among local branches that could be avoided through more central control.

How is the typical public affairs office organized? Again, there is a great deal of variety, much of it dictated by the wide diversity of tasks performed by public agencies. Moreover, beyond the top levels in the executive and legislative branches, information about the organization of public affairs offices is scarce. All that can be said about the following description of the Agriculture Department's Office of Governmental and Public Affairs—which underwent a major reorganization in 1980 and in 1990 was succeeded by the Office of Public Affairs, depicted in Figure 7-2—is that the configurations are not untypical for a large agency directly involved with multiple publics.[34] The fact that the same agency used two different patterns to accomplish the same goals illustrates the old adage that there is always more than one way to skin the proverbial cat. In 1990, as had been the case in 1980, it was the task of Agriculture's public affairs staff to maintain liaison with other governmental units, the mass media, and the public at large. They also coordinated and provided support for communication services rendered by other units within the Agriculture Department. These tasks were accomplished by a staff exceeding 1,200 information specialists throughout the country.

An assistant secretary for governmental and public affairs (now called director/press secretary), appointed by the president, headed the 1980 operation, which combined public affairs and external liaison functions. In other agencies these functions are often kept separate. The secretary was assisted by a director of public affairs, who had the largest staff, a director of congressional affairs, and a director of intergovernmental affairs. Again, in other agencies, responsibilities may be divided somewhat differently. Currently, as Figure 7-2 indicates, there are two deputy directors in Agriculture's Office of Public Affairs. One combines intergovernmental affairs and public liaison; the other is in charge of media relations and various publishing and visual communication functions. Since the director doubles as press secretary, staff agencies include such functions as writing, scheduling, briefing, as well as resource management, information technology, and one assistant charged with confidential matters.

Following the 1980 reorganization, Agriculture added a Special Reports Division, which included directors of Hispanic information, consumer information, international information, and rural information, among others. That division no longer exists, its functions having been absorbed by more generally oriented information units. As Figure 7-2 shows, there is now greater emphasis on dividing work according to the nature of the media and the various technical functions involved in publishing information in the different media. Besides preparing news releases and briefings as well as coordinating releases and briefings from other units, the Office of Public Affairs prepares and coordinates speeches, feature articles, congressional testimony, and broadcasts, including many tailored for special audiences such as women, blacks, or Hispanics. The department also publishes books, magazines, brochures, technical reports, and newsletters that must be edited and coordinated, and has film, radio, and television units that produce training films, videotapes, and radio and television spots.

The major reorganization in 1980 was guided by two widely prevalent concerns. One was the realization that public affairs considerations must be part of all major decisions and that public affairs personnel must therefore be centrally located and given sufficient prestige and authority to be consulted in decision making at the highest levels. The director of public information should not, as often happens, be the odd person out. For this reason, the Office of Governmental and Public Affairs was made part of the secretary of Agriculture's office. The second concern relates to the common difficulty of coordinating an agency's diverse and far-flung activities. Many issues relating to external liaison and information activities originate at local levels and can best be resolved there, but local solutions must also be coordinated with the efforts of the agency as a whole and with the work of related agencies at local, state, and federal levels. The Agriculture Department's structures attempted to provide this coordination without impeding diversity.[35]

Public Relations Staffs at Work

Message Channels. Modern public relations agents use a vast array of techniques to disseminate messages, ranging from personal contacts and mass-media channels to videocassettes, direct mail, computer services, and conferences. Contacts may also be made through appearances at congressional hearings, public exhibits, speeches before key organizations, and speeches by supportive congressmen who then insert them into the *Congressional Record*. When agencies do not wish to be tied directly to particular messages, they may release them surreptitiously as leaks planted by their own staffs or cooperating individuals.

As Table 7-1 shows, dissemination formats vary in such factors as cost effectiveness, update flexibility, and the ability to individualize messages. Videotapes that explain a program, for example, are relatively inexpensive to create and keep current. The Social Security Administration uses them extensively, although they lack the personal touch that might come from direct telephone contact with a Social Security client. Recorded telephone messages not only have the advantages of low cost and round-the-clock access but also can be offered in multilingual versions. However, they also lack the personal contact that may be essential. Other tactics are weekly news bulletins or in-house magazines and newsletters that keep staffs informed of the agency's goals. When issues are very complex, news briefings may be given to explain the story to reporters. Nonetheless time and space constraints in the mass media may make it impossible to supply audiences with needed details.

Agencies such as the Treasury Department, the Postal Service, and the military often use paid mass media advertisements or free advertising donated by the media, which are known as public service advertisements, or PSAs. Both radio and television at the national and local level air thousands of PSAs each year. Among them are appeals by the Environmental Protection Agency for automobile pollution inspection, pleas by the Internal Revenue Service to file returns early, the Forest Service's Smokey the Bear campaign urging caution to prevent forest fires, and the Postal Service's eagle promising to deliver packages more swiftly and cheaply than competing private carriers. Judged by the volume of its messages, the national government ranks among the top twenty-five advertisers in the nation.[36] Table 7-1 indicates the variety of advertising media available for government messages and explains their advantages and disadvantages.

Public agencies must often advertise in order to attract clients or potential recruits. For example, with the country depending on volunteers for its branches of the military or for social services like the Peace Corps or Volunteers in Service to America (VISTA), it is cheaper to reach potential candidates through advertising rather than other recruiting devices. Similarly, advertising is essential to compete with other agencies

Table 7-1   Advantages and Disadvantages of Advertising Media

Media	Advantages	Disadvantages
Wire services	Wide circulation among all mass media; story release dates spread over several days	Multiple versions of story; no control over multiple editing processes; hard to gain access
Newspapers	Wide circulation among demographically diverse audiences; frequent publication; home deliveries; relatively attentive audiences; valued because it costs money	Short shelf life; competition among many advertisements; not selectively targeted
Magazines	Selective targeting; long shelf life; relatively attentive audiences; excellent reproduction capabilities	Focus on unduly narrow audience; high costs; long lead time; cannot deal with rapidly moving events
Radio	Large audiences with some selectivity; message can be easily changed; relatively low cost; free time for PSA's	Unsuitable for complex messages; difficult to memorize; brief life span; competition from other media
Television	Extremely wide audience; low cost per client; joint audio and visual effects; free time for PSA's	Unsuitable for complex messages; brief life span; competition from other media; high costs; hard to create
Direct mail and videotapes	Highly selective circulation to targets chosen by advertiser; personalized approach creates goodwill; easy to measure success	Rejected as junk mail; expensive to create mailing lists and circulate; content not readily changed
Billboards and posters	Repeated exposure to targeted audiences; size may permit more graphic detail; cannot be discarded by audience	Message must be brief and simple; high cost of renting advertising space; low prestige of channel

Source: Compiled by author.

and government entities for a share of tourist, convention, and trade money. Many states and cities now have convention and visitor's bureaus with multimillion-dollar budgets. Audience surveys suggest that the public does pay attention to government advertisements, particularly when they relate to health and safety matters.[37]

Target Audiences.   To determine appropriate information for audiences being targeted, their needs, desires, and proclivities are investigated with the aid of social science research tools such as surveys, focus groups, interviews, and ethnographic observations. For example, the Parks and Recreation Division of Minnesota's Department of Natural Resources successfully used surveys to discover what types of facilities would revive fading attendance at public parks. When state and local government officials wanted to build a new airport in Denver, Colorado, they astutely used polling to establish that the public was eager to have the airport.[38] The polls supplemented other more conventional activities designed to position the

Figure 7-3 Three Layers of Major Publics

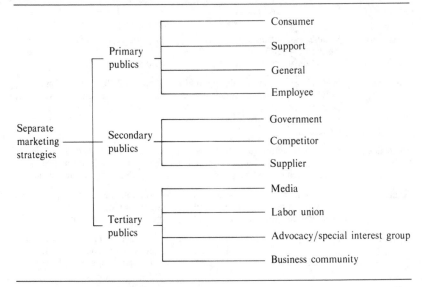

Source: John L. Crompton and Charles W. Lamb, Jr., *Marketing Government and Social Services* (New York: Wiley, © 1986), 34. Reprinted with permission.

issue appropriately on the public agenda and to promote it. After polls have been analyzed, various public relations strategies are developed for diverse target groups such as young people, medical experts, tobacco growers, or congressmen. Direct-mail campaigns or fliers distributed house to house have also been used to influence the behavior of external publics. Good public relations also involves evaluation of the results. Such evaluations are built into the overall research design.[39]

Problems posed by the diversity of the publics to which agencies must appeal are highlighted in *Marketing Government and Social Services* by John Crompton and Charles Lamb.[40] Figure 7-3 presents a diagram in which major publics are classified in three layers: primary, secondary, and tertiary. Depending on the nature of the agency and the particular problem, the composition of each layer will vary. For example, media publics in the tertiary layer might well be primary in many situations. Each public in each layer may require different marketing strategies.

"Benefits Sought by the Major Publics of a High School" on pages 258-259 illustrates what might be involved in handling the public relations activities of a public high school. The box identifies the various publics and suggests the qualities or benefits that would favorably impress each of them. For example, parents might be inclined to support the school primarily because they have learned about its excellent college preparation program, while the general public would be more responsive to appeals indicating that the school's excellence raises local property values. This box highlights the fact that successful marketing is grounded in thorough knowledge of prospective clients rather than in a probably futile effort to sell a service on terms that best suit the agency's needs.

Public relations activities that tell publics what they want to hear are often condemned as blue smoke and mirrors. But at its professional best such image building should not be a sham. Rather, public relations professionals should research what their various clients want prompted chiefly by the kind of concern with public opinion that democracy prizes. Then they should advise their agency to strive to implement these goals so that the image—the beliefs, ideas, and impressions conveyed by the agency—matches the reality. When that happens, public relations activities become an exercise in responsiveness rather than manipulation. Unfortunately, this ideal is not practiced often enough.

Interactions with the Press

The Love-Hate Relationship

The dearth of readily available official channels for external communication forces government agencies to rely on the mass media. Their relationship is frequently uneasy because the two institutions are dependent on each other, yet the pursuit of their diverse goals produces serious conflicts of interest between them. The primary goal of most of the media is to produce interesting stories, preferably full of conflict and evil and heartbreak with only minor concern about their positive or negative consequences on the institutions and people featured in the story. Moreover, the role model favored by American media casts them as watchdogs over government, charged with ferreting out and publicizing misbehavior in the public sector. Hence, there are strong pressures to produce negative coverage.

Government agencies, by contrast, are very much concerned about the political consequences of coverage. Publicity officials therefore try to entice the media to cover stories that agencies wish to publicize, irrespective of their entertainment values, and to do so from perspectives that favor the agency's positions. Agencies also seek to prevent the media from prying into matters that they want to keep out of the limelight, such as the major computer problems at the Internal Revenue Service in 1986 and the military maneuvers during the Persian Gulf hostilities in 1991. Many of the conflicts arising from the divergent goals of the media and government are muted because of the symbiotic relationship between these institutions and their understanding of each other's goals and needs.

Given the structure of America's national news, with its heavy reliance on political stories and its penchant for quoting official sources, government

Benefits Sought by the Major Publics of a High School

Primary Publics

Consumer publics—Those who directly benefit from the services such as students and parents. Benefits they seek could include:
- Vocational skills
- Development of self-confidence and self-esteem
- Knowledge necessary to be an informed citizen
- Preparation for college

Support publics—Those who provide funds for the school such as school boards, foundations, civic groups, parent-teacher organizations, and alumni associations. Benefits they seek could include:
- Evidence that resources are efficiently and effectively used
- Increase in personal stature and reputation in the community
- Meeting commitments that they made to constituents when they were placed in the role of resource provider
- Satisfaction of contributing to students' educational process through allocation of resources

General publics—Consists of nonusers as well as users. They provide the tax support base either directly through their vote in bond referendums (in which case they should be viewed as a *support public*) or through more indirect influence on their elected representatives. Benefits they seek could include:
- Satisfaction of contributing to the education of young people
- Evidence that resources are being efficiently and effectively used
- Evidence that the curriculum is consistent with the citizen's perception of educational priorities
- Increase in property values because the community is recognized as having an excellent school system

Employee publics—Those who work for the school. If their needs are well served, they will be inclined to serve the students' needs well. The commitment, skill, and enthusiasm of groups such as teachers, administrators, janitors, and health and safety personnel will ultimately affect how the school is judged. Benefits they seek could include:
- Recognition of their contribution
- An equitable work load that is challenging but not onerous
- Good remuneration and security
- Opportunities for personal growth, training, and advancement
- Pleasant working environment

Secondary Publics

Government publics—Legislatures, aid-granting agencies, and licensing and accreditation agencies. Benefits they seek could include:
- Evidence of a superior system and staff
- Evidence that resources are being efficiently and effectively allocated
- Noncontroversial programs that are unlikely to arouse public criticism

continued

Competitor publics—Alternative private schools in the area, other school systems, and other public service agencies. Emphasis is likely to be on securing passive acceptance rather than active support. Benefits they seek could include:

- Compatibility of the services offered with their own operations, emphasizing complementary rather than competitive dimensions of the services
- If competitors are seeking only passive acceptance, the agency need only emphasize how it will not hurt them rather than what benefits it will bring to them.

Supplier publics—Textbook publishers, equipment and furnishing suppliers, and contractors. Benefits they seek could include:

- Opportunities to sell their products and services

Tertiary Publics

Media publics—Broadcast and print media. Benefits they seek could include:
- News items of interest to their publics
- Feature and human interest stories
- Sports activities

Labor unions—Professional and janitorial staff. Benefits they seek could include:
- Improved working conditions for their members
- Clearly defined job responsibilities
- Higher salaries
- A voice in administering the school

Advocacy and special interest group publics—Examples include handicapped groups, advocates of specific subject areas, athletic booster groups, groups concerned with raising academic standards, and advocates for gifted and talented students. Benefits they seek will vary according to their mission. A handicapped group, for example, may seek:

- Mainstreaming, which ensures that the handicapped will be integrated with other children in classes
- Particular physical design features incorporated in the school to accommodate the handicapped
- Sports programs for the handicapped

Business community publics—Future employers in the community and establishments of higher education. Benefits they seek could include:

- Cooperation with school classes to offer "live" project experiences
- Students with the basic skills required to function effectively in the workforce (or in higher education)
- Students with positive attitudes toward work (or higher education)

Source: John L. Crompton and Charles W. Lamb, Jr., *Marketing Government and Social Services* (New York: Wiley, © 1986), 35-36. Reprinted with permission.

officials are the main fountain of news. One-fifth to one-third of the content of American newspapers is taken either verbatim from information supplied by the government or is adapted from this information.[41] Washington reporters contact government press officers for almost half of their stories.[42] Given the limited resources of the news media, it would be impossible for them to gather this information on their own. When stories about government policies and activities are expertly prepared to fit the needs of the particular medium for which they are intended, they can be godsends. As Pulitzer Prize-winning editor Harry S. Ashmore has noted: "The media as presently constituted could not function without the array of skills and resources provided them without cost in the name of public relations; and this consideration is compounded by their further reliance on advertising or political favors derived from the same sources." [43]

This dependence on government information makes its public relations officials, whether professional or serving in this capacity by virtue of high positions, important and powerful communicators. Although newspeople need the information and eagerly use public relations output, they do not like to acknowledge their dependence on it. Instead, they prefer to condemn public relations activities and bemoan their high costs.[44]

Government agencies are equally dependent on the media and equally vocal about their practices. Bureaucrats need the media to reach the various targets to which their external communications are directed. These include targets within government who cannot be contacted easily, such as the millions of low-level bureaucrats, or targets who are more likely to be persuaded by widely publicized messages that bring additional audiences into the picture. They also include nongovernmental targets, particularly client publics and interest groups. Most importantly, public relations staffs rely on the media to carry messages that will help their agencies gain the political supporters and widespread approval that are often necessary to carry out policies in the face of political obstacles. The mass media are particularly useful because they reach sizable audiences and lend a cloak of credibility to political messages that direct promotions lack. Moreover, unlike advertisements, the direct costs of gaining access to mass media audiences are normally small.

The Race for Press Attention

Strategies designed to gain media attention are well illustrated by the efforts of postal authorities to reorganize the service, in the face of strong opposition, during the Nixon administration. The would-be reformers launched a massive national, regional, and local media campaign, supplemented by internal policy changes, designed to generate pressure for a major restructuring of the Postal Service. A number of measures were taken to propel postal reform onto the congressional agenda and to overcome objections from postal unions and other hostile groups. As Martin Linsky notes, the strategy included "plans to utilize all the available media, national and local, print and electronic, in all their available slots: letters to the editor, editorials, news stories, feature articles by the postmaster general, and even appearances on entertainment television. . . . It was a saturation strategy in which press support, or at least press cooperation, was crucial." [45] Preparatory work included background briefings for newspaper editorial boards, press briefings and information packets, with special packets for editorial writers, newspaper advertisements, and speeches by high-level postal officials to various media groups. The effort yielded hundreds of editorials as well as a large number of op-ed pieces and cartoons, along with ample news stories, most of them favorable. Although the odds for success seemed slim at the start of the campaign, the reformers prevailed in the end. They credited their media campaign with turning the tide in their favor.

Depending on the interest of journalists, and on the public relations personnel and policies of each office, contacts between public agencies and media institutions range from constant to intermittent to no contact at all. *Press releases* are the most common method for submitting information to the media in hopes of enticing them to publish it. Nearly all government offices prepare press releases routinely, and media institutions, particularly those in Washington, D.C., receive them by the ton. Most of them are discarded, often with only minimal attention to their content, but the occasional successes encourage agencies to maintain the barrage. Several factors increase the chances for publication of press releases, including the expertise with which the release is prepared, its newsworthiness, competition from other news stories clamoring simultaneously for scarce time and space, and the salience of the story for the particular media market. Stories of local concern are more likely to be selected, particularly in areas outside the major media markets.

Many of the larger agencies also routinely conduct *press briefings,* often on a daily basis. Briefings are more likely to pay off in publicity when the media invest the time of their reporters to attend the briefing. Moreover, the opportunity for reporters to ask questions also better meets the needs of the press. Skilled public affairs officials are often able to anticipate correctly what questions will be asked so that they can provide detailed answers. Preparation of replies also permits them to plan the political thrust of their responses to enhance the interests of the agency.

For a variety of political reasons, agencies occasionally impose restrictions on publishing the news released at a briefing, which is then termed a *"backgrounder."* Agencies may stipulate that the name of the official who disclosed the information is not to be released, although the story may be published in full. It is then usually attributed vaguely to an "official source," a "high government official," or an "undisclosed source." At other times, agencies may prohibit direct quotation of the briefing official and any mention of sources. Media people may also be told that the information is not for publication and is being given to them confidentially to enhance their understanding of unfolding events. The memo on page 263 shows guidelines established by the Department of State for the conduct of press relations by its employees.

Restraints requested by government agencies are generally considered informal yet binding agreements. The penalty for nonadherence is greater restraint on disclosures of information either to the indiscreet reporter or to the press in general. However, in recent years several media institutions and individual reporters have refused to attend backgrounders or to follow the guidelines because they believe that government officials use the technique to escape responsibility for the accuracy of the released information.

Much information is also passed on informally to reporters, sometimes at the agency's behest and sometimes contrary to its wishes. *Informal relations* with the press are more likely to involve high-level bureaucrats responsible for major policy decisions and therefore in regular contact with the press rather than people at the bottom of the hierarchy.[46] The content of informal transmissions, which often entail leaks, ranges from insignificant gossip to important policy-driving messages. For example, during the Love Canal investigation, no action was taken to relocate potentially endangered residents until after a Justice Department study about the hazards was leaked to the press. The leak was designed to pressure a reluctant EPA to act contrary to its own judgment when other pressures had failed. Hence, the press became a willing and effective tool for EPA's opponents.[47]

During crises, such as an airplane crash or reports of poisoned food supplies or an impending military deployment, there is a massive speedup of all of the functions performed by public affairs officers of the agencies involved in the event. Special information offices may be set up at the disaster sites, as the Nuclear Regulatory Commission did during a nuclear energy plant emergency at Three Mile Island, Pennsylvania, in 1979. The principal challenge faced by public affairs officials under crisis conditions is to obtain and release accurate information without causing unwarranted panic or making recovery efforts more difficult. Explaining often highly technical information under these circumstances can be exceedingly difficult. Imagine the bafflement of reporters who heard Harold Denton, the Nuclear Regulatory Commission's chief spokesperson, offer a correction to a false report that the hydrogen bubble in the Three Mile Island nuclear reactor was about to explode. Said Denton:

> The oxygen generation rate that I was assuming yesterday when I was reporting on the potential detonation inside the vessel is, it now appears to have been, too conservative. There's an emerging consen-

Limits on the Release of Information

DEPARTMENT OF STATE
Washington, D.C. 20520

February 16, 1982

MEMORANDUM FOR: All Public Affairs Officers
 FROM: Rush Taylor, Director,
 Office of Press Relations

From recent discussions with public affairs officers and other department officers, we have discovered that considerable confusion exists regarding the ground rules for conversations with reporters, correspondents, and journalists.

What exactly does "background" mean? What is "deep background"? When can one be quoted and when should one's remarks be attributed to "an administration official"? When talking on the telephone with a journalist, what ground rules should be used?

Below is an extract from a memorandum circulated some years ago, which deals with these and other questions. I recommend it for general circulation among officers in your bureau.

--"ON THE RECORD" means that you can be quoted by name and title. As a general proposition, and with the exception of the department spokesman, officers are on the record only in speeches, congressional testimony, or in formal press conferences.

--"BACKGROUND" This is the most common basis on which to talk to newsmen. As its name implies, the rule was developed to permit officials to describe facts and policy more fully in a more informal way than they can on the record. In theory, quotes are not to be used from a background discussion on the telephone or in the office, and the results of the conversation must be attributed to "state department officials," or "U.S. officials," or "administration sources," or "diplomatic sources," or anything you and the newsmen agree to by way of identification.

The burden is on the officer to establish at the outset the fact that the conversation is on background and the nature of the attribution he desires.

--"DEEP BACKGROUND" This, too, is a common basis on which to talk to newsmen. When you set this rule at the outset of a conversation, it means that the newsman cannot give any specific attribution to what he writes, but must couch his story in terms of "it is understood that . . ." or "it has been learned that. . .".

Obviously this ground rule permits you somewhat greater scope for frankness. But it also asks the newsman to assume a greater personal burden of responsibility for what he writes since there is no visible source for the facts. In turn, the officer assumes an even greater burden of moral responsibility not to mislead or misinform the reporter.

--"OFF THE RECORD" Technically, this means that the newsman can't use what he is told, except for such things as planning purposes: "Off the record, the secretary is going to New York to give a speech on the 13th" means the reporter can't print that news, but he can make plans to be in New York to cover the speech. Nothing substantive should be discussed "off the record" for the good and sufficient reason that nothing substantive ever stays off the record.

Source: Adapted from Stephen Hess, *The Government/Press Connection* (Washington, D.C.: Brookings Institution, 1984), 118-119.

sus of technical opinion that the—for situations such as this where there's high oxygen overpressure in a vessel, that the oxygen evolution rate is very low, and our numbers for the rate of oxygen yesterday—I think I quoted a number on the order of 1 percent a day—is very, very conservative, and the actual rate is much lower than that.[48]

Media Impact on Public Policies

Martin Linsky concludes his analysis of press impact on federal policy making by pointing out that "policymakers will be more successful at doing their jobs if they do better in their relations with the press. . . . Having more policymakers who are skilled at managing the media will make for better government." [49] A poll that he and his associates conducted among officials who served at levels comparable to assistant secretary or above in administrative agencies during the period ranging from the Johnson administration in the 1960s to the first Reagan term shows that these officials agreed about the importance of skillful handling of the media aspects of their work.[50]

Most of the officials polled considered time spent with the press as a resource that enhanced job performance rather than as an unwelcome drain on their time. Ninety-seven percent agreed that the press has an impact on federal policy, with the majority stating that the impact is significant.[51] Three out of four of these officials therefore reported that they had tried to get media coverage for their agency and its activities. Nearly all had used the media to obtain information about their policy area. Close to half of the officials had spent five hours or more a week dealing with press matters and a quarter had spent between five and ten.[52] However, they usually denied that their own decisions had been affected by media coverage, probably because this would be an admission of lack of steadfastness in the face of pressure.[53]

Linsky's analysis sheds light on the areas in which press impact on the work of federal agencies appears to be most significant. Table 7-2 presents some of the evidence. The greatest impact apparently comes early in the policy-making process when media coverage may determine which issues will receive public attention and move to the policy agenda and when media framing determines the images by which these issues will be appraised. This is the point at which public affairs professionals can have their greatest influence if they are able to seize the initiative from the media and define the issues to be addressed and the facets to be explored. Experienced government officials believe that this happens all too rarely. Linsky notes that "senior federal officials as a whole wait too long before involving their public affairs people in the policymaking process. As a result, policymaking is done without adequate attention to the way the policy will be received and the way it ought to be presented." [54]

Table 7-2   Press Impact on Policy Making (in percent)

Question: When an issue in your office or agency received what you saw as positive or negative coverage in the *mass media*, did that coverage:	*Positive coverage*	*Negative coverage*
■ Increase your chances for successfully attaining your policy goals regarding the issue	78.5	6.4
■ Decrease your chances for successfully attaining your policy goals regarding the issue	4.8	71.4
■ Increase the speed with which the issue is considered and acted upon	38.8	36.0
■ Decrease the speed with which the issue is considered and acted upon	9.9	36.2
■ Make action on the issue easier	63.1	9.6
■ Make action on the issue more difficult	5.7	67.9
■ Increase the number of policy options considered	18.3	27.8
■ Decrease the number of policy options considered	15.8	27.5
■ Reshape the policy options considered	10.3	39.9
■ Cause you to reassess your policy position on the issue	7.6	49.0
■ Galvanize outside support	50.1	18.6
■ Undermine outside support	5.7	65.7
■ Move responsibility for the issue to a more senior official or officials	9.7	43.0
■ Increase the importance of the issue within the bureaucracy	26.2	49.0
■ Cause the public and/or other officials to assume the information contained in the coverage is accurate	31.7	33.8
■ Have long term effects on your career	23.2	22.1
■ Affect your credibility on other issues	22.3	32.6
■ Have no effect	16.8	9.0

Source: Reprinted from *Impact: How the Press Affects Federal Policymaking* by Martin Linsky, by permission of W. W. Norton & Company, Inc. Copyright © 1986 by the Institute of Politics at Harvard University, 236.

Note: Respondents were asked to check the statements that occurred most frequently in each category of coverage.

One reason for neglect of this aspect of policy making is that high-level officials often distrust public affairs staffs, whom they suspect of spineless catering to media whims. Moreover, these officials often believe that a meritorious policy will sell itself and does not require publicity or advocacy by the mass media. As mentioned earlier, public affairs officials are often excluded from early policy considerations but then are expected to rescue the policy from public disdain when its image has been damaged beyond repair.

Once the media pay massive attention to an issue, the decision-making process tends to accelerate. Public officials, eager to appear efficient or to move the issue out of the limelight, try to resolve it with uncommon haste, often bypassing normal procedures. When media coverage is extraordinarily intense or negative, decision making is frequently moved up the ladder in the bureaucratic hierarchy, which endows the decision with more prestige and authority than if it were made at lower levels.[55]

While media coverage can be an important asset, it can also be a liability. As Table 7-2 suggests, when coverage is negative, as happens frequently, the agency's work may be hurt seriously. Publication of a story about an agency that runs counter to its plans may force a reactive stance, denying the agency the opportunity to be the leader in the interaction. For example, when the media focused on chemical pollution at Love Canal, New York, the Environmental Protection Agency felt pressured into action that it deemed precipitous and unwise.[56]

Similarly, when the media frame an issue in ways that are likely to antagonize the public, the policy may fail. This happened when the Social Security Administration devised a new system to catch cheaters. The agency hoped that the media would focus on the savings to taxpayers. Instead, the media pointed out that the system amounted to purging the welfare rolls of people whose requests for aid seemed flawed. Hardships for deserving people were likely.[57] Media publicity may also generate opposition to the agency that would otherwise remain dormant. Efforts to attract media publicity may consume resources needed for other purposes and agency goals.

To get and retain coverage, agencies have to adapt their information strategies to the mutually acknowledged needs of the media for exciting stories. This means that uncommon rather than common occurrences must be emphasized. If important stories that the agencies wish to publicize lack conflict, wrongdoing, and emotion-wrenching events, if they are unspectacular and mundane, agency personnel may withhold them or feel forced to create excitement artificially. They may do this either by adding unwarranted drama or creating events solely for publicity purposes. Consequently, from the perspective of good policy, stories that need attention may be ignored or emphasis may be placed on the wrong facets of the story. The results can be politically disastrous.

To avoid boring mass media audiences, news stories must be told in simplified general terms. Technical points and language must be omitted. Because the media, particularly television news, lack the time or space to explore important issues, much of the context of the story must be excluded. The positions taken by the agency must appear to be unambiguous and often uncompromising. Given the complexity of many of the issues about which media audiences must be informed, such as environmental pollution or foreign policies, this is difficult to do. Widely publicized firm stands may reduce the flexibility that is essential for political compromise. As has been said about Members of Congress, the roles of media show horse and government work horse are often antagonistic and therefore defy successful combination.

Public Information Campaigns

General Nature and History

Despite a political culture that disdains activities smacking of propaganda, communication campaigns run by governmental agencies to shape public attitudes about various issues have been legion. Among them have been campaigns advocating stands on such controversial issues as disarmament, communism, and civil rights; campaigns supporting conservation issues, including forest-fire prevention and judicious energy use; and campaigns promoting healthful behavior such as securing prenatal care and cancer prevention.[58] The term "social marketing" is often used for campaigns designed primarily to foster the welfare of the community as a whole. Some social marketing campaigns are one-shot affairs, but most deal with persistent situations that require periodic campaigns.

Modern public information campaigns are run much more effectively than in the past because a great deal more is known about the process of persuasion and more sophisticated technologies are available to carry messages far afield. Modern technologies range from satellite relays that permit electronic transmissions to isolated areas to transistor radios carried by backpackers in the wilderness to visitors traveling by airplane to agricultural hinterlands who can deliver messages by word-of-mouth and are equipped to give on-site demonstrations of new farming and forestation techniques. Modern computer technologies make it possible to target messages to specific audiences whose needs have been carefully assessed and recorded. Known as "segmentation" in marketing circles, this process is considered an essential element in designing effective messages to persuade people with varying psychological characteristics. Persuasion fails when communicators do not understand the psychological aspects of attitude changes and do not know the diverse techniques required to produce such changes in different audiences.

Even though the elements of persuasion are better understood and message delivery more efficient, success rates remain limited because adoption of change is a multistep process. Failure lurks at every step, ranging from the inability to attract the attention of target audiences and resolve comprehension problems to the inability to produce or maintain the desired attitudinal or behavioral changes. An input-output matrix developed by psychologist William McGuire, depicted in Figure 7-4, illustrates the problems.[59] The persuasion input factors listed across the top of the matrix are communication variables. They include the source of the communication, the message, the channel, the receiver, and the goal or destination. Inclusion of these variables in the matrix indicates that the impact of persuasive communications will vary, depending on such factors as the credibility of the source, the type of information presented in the

Figure 7-4 Communication/Persuasion Model as an Input/Output Matrix

Input: independent (communication) variables ⟍ Output: dependent variables (Response steps mediating persuasion)	Source — number, unanimity, demographics, attractiveness, credibility	Message — type appeal, type information, inclusion/omission, organization, repetitiveness	Channel — modality, directness, context	Receiver — demographics, ability, personality, life style	Destination — immediacy/delay, prevention/cessation, direct/immunization
Exposure to the communication					
Attending to it					
Liking, becoming interested in it					
Comprehending it .(learning what)					
Skill acquisition (learning how)					
Yielding to it (attitude change)					
Memory storage of content and/or agreement					
Information search and retrieval					
Deciding on basis of retrieval					
Behaving in accord with decision					
Reinforcement of desired acts					
Post-behavioral consolidating					

Source: William J. McGuire, "Theoretical Foundations of Campaigns," Ronald E. Rice and Charles K. Atkin, eds., *Public Communication Campaigns*, 2d ed., (Newbury Park, Calif.: Sage, 1989), 45. Reprinted with permission.

message, the modality of the channel in which it is carried, such as television versus radio, the personality of the message receiver, and the type of behavior required for compliance, such as stopping an existing behavior or preventing it before it has started.

For example, in the well-known Smokey the Bear campaign, launched in 1942 to prevent forest fires, the source of the communication was a cartoon of a bear dressed like a forest ranger.[60] The message, by now familiar to most Americans, was "Remember, Only You Can Prevent Forest Fires." It was publicized through repeated million-dollar campaigns, featured on radio, television, and billboards as well as in newspapers and magazines. Smokey also participated in the annual Rose Bowl Parade and in Macy's Thanksgiving Day Parade, both nationally televised events. Children were offered membership in a Smokey the Bear Junior Forest Ranger Program that distributes an official fire-prevention kit to them.

As behooves a psychologist, McGuire also emphasizes that the knowledge, aspirations, motivations, and feelings people bring to each situation strongly affect the reception of and reaction to the information that has been presented or evoked from their memories by the information stimulus. These predispositions must be considered in designing effective communication campaigns.[61] Inability to relate campaigns to people's lives and to motivate them to change socially harmful behavior is the Achilles' heel of most public communication campaigns. Ultimate success often hinges on personal contact with audience members, which is normally too difficult to organize and too costly to provide.

The twelve outputs sought from the communication inputs, deemed essential for successful persuasion, range from securing initial exposure to the communication to designing messages that consolidate the changed behavior. How does the Smokey the Bear campaign measure up on these elements? Although no comprehensive evaluation of its success has been made, given the fact that the forest-ranger bear is as familiar to Americans of all ages as most Walt Disney characters, the campaign seems to have achieved the first four output objectives shown in Figure 7-4. Ninety-eight percent of the public were able to identify Smokey in a 1976 poll.[62] The next eight steps shown in Figure 7-4 seem to have been achieved as well. Acreage lost through wildfires dropped from thirty million per year in 1942 to less than five million thirty years later. And the campaign objectives were reinforced through the continuous campaign year after year.

McGuire's input/output matrix provides a useful checklist for constructing public information campaigns and evaluating their successes and failures at each step. Planning with all twelve output steps in mind helps avoid tactics that may be beneficial in generating success at early campaign stages but are counterproductive for the crucial final steps. Getting a public's attention is worthless if nothing happens after the initial message has been noted.

Four Campaign Phases

The organization of modern public information campaigns involves four main phases. Initially, the problem requiring action needs to be carefully analyzed so that goals for the campaign can be set. This phase may require extensive collections of data about the social, political, and economic environment in which the problem is occurring. Surveys of the target population and community leaders and organizations are common, as are analyses of past campaigns and community resources to sustain them. These steps are especially important for campaigns directed to audiences in Third World countries.

The second phase involves choosing strategies to achieve these goals. It may be advisable to run a series of pretests to determine how well various types of messages fit the information-processing styles of the target audiences and impart the desired information. For example, the Treasury Department has produced television sketches that mimic popular television comedies, which are to be shown to selected audiences to induce them to enroll in payroll savings plans at their workplaces. The characters in the sketches extol the virtues of saving through U.S. government savings bonds. Test runs have shown that using formats and actors with whom audiences are known to identify conditions them to be receptive to the message.[63]

Selection of specific persuasion strategies poses touchy ethical issues. How much advocacy is appropriate in campaigns conducted by public officials who seek to foster important policy goals such as the sale of government securities, military recruitment, protection of the health of various population groups, or protection of the environment? If it is ethical for government to market public causes, must it follow stricter criteria than private marketing when it comes to questions of good taste and decorum? For example, are sexual themes permissible? Must special efforts be made to keep marketing messages acceptable to racial and ethnic minorities? How much humor is appropriate? Must there be rigid standards to avoid promising too much too soon? The answers are difficult.

Allegations of ethical violations have been common. For example, the Federal Trade Commission has received complaints alleging that military recruitment messages raise undue expectations that enlistees will travel widely throughout the world, receive training that will lead to profitable civilian jobs, and have interesting and fulfilling military duties. Similarly, advertisements for long-term government bonds have been criticized for failure to explain that the face value of the bond does not reflect the likelihood that its buying power will be sharply diminished at the time of redemption.[64]

When strategies have been chosen and appropriate message transmission channels secured, the third phase—the actual campaign—can begin. It usually starts with messages designed to make target publics aware of the issues involved in the campaign. This constitutes agenda setting. Given the large number of messages with which people are now bombarded, gaining attention is no easy feat. Once the target public has been alerted, the issue needs to be framed in ways that make the message relevant, understandable, and logical to lay people. Thus Smokey the Bear told people that they personally could prevent forest fires. Messages must motivate the audience to heed the advice and should therefore be linked to people's aspirations. The Smokey the Bear campaign emphasized the value of public parks to average Americans and the high costs of wildfires. It also provided the necessary implementing information that permits audiences to carry out the recommendations of the campaign. Since the behavior must be sustained over prolonged periods of time, reminders to maintain the desired behavior have been essential.

Knowledge by itself is not enough. In public health campaigns, professionals must motivate people at risk so that they are willing to change ingrained behavior, even though this may be physically and psychologically taxing. Motivating them by promising a future benefit such as better health or longer life is often unsuccessful. For instance, in a campaign to lower the intake of dietary fats, it is not enough to alert the public to the fact that a high-fat diet may be dangerous. After public awareness has been generated, public health officials must explain in detail various aspects of the problem. This is exceedingly difficult because the issues are complex and not easily explained to lay people. Public health professionals must also provide "implementing information" that teaches at-risk publics the steps necessary to reduce dietary fats. That task is equally difficult. Finally, most difficult of all, people must be taught to continue the desired behavior indefinitely. Because the behavior involves loss of gratification, backsliding is the rule rather than the exception.

At the end of each campaign, in the fourth phase, instruments to evaluate its success must be designed and applied. This is particularly important for public information campaigns that require frequent repetition and therefore need new funding periodically. Careful evaluation should indicate which features of the campaign should be retained and which should be dropped or altered.[65]

Agencies as Lobbyists and Lobby Targets

Assessing the Lobby Landscape

When public relations activities are highly structured and directed toward achieving specified responses and actions, they are called "lobbying." The term was originally used only to describe interest-group efforts to influence legislation. Advocates of special interests would gather in the lobbies of legislative assemblies to plead their causes when the members emerged from the chambers. Nowadays the term is used more broadly to apply to well-organized pleadings by government outsiders and insiders designed to influence all phases of the government process. This more comprehensive use of the term obscures the boundary between lobbying and other public relations activities.[66]

Although lobbying is a hallowed tactic in American politics, protected by First Amendment free-speech guarantees, it is prone to major abuses. Therefore, steps have been taken to forestall misconduct by lobbyists, including a requirement of compulsory registration. The Administrative Procedure Act and related court decisions impose legal restrictions designed to limit the power of lobbies to influence the operations of regulatory agencies. Nonetheless, the persuasive power of lobbies remains awesome.

For obvious reasons, Washington, D.C., the center of American government, is the primary site for lobbying activities. In addition to the many federal agencies that maintain lobbying staffs in the nation's capital, large state governments, governmental units, and most major cities, such as Chicago and Detroit, have their own Washington lobbyists. The same is true for organizations such as the U.S. Conference of Mayors, the National Association of Counties, and the National Conference of State Legislatures. As Hugh Heclo states, "Today, not only do governors or mayors as groups have their own specialized staffs permanently stationed in Washington, but large state governments, and individual cities frequently have their own Washington offices or hired representatives." [67]

Just as governmental activities have multiplied, so has the scope of interests for which people are likely to lobby. Specialized rather than general interest lobby groups have proliferated. It is difficult to keep track of all these crosscutting ventures and determine who wields power and who has influenced a particular decision.[68] As discussed in Chapter 5, Heclo claims that these amorphous webs of communication and influence, which he calls "issue networks," determine public policies on many issues. Case studies of particular lobbying campaigns largely support this conclusion.[69] Participants in such networks range from the powerful to the powerless, but all share, according to Heclo, a "detailed understanding of specialized issues that comes from sustained attention to a given policy debate." [70] It is their knowledge of particular issues and political processes that gives them influence and convinces the targets of their pleadings to give them serious consideration.

Many causes for which public agencies lobby are also of concern to private and semipublic groups with their own lobbyists. Trade and professional associations are examples. As discussed in Chapter 5, this has led to numerous coalitions between public and private sector lobbyists. Before joining a coalition, public administrators need to assess the costs and benefits of pursuing the coalition's chosen strategies. Such assessments involve gathering information about many technical, practical, and political factors. What sorts of coalitions have been formed in the issue area in question? Who are the dominant players and how much political clout do they have? What are the soundest policies from the agency's perspectives? How many resources should be devoted to this policy? Will policy makers lose touch with the general public if they work closely with interest-group representatives? Will they lose credibility?

Ethical questions arise as well, especially when public agencies combine forces with private sector lobbies on behalf of controversial issues. Is it democratic to align with one policy faction and give it access to policy makers when denying similar access to the opposition? Would it be more democratic to create opportunities for multiple advocacies, with special efforts to elicit minority viewpoints? Do people most likely to be affected by the policy deserve special consideration? Or should the solution that an agency's leadership deems best for the country in general be preferred?

Coping with Lobby Assaults

In addition to their own lobbying activities, public agencies are heavily involved in coping with such activities directed at their programs. That may entail counter-lobbying to balance the effects of hostile attacks, or dealing with lobbyists who contact the agency. In most instances, it becomes necessary to respond to data-based arguments. As Heclo points out, because of the complex, far-reaching decisions that administrators are now forced to make, "Knowing what is right becomes crucial, and since no one knows that for sure, going through the process of dealing with those who are judged knowledgeable (or at least continuously concerned) becomes even more crucial." [71]

As discussed in Chapter 2, many private sector lobby groups are expert in researching data relevant to the performance of public sector organizations but often unavailable to them because of limited resources. Moreover, these data are often packaged in ways that make it very tempting for public agencies to use them without much additional scrutiny. For example, public officials have been unable to generate their own reliable data to assess the oil reserves controlled by major American oil companies. Such data are needed to plan defense and regulatory policies.

When lobbyists for the oil companies approach federal agencies with information concerning these reserves, or when these data are available only from associations like the American Petroleum Institute, the temptation to base policy on industry-controlled information is well-nigh irresistible. The costs of verifying industry-supplied information are often staggering. It may indeed be impossible to verify data for privately controlled resources. When access to such information is blocked, public sector agencies may be forced to rely on the inferences drawn by lobby groups from the data base. For example, an inference that oil supplies are scarce may have to be made without an opportunity to inspect the actual data.

Private sector lobby groups have used various communication tactics to influence public policy on many fronts and in diverse ways. They have been able to shift an agency's activities to new directions or prevent such shifts. For example, labor unions have been very influential in getting OSHA to enforce occupational health regulations by publicly calling attention to lagging performance. John Scholz and Feng Hong Wei report that investigators, after analyzing annual enforcement data from 1976 through 1983 for all fifty states, concluded that "direct labor interaction through the filing of complaints had the most consistent effect on all enforcement output." [72]

Since Congress can control the activities of most federal agencies, it has become a magnet that attracts private lobby groups as well as intergovernmental lobbies. In the hope of influencing policies and actions, the bipartisan congressional Environmental and Energy Study Conference, for instance, distributes information on environmental issues to Congress. The conference also holds meetings, briefings, and workshops on environmental issues, to which it invites members of the executive branch. Its activities are germane to the interests of various administrative agencies.[73]

At times, the two-step lobby approach, in which lobbyists try to contact administrative agencies via the congressional route, escalates to three or more steps. Lobbies, including several organized by incumbent members of Congress, may attempt to mobilize various general publics, urging them to pressure Congress to adopt desired policies and implement them through administrative agencies. For example, the Congressional Space Caucus has contacted scientists throughout the nation, urging them to lobby Congress on behalf of various space issues. The caucus sponsors briefings and speeches by public officials, in addition to producing reports, information kits, and brochures. Similarly, the Congressional Black Caucus created an "action alert communication network" in order to mobilize members of more than 150 black grass-roots organizations. These organizations inform fellow citizens about issues of concern to the caucus, besides lobbying Congress directly. The influence exercised in Congress by the Congressional Black Caucus was enhanced by its ability to demonstrate that it represents the views of a large segment of the black community.[74]

Case Study—Creating the Department of Education

The creation of a separate cabinet-level Department of Education in 1979 illustrates the array of lobbying activities required to promote an issue successfully. It also shows how government agencies collaborate formally and informally with private sector interest groups. The participation of such groups may lend the operation an aura of being legitimated by public opinion.[75] The case is also a perfect example of issue-network coalition building and the battles that can develop among competing networks.[76]

President Carter and Vice President Mondale favored the bill to carve the Education Department out of the Department of Health, Education and Welfare for many reasons. In addition to having made campaign pledges to the National Education Association (NEA), a powerful interest group, the Carter administration sought to stress the importance of education and also needed to show political strength by successfully pushing a controversial program through Congress. The opposition included powerful members of Congress and the executive branch, who opposed fragmentation of cabinet departments, and powerful private sector interest groups, most importantly the American Federation of Teachers (AFT). Aside from specific objections to separating the education programs from health and welfare functions, there was also the usual concern, as David Stephens notes, that "[r]eorganization meant new lines of command, new procedures, new faces, the reshuffling of committee responsibilities, and the possibility, during the bureaucratic shakedown and in the future, that interest groups would lose their access to power." [77]

As often happens, a large part of the lobbying burden was borne by the private sector interest group, in this case the NEA, which mobilized its members, its lobbyists in Washington, and its closest allies among education interest groups. NEA also promoted and financed the establishment of a "citizen committee" of prominent people in education, labor, civil rights, government, and business to speak and pressure on behalf of the cause. Lobbying efforts inside government circles were also orchestrated by NEA. For example, its officials enlisted the help of prominent administration insiders, notably presidential adviser Hamilton Jordan, to use their influence to win over prominent opponents such as Burt Lance, then director of the Office of Management and Budget. OMB had been given the task of assessing the advisability of a Department of Education and was to report its findings to the president.

Throughout the two-year battle for passage of the bill to establish the department, the NEA's Washington office became the chief source of information for Congress. NEA representatives met with members and staffs of the relevant Senate and House committees; they wrote letters and made phone calls to support particular provisions of the legislation. NEA officials also held frequent meetings with OMB and the White House staff. Since the House Government Operations committee was handling the bill, they kept its staff informed about congressional views on the legislation. The midterm elections provided an excellent opportunity to pressure legislators. NEA members kept in constant touch with candidates and incumbents. The NEA Political Action Committee raised over $3 million for sympathetic legislators.

The White House also fought a steadily growing lobbying campaign. In fact, the president ultimately devoted more time to lobbying for the education department bill than for any other issue except the Panama Canal treaties. The president reviewed lobbying efforts on behalf of the Education Department on a weekly basis, and the vice president was involved with these efforts almost daily. The White House also established a special task force to contact and pressure legislators. It included members of the White House legislative liaison team, members of the Domestic Policy staff, other White House units, and members of OMB. When needed, the task force was authorized to request direct help from the president or vice president. It was urged to cooperate closely with the floor leaders of the legislation and other strong supporters. As it turned out, task-force representatives met several times weekly with representatives of interest groups to discuss tactics and exchange information.

When the vote in the House Government Operations committee, which was handling the bill, resulted in a tie—eighteen votes for it and eighteen against—lobbying efforts turned the tide by winning over undecided members and holding on to wavering supporters. In view of the close vote in committee, the opposition stepped up its lobbying campaign to stop the bill on the floor of Congress. The NEA responded in kind.

During the final stages of legislative activities concerned with the bill, the president and vice president personally contacted legislators via telephone or in their offices to drum up support. Cabinet members, including HEW Secretary Joseph Califano, who had initially opposed a separate department, were drafted to pressure members of Congress to support the legislation. NEA staff prepared target lists of key legislators to be visited by lobby groups, including teachers specially flown in. A constant check of congressional attendance was kept to make sure that no legislative vote would be lost through absenteeism.

The bill to create the department finally passed the House on July 11, 1979, after more than thirty hours of debate, by the narrow margin of 210 to 206 votes. It sailed more comfortably through the Senate on September 24, 1979, by 69 affirmative votes, balanced by 22 negative ones. Three days later, it passed comfortably through a conference committee that ironed out differences between the House and Senate bills. The bill was a victory for the private-public sector coalition of lobby groups supporting the president's views.

Summary and Conclusions

In American political culture, democracy means that government must communicate with private and public sector publics about its policies, seeking dialogue, understanding, and ultimately consensus. It also means honest messages, respect for many different points of view, and abstinence from pressure tactics to win consensus. Herein lies the dilemma of public relations activities by government officials. They satisfy the first criterion but seem to violate the second. On the one hand, they are recognized as essential for the conduct of an open government. On the other hand, they are viewed as a form of intellectual coercion designed to brainwash publics into acquiescing to the views and wishes of government.

These ambivalent feelings have led to a schizoid approach to government public relations. They are undertaken on a wide scale and deemed essential, yet they are officially disparaged and hidden under ambiguous, often misleading labels. Despite the pretense that public information functions can be clearly separated from public relations activities, the facts prove otherwise. Because officials are reluctant to create appropriate structures to cope with ongoing public relations activities, the structures used are not as well designed as they might be if the reality of the situation were acknowledged.

The second section of the chapter examines the strategies and tactics used for image building and persuasion. The choice of particular strategies and tactics must vary, depending on the targets to which the messages are directed, the available resources, and the situational constraints at the time public relations messages are dispatched. For most agencies, the key targets to be reached by public relations activities are legislatures, chief executives and their staffs, and the public at large.

Because extensive knowledge is needed about an agency's internal workings and social, political, and economic conditions in its environment, an agency's staff usually includes public relations experts. For their external communications, many agencies also create separate offices whose structures are generally determined by the special needs of the agency as well as the goals and preferences of the leadership. As a result, their patterns vary greatly.

The mass media have become a major channel for disseminating information to widely dispersed publics. Government agencies have established regularized procedures for contacting the press, and press institutions have been structured to take advantage of these opportunities. However, the interactions between them are tempestuous because of conflicting goals. Government officials want stories that will show them and their programs in a favorable light, emphasizing aspects that are most helpful from a governmental perspective. The media are primarily interested in exciting, appealing stories, with a distinct preference for those critical of government. Since the media do like to cover news about government, and government officials feel strongly that they need publicity, the two institutions manage to reach a compromise on many of their differences and establish workable relationships.

The final sections of the chapter describe specific government efforts to use techniques of persuasion to accomplish public policy objectives. The difficulties in designing and executing public information campaigns are outlined as they might be experienced in campaigns on behalf of health and safety or to win compliance with postal and internal revenue regulations. Lobbying is never a one-directional enterprise. Public agencies are on the receiving end as often as they are on the sending end—perhaps more often. The chapter delineates some of the problems faced in coping with lobby efforts directed at public agencies.

The major message of this chapter is that public information and public relations activities are essential to the successful conduct of American government and that the disdain in which they are often held is totally unwarranted and harmful. It promotes hypocrisy and subterfuges when public relations activities are undertaken. The time is therefore ripe to mount concerted efforts to put public relations activities into proper perspective.

The necessity for effective public relations springs from American political culture and from the fragmentation of American government. When mass media publicize problems, cynicism and condemnation abound because most Americans postulate perfection as an achievable ideal. They equate failures with avoidable shortcomings or misdeeds of people and institutions. If blame automatically attaches to failures, it becomes necessary to deflect attention from them and carve positive images into the public's consciousness to sustain the support that is essential for public agencies.

To get funding and supportive legislation, public agencies must woo Congress and the executive branch and also gain the support of the courts and the public. Their work takes place in a contentious environment. American government is structured to encourage a multitude of conflicting interests to speak out and be heeded, at least partially, by elective officials. To achieve their goals, public sector agencies must compete for resources in this melee of clashing interests and power plays, minimizing their weakness and emphasizing strengths.

In these political battles, the press can be a powerful ally as well as a dangerous foe. The interaction between private sector media and public sector agencies therefore deserves more study than it has received thus far. We need to know more about the role played by the press in setting the public policy agenda and in promoting or hindering public agency goals. This is a matter of great interest and concern to executives in public agencies as well as to scholars and the American public.

Notes

1. Jameson W. Doig and Erwin C. Hargrove, *Leadership and Innovation: A Biographical Perspective on Entrepreneurs in Government* (Baltimore: Johns Hopkins University Press, 1987), 14-17.
2. Ibid., 183.
3. James Q. Wilson, *Bureaucracy: What Government Agencies Do and Why They Do It* (New York: Basic Books, 1989), 204.
4. Herbert Kaufman, *The Administrative Behavior of Federal Bureau Chiefs* (Washington, D.C.: Brookings Institution, 1981), 76.
5. J. William Fulbright, *The Pentagon Propaganda Machine* (New York: Vintage Books, 1971).
6. *The Washington Lobby,* 5th ed. (Washington, D.C.: Congressional Quarterly Inc., 1987), 33-41. Various limitations on private sector lobbying are discussed. The major law, the 1946 Federal Regulation of Lobbying Act, is so vague that its provisions concerning registration and spending limits are almost unenforceable.
7. John L. Crompton and Charles W. Lamb, Jr., *Marketing Government and Social Services* (New York: Wiley, 1986), 394-395.
8. Lewis M. Helm, Ray Eldon Hiebert, Michael R. Naver, and Kenneth Rabin, eds., *Informing the People* (New York: Longman, 1981), 169.
9. Leslie H. Gelb, "Speakes Defines His Role in Shaping Events," *New York Times,* October 10, 1986.
10. Jeffrey Pfeffer, *Power in Organizations* (Marshfield, Mass.: Pitman, 1981), 180.
11. Crompton and Lamb, *Marketing Government and Social Services,* 217.
12. Murray Edelman, *Constructing the Political Spectacle* (Chicago: University of Chicago Press, 1988), 103-104.
13. Ibid., 104.
14. Pfeffer, *Power in Organizations,* 184.
15. For example, see Edelman, *Constructing the Political Spectacle,* 104.
16. Stephen Hess, *The Government/Press Connection* (Washington, D.C.: Brookings Institution, 1984), 118-121.
17. Ibid., 24-26.
18. Martha Derthick, *Agency Under Stress: The Social Security Administration and American Government* (Washington, D.C.: Brookings Institution, 1990), 183.
19. Andrew C. Gordon and John P. Heinz, eds., *Public Access to Information* (New Brunswick, N.J.: Transaction, 1979), 189-222, 280-308.
20. Martin Linsky, *Impact: How the Press Affects Federal Policymaking* (New York: Norton, 1986), 81-82.
21. Charles Peters, "From Ouagadougou to Cape Canaveral: Why the Bad News Doesn't Travel Up," *Washington Monthly* 18 (April 1986): 29.
22. Ibid., 28.
23. *The Washington Lobby,* 14.
24. Charles H. Levine and James A. Thurber, "Reagan and the Intergovernmental Lobby: Iron Triangles, Cozy Subsystems, and Political Conflict," in *Interest Group Politics,* 2d ed., Allan J. Cigler and Burdett A. Loomis, eds. (Washington, D.C.: CQ Press, 1986), 202-220.
25. Wilson, *Bureaucracy: What Government Agencies Do and Why They Do It,* 27.
26. See Martha S. Feldman, *Order without Design: Information Production and Policy Making* (Stanford, Calif.: Stanford University Press, 1989). The major

considerations that go into report writing are discussed on pages 61-69.

27. David L. Altheide and John M. Johnson, *Bureaucratic Propaganda* (Boston: Allyn and Bacon, 1980), 4-17.

28. Ibid., 19.

29. Kaufman, *The Administrative Behavior of Federal Bureau Chiefs,* 65.

30. Richard Chackerian and Gilbert Abcarian, *Bureaucratic Power in Society* (Chicago: Hall, 1984), 45.

31. Ronald E. Rice and Charles K. Atkin, eds., *Public Communication Campaigns,* 2d ed. (Newbury Park, Calif.: Sage, 1989), 224-225.

32. Kaufman, *The Administrative Behavior of Federal Bureau Chiefs,* 65-66.

33. Edward Cowan, "Problems with Government Advocacy: A Journalist's View," in *Informing the People,* Lewis M. Helm, Ray Eldon Hiebert, Michael R. Naver, and Kenneth Rabin, eds. (New York: Longman, 1981), 48.

34. All data about the department come from Edie Fraser and Wes Pedersen, "Department of Agriculture: A Structural Model," in *Informing the People,* 283-286. The 1990 chart was supplied by the staff of the Office of Public Affairs.

35. Hess, *The Government/Press Connection,* 13-14.

36. Crompton and Lamb, *Marketing Government and Social Services,* 380.

37. Rice and Atkin, *Public Communication Campaigns,* chaps. 5, 7, 10, 12, 13.

38. Fred Ciruli, Ciruli Associates, Denver, Colorado, personal communication.

39. Rice and Atkin, *Public Communication Campaigns,* 151-195.

40. John L. Crompton and Charles W. Lamb, Jr., *Marketing Government and Social Services* (New York: Wiley, 1986).

41. Scott M. Cutlip, "Government and the Public Information System," in *Informing the People,* 32; Leon Sigal, *Reporters and Officials: The Organization and Politics of Newsmaking* (Lexington, Mass.: D.C. Heath, 1973), 21.

42. Stephen Hess, *The Washington Reporters* (Washington, D.C.: Brookings Institution, 1981), 18.

43. Quoted in Cutlip, "Government and the Public Information System," 23.

44. Ibid., 30.

45. Linsky, *Impact: How the Press Affects Federal Policymaking,* 203.

46. Hess, *The Government/Press Connection,* 75.

47. Linsky, *Impact: How the Press Affects Federal Policymaking,* 73-75.

48. Casey Bukro, "How Accurate Was Press about Three Mile Island?" *Chicago Tribune,* March 30, 1980.

49. Linsky, *Impact: How the Press Affects Federal Policymaking,* 203.

50. The final sample size was 483. However, 10 percent of the sample population lacked administrative experience in the executive branch.

51. Linsky, *Impact: How the Press Affects Federal Policymaking,* 84.

52. Ibid., 81-82.

53. Ibid., 87.

54. Ibid., 125.

55. Ibid., 87.

56. Ibid., 67, 79.

57. Ibid., 52-60.

58. For a history of public communication campaigns, see William Paisley, "Public Communication Campaigns: The American Experience," in Rice and Atkin, *Public Communication Campaigns,* 15-38.

59. Rice and Atkin, *Public Communication Campaigns,* 151-195.

60. Ibid., 215-217.

61. William J. McGuire, "Theoretical Foundations of Campaigns," in Rice and

Atkin, *Public Communication Campaigns,* 44-65.
62. Rice and Atkin, *Public Communication Campaigns,* 216.
63. Richard Marin, "Selling Uncle Sam for a Laugh," *Insight,* February 29, 1988, 46.
64. Cowan, "Problems with Government Advocacy," 39-40.
65. Rice and Atkin, *Public Communication Campaigns,* chaps. 6, 7, 8.
66. For the argument that public relations and lobbying are part of a seamless web, see Randall Rothenberg, "P.R. Firms Head for Capitol Hill," *New York Times,* January 4, 1991.
67. Hugh Heclo, "Issue Networks and the Executive Establishment," in *The New American Political System,* Anthony King, ed. (Washington, D.C.: American Enterprise Institute, 1978), 95.
68. Ibid., 102.
69. Jeffrey M. Berry, *The Interest Group Society,* 2d ed. (Chicago: Scott, Foresman, 1989), 177-179.
70. Heclo, "Issue Networks and the Executive Establishment," 99.
71. Ibid., 103.
72. John T. Scholz and Feng Heng Wei, "Regulatory Enforcement in a Federalist System," *American Political Science Review* 80 (December 1986): 1262.
73. Susan Webb Hammond, Daniel P. Mulhollan, and Arthur G. Stevens, Jr., "Informal Congressional Caucuses and Agenda Setting," *Western Political Quarterly* 38 (December 1985): 592.
74. Ibid., 693-695.
75. David Stephens, "President Carter, the Congress, and NEA: Creating the Department of Education," *Political Science Quarterly* 98 (Winter 1983-1984): 641-663.
76. Ibid., 658.
77. Ibid., 647.

External Communications: Serving Clients

General Concerns

Significance and Scope of Public Encounters

Contacts between citizens and public agencies are the most frequent form of political participation at all levels of American government. These encounters are particularly significant because their quality affects the level of public satisfaction with government services that have a profound impact on people's lives. Through these contacts government officials also obtain feedback about the impact of policies on individual citizens, inequities in service, and the adequacy of bureaucratic routines. Such data may provide clues to improving client services. Perhaps most significant for democratic politics, as Charles Goodsell points out, these encounters are a way to keep unelected bureaucrats moderately accountable and responsive to the public "as they communicate to transact matters of mutual interest." [1] Citizens have the opportunity to question officials and form impressions about how well their government functions. These assessments can be relayed, directly or indirectly, to appropriate decision makers. [2]

Citizen contacts with government bureaucracies range from fleeting encounters on trivial matters, such as paying for a dog license at city hall, to life-and-death issues, such as public assistance to pay for life-saving treatment in a medical crisis. In a national survey conducted in the mid-1970s, 58 percent of the respondents reported contact with at least one of seven types of public agencies rendering crucial services to citizens. [3] The services included workmen's compensation, employment assistance including job training, unemployment insurance, welfare, medical care including hospitalization, and various retirement benefits. The number and percentage of citizens whose lives are strongly affected by the quality of such services have continued to rise steadily. When other services are included, such as dealing with tax-collecting agencies, postal workers, or police officers, significant encounters between government workers and citizens are nearly universal.

Despite their importance and pervasiveness, public encounters have not received extensive study except in professionally specialized situations, such as relations between nurses and patients, police officers and offenders, and teachers and students.[4] Nonetheless, a few studies have focused more generally on encounters between street-level bureaucrats and citizens when they first apply for various public services.[5] From the client's perspective, these bureaucrats are often the most significant officials because they are the first link in the chain of command, filling the important role of boundary spanner between citizens and public agencies. They usually make the initial determination about the citizen's eligibility and need for particular public services. As political scientist Jeffrey Prottas points out in his study of street-level bureaucrats, their gatekeeping powers shape the work of their agencies. "In general, the street-level bureaucrat's autonomy is a result of his control of the flow of information between the organization and its clients. The bureaucrat is the client's major source of information about the rules and procedures of the agency. At the same time he is the agency's major source of information about the circumstances of individual clients." [6]

Types of Public Encounters

Encounters between citizens and officials come in many types and shapes, and their particular characteristics affect the substance and manner of the communication and its effects. As Figure 8-1 shows, important variables include the general sociocultural environment in which the encounter takes place, the characteristics of the agency, its officials and clients, and the nature and size of the client pool. If the prevailing cultural norms endorse open, uninhibited communication, and if clients and officials have no trouble communicating and cooperating with each other, problems are minimal. It also helps if their goals are shared and if officials find it easy to accommodate the client within the goals and resources of the agency.

The characteristics of the institutional climate in which the encounter takes place are particularly important. For instance, large social service agencies dominated by a single profession tend to be more impervious to external controls, more authoritarian in their proceedings, and less disposed to accommodate clients' wishes than most other types of agencies.[7] As Evelyn Brodkin points out, "As soon as an issue is institutionally defined as requiring scientific advice and expertise, the scope of legitimate participants is drastically reduced." [8] Clients in turn become more submissive.

Figure 8-1 Dynamics of Official-Client Communication

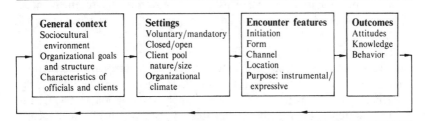

General context	Settings	Encounter features	Outcomes
Sociocultural environment	Voluntary/mandatory	Initiation	Attitudes
Organizational goals and structure	Closed/open	Form	Knowledge
Characteristics of officials and clients	Client pool nature/size	Channel	Behavior
	Organizational climate	Location	
		Purpose: instrumental/ expressive	

Source: Adapted from Elihu Katz and Brenda Danet, "Communication Between Bureaucracy and the Public," Ithiel de Sola Pool and Wilbur Schramm, eds., *Handbook of Communication* (Chicago: Rand-McNally, 1973), 668.

Jeffrey Prottas, who investigated bureaucratic encounters in veterans' hospitals, found that

> medical situations tend to make people unusually passive and malleable. People will generally accept what is told them in a hospital or clinic and do what they are told even when they don't understand it. This minimizes what might otherwise be a check on the system, especially when combined with the fact that the clientele of the VA hospital is generally not skilled at dealing with large and impersonal bureaucracies. . . . This sort of client is unusually lacking in aggression and information, the qualities that provide clients of large bureaucracies with leverage. For these reasons, clients of the VA hospital play an unusually small role in checking the behavior of those they deal with. All the factors work against them.[9]

Organizational settings may range from total involvement to occasional contact. People in prisons, for example, are forced into constant contact with public officials. Because the prisoners' involvement is total and involuntary and therefore often breeds resentment, they are much more likely to develop hostile relationships with public officials than people in brief and casual contact with postal employees or public transportation personnel. Between these two extremes are intermediate institutional relationships, such as encounters in schools and in the military, which involve some compulsion but also permit citizen contacts outside the institutional setting, and semicompulsory contacts with welfare workers or employment counselors.

Public encounters also vary in terms of who initiates them. Citizens usually initiate contacts with public aid agencies, whereas government initiates the contact in matters involving the regulation of harmful behavior or the maintenance of public order, such as policing compliance with environmental regulations or arresting traffic-law violators. From the citizens' perspective, contacts initiated by government are frequently regarded as involuntary or even coercive, which generates resentment and impairs open communication. This is why governments routinely make disclosure of information compulsory and often inflict severe penalties if it is withheld.

The major purposes of public encounters also vary, the tone of the messages and the degree of firmness reflecting diverse social situations. Encounters may be primarily instrumental. The goal might be to exchange information, as happens when citizens supply information to the Census Bureau, which subsequently is available to them in the form of census reports. Or the goal may be to obtain services for citizens, such as medical care, or to obtain resources from the citizen, such as tax money or military service. Alternatively, the purpose of the encounter may be purely expressive, allowing citizens and officials to signal their reactions to each other and to a particular situation. A letter to the Internal Revenue Service complaining about high tax rates, without expectations that it will produce any changes, is an example. With little at stake, the sender may indulge in strong language that might be deemed counterproductive in other situations. The objective may be a combination of instrumental and expressive purposes, as happens when people are dissatisfied with government services and request specific improvements. A request for better patrolling of local parks by police is an example.

The physical locus and medium of communication may vary as well. For example, communication may take place on the street, as it does when citizens encounter police or sanitary workers, or in offices, ranging from pleasant to daunting, or in the citizen's home. As discussed in Chapter 3, the messages conveyed through the physical appearance and maintenance of an office are important factors in communication flows. When clients queue up in front of an open counter, with long lines of people waiting, in a dingy, hot, and windowless room, the prospects for a satisfying exchange of information are diminished.

As previously noted, the characteristics of each medium of communication strongly affect the nature of the encounter. The impact of a recruiting poster in a military installation will differ from the same message delivered by a drill sergeant. Encounters may be conducted face to face, via telephone conversations, or through written, printed, or broadcast messages made available through direct contact between clients and agencies or through mass media channels. Max Weber considered written communications best, claiming that they would insulate officials from improper interpersonal influences that might make it difficult to treat clients neutrally. Current American practice, contrary to Weber's recommendations, appears to favor personal or telephone encounters between citizens and bureaucrats, judging from interviews I obtained with officials at the Social Security Administration, the Consumer Products Safety Commission, and Marine Corps recruitment offices. Citizens may conduct their own encounters or act through a chosen legal or political advocate.

Outreach Programs

Although there are millions of public encounters, large numbers of them never take place because potential clients are uninformed or misinformed about a program from which they ought to benefit. Usually this indicates the government's lack of effective outreach efforts. Missed contacts with public agencies are especially damaging at lower socioeconomic levels, where many potential clients are unaware of the existence of such services as health care, food supplements, housing subsidies, and care for the elderly. Political scientist Bryan Jones and his associates developed a mathematical model to indicate the quantitative relationship between socioeconomic well-being and the propensity to contact government agencies to secure city services.[10] The model suggests that increased socioeconomic status leads to more requests for services because people at higher levels know more about government services and how to obtain them. The request curve dips only when socioeconomic well-being is great enough to obviate the need for government services. Empirical tests of citizens' contacts with local public agencies in Detroit indicated that the model was reasonably accurate for the Department of Building and Safety Engineering, the Sanitation Division, and the Environmental Enforcement Division.[11]

Congressional Budget Office data substantiate that programs designed for the poor are underused. For example, only 41 percent of eligible households received food stamps in 1984.[12] Nearly 30 million people were eligible for benefits under the program in that year. The low participation rate was blamed on a combination of factors, including the failure to alert people to the availability of the program and to inform them adequately about the required procedures. An earlier outreach program designed to educate potential food-stamp recipients had been discontinued in 1981. The usual bureaucratic barriers were a deterrent, as was the stigma associated with receiving public assistance. Some people decided against applying because they anticipated only small benefits.

The record was equally dismal for the Supplemental Security Income Program created to help 3.5 million elderly poor achieve a minimum income of 75 percent of the officially designated poverty level.[13] In 1988, experts estimated that only roughly half of the people eligible to receive aid were actually receiving it. Congress, which often authorizes programs without making sure that resources are adequate to implement them, had failed to fund $10 million requested for outreach programs to inform the elderly poor.[14] Nonetheless, outreach programs were instituted in Pittsburgh, El Paso, and Oklahoma City through collaboration between the Federal Administration on Aging and the American Association of Retired Persons, a major lobby group. When a nationwide sample of eligible nonparticipants was interviewed in the fall of 1987, 55 percent of the respondents said they had never heard of the program; 62 percent said that they did not know where to apply or could not get there. Others objected to taking government aid or considered the benefits too paltry to apply. Obviously, assuming genuine concern about getting these benefits to the needy, extensive outreach activities were required to let people know that the programs existed.

The problem is of long standing. Daniel Katz and his associates reported marked underutilization of a number of public services in their 1975 study. For example, 30 percent of the respondents in a nationwide poll felt that they needed job training but, due largely to communication problems, only 9 percent had received it.[15] Even when potential clients were aware of services, they often lacked adequate information about how to go about obtaining benefits. In general, lower-class and socially deprived people, especially women, were more apt to be uninformed about benefits available to them and less adept in getting them even when they were aware. Bureaucrats, more likely to be drawn from the middle class, empathized more readily with middle-class clients.[16]

Encounters and the Quality of Government

In terms of democratic theory, as previously noted, accountability and responsiveness are the most important reasons for communication between public officials and citizens. Aspects of their relationship were discussed in Chapter 7 under the heading of "public information." Whereas the focus in that chapter was on communication by public and private sector agencies to provide information and influence public policy, the focus shifts in this chapter to interactions between citizens who must deal with government to solve individual problems. Although individual clients are the center of attention, broader issues are involved because public bureaucracies have an obligation to perform their duties well.[17] From the citizen's perspective, issues of accountability and responsiveness may have the most profound political consequences because they indicate the government's concern for the public. The crucial questions are whether citizen encounters with bureaucrats will elicit any response and whether the response is satisfactory to the citizen. Responsiveness rates vary among agencies but are generally poorer in the public sector than in their private sector counterparts, often for reasons beyond the control of individual agencies. When agencies are flooded with more demands than they are equipped to handle, as is common in the public sector, responsiveness is bound to suffer.

Some agencies ignore messages from citizens or delay responses excessively, especially when the messages are unsolicited. Some treat citizens with condescension or rudeness, secure in the knowledge that retribution is unlikely. However, contrary to the suspicions of some critics of public bureaucracies, the degree of responsiveness is not linked to political clout. For example, a study of responsiveness in Chicago and Houston showed that treatment of requests depended on the nature of available programs rather than on the political clout of the official whom the citizen had asked to intercede on his or her behalf. The process was more political in Chicago than in Houston, but outcomes, in terms of services rendered to citizens, were similar.[18] As exchange theories predict, agencies that rely on citizen input and are structured accordingly are generally most responsive. Examples are the Detroit housing and safety bureaus mentioned earlier, rabies control departments that depend on citizens for information about stray animals, and water departments that are eager to be notified about broken water mains.

Aside from concerns about responsiveness, client communication is also a practical matter because government agencies need massive amounts of information to perform the ever-increasing array of services rendered to individual citizens. If public employment agencies fail to get adequate data from job-seekers about their qualifications and expectations, placement efforts are likely to go for naught. If physicians hired for a government psychiatric facility cannot communicate with patients in languages that they understand, the services will, at best, be seriously impaired. At worst, they may become useless. If people fail to file tax returns because they are baffled by the instructions supplied by the Internal Revenue Service, or if error rates are unduly high because of communication difficulties, government resources are diminished.

Many agencies depend on citizens as their eyes and ears. An example is provided by Detroit's building and safety bureaus: 93 percent of the actions of the Housing Improvement Bureau, 72 percent of the actions of the Electrical Inspection Bureau, and 65 percent of the activities of the Bureau of Buildings were initiated as the result of information volunteered by individual citizens.[19] Citizens also perform a service by reporting crimes, safety hazards, and other conditions requiring attention from government officials.[20] If citizens do not know the appropriate channels and format for conveying these messages, the quality of public services suffers. Outreach programs by police departments that encourage citizens to call a toll-free number and often guarantee anonymity are among the examples of overcoming communication problems.

Strains Inherent in Bureaucratic Settings

Resistance to Categorization. Interchanges between citizens and bureaucracies involve one of the toughest problems faced by bureaucracies—humane interactions in a bureaucratic context. There are inherent tensions between bureaucratic categorization and democratic individualism. It is part of America's democratic credo that every individual is unique and deserves to be treated accordingly. Americans do not want to be mere numbers or an impersonal "case." However, standardization is the essence of bureaucracy. Clients must be categorized so that members of each group will be treated equally because they share relevant characteristics, even though they may differ in many important respects. As Max Weber recommended, interchanges between officials and the public should be universalistic, task-oriented, and emotionally neutral. Just as clients should not seek individualized treatment or personal favors, officials should resist bestowing them.

While impersonal treatment does enhance efficiency from a variety of perspectives, including protecting public agencies from charges of unfairness and favoritism, the communication environment thereby created is often undesirable. Clients may feel demeaned and depersonalized, even to the point of shunning the services to which they are entitled.[21] Poor clients are most vulnerable to the harm done by impersonal treatment. Upscale clients, familiar with impersonal dealings, can cope more readily with the lack of personal attention, as they have other sources of ego and social support. Feelings of rejection are one reason why so many public welfare services are underused by the very clients who need them most. This makes outreach programs absolutely essential.

Bureaucrats as Masters. Another major problem plaguing relationships between public officials and citizens springs from their unequal power resources. Moreover, contrary to democratic tenets that designate citizens as masters and public officials as their servants, bureaucrats are the de facto masters. Citizens neither elect them, control their stay in office, nor determine their mode of operation.[22] The bureaucrats' dominant status is particularly galling in that citizens frequently have a much larger stake in the interactions than those who serve them. For the public official, each citizen represents one case among many that must be resolved according to bureaucratic rules. For the citizen, it constitutes his or her only case. If it is poorly handled, the citizen whose life is affected bears the major burden, *not* the bureaucrat.

The power of bureaucrats stems from their official position which authorizes them to exercise the legal powers pertaining to that office. The precise interpretation of these powers may ultimately rest with courts of law, but initial determinations, which usually go unchallenged, are made by incumbents of the office. Generally, the agency's goals and the priorities of the officeholder, rather than the client's wishes, guide these determinations.[23] As political scientist Michael Lipsky has pointed out, bureaucrats at the lowest level of the hierarchy, such as police officers on the beat or welfare caseworkers, commonly determine the policies that affect citizens most immediately. By determining what action will be taken and choosing among multiple legitimate objectives and specific tasks authorized by their jobs, they give operational meaning to broader public policies.[24] It is difficult for clients to challenge street-level policy making because it develops case by case and is therefore hard to pinpoint.[25]

Citizens, particularly those who are not well educated, are also at a disadvantage in the relationship because bureaucrats control the information needed to challenge them. Their knowledge of the rules and regulations is vastly superior, enabling them to impose their perceptions of situations and solutions on clients. Even when citizens have access to the information, it is usually couched in bureaucratic language that is difficult for the uninitiated to understand.[26] With citizens thrust into positions of inferiority and often treated accordingly, the public encounter generally amounts to a duel of unequals. When citizens are clients, notes Murray Edelman, they occupy "the lowest rung of the organization's internal class structure." [27] In an effort to even the score, some public institutions, such as hospitals and nursing homes, employ ombudsmen to act as advocates for the clients.[28]

Citizen control is further weakened by the monopoly status and financial security of many public service providers. The private sector, where market conditions prevail, usually offers choices among service providers. To survive financially, these providers must compete for the favor of prospective clients. By contrast, service providers in the public sector face little or no competition. Since they are supported by public funds, they are less dependent on their customers. As a result, consumers of public services have little or no choice among service providers, who lack economic incentives to serve them well. There is only one Social Security Administration, one Occupational Health and Safety Administration, one Immigration and Naturalization Service. While people in large cities may have the option of dealing with various offices of these agencies, in most locations this is not the case. Consumers needing services, or compelled by law to use these services, must deal with these monopolies according to the agency's interpretation of bureaucratic rules.

Most agencies have more clients than they can handle comfortably and inadequate resources to meet their needs. This imbalance affects the criteria by which excellence in performance is judged. Bureaucrats receive credit for doing their job well if cases are handled at minimum expense to the government and if all agency rules are followed. Whenever bureaucrats deviate from the rules or spend beyond budgeted resources in order to better serve the client, they face possible reprimands. The official's personal goal to win praise from superiors and the agency's goal to be efficient from an organizational standpoint thus conflict with the goals of the clientele being served. These tensions diminish the quality of treatment accorded to clients, including the quality of communication.[29]

Bureaucratic structures make it very tempting to be unresponsive to clients. Police officers, for example, get no credit for being courteous and helpful to the citizens they encounter. Medical staffs in public hospitals are not likely to win official plaudits for spending time to reassure anxious

patients or their relatives. When goals conflict, status and career advancement are more important to most bureaucrats than satisfaction from doing
their particular job. "Personal autonomy, a service ethic, and the inner
rewards of work tend to give way to the extrinsic rewards of career
advancement and organizational status," according to Clarence Stone.[30]
The sheer fact of bureaucratization decreases individual pride in work and
makes officials feel like cogs in a machine. However, the desire to use the
agency for personal advancement is held partly in check by bureaucratic
rules and regulations as well as by norms of professional ethics.[31]

Unresponsiveness, which has been called a problem of mammoth scope,
may take many forms in addition to outright failure to respond.[32] One of the
most common forms is delay.[33] This may mean keeping people waiting in
offices, failing to respond to inquiries, or failing to communicate decisions for
weeks or months. Many agencies are notorious for keeping clients waiting.
Courts, because of vastly excessive case loads, are among the worst.[34] By
contrast, agencies such as the National Park Service and the Public Health
Service consider it a matter of pride that their waiting periods are
comparatively brief. These agencies will respond to inquiries within three
weeks.[35] The explanation may be that the Park Service needs clients to
justify its activities and the Public Health Service cannot risk major health
disasters that might have been prevented by quick action. Most other public
agencies, with less to gain from promptness, take longer unless a client can
persuade a well-placed advocate to intercede. Keeping clients waiting is
usually due to understaffing, but it may also be a deliberate effort to
discourage contact so that the agency's workload will decrease.

Exchange theory explains why elective officials are more likely than
bureaucrats to respond promptly to client contacts. In exchange for help,
the client can give the elective official her or his vote. In most situations,
the client has little to offer the bureaucrat in exchange for the requested
services. Burdensome rules and procedures and the inadequacy of many
public services tend to fray everyone's temper. Resentful citizens may then
vent their wrath on the bureaucrats they encounter, further straining the
relationship. In turn, bureaucrats feel maligned when they have little
control over the matters that have aroused the client's ire.[36]

Of course, citizens often play more influential roles than indicated thus
far. Political scientist Kathy Ferguson, for example, cites three different
roles that citizens can assume in their interactions with bureaucrats.
Citizens may be clients, constituents, or consumers. "Clients," she states,
"are those who must interact actively with bureaucracies upon which they
are dependent but over which they exercise little or no control; for example,
the relationship between the poor and state welfare bureaucracies is a client
relationship." [37]

By contrast, constituents enjoy more power because they deal with
bureaucracies through organized bodies. "Constituents are organized

groups who are interdependent with a bureaucracy and who are able to exercise significant control over it; for example, the relationship between the Farm Bureau and the Department of Agriculture is a constituent relationship." [38] Farmers who push their demands through their representatives in the Farm Bureau are quite likely to have a major impact on agricultural policies and the actions of farm agencies. In public utility commission proceedings, citizen groups have been moderately influential, whereas demands by individual citizens have been ignored.[39]

"Consumers are those who purchase goods and services through the market," Ferguson continues. "Because consumers render payment in money rather than in some less tangible form such as time, dignity, or autonomy, their dependency on the organization supplying the good or service is less acute." [40] Many adult education programs, which depend partly on fees paid by students and partly on public subsidies, represent consumer relationships. In many instances, consumers are under no obligation to buy the services. When constituent and consumer relationships exist between citizens and government agencies, communication problems, though similar to those faced in client relationships, are usually far less serious. Since the discussion in this chapter emphasizes client relationships, it deals with problems at their severest level.

Common Communication Difficulties

Aside from the communication problems arising from the tensions inherent in bureaucratic settings, more routine problems occur as well. They fall into two major categories. The first is caused by difficulties that happen when large numbers of people in huge complex organizational systems must communicate effectively by exchanging complicated messages. The second type of problem arises from the interpersonal tensions existing between bureaucrats and large numbers of their clients because of social, cultural, and status gaps and conflicting interests.

Transmission Problems

Message Channels and Formats. At the most basic level, communication depends on the existence of adequate channels through which government can contact citizens reliably and vice versa. The mass media, of course, serve as major channels, although they are geared primarily to distributing very general, often sketchy messages, and their performance is erratic. When laws are passed to guide the behavior of citizens, such as those concerning professional or business standards or regulating the operation of motor vehicles or the sale of property, mass media channels are often silent or omit crucial details. Direct channels of transmission to the public that automatically reach most members of the relevant client groups are usually nonexistent. Unofficial sources, such as trade publications or lobby-group information, fill that gap only partially.

Even when channels are provided, they usually do not carry all of the information that citizens need to receive and transmit. Government agencies, such as the Internal Revenue Service and the Social Security Administration and comparable agencies at state and local levels, provide regular public information services, including mass mailings. Unfortunately much of this material is not readily usable. Moreover, staffs who deal with the public are often poorly trained, further complicating information transmission. For example, during the 1987 tax season, the Internal Revenue Service acknowledged that only 61 percent of clients who requested help got complete and accurate information. The General Accounting Office pegged the figure at 57 percent.[41]

Government attempts to standardize information flows between citizens and particular agencies by mandating the formats have also been flawed. A list of citizen complaints, compiled by the Commission on Federal Paperwork, pointed out that forms and reports required from the public are too complex and that too many of them must be filled out at the same time. People also complained that they were required to file an excessive number of copies. Because there were no central data files shared by national, state, and local agencies, there was unnecessary duplication of required reports. The complainants believed that record-keeping for agencies at various levels should be more standardized in format and substance. They also thought that information was frequently misused and that confidential information was not properly safeguarded.[42]

The Ombudsman Role.   To ease the citizen's task in communicating needed information in the appropriate form to public agencies, some agencies and institutions have created the position of *ombudsman*. Others have established proxy advocacy offices. Ombudsmen are experts on bureaucratic procedures within particular agencies. They serve as agents for individual citizens, helping them to collect needed information and transmitting their messages, including questions and complaints, to appropriate employees within a particular organization. However, ombudsmen's efforts are largely directed toward solving individual problems rather than initiating broad reforms of procedures or policy.[43] Proxy advocacy offices have been used mainly to represent consumer interests in public utility commission proceedings. Their primary focus has been on policy issues, such as the level of utility rates, and they have often won victories for citizens in these areas. They have not generally articulated the interests of individual citizens.[44]

A survey of American ombudsmen indicates that most of them react primarily to citizen-initiated requests for help rather than initiating inquiries on their own.[45] One might expect this approach to work to the disadvantage of knowledge-poor groups, based on the assumption that they would be least likely to contact ombudsmen. But that is not the case. The ombudsman survey also disclosed that many requests for help come from traditionally underrepresented segments of society, such as women, the elderly, and racial minorities. Ombudsmen thus serve as important communication links between the bureaucracy and otherwise mute clienteles.[46]

The ombudsmen's effectiveness depends to a large extent on their power and position within an organization and on their professional skills and the resources available to do their job. If their position is subject to control by the organization's hierarchy, it is considerably weaker than if the position is independent. Similarly, if ombudsmen have ways to compel officials to disclose information needed by clients or to pay heed to client messages, they are powerful. If they lack such powers, their effectiveness may be sharply limited.[47]

Legislators serve as informal ombudsmen when they engage in casework. They are among the most powerful practitioners of the art. Their influence on bureaucrats is enhanced if they serve on committees that control the resources and powers of the bureaucrat's agency.[48] Similarly, local city council representatives often consider their ombudsman role paramount. In a 1980 survey, Chicago aldermen claimed that, on average, they spent 60 percent of their time as advocates for citizens who had requested their help.[49] The unwritten expectation is that the representative who has procured the services will be compensated by receiving the constituent's vote.

Coping with Bureaucratic Jargon

Gobbledygook Problems. Expressing complex rules and procedures in simple language that average people can understand is among the most intractable communication problems faced by public agencies. Internal Revenue Service codes and instructions and consumer credit regulations provide many examples of what has been called gobbledygook, federalese, or doublespeak.

Complicating the problem is the vagueness of laws and regulations, which is often intentional because lawmakers could not agree on certain provisions or have wanted to ensure flexibility in interpretation. Administrators welcome this flexibility because it allows them to exert greater influence and control over programs.[50] But it also means that laws and regulations defining the nature of programs and implementation methods often receive conflicting or wrong interpretations, intentionally or not.

For example, in 1989 when the Social Security Administration investigated a sharp rise in the number of homeless, aged, and mentally and physically impaired people suspended from its disability-pension rolls, it discovered that staff members had misinterpreted the procedures.[51] As a result of these misinterpretations, which were attributable to vagueness in the law and inadequate time to prepare for its implementation, three-quarters of 1,500 suspensions that were investigated turned out to be inappropriate. Two-thirds of the wrongfully excluded clients were ultimately reinstated, but in some cases it took six months or more. Some reinstatements were never made because frail and otherwise incapacitated clients found it too difficult to submit the required verified annual reports about their financial status.[52]

Agencies vary widely in the clarity and attractiveness of the communications directed toward their clients. To assess the quality of bureaucratic communications, in 1980 a group of social scientists examined 157 documents dealing with wildlife, public parks, tax, and welfare regulations in the fifty states and the District of Columbia.[53] The sample documents were judged on how well they conveyed their messages to average citizens and on their tone, which might affect citizens' reactions to them. Readability was also assessed, using an index that gauges sentence length and polysyllabic words to determine the grade level of reading competence required. Clarity was judged by such features as logic of presentation, use of defined technical terms, typography, and layout. Tone was judged by such factors as whether messages ordered or requested people to act, whether messages sounded patronizing, and whether there was an emphasis on penalties or rewards. Judges also noted whether the message suggested disdain or respect for the audience.[54]

Overall, the research team found substantial variations in these communications. The readability index showed that wildlife and park regulations were written at a twelfth-grade reading level, indicating that comprehension requires a high school education. State income-tax regulations were at a level two years beyond high school, and welfare documents at a reading level five years beyond high school. Obviously all of these levels are beyond the competence of average Americans, particularly those who did not progress beyond a grade-school education.[55] Scores on communication effectiveness, judged by whether a document is readable, clear, and usable, showed welfare documents to be the least effective. Difficult words such as "vendor," "incapacitate," and "encumbrance" were common. Documents concerning wildlife protection had the highest effectiveness scores.

When it came to tone, welfare and tax documents were most negative, although positive and negative tones were almost even in these scores. Exchange theory may explain these rankings. As Hasenfeld and Steinmetz point out, "The dependence of the client on an official is directly proportional to the client's need for the resources controlled by the official and inversely proportional to the availability of the resources elsewhere."[56] Citizens have no burning need for state services involving hunting, fishing, and visiting public parks. With respect to these services, they are consumers rather than clients. To entice them to use these services, state officials therefore try to be pleasant and informative. The reverse is true for paying taxes and trying to obtain welfare support. Because citizens are compelled to use the service, officials need not cater to them.

Moreover, several observers contend that the language used in the relevant documents and the strict regulations are deliberately designed to discourage clients. The costs of welfare are high for agencies, who are always short of funds, and the need to collect taxes is pressing. Discouraging prospective clients from applying for welfare and scaring taxpayers into paying the full amount of their obligation, or possibly more, may be advantageous.[57] If this can be done implicitly, rather than explicitly through laws or explicit directives, the political costs are minimized.

The researchers concluded from their analysis that bureaucratic language is worse than it need be. It is possible to state rules clearly and concisely judging from the many examples of good communication. Overall, the quality of documents was better than generally believed, but bad practices were unfortunately most common in areas where clarity and an encouraging tone were most needed.[58]

In 1987, to follow up on research into the clarity of messages disseminated to the public by government agencies, my research assistants and I analyzed the content of randomly selected, widely circulated brochures produced by three federal agencies: the Consumer Product Safety Commission, the U.S. Army, and the Internal Revenue Service.[59] A widely used test—the Flesch index of readability—was applied to these documents. The index gauges readability, based on such measures as sentence length and complexity, word difficulty, and logic of presentation. The analysis revealed that one-third of the documents were easy, fairly easy, or average in readability. Most Americans would be able to use them successfully. But two-thirds of the documents were difficult or fairly difficult, placing them beyond the comprehension capabilities of average people. *All* forms obtained from the Internal Revenue Service were difficult; there was a mixture of levels of difficulty for the other agencies. Figure 8-2 shows a sample instruction page from the tightly spaced sixty-four page Form 1040 tax guide for the 1990 tax year.

The Tower of Babel. Problems of message transmission are bad enough when all parties speak the same language. They become well-nigh insurmountable in a multilingual society such as the contemporary United States, which has become like a tower of Babel with many recent immigrants failing to master English. In the Los Angeles area, where large numbers of immigrants are concentrated, the court system alone employs more than 400 interpreters to handle some eighty languages and dialects, ranging from Albanian to Wolof, Yoruba, and a multiplicity of Chinese dialects. It is not uncommon for plaintiffs, defendants, and witnesses to speak different languages, requiring the presence of several interpreters.

Figure 8-2   Page of Instructions for IRS Form 1040, 1990

Earned income (such as wages and tips) from sources outside the United States (Form 2555).

Unearned income (such as interest, dividends, and pensions) from sources outside the United States unless exempt by law or a tax treaty.

Director's fees.

Fees received as an executor or administrator of an estate.

Embezzled or other illegal income.

U.S. Citizens Living Abroad

Generally, foreign source income must be reported. Get **Pub. 54,** Tax Guide for U.S. Citizens and Resident Aliens Abroad, for more details.

Examples of Income You Do Not Report

(Do not include these amounts when you decide if you must file a return.)

Welfare benefits.

Disability retirement payments (and other benefits) paid by the Veterans' Administration.

Workers' compensation benefits, insurance, damages, etc., for injury or sickness. (Punitive damages received in cases not involving physical injury or sickness usually must be reported as income. Get **Pub. 525,** Taxable and Nontaxable Income.)

Child support.

Gifts, money, or other property you inherited or that was willed to you.

Dividends on veterans' life insurance.

Life insurance proceeds received because of a person's death.

Amounts you received from insurance because you lost the use of your home due to fire or other casualty to the extent the amounts were more than the cost of your normal expenses while living in your home. (Reimbursements for normal living expenses must be reported as income.)

Certain amounts received as a scholarship (see the instructions for line 7).

Cancellation of certain student loans if, under the terms of the loan, the student performs certain professional services for any of a broad class of employers (get **Pub. 520,** Scholarships and Fellowships).

Community Property States

Community property states are: Arizona, California, Idaho, Louisiana, Nevada, New Mexico, Texas, Washington, and Wisconsin.

If you and your spouse live in a community property state, you must follow state law to determine what is community income and what is separate income. However, different rules could apply if:

• you and your spouse lived apart all year,
• you do not file a joint return, and
• none of the community income you earn is transferred to your spouse.

For details, get **Pub. 555,** Federal Tax Information on Community Property.

Rounding Off to Whole Dollars

You may round off cents to the nearest whole dollar on your return and schedules. To do so, drop amounts under 50 cents and

Page 12

increase amounts from 50 to 99 cents to the next dollar. For example, $1.39 becomes $1 and $2.50 becomes $3.

If you do round off, do so for all amounts. However, if you have to add two or more amounts to figure the amount to enter on a line, include cents when adding and only round off the total. **Example.** You received two W-2 forms, one showing wages of $5,000.55 and one showing wages of $18,500.73. On Form 1040, line 7, would enter $23,501 ($5,000.55 + $18,500.73 = $23,501.28).

Line 7

Wages, Salaries, Tips, etc.

Show the total of all wages, salaries, fees, commissions, tips, bonuses, supplemental unemployment benefits, and other amounts you were paid before taxes, insurance, etc., were taken out. For a joint return, be sure to include your spouse's income on line 7.

Include in this total:

• The amount that should be shown in Box 10 on **Form W-2.** Report all wages, salaries, and tips you received, even if you do not have a Form W-2.

• Tips received that you did not report to your employer. (Show any social security tax due on these tips on line 51—see the instructions on page 22.)

You must report as income the amount of allocated tips shown on your W-2 form(s) unless you can prove a lesser amount with adequate records. Allocated tips should be shown in Box 7 of your W-2 form(s). They are not included in Box 10 of your W-2 form(s). For information on allocated tips, get **Pub. 531,** Reporting Income From Tips.

• Corrective distributions of excess salary deferrals.

• Corrective distributions of excess contributions and excess aggregate contributions to a retirement plan.

• Disability pensions if you have not reached the minimum retirement age set by your employer.

Note: Disability pensions received after you reach your employer's minimum retirement age and other pensions shown on **Form W-2P** (other than payments from an IRA) are reported on lines 17a and 17b of Form 1040. Payments from an IRA are reported on lines 16a and 16b.

• Payments by insurance companies, etc., not included on Form W-2. If you received sick pay or a disability payment from anyone other than your employer, and it is not included in the wages shown on Form W-2, include it on line 7. Attach a statement showing the name and address of the payer and amount of sick pay or disability income. (Get **Form W-4S** for details on withholding of Federal income tax from your sick pay.)

• Fair market value of meals and living quarters if given by your employer as a matter of your choice and not for your employer's convenience. Don't report the value of meals given to you at work if they were provided for your employer's convenience. Also don't report the value of living quarters you had to accept on your employer's business premises as a condition of employment.

• Strike and lockout benefits paid by a union from union dues. Include cash and the fair market value of goods received. Don't report benefits that were gifts.

• Any amount your employer paid for your moving expenses (including the value of services furnished in kind) that is not included in Box 10 on Form W-2.

Note: You must report on line 7 all wages, salaries, etc., paid for your personal services, even if the income was signed over to a trust (including an IRA), another person, a corporation, or a tax-exempt organization.

For more details on reporting income received in the form of goods, property, meals, stock options, etc., get **Pub. 525,** Taxable and Nontaxable Income.

Statutory Employees. If you were a statutory employee, the "Statutory employee" box in Box 6 of your W-2 form should be checked. Statutory employees include full time life insurance salespeople, certain agent or commission drivers and traveling salespeople, and certain homeworkers.

If you are deducting business expenses as a statutory employee, report the amount shown in Box 10 of your W-2 form and your expenses on Schedule C. If you are not deducting business expenses, report your income on line 7.

Employer-Provided Vehicle. If you used an employer-provided vehicle for both personal and business purposes and 100% of the annual lease value of the vehicle was included in the wages box (Box 10) of your W-2 form, you may be able to deduct the business use of the vehicle on Schedule A. But you must use **Form 2106,** Employee Business Expenses, to do so. (The total annual lease value of the vehicle should be shown in Box 16 of your W-2 form or on a separate statement.) For more details, get Pub. 525.

Excess Salary Deferrals. If you chose to have your employer contribute part of your pay to certain retirement plans (such as a 401(k) or the Federal Thrift Savings Fund) instead of having it paid to you, your W-2 form should have the "Deferred compensation" box in Box 6 checked. The amount deferred should be shown in Box 17. The total amount that may be deferred for 1990 under all plans is generally limited to $7,979. But amounts deferred under a tax-sheltered annuity plan may have a higher limit. For details, get **Pub. 575,** Pension and Annuity Income (Including Simplified General Rule). Any amount deferred in excess of these limits must be reported on Form 1040, line 7.

Caution: You may not deduct the amount deferred. It is not included in Box 10 of your W-2 form.

Employer-Provided Dependent Care Benefits (DCB). If you received benefits under your employer's dependent care plan, you may be able to exclude part or all of them from your income. But you must use **Form 2441,** Child and Dependent Care Expenses, to do so. The benefits should be shown in Box 15 of your W-2 form(s).

First, go to Form 2441 and complete Parts I and III. Line 25 of that form shows any excluded benefits. Line 26 shows the taxable benefits, if any. Include the taxable benefits from line 26 on Form 1040, line 7. On the dotted line next to line 7, write "DCB."

Whenever translations are required in court cases and other proceedings, only the words are translated, stripped of paralinguistic cues to emotions, hesitancy, or credibility. Much crucial information is thereby lost. Translation becomes a major problem in most agencies because their capabilities are limited to a few relatively common languages such as Spanish, Polish, or Japanese. Speakers of other languages find it difficult to contact such agencies by telephone or even in person. The mere identification of the language or dialect in which the speaker is trying to communicate can be a major puzzle.

Many agencies, such as the Internal Revenue Service and the Social Security Administration, operate bilingually, with Spanish the most common second language. It is obviously impossible to expand such programs to encompass all languages spoken by clients of these agencies. Those who do not understand English often cannot follow a doctor's instructions, are unable to complete forms, and cannot read insurance or job contracts. When speed is of the essence, as in hospital emergency rooms or police stations when a crime in progress is reported, language barriers can lead to disasters. Other than trying to hire people with varied language skills, little has been done to resolve the problem. No quick and easy cure is now on the horizon.

The Impact of Differential Cognitive Skills. Comprehension problems are made worse because many American adults are functionally illiterate, unable to comprehend simple instructions, let alone the complex directions on income-tax forms or welfare applications. The lack of information and comprehension skills that traditionally plagues economically and socially disadvantaged groups in American society is a self-perpetuating problem that deprives these groups of political influence and access to social and economic resources. As Bryan Jones states, "Cognitive skills develop in a sociospatial context, so that there exist spatial concentrations of individuals with substantial skills as well as concentrations of individuals with low information about influencing governmental decisions." [60]

Individuals in a social milieu that emphasizes the acquisition of political information will tend to acquire it even when the information is complex, lengthy, and poorly presented. Those who do not live in such a milieu will tend to ignore such information. Some agencies, such as the Social Security Administration and the Internal Revenue Service, provide help in completing forms, but such services are relatively rare. As indicated, they are often of low quality so that information seekers receive misinformation in addition to wasting time in efforts to reach overburdened officials.

In part, acquisition of new information hinges on the availability of appropriate mental images acquired through earlier learning. Thus poorly informed people, regardless of the extent of their exposure to information, lack the incentive and predisposition to learn much new information, whereas the already well-informed absorb it with ease because it fits readily into their established knowledge base. Over a lifetime, information-rich people get richer, while the information-poor remain poor. Thus, the knowledge gap between the privileged and underprivileged widens.[61]

Knowledgeable clients have a distinct advantage. They are more likely to understand complex rules and regulations, including appeals procedures, without depending on interpretations supplied, or omitted, by bureaucrats.[62] They are better able to make believable threats, such as threatening to appeal to the bureaucrat's superior. Their intellectual and financial resources may allow them to move from client to constituent status by developing effective lobbying groups.

Bridging Interpersonal Differences

Gaps in Social and Cultural Status. Differential cognitive skills often parallel social and cultural disparities and indeed may be caused by them. Bridging these gaps poses serious problems in client communication because relationships are perceived differently when viewed through diverse social and cultural lenses. For example, a client's cultural background may make him or her submissive to public officials. Accordingly, the individual may fail to correct the official's obvious misstatement of facts. Offers of gifts to officials, which are customary in many cultures, may be regarded as bribes in the American context. Scorn may therefore be heaped on clients who offer gifts.[63]

Bridging social and cultural gaps is made more difficult because of prevailing stereotypes about population groups. For example, many Americans tend to blame the poor for their plight, characterizing them as lazy and lacking in self-respect and motivation. People who suffer from sexually transmitted diseases or those with prison records or records as substance abusers are scorned for their alleged failings.[64] When such attitudes are prevalent in the political culture, they are difficult to overcome. Officials who disdain their clients are not likely to interact well with them and establish open lines of communication. The fact that many bureaucrats now come from groups with firsthand experience with major social ills is lessening this problem somewhat.[65]

Disdain and the hostility that often accompanies it cut both ways, of course. For example, in many poor neighborhoods citizens dislike the police as much as or more than the police dislike suspects and convicted offenders. When police-community relations deteriorate, it becomes difficult for the police to induce citizens to supply information that is essential to law enforcement. Similarly, bureaucrats involved in enforcing drug laws or in checking on truancy or on the whereabouts of errant fathers who do not support their children find it difficult to get community cooperation.

Many of these tensions surface during face-to-face encounters in public offices, making it excruciatingly difficult to elicit the information needed to categorize clients properly and to initiate the required procedures so that services can commence. Clients often hedge their answers when they suspect rightly or wrongly that questions have hidden meanings. For example, a mother applying for welfare is likely to tell officials that her children are healthy to avoid any suspicion that she is an unfit mother. If the children are really ill, the mother's lack of candor may discourage the official from recommending needed health services for the children.[66]

Playing Encounter Games—The Client's Move

When clients are knowledgeable about the bureaucratic system, encounters may become ritual battles between clients who try to gain maximum benefits and officials who seek to husband their agency's resources. Whether the stakes in this battle of conflicting interests are high or low depends on how much discretion the particular situation and its rules allow to the official. As discussed earlier, bureaucrats usually hold a huge advantage because of their legal status, ready access to information, control of the resources wanted by the client, and lack of competition from alternative service providers.

Attempts to bargain with officials for better treatment are most common in three types of situations in which officials enjoy discretion.[67] One of these occurs when benefits or services are not automatic so that the client must request services, including submitting evidence that they are needed. For example, clients requesting an interest-free loan after a hurricane must provide evidence of serious damage to their home that is satisfactory to the official handling the case. Secondly, appeals are common when the benefits sought are not a matter of right so that the official has discretion to grant or refuse their request. Admission to a job training program or a public works program is an example. Thirdly, attempts to bargain with officials occur when a request has been refused and the client seeks a reversal of the decision. In addition, clients occasionally make personal appeals for services when they are unaware that such appeals are not needed or when they are trying to pull strings—to gain special favors by extra effort.

When citizens contact public officials requesting specific actions, how do they attempt to control a situation in which they are the underdogs? What sorts of manipulative communication strategies should bureaucrats expect? To find out, a research team looked at letters written to Israeli customs officials by Israeli citizens pleading for lowered duties on goods sent to them from abroad.[68] The researchers discovered that appeals were both positive and negative. Clients promised rewards for favorable action and threatened penalties for refusals. In each case, the reward or threat invoked one or several wellsprings of human motivation, with people from different sociocultural groups showing distinctive ways of operating. There were references to the self-interest of the official or the public that would be served by granting the request. There were appeals to the altruism or empathy of the official and to legal or moral norms, such as a claim that the client had a legal right to import the goods free of charge or at a lower rate.

There were also threats of physical harm to authorities, warnings that certain benefits would be withheld or withdrawn from a noncompliant official or that superiors would be notified about the official's allegedly inappropriate behavior. All of these exemplify an appeal to the official's self-interest. Offers of reward ranged from the material, such as an outright bribe, to the symbolic, such as an invocation of divine blessings. At times, clients referred to the norms governing their relationship with the official by alleging that certain behavior was owed to citizens as a moral or legal duty, either by the official or by society. Clients also pledged to reward the official or society with cooperative behavior if the official would keep her or his part of the bargain. In other letters, clients appealed to the official's sense of pity for their presumably unusual plight, either with or without offering a material or symbolic reward. The researchers did not report the results of the various types of appeals, leaving open the question of what strategy works well and what does not.

Playing Encounter Games—The Bureaucrat's Move. The bureaucrat's arsenal of communication resources to cope with clients' ploys is heavily stocked, outweighing by far the clients' resources.[69] Client demands can be reduced, delayed, or rejected in a number of ways. Responding with jargon, for one, makes it difficult for clients to assess the situation and contest it if necessary. Jargon used in denying Medicare claims provides many examples. When technical medical terms are used to describe conditions excluded from coverage, few applicants can decipher the message. The stock paragraphs that bureaucrats use to assemble rejection letters often make it difficult or impossible to figure out Medicare payment criteria and to detect errors. The client's efforts to get services may also be short-circuited by conveying the impression that application procedures are arduous and humiliating and that a favorable outcome is unlikely. This type of advice is usually informal and remains unrecorded so that it is not subject to a superior's scrutiny and control. It therefore enables officials to use the client encounter to weed out potential clients who seem undesirable or whose eligibility for the service is indeed questionable.[70]

Another tactic for discouraging client requests consists of evading decisions and dispatching clients to various offices within the agency where help is unlikely or sending them to other agencies in the hope that frustration will end their efforts. This is known colloquially as giving them the runaround. When errors occur and elicit client complaints, agencies may take a long time to make corrections. For example, it has taken years to correct the duplication of a social security number issued to two different individuals or to have a name removed from voter registration lists after the voter has moved to another state. A claim of error suggests that some bureaucrat deserves blame for making incorrect discretionary judgments or for misapplying official rules or handling tasks carelessly. Like most people, bureaucrats are loath to correct errors that amount to a tacit admission that they failed to perform their duties properly.

Officials can also discourage undesirable clients by withholding information and evading questions. For instance, nurses in a public health clinic may claim to be too busy to answer questions or pass them off as requiring answers by a physician. The range of topics covered in conversations between officials and clients can be controlled by eliciting information only through highly structured interviews and allowing no side comments. Office hours may be scheduled at inconvenient times, and forms may be made deliberately complex with little assistance provided for completing them. No help may be forthcoming in securing necessary documents. To obtain food stamps, for example, the 1984 rules required at least sixty pieces of information about the applicant's household size, income, living expenses, and assets. Applicants had to present the required information within thirty days of filing their application, with a possible extension for another thirty days in some states.[71]

Clients may also be discouraged by making them feel uncomfortable. They may feel degraded when addressed by their first names by officials whom they must address more formally, or when they are forced to discuss intimate details of their lives in an open setting where others can listen. Bureaucrats can use their power to categorize clients to manipulate their eligibility for services and benefits of various kinds. A simple stomachache that a health professional classifies as major abdominal pain may allow a veteran to see a physician rather than a nurse practitioner with less medical training at a veterans' hospital. Conversely, by categorizing major abdominal pain as a simple stomachache, a patient who ought to see a physician may be shunted off to a nurse practitioner. Labels may be used to determine the disposition of clients by putting them into stigmatizing classifications such as "mentally disturbed" or "troublemakers." While these classifications may be based on bona fide appraisals, they often spring from misunderstanding the client's culture. They can also be used to punish disagreeable clients and reduce their effectiveness in coping with bureaucracies.[72]

Likable clients who are cooperative and deferential may receive extra advice and encouragement. For example, they may be told that they are eligible for the little-known supplemental medical-aid program that may add as much as 15 percent to their welfare payment. Officials may even steer favored applicants to a particular doctor who is known to be very generous in certifying the client's eligibility for this program.[73] Favored clients may be told about exceptions to the rules and how to make themselves eligible for them. They may not be questioned about income from occasional jobs that might reduce their benefits. They may be beckoned to move to the head of a waiting line, as happens routinely when lawyers go to traffic court with their clients.

One may ask how it is possible for either clients or officials to modify procedures when bureaucratic rules prescribe what is to be done.[74] The answer is that rules are nearly always imprecise enough so that transactions can be shaped by the way questions are structured and information about opportunities is provided. Flexibilities in categorization schemes, special procedures for emergencies, and outright bending of rules allow some parties to receive preferential treatment. Clients may be favored because their background is similar to that of the official, because they dress and act in approved ways, because they are emotionally appealing, or because they have powerful sponsors. Conversely, difficult cases involving troublesome clients may be steered away from the agency lest they blemish its record of accomplishments. Overall, states James Wilson, "the imperatives of the situation more than the attitudes of the worker shape the way tasks are performed in welfare offices. The key imperative is to reconcile the wants of a variegated and somewhat suspect group of petitioners with the organizational need for achieving equity and managing the large case load." [75]

The Scope of Citizen Roles

The Evaluation Puzzle

Judgment Criteria. How can one measure the quality of communications between government agencies and their clients? This question has been tackled from several perspectives by government agencies and private researchers. Investigators have asked whether encounters accomplish the intended tasks. Is the encounter effective in conveying messages to target groups, and are these messages understood so that they produce the desired action? The discussion thus far indicates that there are many problems on that score. Messages may also be judged by the relation between input and output. Were costs commensurate with benefits? Telephoning all licensed drivers to inform them about a change in the speed limit on national highways might be a highly effective method of message transmission, but it would not be an efficient use of resources. Many outreach programs have turned out to be excessively costly because response rates have been low.

Critical theorists have judged encounters by the equity of the interchange. Are the questions and responses fair and appropriate? Does the interchange present special advantages or disadvantages to particular clients? As noted, encounters pose grave problems of equity when socioeconomically disadvantaged groups face bureaucracies. When viewed from a critical perspective, encounters between citizens and public officials are prime examples of exploitative relationships.[76] They discriminate against the poor and weak, allowing government officials to dominate the relationship to their own advantage rather than the clients' benefit. In the eyes of critical theorists, there is little hope for improvement. While many complexities could be simplified, the system, by its very nature, will remain forbidding for its clients and therefore inherently inequitable.

The area of evaluation that has received comparatively little attention is the degree of satisfaction that clients experience in their contacts with bureaucrats. Ideally, in a democratic society, bureaucrats should be eager to discover the degree to which citizens are satisfied with services and their encounters with public servants. In reality, when provisions for feedback have been made, they usually have been limited to factual questions about the administration of existing services and the need for new or altered services. For example, in the fall of 1989, the Colorado Department of Revenue commissioned a private firm to gauge how well people understood current tax forms and to discover problems and misunderstandings about procedures. The information gathered through these focus groups then helped the agency in devising plans to encourage the use of short-form tax returns.[77]

Similarly, in April 1989 the Environmental Protection Agency, the Colorado Governor's Office, and the Colorado Departments of Natural Resources and Health sponsored a statewide survey of citizens to assess their policy priorities in environmental protection. The survey disclosed that the public rated hazardous waste, air pollution, loss of wilderness, and endangered plants and animals as the most serious problems. Coloradoans were willing to pay higher taxes and accept increased regulation to cope with these problems, but they were unwilling to undertake cleanups that might increase unemployment in the state or infringe on private property rights.

While such questions shed light on the kinds of policies and procedures likely to produce a satisfied public, they are not direct measures of citizen satisfaction. On the whole, public agencies have avoided asking questions about client satisfaction with bureaucracies. One major reason for this reluctance—the desire to protect agencies from public criticism—has already been mentioned.[78] Additionally, in the bureaucratic compensation structure, client satisfaction has not been a criterion for rewarding bureaucrats. Rather, evaluations of public services and the concomitant rewards for good performance have been concerned primarily with cost effectiveness and administrative efficiency. Public agencies have therefore structured their services to enable them to score well on these criteria.[79]

The desire to please official evaluators has led to the common practice of "creaming" client pools. By taking care of large numbers of easy cases and ignoring difficult ones, agencies are able to show that they serve a maximum number of clients with relatively few difficulties and failures. Employment agencies, for example, routinely concentrate on the most readily employable people, leaving the hard-core unemployed behind. Welfare agencies concentrate on simple cases, preferably working with people who pose no communication or missing documentation problems.[80] Similarly, when the norms of bureaucratic culture suggest that "getting work done" means completion of paperwork for purposes of evaluation, talking with clients becomes a time-consuming nuisance.[81] Accordingly, clients are often kept waiting while the officials attend to the paperwork.

Most of the information about citizens' appraisals of public services and encounters is transmitted to officials through relatively informal, unsystematic personal contacts or through written or telephoned complaints and comments.[82] Public officials often prefer these informal approaches to attitude measurement to more formal types of tests. For example, when 279 Florida city managers and mayors were interviewed in 1985, 88 percent said that informal contacts with the public provided them with a good deal of information about citizen wants and needs. Eighty percent of these officials also deemed information from letters or telephone calls quite helpful. By contrast, only 48 percent of them found systematic program evaluations helpful in conveying this type of information.[83]

Evaluation Scores—General Data. Given the fact that client satisfaction is a low priority for most bureaucrats and also that there are many reasons for neglecting client concerns, and given the harsh criticism of welfare bureaucracies in the media and in much of the social science literature, one would expect client evaluations of encounters and services to be unfavorable. This is not the case. Although public opinion polls show that people generally feel negatively about bureaucracies, they give high marks to specific agencies and officials. Barbara Nelson concluded from a review of polls covering various welfare services that "clients consistently found agency personnel friendly, empathetic, and humane." [84]

Similarly, after a critical review of a variety of polls in which people assessed their encounters with public social service agencies, Charles Goodsell concluded:

> The survey results described in the preceding section show favorable response rates on questions concerning bureaucratic performance that are almost never below 50 percent, usually above 70 percent, and not infrequently in the 80 and 90 percent ranges. In light of attacks on bureaucracy's treatment of clients, the consistency with which citizens evaluate their personal experiences with public agencies in a positive light is remarkable.[85]

Moreover, the review of evaluation studies showed that a variety of encounter dimensions, such as courtesy and respect shown, speed of service, and complaint handling in different types of services rated

> high levels of approval . . . at the town, city, county, state, and federal levels. . . . In most instances bureaucratic personnel are described as helpful, efficient, fair, considerate, and courteous. They are, furthermore, usually perceived as trying to assist, ready to listen, and even willing to adapt the rules and look out for client interests . . . an

almost complete contradiction of the hate image depicted in popular media and academic writing.[86]

The explanation for this puzzle of bad general evaluations and good specific ones seems to lie in stereotyped thinking. Average Americans, familiar with media accounts of bureaucratic incompetence and callousness, hold negative stereotypes on this subject and express them when asked, but they judge particular services on the basis of their own experiences.[87] When it comes to services for the unemployed, the retired, the sick, the disabled, and the poor, apparently these experiences are usually quite positive in the absolute or relative sense for the vast majority of clients.[88] Given the negative expectations produced by negative stereotypes, the positive appraisals may reflect the fact that the actual service is usually better than expected and is therefore positively evaluated. Moreover, people are prone to evaluate events in their lives positively because that is psychologically comfortable. Their actual behavior may suggest that they feel otherwise. For instance, they may express satisfaction with their job while exhibiting high rates of absenteeism and job turnover.[89]

Given the massive American entitlement programs, social service agencies are able to provide some help for most applicants, including the most needy. These clients, who may have approached their encounters with public agencies with considerable fears and doubts, are apt to feel a sense of relief and gratitude. Survey data collected in 1972 indicated that only 10.6 percent of the applicants to the sixteen major welfare programs existing at the time were rejected outright.[90] The common perception, shared by rich and poor alike, that those who depend on public assistance should be quiescent and thankful may be another factor in expressed satisfaction by welfare clients. Negative evaluations of bureaucracies increased when the agencies were farther removed from survey respondents. Washington bureaucrats, for example, were called incompetent and untrustworthy much more often than those at the state and local levels. Stereotypes of remote bureaucrats were not improved by positive personal experiences. However, they deteriorated in the wake of negative personal experiences.

Evaluation Scores—Communication Data. Citizen evaluations of bureaucracies will hinge partly on the nature of the questions asked. These may relate to the quality of the personal interactions between bureaucrats and clients during their encounter, the adequacy of the information given, a general evaluation of the bureaucrats' competence, or satisfaction with the final disposition of the case. The vast majority of surveys have focused on the last point, evaluating satisfaction with the substance of bureaucratic performance. However, questions relating to the quality of the encounter have also been asked occasionally. Charles Goodsell, for example, interviewed a random sample of 240 welfare clients in San Francisco, St. Louis,

Duluth, and Evansville, Indiana, immediately after they had completed a visit to either the main Social Security office, the Unemployment Compensation office, or the Public Assistance office for Aid to Families with Dependent Children. Based on these interviews, Goodsell reported that 66 percent of the people he interviewed as they left Social Security offices said that their caseworkers had been very courteous. Sixty-eight percent were satisfied with the official's willingness to listen to them. Usual waiting time was thirty minutes or less. Only five percent of the clients waited for more than one hour to be served.[91]

To focus more directly on communication aspects of public encounters, my research assistants and I ran a small pilot study in June 1988 patterned on Goodsell's approach, conducting exit interviews at thirty-minute intervals with randomly selected clients at two Social Security offices in Chicago in low-income neighborhoods. When clients emerged from the office, they were asked to respond to a series of open-ended questions about the quality and tone of communication between themselves and public officials and their feelings about the encounter. A total of 71 clients were requested to participate, of whom 9 (13 percent) refused outright, usually claiming to be in a hurry to leave. Difficulties in communicating with non-English-speaking people, other than Spanish speakers, further reduced the pool of completed, usable interviews to 43, making this a very small pilot study.[92] The group was 16 percent white, 37 percent black, and 47 percent Hispanic. In line with Goodsell's findings, 88 percent reported that they were treated in a friendly, courteous manner. In fact, 55 percent considered the workers in the Social Security office to be friendlier than the employees in their local grocery store.

Ninety-one percent said that Social Security officials paid attention to what they had to say. This indicates that officials had mastered important listening skills. At the very least, they could convey the impression that they were attentive. When asked whether the officials explained what they were doing, 86 percent said they did and 98 percent claimed to understand the explanation. Moreover, 91 percent said that they found it easy, rather than difficult, to comprehend the information. Even when one discounts this figure somewhat because people might be embarrassed about admitting comprehension problems, it suggests high levels of success in transmitting information. Receiving explanations of Social Security rules and procedures is apparently important because 15 percent of the clients indicated that they lacked essential information prior to their encounter with office personnel. When asked about their major sources of information about Social Security matters, 35 percent named office personnel, 30 percent relied on printed information, and the remainder relied on friends or other informants.

In terms of the substance of the transaction, only 64 percent of the respondents thought they had accomplished as much as they had hoped during this visit. Among those who felt the encounter had not met their expectations, 46 percent blamed the official while the remainder felt that circumstances beyond the control of the official had caused the problem. For 47 percent, there was little dissatisfaction about being forced to wait in line. The fact that average waiting time was only five minutes and that waits of thirty minutes or more were rare may account for the lack of resentment. Overall, 49 percent could not think of any aspect of their visit that might be characterized as unpleasant.

The Pros and Cons of Client Consultations

In recent years, attention to matters concerning public satisfaction with bureaucracies has increased, partly as a result of the work of organizations dealing with welfare rights and civil rights. Client demands for participation in public agency decision making have become more strident, and political forces supporting these demands have become better organized. New political norms have emerged that emphasize the public's right to receive more respectful treatment, to be consulted about services, and to be kept informed about agency performance. However, resources made available for improving public encounters and increasing consultations have not kept up with demands.

The Pruitt-Igoe Case

The Pruitt-Igoe public housing project is often cited as a classic case of disastrous consequences when concern with client satisfaction is slighted and client communication is inadequate.[93] The project, built in St. Louis in the 1950s, consisted of thirty-three apartment buildings, each eleven stories high. It was designed by a well-known architect and managed by a professional army psychologist. At its inception it was "hailed as the most progressive poor people's housing project in the United States."[94] In addition to modern appliances in each apartment, its unique features included speedy elevators that stopped at three-floor intervals only. At each stop were community centers where residents could meet and enjoy each other's company.

Contrary to the expectations of the designers, the community centers soon deteriorated into hangouts for young punks who assaulted people when they emerged from the elevators. The lack of ground-floor toilets led children to use the elevators for this purpose so that they became filthy. Gangs began to take over the buildings, which gradually became totally unsafe and uninhabitable. Rent collection and building repairs became impossible. By 1974 the city decided to dynamite the entire complex.

Postmortems on the causes of the failure concluded, as Everett and Rekha Rogers report, that "the main problem, in addition to architectural blunders, was the lack of participation afforded residents in designing and governing" the project.[95] To forestall similar disasters, subsequent housing projects built in St. Louis allowed for far greater citizen input about their design and management. The results have been at least marginally better.

The Limits of Pluralist Control

The case does raise questions, however, about the nature and scope of desirable citizen input into public ventures. What information should have been provided to citizens in advance of construction? Would prospective clients have known how to respond to questions about the advisability of constructing high-rise buildings, features needed for adequate elevator service, and the ground-level public toilet requirement? Should "expert" or client views be more important in building projects, assuming that they differ? In weighing the answers to such questions, on must remember that agencies receive advice from many quarters. In the case of public utility regulation, for example, the advice of citizens is balanced by that of industry representatives and regulatory commission members and their staffs. The advice of the more technically experienced people is likely to prevail in certain instances over the opposition of citizen boards.[96] The same holds true for occupational licensing boards, where members representing the general public have no influence because they lack expertise.[97]

More generally, what portion of available resources should be devoted to securing and catering to citizen input and on what sorts of policies should they be consulted and local control prevail? The answers to such questions are particularly difficult when controversial public services are concerned, such as busing to provide school integration, health services for mental patients or AIDS victims, or when communities are unwilling to host dangerous or disagreeable service such as prisons, nuclear-waste sites, or garbage dumps.[98]

This last point directs attention to the reverse aspect of client communication and influence. Catering to the particular interests of individual citizens may harm the interests of the larger society. Many contacts between citizens and bureaucracies relate to the citizens' narrowly private concerns. A cross-national analysis of citizen input into public policies revealed that responding sympathetically to such demands may have profound policy consequences. As Alan Zukerman and Darrell West state, "The more widespread contacting is within a country, the more time government officials spend responding to narrow demands. The more successful contacting is, the more government policies center around the production of private goods and public goods with very limited sets of beneficiaries."[99] As has been amply demonstrated in Congress, where casework takes up much of a member's time, important activities of concern to more broadly based constituencies suffer when casework becomes dominant. Moreover, impartiality suffers. When individuals gain access to a government service that is denied to others in similar positions, fairness goes out the window.[100]

A number of scholars have tried to identify the factors important in predicting which citizens are likely to contact government officials and hence garner a disproportionately large share of benefits. The assumption has been that well-educated clients fare best. The research findings are not clear-cut on that score, although outreach efforts, as we have seen, show that the neediest are often least aware of available public assistance. Factors such as need for a particular service, awareness of its existence, and political sophistication are important predictors, but their impact varies so that disadvantaged groups do not necessarily lose out.[101] For example, when it is easy to contact government officials, even disadvantaged citizens who might ordinarily be unaware of available services are likely to do so. In Houston and Dallas, the existence of a central office to receive citizen complaints has increased contacts from the lowest socioeconomic sector.

However, the danger remains that encounters empower the haves more than the have-nots. When encounters become ongoing relationships, such as the relationship between lobbyists and bureaucrats, the danger of government dominated by vocal minorities is real, as explained in the previous chapter.[102] The winners in this political sport of hunting for specialized advantages are usually the well-to-do, the educationally advantaged, and political activists from all socioeconomic levels.[103] It is the squeaky wheel that gets the grease that may be needed elsewhere to prevent major breakdowns.

Summary and Conclusions

Life in the United States entails a large number of contacts between citizens and government officials, ranging from relatively minor matters to services of the greatest significance, involving health, social welfare, and public security. This chapter focuses on the encounters between citizens and bureaucrats that initiate and guide major and minor services to individuals. Despite the importance of these transactions, the communications aspects of rendering services to the public have received relatively little attention.

Establishing a good communication climate is a formidable task in the public sector because bureaucracy is largely inhospitable to free-flowing, open communication based on respect for each client's particular needs and wants. The information elicited from personal encounters, questionnaires, or interpersonal contacts is designed to allow officials to fit each client's case into a predetermined category. Standardized bureaucratic procedures aim to treat all members of a category alike, *not* to provide individualized attention. Most people resent being treated impersonally as just another "case." Socially disadvantaged people are particularly likely to feel rejected and powerless in the presence of officials who, so the theory goes, are their servants.

Numerous factors heighten these feelings of powerlessness and the realization that bureaucrats dominate public encounters. Unlike their clients, bureaucrats know the rules of the encounter game very well and, within limits, enjoy the power to interpret them according to their own inclinations. With no alternative providers, clients who need a particular service are forced to deal with the government agency that supplies it. Moreover, private sector incentives to please clients are absent in the public sector.

Given the large number of important, complex government activities that require interaction with clients, as well as the diversity of both clients and public officials, it is not surprising that many common communication difficulties emerge, such as message transmission problems. The discussion focuses on the inadequacy of channels for exchanging information between citizens and their government, the arduous task of composing comprehensible messages about technically complex matters, the propensity to use overly convoluted language, and the difficulty of coping with the ever-increasing number of non-English-speaking people now living in the United States. The discussion of social, cultural, and status gaps points out that intelligent, well-educated, knowledgeable clients are more likely than their less fortunate fellow citizens to take control of encounters with public officials.

The chapter also details some of the resources available to clients in their efforts to control encounters with public officials and obtain consideration for their views in bureaucratic decision making. Although these resources are insufficient to overcome the advantages enjoyed by bureaucrats, the latter do recognize the need for information from citizens in order to accomplish their work properly and are aware that consultations with citizens prior to administrative decisions may be helpful. However, citizens often lack essential expertise and tend to push their narrow interests without considering the welfare of the larger community.

If this chapter seems to bash bureaucracies in general, and the Social Security Administration in particular, for their communication failures, this is not my intent. Major failures have often been dwarfed by amazing successes. In a typical year (1986), the Social Security Administration, for example, issued 5.7 million new social security cards. It received and posted 230 million earnings reports for the country's 124 million workers. It also processed 6 million applications for benefits and made benefit payments to 41.8 million persons.[104] Additionally, Congress thrust very burdensome new responsibilities on the agency, such as reviewing the eligibility of recipients of disability benefits. That task required checking the health status of 1,203,000 individuals. Congress further complicates the operations of the agency by continually tinkering with its mandate and rules. Between 1977 and 1982, for example, more than 6,200 bills related to the agency's programs were introduced in Congress, forcing the SSA to assess their provisions and take appropriate stands. Sixty-six bills, containing 300 new provisions, were actually enacted.[105]

Major government agencies obviously face staggering tasks in interacting with their publics, even without considering the difficulties inherent in all bureaucratic situations. If responsiveness is poor at times, if many serious errors occur, it may be quite unfair to ask why performance cannot be better. Instead, the question should be: "Why isn't it worse?" American bureaucracies with their limited powers, hemmed in by strict procedural regulations controlled by elected officials who cater to publics with conflicting interests, have more pressing priorities than client relations and responsiveness. Before these priorities can be recast, the underlying structural and functional problems must be resolved. Whether that is worth doing and how it might be accomplished is beyond the confines of this discussion.

Nonetheless, even under present conditions, several areas offer the prospect of improved client communication. Outreach, for one, needs to be done on a bigger scale and more effectively. The task might well be assigned to the growing number of ombudsmen used by the public sector. Simplification of bureaucratic language and bridging of cultural gaps are also promising areas for reform. Since millions could benefit from improved performance in these areas, they are well worth major efforts.

However, empowerment of individual citizens must not be bought at the price of marginalizing the majority and endangering broad general interests. The welfare of the whole must always remain more important than the fate of any of its parts.

Notes

1. Charles T. Goodsell, ed., *The Public Encounter: Where State and Citizen Meet* (Bloomington: Indiana University Press, 1981), 3.
2. For a discussion of the differences between contacts by citizens and other forms of citizen participation, see Alan S. Zukerman and Darrell M. West, "The Political Bases of Citizen Contacting: A Cross-National Analysis," *American Political Science Review* 79 (1985): 117.
3. Daniel Katz, Barbara A. Gutek, Robert L. Kahn, and E. Barton, *Bureaucratic Encounters* (Ann Arbor, Mich.: Institute for Social Research, 1975), 52-59.
4. For a discussion of public encounters in various disciplines and bibliographic information, see Goodsell, *The Public Encounter,* 7-13, and sources cited there,

and Elihu Katz and Brenda Danet, "Communication between Bureaucracy and the Public," in *Handbook of Communication,* Ithiel de Sola Pool and Wilbur Schramm, eds. (Chicago: Rand-McNally, 1973), 666-697.

5. Relevant studies are Michael Lipsky's *Street-Level Bureaucracy: Dilemmas of the Individual in Public Services* (New York: Russell Sage Foundation, 1980), and Jeffrey Prottas, *People Processing: The Street-Level Bureaucrat in Public Service Bureaucracies* (Lexington, Mass.: D.C. Heath, 1979), as well as an earlier study by Elihu Katz and Brenda Danet, *Bureaucracy and the Public* (New York: Basic Books, 1973). Bryan Jones, with Saadia Greenberg and Joseph Drew, in *Service Delivery in the City: Citizen Demand and Bureaucratic Rules* (New York: Longman, 1980), focused more generally on citizen interactions with urban public service bureaucracies.

6. Prottas, *People Processing,* 46.

7. Paul A. Sabatier and Neil Pelkey, "Incorporating Multiple Actors and Guidance Instruments into Models of Regulatory Policymaking," *Administration and Society* 19 (August 1987): 238.

8. Evelyn Z. Brodkin, "Policy Politics: If We Can't Govern, Can We Manage?" *Political Science Quarterly* 102 (1987): 579. The quote is from a 1979 convention paper by Claus Offe.

9. Prottas, *People Processing,* 65.

10. Jones, *Service Delivery in the City,* 50-52.

11. Ibid., 53. Also see Elaine B. Sharp, "Citizen-Demand Making in the Urban Context," *American Journal of Political Science* 28 (November 1984): 654-670, and Steven A. Peterson, "Close Encounters of the Bureaucratic Kind: Older Americans and Bureaucracy," *American Journal of Political Science* 30 (May 1986): 347-356.

12. Martin Tolchin, "Study Says Half of Those Eligible Get Food Stamps," *New York Times,* November 15, 1988.

13. Martin Tolchin, "Federal Aid for Destitute Reaching Just Half of Those Eligible," *New York Times,* May 10, 1988.

14. For a full discussion of this situation, see Martha Derthick, *Agency under Stress: The Social Security Administration in American Government* (Washington, D.C.: Brookings Institution, 1990).

15. Katz et al., *Bureaucratic Encounters,* 59-60.

16. Ibid., 54.

17. Arnold Vedlitz, James A. Dyer, and Roger Durand, "Citizen Contacts with Local Governments: A Comparative View," *American Journal of Political Science* 24 (February 1980): 50.

18. Kenneth R. Mladenka, "Citizen Demands and Urban Services: The Distribution of Bureaucratic Response in Chicago and Houston," *American Journal of Political Science* 25 (November 1981): 693.

19. Jones, *Service Delivery in the City,* 142-144.

20. Ibid., 86-87.

21. Michael T. Harmon and Richard T. Mayer, *Organizational Theory for Public Administration* (Boston: Little-Brown, 1986), 326-331.

22. Citizens' interactions with bureaucrats reflect their lack of power and control. See Jones, *Service Delivery in the City,* 7.

23. John L. Crompton and Charles W. Lamb, Jr., *Marketing Government and Social Services* (New York: Wiley, 1986), 9.

24. Lipsky, *Street-Level Bureaucracy,* 84-86.

25. Brodkin, "Policy Politics," 579, and Scott T. Moore, "The Theory of Street-Level Bureaucracy: A Positive Critique," *Administration and Society* 19 (May

1987): 74-94.

26. Kathy E. Ferguson, *The Feminist Case against Bureaucracy* (Philadelphia: Temple University Press, 1984), 123.

27. Murray Edelman, *The Symbolic Uses of Politics* (Urbana: University of Illinois Press, 1964), 134-146.

28. William T. Gormley, Jr., "The Representation Revolution: Reforming State Regulation through Public Representation," *Administration and Society* 18 (August 1986): 179-196.

29. Larry B. Hill, "Bureaucratic Monitoring Mechanisms," in *The Public Encounter,* Charles T. Goodsell, ed. (Bloomington: Indiana University Press, 1981), 165.

30. Clarence N. Stone, "Attitudinal Tendencies among Officials," in *The Public Encounter,* 56.

31. Yeheskel Hasenfeld and Daniel Steinmetz, "Client-Official Encounters in Social Service Agencies," in *The Public Encounter,* 87.

32. Harvey A. Abrams and Peter Bidney, "When Clients Complain: Bureaucratic Responsiveness in Large Federal Agencies," *Journal of Sociology and Social Welfare* 6 (June 1979): 558.

33. Barry Schwartz, *Queuing and Waiting: Studies in the Social Organization of Access and Delay* (Chicago: University of Chicago Press, 1975), discusses the power plays involved in delays.

34. Ibid., 26.

35. Abrams and Bidney, "When Clients Complain," 559.

36. Hasenfeld and Steinmetz, "Client-Official Encounters in Social Service Agencies," 84. Measures of unresponsiveness are discussed in Abrams and Bidney, "When Clients Complain," 558-561.

37. Ferguson, *The Feminist Case against Bureaucracy,* 123.

38. Ibid., 123-124.

39. Gormley, "The Representation Revolution," 184.

40. Ferguson, *The Feminist Case against Bureaucracy,* 124.

41. Joan Beck, "What if Taxpayers Can't Cope with New Forms and Give Up?" *Chicago Tribune,* May 25, 1987.

42. John M. Stevens and Robert P. McGowan, *Information Systems and Public Management* (New York: Praeger, 1985), 27. William T. Gormley, Jr., "The Representation Revolution," 179-196.

43. Gormley, "The Representation Revolution," 187-188.

44. Ibid., 188-189.

45. Larry B. Hill, "The Citizen Participation-Representation Roles of American Ombudsmen," *Administration and Society* 13 (February 1982): 411.

46. Ibid., 428.

47. Hill, "Bureaucratic Monitoring Mechanisms," 170-181.

48. Abrams and Bidney, "When Clients Complain," 562-574.

49. Mladenka, "Citizen Demands and Urban Services," 697.

50. Brodkin, "Policy Politics," 375-382.

51. The Social Security Disability Program, though small by comparison with other Social Security programs, still involved roughly 4.5 million people at the time of the investigation. For more details, see Derthick, *Agency under Stress.*

52. Martin Tolchin, "Staff Is Cut, Many Lose Social Security," *New York Times,* December 8, 1989.

53. Charles T. Goodsell, Raymond E. Austin, Karen L. Hedblom, and Clarence C. Rose, "Bureaucracy Expresses Itself: How State Documents Address the Public," *Social Science Quarterly* 62 (1981): 576-591.

54. Ibid., 579-581.
55. Ibid., 584.
56. Hasenfeld and Steinmetz, "Client-Official Encounters in Social Service Agencies," 84.
57. Brodkin, "Policy Politics," 585-587.
58. Goodsell et al., "Bureaucracy Expresses Itself," 590-591.
59. Author's unpublished research.
60. Jones, *Service Delivery in the City,* 49.
61. Cecilie Gaziano, "The Knowledge Gap: An Analytical Review of Media Effects," *Communication Research* 10 (October 1983): 447-486, and sources cited there.
62. Hasenfeld and Steinmetz, "Client-Official Encounters in Social Service Agencies," 93.
63. For examples of cultural differences among Western and nonWestern populations, see Elihu Katz, Michael Gurevitch, Brenda Danet, and Tsiyona Peled, "Petitions and Prayers: A Method for the Content Analysis of Persuasive Appeals," *Social Forces* 47 (1969): 447-463.
64. For additional examples, see Stone, "Attitudinal Tendencies among Officials," 54-59.
65. Barbara Nelson, "Client Evaluations of Social Programs," in *The Public Encounter,* 27-29.
66. Prottas, *People Processing,* 138-139.
67. Katz and Danet, *Bureaucracy and the Public,* 175.
68. Katz et al., "Petitions and Prayers," 447. For a similar analysis of Soviet citizens, see Wayne DiFrancesico and Zvi Gitelman, "Soviet Political Culture and 'Covert Participation' in Policy Implementation," *American Political Science Review* 78 (September 1984): 603-621.
69. Hasenfeld and Steinmetz, "Client-Official Encounters in Social Service Agencies," 89; Prottas, *People Processing,* chap. 1.
70. Prottas, *People Processing,* 130.
71. Tolchin, "Federal Aid for Destitute Reaching Just Half of Those Eligible." Excessive documentation requirements, designed to discourage welfare applicants, are discussed in Brodkin, "Policy Politics: If We Can't Govern, Can We Manage?" 583-584.
72. For further discussion of the importance of categorization, see Prottas, *People Processing,* 5-6.
73. Ibid., 32-33.
74. Of course some exceptions are actually built into the rules. For example, veterans receive preferential treatment in grading of civil service examinations.
75. James Q. Wilson, *Bureaucracy: What Government Agencies Do and Why They Do It* (New York: Basic Books, 1989), 53.
76. Goodsell, *The Public Encounter,* 9-10.
77. The research for Colorado agencies was done by Ciruli Associates of Denver.
78. Katz et al., *Bureaucratic Encounters,* 2; Nelson, "Client Evaluations of Social Programs."
79. Hasenfeld and Steinmetz, "Client-Official Encounters in Social Service Agencies," 61.
80. Prottas, *People Processing,* 37.
81. Ferguson, *The Feminist Case against Bureaucracy,* 140-141.
82. Carol Ann Traut and Hal G. Rainey, "The Information Gathering Practices of City Officials," American Political Science Association paper, 1989.
83. Ibid.

84. Nelson, "Client Evaluations of Social Programs," 27-28.
85. Charles T. Goodsell, *The Case for Bureaucracy: A Public Administration Polemic* (Chatham, N.J.: Chatham House, 1985), 21.
86. Ibid., 21, 29. For a critique of such analyses of evaluations on theoretical and methodological grounds, see Yeheskel Hasenfeld, "Citizens' Encounters with Welfare State Bureaucracies," *Social Service Review* 59 (December 1985): 622-635.
87. Katz et al., *Bureaucratic Encounters,* and Lloyd A. Free and Hadley Cantril, *The Political Beliefs of Americans: A Study of Public Opinion* (New York: Simon & Schuster, 1968), report similar discrepancies between overall evaluations and specific judgments.
88. Hasenfeld, "Citizens' Encounters with Welfare State Bureaucracies," 629.
89. Nelson, "Client Evaluations of Social Programs," 34.
90. Ibid., 38.
91. Goodsell, *The Case for Bureaucracy,* 31; the study is reported in full in Charles T. Goodsell, "Conflicting Perceptions of Welfare Bureaucracy," *Social Casework: The Journal of Contemporary Social Work* 61 (June 1980): 354-360.
92. The literature on client perception is reviewed in Goodsell, "Conflicting Perceptions of Welfare Bureaucracy," 356-358.
93. Everett M. Rogers and Rekha Agarwala Rogers, *Communication in Organizations* (New York: Free Press, 1976), 3-6.
94. Ibid., 3.
95. Ibid., 5.
96. William Gormley, John Hoadley, and Charles Williams, "Potential Responsiveness in the Bureaucracy: Views of Public Utility Regulation," *American Political Science Review* 77 (September 1983): 704-715.
97. Gormley, "The Representation Revolution," 185.
98. See Robert D. Miewald and John C. Comer, "Complaining as Participation," *Administration and Society* 17 (1986): 481-499, for a discussion of the pros and cons of citizen participation in the administrative process.
99. Zukerman and West, "The Political Bases of Citizen Contacting," 118. Also see Sidney Tarrow, *Between Center and Periphery: Grassroots Politicians in Italy and France* (New Haven: Yale University Press, 1977).
100. Gortner, Harold F., Julianne Mahler, and Jeanne Bell Nicholson, *Organizational Theory: A Public Perspective* (Chicago: Dorsey, 1987), 277-289. Illustrates this point with a case of parental intervention in school policy.
101. See, for example, Vedlitz et al., "Citizen Contacts with Local Governments."
102. Zukerman and West, "The Political Bases of Citizen Contacting," 118.
103. Zukerman and West, "The Political Bases of Citizen Contacting," 119, examined contacting in Austria, India, Japan, the Netherlands, Yugoslavia, and the United States.
104. Derthick, *Agency under Stress,* 5.
105. Ibid., 75.

C H A P T E R   9

Communication Analysis and Problem Solving

General Concerns

Social scientists have developed numerous approaches and techniques for analyzing and evaluating organizational communication in the public sector. Those that have proved to be particularly useful for public sector agencies will be discussed in this chapter. As indicated at the beginning of this book, its purpose is to provide an introduction to these techniques rather than specific instructions for implementing them. The chapter end notes refer readers to the implementation literature.

Theories

Like all scientific endeavors, the analysis of communications in organizations requires good theories. They provide researchers with directions for determining what phenomena need to be examined in order to answer the questions posed for the analysis, what data must be collected, and what methods of data analysis are likely to be useful.

Several major theoretical approaches that have guided organizational communication research in the past were discussed in Chapter 1. There the focus was on the findings yielded by these research approaches and the motivations that inspired the researchers. In this chapter our concerns are more methodological, focusing on issues of overall research design and data collection. What major theoretical foundations are currently available to undergird organizational communication research? A fourfold classification scheme presented in the opening chapter of the *Handbook of Organizational Communication* is useful.[1] The authors identify four packages of theories and characterize them as mechanistic, psychological, interpretive-symbolic, or systems-interactive. Each package of theories rests on a different set of assumptions and is directed toward examining different aspects of organizational communication.

Research proceeding from theories guided by *mechanistic* perspectives assumes that messages are composed of tangible bits of information that travel from senders to receivers along physically identifiable channels. To analyze communication processes, researchers must therefore examine the mechanics of the process, such as the nature and capacity of the channels linking senders and receivers, noise factors that may produce distortions, and the volume and direction of messages. There is an assumption that communication phenomena are causally linked so that message senders expect to produce effects through the messages that they transmit.[2] Examples of research based on mechanistic principles include much of the work of Karl Deutsch discussed in Chapter 1, as well as the ideas underlying network analysis, which are discussed in Chapter 5.

When theories based on *psychological* perspectives are used, researchers assume that the psychological predispositions of human message senders and receivers determine the nature and format of the messages that will be transmitted and the nature of attention and type of interpretation that they will receive upon reaching their targets. Since human minds are crucial intervening variables in the message-transmission process, research must focus on them. The psychological screens that Deutsch included in his model of communication, depicted in Figure 1-2, are an example of using psychological theories for communication analysis. This figure actually represents a combination of mechanistic and psychological perspectives.

Research proceeding from theories classified as *interpretive-symbolic* is grounded in the notion that the messages traveling through various channels are nothing more than stimuli that lead to communication by creating understanding between the parties exchanging these stimuli. These understandings, developed through an interchange of ideas, are the actual messages, quite apart from the original intent of the message senders and the conceptual filters of the message receivers.[3] Shared perceptions create a sense of organizational existence and make members feel that they are playing distinct roles in the agency. Organizations lack reality without such shared perceptions, which produce such intangible yet very real phenomena as organizational cultures and climates. Obviously, researchers attempting to capture such intangibles need to delve into the shared perceptions of participants in organizational communication. This is done through methods geared to holistic analyses of all the factors involved in a particular situation. Examples are participant observations when a researcher actually works for a while in the agency under study, or ethnographic techniques used by anthropologists to describe people and their cultures.

How does the fourth group of theories differ from the other three? As indicated, mechanistic theories direct researchers to issues related to the transmission of communication stimuli. Psychological theories concentrate on the consequences for communication when psychological filters mediate the responses of individual message receivers. Interpretive-symbolic theories deal with shared perceptions that arise from the interactions of organization members. By contrast, *systems-interaction* theories dwell on message patterns on the assumption that communication patterns exhibited over time are significant indicators of how systems function in a given environment. The research focuses on recurring communication events, such as complaints about unclear messages, rather than on communicators as individuals or interactive groups or on the structures that they have created for communication. Accordingly, recording of message patterns permits investigators to make predictions about pattern repetitions and changes. For example, if one can detect typical patterns in disputes between labor and management, one may be able to predict when a settlement is imminent.[4]

Research Designs

The theory chosen for a particular research project will depend on the researcher's preferences and the nature of the situation under investigation. At times a particular theoretical orientation seems obviously superior; at other times a combination of orientations appears to be best. In many situations each of the theoretical approaches may seem equally promising, although each is likely to illuminate a different facet of the problem. Obviously, the design of a particular research project hinges very heavily on which of these four theoretical orientations is selected. An interpretist theorist would not be concerned primarily with the capacity of a telephone line to handle incoming message traffic, nor would a systems-interaction theorist focus on the degree of emotion generated by particular messages traveling horizontally between organizations.

Once the focus of the investigation has been determined and hypotheses have been formulated in line with the chosen theory or theories, the researcher must decide what body of data should be examined, the time frames and sampling procedures that may be needed to reduce the data to manageable proportions, and the precise ways in which the data are to be gathered. Keeping data bases manageable is particularly important because of the vast number of messages that make up the communication universe of even small organizations.

For example, political scientist Martha Feldman was interested in how administrative agencies produce and then use information. She was intrigued by the fact that although public agencies produce a tremendous number of reports, these are hardly ever used.[5] Based on theories about organizational decision making and information use in inherently ambiguous situations, she formulated a series of hypotheses that might explain the phenomenon. Most of them were in the psychological and interpretive traditions, with some mechanistic approaches also included. As the site of her research she chose a single, relatively small organization—the policy office of the U.S. Department of Energy. To gather data that might support or disconfirm her hypotheses, she observed and participated in operations at the policy office for a period of over a year and a half, keeping records on organizational activities and conversations. These were supplemented by records kept by co-workers at her behest. Her own observations were supplemented by interviews with co-workers representing various occupational roles.[6] The findings supported her hypotheses, revealing a variety of political and organizational reasons that make bureaucratic reports generally unusable for decision makers. The study also produced numerous suggestions for improved utilization of the reports of professional analysts.

Data Collection and Analysis Methods

The most commonly used data-collection methods involve systematic observations, surveys conducted through questionnaires and interviews, and data extraction through content analysis of existing records. Experimental techniques have been used infrequently because it is difficult to simulate organizational settings involving large numbers of people and events. Communication behavior has occasionally been studied in artificially created situations in laboratory settings or in focus groups. The latter engage in free-flowing conversations on predetermined topics.[7]

Systematic observations may entail on-site visits by researchers at predetermined intervals and for fixed periods of time. Alternatively, the behavior may be recorded electronically with or without the actual presence of researchers. Members of the organization may also be asked to observe and record their own behavior in the form of more or less detailed diaries. In general, observation techniques are most suitable for relatively small organizations because of the limited scope of activities that each observer can watch. Among the major problems with the technique are its intrusiveness, which may alter the behavior of subjects under observation, and the difficulty of watching many interactions that may occur simultaneously.

For surveys, questions may be transmitted in person, by mail, or by telephone, or they may be incorporated into computer programs. As in other types of social research, data collection through questionnaires and interviews presents problems because of the difficulty of phrasing questions appropriately and then accurately assessing the meanings of the answers. The latter is a particularly serious problem when people are asked about past events or behavior that they did not record systematically at the time. Retrospective memories and evaluations are notoriously unreliable.

Instead of eliciting data through questioning respondents, researchers may extract data from recorded messages through some form of content analysis. Content may be captured retrospectively from recording devices, such as printed matter, film, or audio tapes. Alternatively, it may be analyzed instantaneously by observers present at its creation. Monitoring to capture content may occur on a random or purposive sampling basis or as part of a continuous effort. For example, the Vanderbilt Television News Archives collect nightly television news continuously but sample other types of political messages, such as presidential addresses. The advantage of continuous recording is that it captures unanticipated events and facilitates time series analyses. The disadvantage is high recording and storage costs.

For data analysis, organizational communication researchers use the same tools as other social scientists, ranging from intuitive approaches to simple as well as sophisticated mathematical procedures. However, in some types of communication research, such as interpretive approaches or network analysis, the use of ordinary statistical techniques may be inappropriate because their assumptions, such as randomness in the selection of survey respondents, are not met.

Communication analysis proceeds from various unexplored assumptions that need more rigorous scrutiny than they have received. For example, topics and themes that occur frequently in a body of messages are presumed to be important to the senders and familiar to the receivers. Value judgments expressed or implied in messages are supposed to reveal the sender's value perceptions, except when there is a discernible reason for deception. When oral communications are analyzed, paralinguistic cues, such as pauses, raised or lowered pitch, laughing, or crying, are given standardized rather than particularized interpretations. In each case, the underlying assumptions are questionable.

In all studies, regardless of focus, theory, or technique, it is essential to incorporate contextual information into the analysis. Organizational communication patterns and practices cannot be fully understood if investigators do not know the cultural, social, economic, and political context in which organizations operate. Peter Monge and Eric Eisenberg state, "In general, an organization performs best when there is a good 'fit' between the nature of its environment and its formal and informal internal structures. Research shows that diverse, turbulent environments require more flexible organic structural arrangements, whereas more placid, stable environments can be coped with by more traditional, mechanistic structures." [8] As we have seen, organizations in the public sector are particularly sensitive to environmental influences.

Turning more specifically to research dealing with organizational communication problems, what has been done to diagnose them and determine the appropriate types of remedies? If communication is as important to the welfare of organizations as we have indicated, it stands to reason that it must be monitored so that it can be managed properly. The Management of communication involves, as Howard Greenbaum and his colleagues point out, "planning, organizing, and controlling communication networks, policies, and activities. . . . Control implies the presence of standards and the knowledge of what is actually happening in the organization." [9] Answers come largely from analyses developed for the private sector, but many are applicable to the public sector, where some have actually been tried.[10]

Communication Audits

History

Several standardized instruments for evaluating communication systems in organizations were developed in the mid-1970s.[11] It was hoped that wide use of these instruments would standardize the collection of evaluation data so that large banks could be built. The findings from subsequent evaluations, called "audits," could then be judged in light of the previously developed standards. Communication performance could be examined across organizations, across time, and across various major changes in organizational structures and functions. The data banks would also enable researchers to test various hypotheses on data drawn from a large sample of organizations instead of relying on individual case studies. Prior to the development of standardized data banks, findings in one organization were difficult to interpret, and their general applicability was difficult to assess without comparable studies to provide a context for interpretation. To make matters worse, with few exceptions, measurements had been made at only one point in time rather than repeatedly over a span of time so that the influence of conditions unique to a particular audit was not apparent. Standard instruments were also expected to reduce the costs of audits, which had heretofore relied on customized evaluation instruments. Additional savings might be possible because audits could lead to preventive steps, lessening the need for correcting malfunctions after the fact.

Three major evaluation programs were developed during this period: (1) the LTT audit system, named after the Finnish initials of the Helsinki Research Institute for Business Economics, where it was developed; (2) the Organizational Communication Development Procedure, known as the OCD audit system; and (3) the International Communication Association audit system, known as the ICA audit, which took its name from the sponsoring association.

The LTT, which has been used primarily in Europe, was developed mainly as a simple single-instrument audit to assess communication climates in organizations. Climates were measured by soliciting employees' opinions and attitudes about working conditions and policies, about upward, downward, and horizontal communication flows, and about the adequacy of communication channels. Employees were also asked about communication improvements that they would favor and the extent of their influence over their work. Altogether, the audit consisted of seventy-five questions, with some provisions for variations to accommodate differences among organizations. The questionnaire took twenty to thirty minutes to complete. The minimum recommended sample size was 150 persons for organizations of more than 500 people. Otherwise, it was recommended that every member of the organization should be questioned. The average time for data processing of questionnaires was estimated at four to eight weeks.

Based on their experience with the LTT audit, a team of Finnish researchers, headed by Osmo A. Wiio, Martti Helsila, and their associates, developed more advanced, yet still comparatively simple, auditing procedures for detecting communication problems in organizations. The OCD questionnaire, like its predecessor, remained limited to seventy-five questions, focusing primarily on objective and subjective communication assessments and respondents' views of the overall climate of the organization. Questions dealt with the availability and demand for information, effectiveness of communication channels, employees' perception of causes of poor communication, suggestions for improvements, degree of satisfaction with the job, and general demographic characteristics of the employees. Following data analysis, the audit provided for initiating corrective measures and subsequent feedback about the communication health of the organization.

The ICA audit, developed by an international team of some 150 researchers, is a multi-instrument research system specifically designed to detect organizational communication problems. There were several reasons for developing such a multifaceted approach. Audits employing a single instrument for data gathering could not capture the richness of organizational life.[12] Moreover, every measuring instrument is flawed in ways that differ from the flaws of other types of instruments. A multimethod approach, it was hoped, would allow weaknesses in the performance of one instrument to be compensated by strengths in the performance of another.

The ICA audit encompasses five separate instruments: (1) a questionnaire that includes standardized and customized questions; (2) interviews with members of the organization; (3) network analysis of the organization's actual communication connections; (4) reports by organization members about incidents in which communication was particularly effective or ineffective; and (5) communication diaries that record all persons with whom an employee was in work-related contact during a one-week period, along with an evaluation of the importance of the contact.

Audit Goals

What could administrators expect to learn from audits? As envisaged, the ICA audit was intended to provide factual and evaluative diagnostic data in all of the major problem areas. It was designed to identify the formal and informal communication networks and the roles played by various individuals in these networks. It would detect underloads and overloads of communication channels. It would provide means to assess the quality of information flowing from various sources and to judge the quality of interpersonal communication relationships. It would describe patterns of actual communication behavior, identifying sources, channels, topics, and length and quality of interactions. It would provide examples of commonly occurring positive and negative communication experiences. After completing their analysis, the auditors were expected to make recommendations for changes in the communication activities if they were needed to resolve problems or improve the organization.

Table 9-1 indicates the kinds of factual and evaluative information about an agency that audits try to elicit. Answers to the questions presented in this table should disclose the organization's communication policies, the structures available for communication, the functions performed by the existing communication system, and the attitudes of personnel at various levels about the organization and its communication system. Questions about these matters are often part of a preliminary survey that provides useful insights for the conduct and evaluation of the subsequent audit.[13]

Table 9-2 focuses on important aspects of communication between individual members of an organization and the organization as a whole. The first part of the table points out the data that investigators should have about the structures available for communication between individuals and the organization and about the types of messages linking the organization to its members. The second part of the table refers to the data needed about members' reactions to the organization and to its communication flows. Tables 9-3 and 9-4 reflect the need for similar descriptive and evaluative information about communication between various units within the organization and about boundary-spanning relationships between the organization and its environment.

If auditors were able to obtain the information specified in Tables 9-1 to 9-4, they should have sufficient diagnostic data to pinpoint problems and devise remedial measures. The data should also provide a base for planning the future development of communication capabilities. Following an audit, three out of four organizations generally have undertaken some type of reform, such as opening new channels of communication, hiring and

Table 9-1   The Existing Communication System

Description

■ Is there an established policy statement concerning a communication program?
   What value is placed on communication?
   What functions are attributed to communication?
   What are the premises underlying the communication program?
   Is there a director of communication?
   Is there an on-going communication program?
   How "open" is the communication system?

■ What structural factors affect the system?
   Organizational design?
   Interdependence of organizational units?
   Are channels clearly defined?
   Are roles clearly defined?
   Are both goals and sub-goals defined?
   Are expectations clear at each level?
   Is the flow of information clearly defined and easily followed?
   Are expectations of vertical and horizontal communication clearly defined?
   Does the structure allow for informal networks?

■ Are components for implementation of the system adequate?
   What forms and means of communication are available?
   What evaluating mechanisms exist?
   What facilitating mechanisms exist?

Appraisal

■ How much of an organization's resources are allocated for communication?
   How much manpower and media?
   Training programs?

■ Does the program reflect human values?
   Are managers and subordinates aware of shared values?
   Do managers and subordinates understand the mission of the total enterprise?
   Do employees feel involvement in the organizational goals?

■ Do employees understand the relationship of their work to the overall goals of the organization?

■ Do employees have a clear understanding of existing communication channels?

■ Do employees have a clear understanding of their roles and the roles of others?
   Do managers and subordinates agree on expectations?

■ Do employees feel that they get timely and adequate information to carry out their tasks?

■ Do employees feel that the organizational structure facilitates communication?

■ How do the employees respond to various media and forms of communication?

■ Does the organization evaluate and adjust its communication program?

■ Does management recognize the multiple functions of communication and evaluate accordingly?

Source: Gerald M. Goldhaber and Donald P. Rogers, *Auditing Organizational Communication Systems: The ICA Communication Audit* (Dubuque, Iowa: Kendall/Hunt, 1979), 3-4. Reprinted with permission.

Table 9-2   Communication Between Individual and Organization

---

Description

■ Is the communication related to both organizational and individual goals?
■ Do mechanisms exist for upward communication?
■ Do mechanisms exist for grievances?
■ What kinds of information are transmitted to subordinates and superiors?
■ Are channels of communication identified as open?
■ What mechanisms exist for interaction at all levels?
■ Do employees have a voice in their own destiny and in the way work is carried out?
■ What is the nature of performance-appraisal procedures?
■ What role do the employees play in decision making?
■ How many levels of management exist?
■ What are the assumptions behind communication directed to employees?
■ Is the employee looked upon as a human resource that can be developed?
■ How well does management know its people?

Appraisal

■ Do employees understand organizational goals and their attitudes toward those goals?
■ How do employees perceive the interest of management toward their (employees) individual goals and needs?
■ Do employees feel that effective upward communication exists?
■ What disparities exist between management and subordinate perception of effective communication?
■ Do employees feel that they can air grievances and suggestions without retaliation by others?
■ Do employees feel that they are "recognized" by the communication transmitted?
■ Do superiors feel that they receive the bad news as well as the good?
■ Are all levels of the organization involved in communication activities?
■ Does management acknowledge and act on communication from subordinates?
■ Is "negotiation" between organizational levels a reality and perceived as such by employees?
■ Do employees feel that their communication means something in terms of having a voice in the way work is carried out?
■ Do employees feel that effective communication takes place in performance-appraisal procedures?
■ Do employees feel that they have an opportunity to be heard in the decision-making process?
■ Do employees feel that the communication directed toward them is designed to help them "grow" in their jobs?
■ What types and content of messages are absent according to employees?
■ To what degree does the system meet stated communication desires of employees?
■ What values are reflected by the communication program?
■ Do employees feel that they get the right information at the right time?
■ What is the perceived communication competence of managers by subordinates?

Source: Gerald M. Goldhaber and Donald P. Rogers, *Auditing Organizational Communication Systems: The ICA Communication Audit* (Dubuque, Iowa: Kendall/Hunt, 1979), 4-5. Reprinted with permission.

Table 9-3   Communication Between Organizational Units

Description

■ What relationships exist between groups in terms of interdependence?
■ What role does each group play in organizational goals?
■ How differentiated are the various units of the organization?
■ How cohesive are the groups?
■ Is there planned interaction between groups?
■ How much integration is required between units?
■ What mechanisms exist to deal with conflict?

Appraisal

■ Are groups aware of interdependence?
■ Do groups understand their role and relationship to other groups?
■ Do groups feel that there is adequate exchange between units?
■ Do groups have a perspective on sub-group and organizational goals?
■ Do groups interact on an informal basis as well as formal?

Source: Gerald M. Goldhaber and Donald P. Rogers, *Auditing Organizational Communication Systems: The ICA Communication Audit* (Dubuque, Iowa: Kendall/Hunt, 1979), 5. Reprinted with permission.

shifting gatekeeping personnel, and instituting more training in communication techniques.[14] A school district audit provides an example. In the wake of an audit, school officials were urged to create the position of a professional director of communication responsible for monitoring the quality of internal and external communication.[15] As part of the job, the director, assisted by a communication committee, was asked to prepare a clear statement of information goals, objectives, and priorities for the school system. To improve downward communication, the auditors recommended revisions in the scheduling, composition, and agenda of the meetings of the district's school principals. The auditors also suggested a telephone hotline for relaying important information to staff members. Public release of that information was to be delayed until all staff members had been informed. To improve upward communication, the auditors recommended a better way for employees to submit suggestions and better follow-up to assure responses from administrators.

Audit Accomplishments

A survey of completed audits shows four areas in which they tend to be particularly useful. One is the *diagnosis of internal communication problems.* For instance, an audit of NASA's Marshall Space Flight Center in Huntsville, Alabama, detected seven major barriers to good communication:

Table 9-4   Transaction Between Organization and Environment

Description

- What type of organization is being examined?
- What information from the environment is necessary for organizational survival?
- What kind of communication is being sent to the external environment and for what reasons?
- What types and forms of communication are used to communicate externally?
- Does the organization recognize change in the environment and convey such knowledge to its members?
- Does the organization monitor the effects of external communication?
- Is relevant information from the external environment conveyed to the proper internal units?
- Does the organization have the capacity to change on the basis of environmental information?
- Does the organization serve a divergent clientele with its communication?
- What image does the organization attempt to project?

Appraisal

- Are all members of the organization aware of the external messages being sent?
- Do members of the organization feel that the external communication represents an accurate and desirable point of view?
- Do members of the organization have knowledge of the elements of the external environment that may affect their role or job?
- Do members of the organization have knowledge of the "large picture" that comes from internal and external environments?
- Are members of the organization flexible enough to change on the basis of external information?
- What is the organization's image to its various publics?
- Are members of the organization aware of societal responsibilities?
- Are members of the organization responsive to a larger environment?

Source: Gerald M. Goldhaber and Donald P. Rogers, *Auditing Organizational Communication Systems: The ICA Communication Audit* (Dubuque, Iowa: Kendall/Hunt, 1979), 5-6. Reprinted with permission.

1. Competition between departments had led to lack of trust and secrecy, impairing lateral communications.

2. Animosity existed between older members of the organization, who were viewed as a cohesive insider group, and newer management employees.

3. Civil service workers below the level of laboratory director suffered from poor morale because they believed that employees of contractors working with them were receiving a higher salary for the same job.

4. Uncertainty about the future pervaded the organization because there were rumors about possible retrenchment and lack of official word from the top.[16]

5. A communication bottleneck existed at the Office of Research and Development Operations because twelve units reported to its director.

6. Coordination of staff offices was deficient because the deputy

director of administration was spending increasing amounts of time at NASA headquarters.

7. Because of the complexity of the work, the number of external contacts was extraordinarily high and therefore burdensome. Contacts had to be maintained with NASA headquarters and field centers, university scientists, and prime and support contractors. Many of these external relations were unsatisfactory because the technical personnel at other agencies were not well qualified.

Audits also help to *keep organizations running efficiently* and improve them through recommended changes in communications systems. The school district changes mentioned earlier are illustrative. Improvements may involve changes in structure, methods of communication, and training, such as workshops on communication. The audit of communication at the Marshall Space Flight Center revealed a successful way to institutionalize regular upward, downward, and horizontal communication. Called the "Monday Notes" system, it allowed department heads to summarize achievements and problems in their unit for the previous week. The summaries went to the top management, who added commentary and then circulated them to all departments. In this way, each department head was kept informed about events in other units. Furthermore, in order to prepare the weekly summaries, department heads consulted their subordinates each week to obtain the needed information.

Audits have also proved valuable in *developing benchmarks* to judge the impact of major changes, such as organizational restructuring or new computerization programs. For example, new technologies, such as electronic mail, have brought about changes in network patterns, flattening organizational hierarchies by increasing vertical links across status levels. They have broadened the reach of organizations to include more distant people. In the process, some linkages have grown in frequency while others have diminished. Communication audits can track such changes and assess their consequences.[17]

Valuable insights may also be derived from *comparing different types of organizations*. For example, comparison of audit data from three health-care institutions, five educational entities, three private enterprises, and five government agencies indicated that government agencies need to receive and send more information than other types of organizations. They also have to tap into more diverse sources. Workers in government agencies also tend to be less satisfied with the performance of their organization compared with the norms for workers in private sector organizations. These differences should be kept in mind when evaluating appraisals provided by public sector employees.[18]

Not all audits are as comprehensive as the ICA audit. Cost considerations and research interests often impose limits, necessitating a scaling down of expectations about research results. For example, evaluations may focus only on network studies, which may be further restricted to dealing solely with selected aspects of information flows, such as channels, feedback, or network members. Alternatively, studies may focus on content, assessing meanings, accuracy, distortions, and similar matters. The focus of the study may also be limited to aspects of an organization's climate, such as employees' attitudes about the communication process. Finally, a number of studies have concentrated on organizational training and development to enhance communication. The level of analysis of these studies also tends to be more restricted than the ICA audit. Some have focused on communication at the individual level only, others on communication among groups, and still others on communication flows in the organization as a whole.

A Closer Look at Research Techniques

We are now ready to take a closer look at several parts of the ICA audit. It should be clear that each of the measuring instruments discussed below has also been used by itself or in combination with other instruments with good results. The package of instruments that form the ICA unit constitute an excellent combination, but the various instruments are clearly separable. The specific content included in the examples presented here is illustrative only, with many variations possible. However, using instruments like those of the ICA audits, which have been validated through previous research, has distinct advantages.

Surveys and Interviews

The ICA survey questionnaire encompasses 122 standard items included in all audits, thirty-four customized items determined by the organization undergoing the audit, and twelve demographic questions, covering gender, age, education, and job-related characteristics, such as rank, length of tenure, and communication training. "Major Survey Targets" on pages 333-335 is an abbreviated version of the actual survey questions and the instructions for answering. For most aspects of the appraisal, respondents are asked to indicate their perceptions of the current status of the organization as well as the status they deem ideal. This allows investigators to identify possibilities for changing communication flows. Five responses are possible for questions about actual and needed information. They range from "very little" to "very great." In organizations no larger than 300 people, the ICA audit usually includes a survey of all employees; otherwise, a representative sample is drawn. The survey takes about forty-five minutes to complete.[19]

Major Survey Targets

Receiving information from others

Instructions: You can receive information about various topics in your organization. For each topic listed, mark your response on the answer sheet that best indicates:

1. the amount of information you *are* receiving on that topic, and
2. the amount of information you *need* to receive on that topic in order to do your job.

Choice categories:

1. This is the amount of information I receive now.
2. This is the amount of information I need to receive. [a]

Topic areas for which information is needed: Respondent's job performance; respondent's job duties; organizational policies; impact of technology on respondent's job; mistakes and failures of respondent's organization; personnel evaluation criteria; handling of respondent's job-related problems; decision criteria regarding respondent's job; promotion and advancement opportunities in respondent's organization; important new products, services, or program developments in respondent's organization; relation of respondent's job to the total organization; specific problems faced by management.

Sending information to others

Instructions: In addition to receiving information, there are many topics on which you can send information to others. For each topic listed, mark your response on the answer sheet that best indicates:

1. the amount of information you *are* sending on that topic, and
2. the amount of information that you *need* to send on that topic in order to do your job.

Choice categories:

1. This is the amount of information I send now.
2. This is the amount of information I need to send. [a]

Topic areas for which information should be sent: Respondent's job-related activities; respondent's perceptions regarding job requirements; job-related problems; complaints about respondent's job or work conditions; requests for information needed for respondent's job; evaluations of respondent's immediate supervisor; requests for clearer work instructions.

Follow-up on information sent

Instructions: Indicate the amount of follow-up that *is* and *needs* to be taken on information you send to the following:

Choice categories:

1. This is the amount of follow-up now.
2. This is the amount of follow-up needed.[a]

Personnel requiring contact: Subordinates; co-workers; immediate supervisor; middle management; top management.

(continues)

continued

Sources of information

Instructions: You *not only* receive various kinds of information, but can receive such information from *various sources* within the organization. For each source listed, mark your response on the answer sheet that best indicates:

1. the amount of information you *are* receiving from that source, and
2. the amount of information you *need* to receive from that source in order to do your job.

Choice categories:

1. This is the amount of information I receive now.
2. This is the amount of information I need to receive. [a]

Information sources: Subordinates, if applicable; co-workers in respondent's unit or department; individuals in *other* units or departments in respondent's organization; immediate supervisor; department meetings; middle management; formal management presentations; top management; the grapevine.

Timeliness of information received from key sources

Instructions: Indicate the extent to which information from the following sources is usually *timely* (you get information when you need it). [a]

Information sources: Subordinates, if applicable; co-workers; immediate supervisor; middle management; top management; grapevine.

Organizational communication relationships

Instructions: A variety of communicative relationships exist in organizations like your own. Employees exchange messages regularly with supervisors, subordinates, and co-workers. Considering your relationships with others in your organization, please mark your response on the answer sheet that best describes the relationship in question. [a]

Relationships: Trust in co-workers; rapport among co-workers; satisfactory relationships with co-workers; trust in immediate supervisor; immediate supervisor's honesty with respondent; immediate supervisor's willingness to listen to respondent; freedom to disagree with immediate supervisor; freedom to inform immediate supervisor about adverse happenings; praise from immediate supervisor for good job performance; friendliness of immediate supervisor toward subordinates; immediate supervisor's understanding of respondent's job needs; satisfactory relationship with immediate supervisor; trust in top management; sincerity of top management in efforts to communicate with employees; satisfactory relationship with top management; encouragement of opinion differences by organization; respondent's participation in decisions affecting respondent's job; respondent's influence on operations in own unit or department; respondent's role in accomplishing organizational goals.

Organizational outcomes

Instructions: One of the most important outcomes of working in an organization is the *satisfaction* one receives or fails to receive through working there. Such satisfaction can relate to the job, one's co-workers, supervisor, or the organization as a whole. Please mark your response on the answer sheet that best indicates the extent to which you are *satisfied*. [a]

continued

Outcomes: Respondent's job; respondent's pay; respondent's progress in the organization to date; respondent's chances for getting ahead in the organization; respondent's opportunity to contribute to the overall success of the organization; the organization's system for recognizing and rewarding outstanding performance; the organization's concern for its members' welfare; the organization's overall communicative efforts; working in respondent's organization; respondent's organization compared with similar organizations; the organization's overall efficiency of operation; the overall quality of the organization's product or service; the organization's achievement of its goals and objectives.

Channels of communication

Instructions: The following questions list a variety of channels through which information is transmitted to employees. Please mark your response on the answer sheet that best indicates:

1. the amount of information you *are* receiving through that channel, and
2. the amount of information you *need* to receive through that channel.

Choice categories:

1. This is the amount of information I receive now.
2. This is the amount of information I need to receive. [a]

Channels: Face-to-face contact between two people; face-to-face contact among more than two people; telephone; written; bulletin boards; internal publications; internal audio-visual media; external media.

Background information

Payment method; gender; work obligation; years employed by organization; years in present job; position level; highest educational level; age; amount of training in communicative skills; salary from organization during past year; number of organizations for which respondent has worked during past ten years; current search for job in another organization.

Source: Adapted from Gerald M. Goldhaber and Donald P. Rogers, *Auditing Organizational Communication Systems: The ICA Communication Audit* (Dubuque, Iowa: Kendall/Hunt, 1979), 35-53. Reprinted with permission.
[a] Coded as very little, little, some, great, very great.

The validity of such surveys has been challenged on several grounds. For example, it has been pointed out that five-point Likert-type scales that measure various degrees of agreement with a statement, though relatively easy to administer, are too crude to give reliable results.[20] Various methods using more finely grained scales have been proposed as alternatives. Some researchers oppose all closed-ended questions and advocate open-ended, free-flowing answers. However, open answers are difficult to code accurately.

On a different level of criticism, it has been claimed that self-assessments of communication behavior are often flawed. Because self-reports contain introspective data, they are likely to diverge substantially from reports of observers. On the other hand, observer data are also problematic because the difficulty in observing and recording all interactions may cause the data to be quite scanty. Thus, they may not be a good yardstick for gauging the reliability of survey responses. The reliability of the scales on the standard items is a better gauge. It has been high for the ICA audit, ranging from .70 to .90. The fact that the scales have proven useful in predicting organizational outcomes also attests to their quality.

To provide an opportunity for further exploration of the survey questionnaire items, the ICA audit also includes personal interviews with selected members of the organization. Having been promised that their responses will be confidential, they are asked a series of open-ended questions (see "The Exploratory Interview Guide" on page 337). The initial interview provides exploratory information to explain the respondent's communication role and behavior in the organization, perceptions about the effectiveness of formal and informal channels and the quality of information, and the respondent's criteria for making these evaluations. A follow-up interview is structured to clarify and expand audit data obtained earlier. The data are then qualitatively analyzed.

Network Analysis

General Features. As discussed in Chapter 5, network analysis aims to capture the interactive aspects of communication that may lead to understanding and convergence of views. According to Frederick Williams and others, "The network paradigm refocused researchers' preoccupations with individuals as independent senders and receivers of messages toward a concept of individuals as nodes in a network of interdependent relationships. Instead of analyzing average values of aggregated individual-level variables, network analysis focuses on patterns of relationships among individuals." [21]

Unlike traditional multivariate descriptive techniques, network analysis does not pool the information gathered from organization members to arrive at a generalized description of the organization. Instead, it preserves the members' individual data sets and describes each person's placement in the organization. Besides indicating who communicates with whom, either reciprocally or nonreciprocally, network analysis also indicates the degree of importance of each of these communication links and shows whether they occur as part of the formal or informal communication network.

If the network is depicted as a matrix, as shown in Tables 5-1, 5-2, and 5-3, it is possible to express numerically the relationships among various senders and receivers—often referred to as *nodes*, who may be individuals, groups, or whole organizations. High numbers indicate intensity of various relationships, such as frequency and importance of contacts or perceptions of influence. When contacts between two nodes seem inconsequential or are not reciprocated, researchers may choose to omit them from the analysis.

The Exploratory Interview Guide

- Describe your job (duties and functions). What decisions do you usually make in your job? What information do you *need* to make those decisions and from where should you get it? What information do you get to make those decisions and from whom? Are there formal (written) or informal policies in your organization that determine how you get this information? Should any policies be added, changed, or abandoned?
- What are the major communication *strengths* of this organization? Be specific. (Begin with the larger system and work down to your work unit.)
- What are the major communication *weaknesses* of this organization? Be specific. (Begin with the larger system and work down to your work unit.)
- Describe the *formal* channels through which you typically receive information about this organization. What kinds of information do you tend to receive? How often?
- Describe the *informal* channels through which you typically receive information about this organization. What kinds of information do you tend to receive? How often?
- How often, if ever, do you receive information about this organization that is of low value or use to you? If and when you do, what kinds of information do you receive? Be specific. From whom do you receive this?
- What would you like to see done to improve information flow in this organization? Why hasn't it been done yet?
- Describe the way decisions are typically made in this organization.
- When conflict occurs in this organization, what is its major cause? How is conflict typically resolved?
- Describe the communicative relationship you have with your immediate supervisor, co-workers, middle management, top management, and subordinates (if appropriate). (Ask for specific examples of *behavioral* evidence of trust and openness— "How do you know that he/she trusts you?" "What has he/she done to indicate that they are being open and frank with you?")
- How do you know when this organization has done a good or bad job in accomplishing its goals? What measures of effectiveness are used in this organization?
- Is there anything else you would like to talk with me about? Is there some other person (or group of people) with whom you think I should talk?

Source: Gerald M. Goldhaber and Donald P. Rogers, *Auditing Organizational Communication Systems: The ICA Communication Audit* (Dubuque, Iowa: Kendall/Hunt, 1979), 31. Reprinted with permission.

Studies of the reliability of sociometric data have shown that patterns of group interaction and indexes derived from them are quite stable, even though individual behavior may vary considerably over time.[22]

However, some caution is needed when using sociometric data based on a one-time survey. Relationships in organizations frequently lack stability, and network patterns shift accordingly. Data gathered at a particular moment may or may not capture customary interaction behavior. Moreover, this behavior may differ, depending on the nature of the issue that is the focus of information exchanges and decisions. Major and minor crises may alter network patterns temporarily or permanently.[23] A single-shot investigation is thus bound to miss a variety of network routines that come into play periodically. Ideally, studies should be repeated, covering multiple points in time. The patterns detected are also determined in part by the nature of the questions asked by the investigator. It is therefore wise to phrase questions in different ways in order to tap diverse thinking patterns.[24]

Level of Analysis Issues. Analysts must determine the level of network structures within the organization on which the analysis will be focused. They can study the entire organization as a network, involving all people, irrespective of whether they know each other. To facilitate analysis, large networks can also be divided into smaller subgroups of structurally equivalent members—those who show identical, or nearly identical, patterns of network relationship. Unlike members of a clique, structurally equivalent network members may not have any relationship to each other.[25] Alternatively, like the ICA auditors, researchers can focus on the personal networks of particular individuals, noting the people with whom the chosen individuals interact most often. Cliques of five to twenty-five people have often been the focus of network research by small-group specialists. As David Knoke and James Kuklinski observe, "The implicit proposition motivating clique analysis is that actors who maintain especially cohesive bonds among themselves are more likely to perform similarly (e.g., to share information, to develop similar preferences, to act in concert)." [26]

Network analysts may face difficult decisions when they must specify the boundaries of organizational networks. Knoke and Kuklinski ask: "Where does one set the limits when collecting data on social networks that in reality may have no obvious limits?" [27] When analysts adopt what has been called a realist perspective, they define the boundaries of organizations in accordance with the perceptions of all or most of its members. But analysts may also allow the purpose of their investigation to guide their boundary definition. For example, the analysis could be limited to networks of civil servants at a particular grade. If one uses a snowball-sampling approach to network analysis, in which one traces the nodes with whom a particular respondent communicates, and then traces the nodes of these nodes, where should one stop? After the second level, the fifth, the tenth?

According to Knoke and Kuklinski, "The decision about where to draw the boundary must ultimately be set by social-theoretic considerations of the phenomenon under investigation." [28] Since restricted samples lead to distortions, it is always wise to err in the direction of broadening the network. If the focus is too narrow, it may capture only truncated network structures. On the other hand, if the focus is too wide, it may be impossible to collect and handle all of the data. For example, when a network includes

5,000 people, it encompasses 25,000,000 linkage possibilities. Current computer programs cannot handle such massive data sets effectively.[29]

Sociometric Instruments. Networks are best studied through sociometric measures that reveal how communication travels among senders and receivers. When interrelations are measured, data are usually derived from social science sources such as questionnaires, interviews, diaries, focus groups, and on-site observations. Data are normally gathered from each member of an organization, *not* merely a random sample. Researchers ascertain how often the members communicate with specific colleagues and how this information moves through the network. In many studies, researchers also inquire about who ordinarily initiates the information exchange and the nature and importance of network messages.[30]

Table 9-5 presents the form used in the ICA audit to instruct participants about the purpose of network analysis and the data required from them. Respondents are requested to name individuals inside and outside the organization with whom they typically communicate about organizational matters. To make the task easier, the respondents receive name lists that classify all members according to rank within the organization. In very large organizations a name list is usually not provided because of its excessive length.

These self-reports become the basic data for the analysis. In place of these data, which some investigators distrust as potentially flawed, it is, of course, possible to obtain contact data through direct observations or scanning records of past communications. Using archival data has the added advantage of covering long time periods, providing insights on networking under the impact of diverse contextual factors, such as major economic, political, and personal changes.

Data Analysis. After the data about links among organization members have been collected, a computer program can be used to identify formal and informal networks. Data analysis poses several difficult problems. One is the fact that data collections have to be massive because network analysis currently requires receiving data from all members of the organization, or at least from 90 percent of them, to obtain a sufficiently clear picture of interrelationships. A moderately sized network of 1,000 people could have as many as half a million links.[31] This problem may be alleviated when suitable sampling programs are developed.[32]

A number of computer programs have been written to cope with the massive amount of data generated by network analysis. The computer program developed for the ICA audit is called NEGOPY—a combination of the words "negative" and "entropy"—which signifies that network structures create order within a system and that order can be conceptualized as negative entropy (the negation of uncertainty). The program was

Table 9-5   Network Analysis in the International Communication Association Audit System

As part of our study we would like you to complete this communication flow form. Although people's names are included here, *your individual responses will not be made available to anyone in the organization.* The purpose of this part of the audit is to quickly and efficiently assess the ability of the communication network to provide people with the information they need to do their jobs effectively and happily.

As you complete this form, we want you to think about the people you usually communicate with in a typical work day. This includes face-to-face interaction, telephone calls, and written memos.

You will notice that we have asked about two different channels of communication. In the first, we want you to think of the times you communicate (sending and receiving) about work-related matters through the *formal organizational structure,* such as committee or staff meetings, memos, oral or written official notices, and business communications.

In the second question, we want you to think of the times you communicate through the *informal (grapevine) structure,* such as chance conversations, spontaneous meetings, personal notes, and phone calls.

To fill in the form, you should:

1. Find your name on the list and circle it.
2. Write the I.D. number found to the right of your name.
3. Scan the list of names until you locate a person with whom you usually communicate in a typical work day.
4. Decide whether each communication is part of either the formal or informal structure.
5. Write the number of communications that typically take place in the space beside the appropriate heading (formal and/or informal).
6. For the persons with whom you typically communicate, decide how important these communications *usually* are to you. Next to the number of communications, for either or both of the channels you have chosen, circle:

   "1" if they are usually *not at all important*
   "2" if they are *somewhat important*
   "3" if they are *fairly important*
   "4" if they are *very important*
   "5" if they are *extremely important*

7. Continue this process for each person on the questionnaire for which you feel that you communicate each day.

Example

During the typical work day I usually communicate about work-related matters with the following people through the:

	I.D.	Formal organizational structure	Informal organizational structure
Jones, Charles, clerk	2056	— 2 — 1 2 3 4 ⑤	— — — 1 2 3 4 5
Smith, Harry, manager	2057	— 5 — 1 2 ③ 4 5	— 2 — 1 ② 3 4 5

In this example, the person filling out the form indicated that he or she communicated two times a day with Charles Jones in business meetings or through official memos and these are extremely important to him or her. In another example, the respondent indicated that he or she typically communicated with Harry Smith about five times a day using formal channels and about twice a day using informal channels. In the first case the interactions were usually fairly important and in the second case only somewhat important.

Source: Gerald M. Goldhaber and Donald P. Rogers, *Auditing Organizational Communication Systems: The ICA Communication Audit* (Dubuque, Iowa: Kendall/Hunt, 1979), 166. Reprinted with permission.

developed by communications scholar William Richards, drawing on matrix analysis and graph theory. An example of this type of research is John Kessel's study of the Reagan and Carter White House presented in Chapter 5, along with illustrations of matrixes (Tables 5-1, 5-2, 5-3) and graphs (Figures 5-1, 5-2, 5-3, 5-4). Because it does not use the complete matrix of data for calculating network connections, NEGOPY can efficiently handle data involving organizations of up to 4,096 members and up to 80,000 links.[33] The program identifies patterns to produce a description of the organization, consisting of a list of the network groupings in the organization and a description of the roles of all individual members. This is known as a "topological" description.[34] NEGOPY also provides descriptive statistics of several subsystems within the organization at various levels of analysis, including the direction and magnitude of network relationships.

To relate the NEGOPY network analysis results to the organization, another computer program, called NETCHART, superimposes the actual network features found by the computer program over the formal organization reporting chart to determine the nature of divergencies. The findings provide insights about how well actual communication flows are serving the organization and may suggest needed changes to remedy deficiencies. Examining actual communication flows and comparing them with the formal organization chart is called *H technique,* which stands for holistic analysis of all aspects of the system. Scholars with a bent toward interpretive theories favor holistic analysis. The alternative technique is mechanistic analysis, called *M technique.* Users of this technique start with the formal organization chart and attempt to analyze information flows among formally designated positions. Since M technique rests on the assumption that communication flows follow established organization patterns, investigators are more apt to miss actual patterns and merely show the formal ones. As is true in many social scientific investigations, the nature of the data collected and the coding scheme adopted may predetermine the findings.[35]

The ICA network analysis begins with the collection of descriptive data about the full set of communication relationships among members of an organization. This includes the nature and frequency of communication with other members and the roles individual members perform within particular networks as well as within the organization as a whole. All of these data are then used to define the network groupings that are functioning parts of the whole organization. Basing groupings on descriptive data differs from most other methods of network analysis, where investigators define networks a priori. Richards's a posteriori approach provides greater assurance that emerging and changing network configurations will be noted and used in structuring the analysis.

Network data can be processed in many different ways. One recent overview mentions such possibilities as sociometric analysis, graph-theoretical analysis, matrix analysis, factor analysis, block-modeling techniques, multidimensional scaling techniques, and cluster analysis.[36] Conventional statistical methods can be used to describe the properties of various aspects of the network structures.[37] However, since network data violate the random-sampling assumptions that underlie statistical inference, conventional statistical analyses are problematic.[38] Nevertheless, they are frequently used.

Findings.   The results of network analysis, as illustrated in Chapter 5, can be presented as matrixes or sociograms.[39] The analysis can focus on dyadic (two-person), group, or organizational relationships. It can reveal network characteristics, such as the centrality of various nodes within the network, the accessibility of particular nodes to other nodes, and the reciprocity, strength, and frequency of relationships.[40] The individuals who occupy key roles in organizations, such as gatekeepers, liaisons, or isolates, can be identified.

Common indexes derived from network data include an index of *network cohesion* that shows the proportion of network relations that are reciprocated. When such an index includes asymmetric ties, it is called an index of *network density*. One can also derive an index of *network multiplexity,* which indicates multiple types of relationships, such as communication about a variety of issues among nodes. An index of *communication intensity* can be created that combines measures of frequency of contacts, average frequency of individual contacts, response satisfaction, and response importance. An index of *actor multiplexity* can measure the proportion of an individual actor's ties with other actors in the network that occur through various networks. Such an index takes account of the fact that linkages among network members involve multiple kinds of relationships and that individuals belong to more than one group. An *ego network density* index measures the density of networks clustering around a particular individual, presumably supporting his or her ego. There are also indexes of *network centrality* that measure the degree to which an actor is enmeshed in various relationships occurring within the network. Finally, indexes of an *actor's prestige* have been devised. For example, actors who receive more communications than they send are generally considered to have high prestige. This is especially true if their contactors also enjoy high prestige.[41]

The various indexes permit analysts to determine how well coordinated the communication network is overall and within various units of the organization. They can tell which communication roles are adequately handled and where additional liaisons and gatekeepers are required. The charts developed from the data reveal isolates who need to be integrated into the communication system. It is also possible to compare actual with anticipated networks and to make organizational changes that will match expectations and actualities more closely. Finally, a combination of network data and other communication data collected from audits provides leads to answering many intriguing questions about the relationship between an individual's network roles and position and other communication behaviors and evaluations. This is why small-group researchers, sociometricians, political scientists, and anthropologists have long been interested in network analysis.[42]

What key questions should network analysts ask if they wish to assess the appropriateness of network structures for achieving the goals of the organization? At the institutional level, one might explore the question of whether alternative structures would enhance organizational effectiveness and minimize distortion. Groups would have to be judged on the basis of how well connected they are and whether they suffer from communication overloads or underloads. At the group level, one might investigate the network roles played by members and judge whether or not the best person is performing a particular role. At the individual level, one might be concerned with isolates and the impact of their isolation on the welfare of the organization. Gerald Goldhaber has recommended, as a general rule, that existing well-functioning network structures be used as a guide for structuring the work in the organization rather than trying to fit communication patterns into a predetermined mold. That seems wise counsel, indeed, because network structures are adaptations to the social context in which individuals are operating, and such social contexts are highly resistant to change.[43]

Small-Group Communication Analysis

Various forms of network analyses have been used extensively to study interactions in small groups. Since many of the most important interactions in organizations, such as planning and decision making, generally take place in existing cliques or in small groups constituted for specific purposes, it is not surprising that specialized tools have been developed. Several focus on the nature of the messages exchanged among nodes.

Interaction measures may simply record whether or not a message has elicited a response, or they may entail elaborate coding schemes that identify the nature of the response either generically or specifically. *Interaction Process Analysis,* designed by Robert F. Bales, has been used to study public sector groups, such as legislative committees and party caucuses.[44] As Table 9-6 shows, Bales's analysis classifies verbal interactions into four major categories: questions, answers, positive reactions, and negative reactions. Each of these categories has three subcategories. Questions, for example, are subdivided into requests for information, expressions of opinions, and suggestions. Positive and negative reactions are categorized according to the state of agreement or disagreement, the state of tension, and the degree of antagonism.

Table 9-6   Bales Interaction Process Analysis

Reaction display	Functional remarks
Positive reactions	**Questions**
■ Shows solidarity	■ Asks for information
■ Shows tension release	■ Asks for opinions
■ Shows agreement	■ Asks for suggestions
Negative reactions	**Answers**
■ Shows disagreement	■ Gives information
■ Shows tension	■ Gives options
■ Shows antagonism	■ Gives suggestions

Source: Compiled by the author from data in Robert F. Bales, *Interaction Process Analysis* (Reading, Mass.: Addison-Wesley, 1950).

Bales claimed that the twelve categories are adequate to score all major aspects of interactions within small groups. His version of interaction process analysis has been used, for example, to analyze discussions in congressional committees, to gauge the role played by emotion-laden messages, and to measure to what extent discussions focused on solving problems rather than merely exchanging views.[45] In successfully functioning groups, 50 percent of all remarks during encounters are normally answers; the rest are questions and reactions. In most encounters, the ratio between positive and negative reactions is two to one. High rates of disagreement and antagonism spell trouble. However, too much agreement and lack of disagreement may indicate that group members are not really involved in the interactions or that the climate is inhibiting or threatening. When groups interact well, the rate of suggestions climbs, often accompanied by an increase in negative reactions.[46]

Other types of interaction process analysis have focused on the social dimensions of the interactions, on logical strategies used by the communicators, and on the interrelation between messages and responses. A number of analyses have focused on various message strategies that led to desired or undesired outcomes during bargaining and decision making. Proposals made by group members have been scored in *Carr's Interaction Diagrams.* Each proposal is given a rating reflecting its contribution to solving the group's problems. The result of scoring is then depicted in the form of a diagram. The climate created through messages has been gauged through *Sign Process Analysis,* which records the distribution of positive, negative, and neutral substantive remarks exchanged by group members in the course of their interactions. Various sociometric analyses of communications have been used to discover interpersonal affinities and rejections within groups. These measurements have been used to form groups composed of people favorably disposed to each other who will presumably work well together.

Semantic Network Analysis. In recent years, researchers have moved beyond merely tracing the path of messages and have begun to focus on their content as indicators of linkages. James Danowski has developed a technique called *Word Network Analysis,* which uses computerized content analysis to detect the sharing of words and concepts among message senders.[47] This approach, particularly if it focuses on consensual meanings developed by network members, rather than only on the shared words and word groups that are detected in their messages, promises to provide fresh insights into the manner in which organizations develop common concepts and reach consensus. Semantic Network Analysis is a potentially highly productive way to test the existence, growth, and nature of organizational cultures and subcultures. It also makes it possible to assess how well particular individuals are likely to fit into a culture.[48]

Communication Diaries and Reports

ICA audit data are further enhanced by diaries of communication activities that participants are asked to maintain over a one-week period. All communications received and sent are included, such as conversations, phone calls, meetings, and written messages. Forms are provided to simplify diary keeping and assure equivalence among diaries. "Communication Profile of a Senate Staff Member" on page 346 presents the information gleaned from the diary of an employee in a U.S. senator's office in 1975.[49] The diary indicates that the staff member averaged sixty-seven interactions each day. Depending on the employee's designated role, this may be an overload or an underload for that particular job or in relation to other jobs. Most interactions were face to face and dealt with legislative matters; most lasted less than three minutes and were perceived as useful. However, only 40 percent were perceived as important. If reduction in contacts seemed indicated, unimportant contacts might have been eliminated selectively.

Data gathered from individual diaries were combined into a collective portrait of communication activities in the senator's office. Among other things, this portrait showed that 86 percent of all recorded interactions were conducted face to face or by telephone. Only 14 percent used intercoms and written channels, but these channels were perceived as more useful and more important than the others. Eighty-eight percent of the reported failures in communication occurred in telephone conversations, raising questions about possible problems when this important channel is used.

Forty-two percent of the interactions dealing with legislative matters, 27 percent of the interactions dealing with constituent matters, as well as 8 percent of contacts related to incidental matters, were perceived as

Communication Profile of a Senate Staff Member

Week-at-a-glance[a]
- Number of interactions during the week—268
- Average interactions per day—67
- Share of total office interactions during the week—6.7%
- Normal share of interactions for staff member—2.6%
- Interactions initiated by staff member—49.6%
  N=268

Types of interactions[b]
- Face-to-face interactions—167/63.0%
- Telephone calls—62/23.4%
- Written communications—21/7.9%
- Intercom communications—15/5.7%
  N=265

Subject of interactions[b]
- Legislative—167/66.8%
- Constituency—35/14.0%
- Incidental—3/1.2%
- Other—45/18.0%
  N=250

Length of interactions[b]
- Less than three minutes—176/66.1%
- Three to fifteen minutes—69/25.9%
- Fifteen minutes to one hour—8/3.0%
- Longer than one hour—13/4.9%
  N=266

Importance of interactions
- Useful interactions—63.1%
- Important interactions—41.8%
- Private interactions—8.6%
- Interactions in conference—7.0%

Source: Adapted from Gerald M. Goldhaber and Donald P. Rogers, *Auditing Organizational Communication Systems: The ICA Communication Audit* (Dubuque, Iowa: Kendall/Hunt, 1979), 162. Reprinted with permission.

[a] When the week studied was tabulated, one day's worth of data was lost because of computer problems. Thus, the data reflect a four-day week.

[b] Number/percent.

---

important. Nonetheless, only one-third of all transactions were deemed useful. This suggests again that it may be possible to prune message flows so that unproductive transactions are reduced. Most interactions were brief. Sixty-three percent lasted less than three minutes; only 1 percent lasted for more than one hour. As Goldhaber and Rogers point out, "Longer interactions tended to be initiated by others, tended to lose their utility but gain importance, tended more often to be about legislative matters and be more often of the face-to-face variety." [50]

The ICA audit also includes a *Critical Incident Analysis,* which is based on descriptions supplied by respondents when they are asked to give examples of typical successful and unsuccessful work-related communication incidents. The form asks respondents to "describe the communicative experience, the circumstances leading up to it, what the person did that made him/her an effective or ineffective communicator, and the results (outcome) of what the person did." [51] The respondents are asked whether the experience related to a subordinate, a co-worker, an immediate supervisor, middle or top management. The data provided by the narrative supply rich details that enhance the meaningfulness of the quantitative data obtained through the surveys. The Critical Incident Analysis also permits the development of good and bad examples of communications within the organization.

Content Analysis

The ICA audit encompasses open-ended responses and discursive reports, in addition to the closed-ended survey responses. Examples are the intensive interviews discussed earlier and the Critical Incident reports. Content of these responses, reports, and other messages may be analyzed intuitively, based on techniques for interpreting messages that humans learn from interacting with others throughout their lives. This more or less subjective judgmental approach, called "qualitative" analysis, has been plagued by unresolved scholarly disputes about the meanings that should be attributed to messages. Should it be the meaning of the sender, the receiver, or a spin-off produced through interactions, as interpretist scholars would contend? When messages carry multiple meanings, as many do, which meaning or meanings should be recorded?

"Quantitative" analysis, as distinguished from "qualitative" analysis, involves systematic examination of content after objective criteria have been established for defining the elements to be detected and the indicators that signal the presence or absence of these elements. For example, a study of the respect shown by Commerce Department employees for congressional rules might be based on scrutiny of all annual reports of the department. Every reference to congressional rule making might be evaluated and scored on a five-point scale ranging from "great" respect to "no" respect. Just as qualitative analysis has quantitative aspects because investigators note the presence or absence of specified content characteristics, the reverse is also true. For example, deciding whether specified criteria are present or absent often involves subjective considerations. For instance, should a complaint that Congress ignores the department be judged as a comment on rule making? At what point does "great" respect become "somewhat great" or "neutral"?

Systematic, quantitative recording of data guards against errors arising from more casual procedures, making it possible to gather large data bases and subject them to rigorous quantitative analyses. For example, factor analysis may reveal clusters of concepts that would escape the intuitive analyst. Multiple regression analysis may permit predictions about changes in communication variables that can be expected from various changes in the communication situation. Mathematical models can be developed to undertake sophisticated analyses that may aid in restructuring ineffective communication networks. The price to be paid for increased rigor, however, may be an overly mechanical analysis that distorts the meanings that the content is likely to convey.

Content analysis involves a series of important steps, beginning with selection of the body of data to be examined to shed light on the research hypothesis. The next decision involves selection of the unit of analysis, which may range from parts of a sentence to entire documents or groups of documents. Generally, qualitative analysts use the larger units, while quantitative analysts prefer the smaller ones. After the unit of analysis has been chosen, codes and indexes must be developed to identify the content variables that the investigator wishes to record. This is a crucial aspect of content analysis because the ultimate value of most of these studies hinges on the insight and skill with which important variables have been identified and defined so that they are mutually exclusive while covering all of the variables essential to the investigation.

It is often difficult to identify all of the elements of content variables that should be recorded—"coded" is the technical term. For example, a researcher may want to investigate how frequently race identification is included in an agency's personnel files. Should a mention of the client's address be considered racial identification when it refers to a section of town that is known to be overwhelmingly populated by a single race? Should identification of the client as a member of a racially oriented organization be deemed racial identification? Is the inclusion of a client's photograph a form of racial identification? Such questions illustrate the difficulty of making coding decisions. They also make it clear that the outcome of a study depends, to a great extent, on the coding decisions that have been made.

To permit the making of accurate coding decisions, researchers must define coding categories carefully enough to eliminate, as much as possible, doubt about category assignments. How successfully this has been done can be checked through various reliability tests that check "intercoder reliability." When categories are well defined, the coding process can become so mechanical that computers can do the job. While perfect agreement on coding decisions is rare because it is difficult to specify all contingencies and subtleties, one would normally expect coders to be in agreement about 80 percent or more of their decisions. "Intracoder reliability" refers to the ability of coders to replicate their own decisions after a lengthy period of time. For well-trained coders, it should be even higher than intercoder agreement. When agreements drop below acceptable levels, categories may have to be redefined or even redesigned.[52]

Research Needs

It seems appropriate to conclude a discussion of research approaches and methods with a brief inventory of the arenas in which research is badly needed. If improvement in public sector communication is a major goal, then a vast increase in the number of audits of such organizations is needed. At present, most audit procedures have been designed by communication scholars, primarily for private sector organizations. Their usefulness for the public sector could undoubtedly be enhanced by research-based design changes that take into account the unique character of the public sector. The addition of questions that may shed more light on politically relevant characteristics is one example.

Aside from formal audits, case studies focusing on communication within public agencies and in important policy domains are urgently needed. As part of the research for this book, I combed the literature dealing with specific public agencies for information about communication issues and problems. The yield was discouragingly low. Communication problems and patterns were mentioned occasionally but very rarely rated more than cursory discussion.[53]

Public sector organizations are particularly concerned with external communication because of their openness to public scrutiny, their contacts with literally millions of people, and their accountability to the public. Yet they are prevented from a systematic and thoughtful tackling of external communication issues involving public relations because of the cultural reluctance to accept persuasive communication as essential and not inherently dishonest. A resumption of research begun in the 1960s in the areas of image formation and public relations might enable agencies to convey a more positive image and to reduce the barriers between organizations and their clients.[54]

A number of endemic organizational communication problems also require more attention from researchers. These include network-related problems of message overload or underload for key individuals or groups, failure to make the most advantageous connections and avoid the disadvantageous, and finding the most efficient ways to route routine and nonroutine messages. Distortion problems that are fostered by the hierarchical structure of organizations, task specialization, and excessive centralization or decentralization also need to be addressed, as do problems of client communication during public information campaigns and during public service-related encounters between citizens and bureaucrats.

When communication failures lead to major difficulties like the Challenger disaster or Operation Urgent Fury, the analysis of reasons for failure has usually been quite primitive. One rarely sees theory-based analyses that take into consideration important contributing factors, such as the context, including political and psychological elements, in which communication occurred, the diversity of meanings inherent in messages, and the relationships between message senders and receivers. Much more research and new theories are needed to achieve a fuller understanding of what is happening and how failures might be prevented.

Finally, it is important to carry out more comparative research to understand the impact of various cultural and subcultural elements on organizational communication. This includes comparing American organizations with those in other societies, as well as comparing organizations at state and local levels in different parts of the United States. Since the nature of an organization may affect communication patterns, comparisons of large and small organizations or high- and low-technology organizations may be useful. It is also important to analyze the impact of new communication technologies on various aspects of organizational communication. For example, before-and-after studies are needed to determine the impact of computerization and other technologies on communication patterns and organizational power structures.

Summary and Conclusions

The chapter opens with a broad discussion of the essential aspects of research on organizational communication, followed by a description of diagnostic research designed to detect problems in this area. The opening section emphasizes that research must be theory based and briefly describes research approaches based on mechanistic, psychological, interpretive, and systems-interaction theories. Common methods of data collection and their advantages and disadvantages for organizational communication research are outlined. These include familiar social science approaches, such as participant observations, surveys and interviews, experimental studies, and content-analytic research.

As an example of diagnostic research, the chapter focuses on the ICA audit system, a sophisticated, multi-instrument audit that has been used to diagnose communication problems in numerous organizations. The ICA audit is composed of five instruments. One is a questionnaire that assesses the perceptions of organization members regarding various communication features present in the organization. To gain deeper insight into the conditions underlying the questionnaire responses, the audit provides for personal interviews with selected organization members. Members are also asked to keep diaries for one week in which they record and evaluate the usefulness of their contacts with others in the organization. They are requested to report extensively on communication incidents that they deem critical to the organization's functioning.

The fifth ICA audit instrument, network analysis, is described in more detail than the other procedures because of the unique role of this research technique in organizational communication analysis. Unlike the other instruments, which focus on individuals' perceptions about the organization, network analysis focuses on the interaction structures created by individual communications. Various types of network indexes that can be created through specially designed computer programs are discussed, along with some of the major problems in designing network analysis research. A brief section deals with network analysis methods, such as Robert F. Bales's Interaction Process Analysis, which were developed specifically for assessing interactions in small groups.

Since content analysis is a frequently employed technique in organizational communication research, its main features are discussed briefly. The differences between qualitative and quantitative analysis methods are explained, and their respective merits and shortcomings are noted. Other problems touched upon are the difficulties in determining the unit of analysis and devising coding categories.

The chapter ends with a brief overview of research needs. More audits of public sector organizations are recommended, possibly with new instruments specifically designed for public sector institutions. There is also a need for research on various aspects of public information dissemination and more scholarly scrutiny of public encounters. Major communication failures deserve more sophisticated analysis, as do more routine communication problems such as overloads, distortions, and network inadequacies. The goal for all these research endeavors, beyond their social-scientific contributions, should be improvement of communication in public sector organizations. Given the importance of these organizations to the nation's welfare, they deserve the very best efforts of the social science community.

Notes

1. Kathleen J. Krone, Frederic M. Jablin, and Linda L. Putnam, "Communication Theory and Organizational Communication: Multiple Perspectives," in *Handbook of Organizational Communication,* Frederic M. Jablin, Linda L. Putnam, Karlene H. Roberts, and Lyman W. Porter, eds. (Newbury Park, Calif.: Sage, 1987), 18-40.
2. Ibid., 22.

3. Ibid., 28.

4. Linda L. Putnam and Thomas S. Jones, "Reciprocity in Negotiations: An Analysis of Bargaining Interaction," *Communication Monographs* 49 (1982): 171-191.

5. Martha S. Feldman, *Order without Design: Information Production and Policy Making* (Stanford, Calif.: Stanford University Press, 1989), 1-2.

6. Ibid., 27-34.

7. Focus groups are discussed in David W. Stewart and Prem N. Shamdasani, *Focus Groups: Theory and Practice* (Newbury Park, Calif.: Sage, 1990).

8. Peter R. Monge and Eric M. Eisenberg, "Emergent Communication Networks," in *Handbook of Organizational Communication* (Newbury Park, Calif.: Sage, 1987), 318.

9. Howard H. Greenbaum, Susan A. Hellweg, and Raymond L. Falcione, "Organizational Communication Evaluation: An Overview, 1950-1981," in *Handbook of Organizational Communication,* Gerald M. Goldhaber and George A. Barnett, eds. (Norwood, N.J.: Ablex, 1988), 278-279.

10. Ibid. When researchers surveyed Fortune 500 companies in the early 1980s, 45 percent of them had used organizational communication audits and deemed them important as a regular procedure for evaluating the health of their companies.

11. Ibid., 275-317. The authors provide a comprehensive overview of evaluations between 1950 and 1981.

12. Osmo A. Wiio, Gerald M. Goldhaber, and Michael P. Yates, "Organizational Communication Research: Time for Reflection?" in *Communication Yearbook 4,* Dan Nimmo, ed. (New Brunswick, N.J.: Transaction Books, 1980), 85.

13. Gerald M. Goldhaber, *Organizational Communication,* 3d ed. (Dubuque, Iowa: Wm. C. Brown, 1983), 377-379.

14. Gerald M. Goldhaber and Donald P. Rogers, *Auditing Organizational Communication Systems: The ICA Communication Audit* (Dubuque, Iowa: Kendall/Hunt, 1979), 11.

15. Ibid., 204.

16. Phillip K. Tompkins, "Management Qua Communication in Rocket Research and Development," *Communication Monographs* 41 (March 1977): 15.

17. Monge and Eisenberg, 320-321.

18. Wiio et al., 88-89. For nuts-and-bolts audit information and a series of case studies, see Seymour Hamilton, *A Communication Audit Handbook* (New York: Longman, 1987).

19. Goldhaber and Rogers, 35-36.

20. George A. Barnett, Donna M. Hamlin, and James A. Danowski, "The Use of Fractionation Scales for Communication Audits," in *Communication Yearbook 5,* Michael Burgoon, ed. (New Brunswick, N.J.: Transaction, 1982), 455-471, discuss this problem at length. Also see Nancy Wyatt and Gerald M. Phillips, *Studying Organizational Communication: A Case Study of the Farmers Home Administration* (Norwood, N.J.: Ablex, 1988).

21. Frederick Williams, Ronald E. Rice, and Everett M. Rogers, *Research Methods and the New Media* (New York: Free Press, 1988), 164.

22. Louise H. Kidder, *Seltiz, Wrightsman and Cook's Research Methods in Social Relations,* 4th ed. (New York: Holt, Rinehart and Winston, 1981), 191.

23. James A. Danowski and Paul Edison-Swift, "Crisis Effects on Intraorganizational Computer-Based Communication," *Communication Research* 12 (April 1985): 259-270.

24. Network analyses often miss important nonroutine relationships that may yield

exceptionally valuable new information. What is involved is the concept of "the strength of weak ties" mentioned in Chapter 5.

25. David Knoke and James H. Kuklinski, *Network Analysis* (Beverly Hills, Calif.: Sage, 1987), 59-60.

26. Ibid., 56.

27. Ibid., 22.

28. Ibid., 23.

29. William Richards and George Lindsey, "Social Network Analysis: An Overview of Recent Developments," in *Communication and Control in Society,* Klaus Krippendorff, ed. (New York: Gordon and Breach, 1982), 59.

30. Examples can be found in Everett M. Rogers and Rekha Agarwala Rogers, *Communication in Organizations* (New York: Free Press, 1976), 124-125.

31. Goldhaber and Rogers, 165.

32. Monge and Eisenberg, 330; also see Knoke and Kuklinski, 26-30, for a discussion of attempts at sampling large populations.

33. Rolf T. Wigand, "Communication Network Analysis: History and Overview," in *Handbook of Organizational Communication* (Norwood, N.J.: Ablex, 1988), 337.

34. The program contains detailed lists of characteristics for identifying various roles and network characteristics.

35. William D. Richards, Jr., "Data, Models, and Assumptions in Network Analysis," in *Organizational Communication: Traditional Themes and New Directions,* Robert D. McPhee and Phillip K. Tompkins, eds. (Beverly Hills, Calif.: Sage, 1985), 113; also Goldhaber and Rogers, 165.

36. Wigand, 328-336. The author provides brief descriptions of the use of these techniques for network analysis. The possibilities of graphic computerized representations of networks are discussed and illustrated in J. David Johnson, "On the Use of Communication Gradients," in *Handbook of Organizational Communication* (Norwood, N.J.: Ablex, 1988), 361-383.

37. Richards and Lindsey, 64-69; Wigand, 337-342.

38. Knoke and Kuklinski, 30.

39. For a discussion of the advantages and disadvantages of various types of sociograms, see Wigand, 328-331.

40. Goldhaber, 411.

41. Knoke and Kuklinski, 50-56.

42. For an extensive list of earlier studies relevant to political science research, see the bibliography in Edward O. Lauman and David Knoke, *The Organizational State: Social Choice in National Policy Domains* (Madison: University of Wisconsin Press, 1987), and the bibliography in Knoke and Kuklinski.

43. Goldhaber, 59-60.

44. Robert F. Bales, *Interaction Process Analysis* (Reading, Mass.: Addison-Wesley, 1950).

45. Interaction process analyses are discussed in Doris A. Graber, *Verbal Behavior and Politics* (Urbana: University of Illinois Press, 1976), 225-229.

46. Goldhaber, 287.

47. James Danowski, "Organizational Media Theory," in *Communication Yearbook 14,* James A. Anderson, ed. (Newbury Park, Calif.: Sage, 1991), 187-207. The article reports numerous research projects in which automated content analysis revealed word network characteristics.

48. Monge and Eisenberg, 332-334.

49. Goldhaber and Rogers, 162.

50. Ibid., 163.

51. Ibid., 37.

52. For details on content analysis, see Ole Holsti, *Content Analysis for the Social Sciences and Humanities* (Reading, Mass.: Addison-Wesley, 1969), which remains the best book on the technique.

53. For examples of what needs to be done, see Lauman and Knoke, *The Organizational State;* Feldman, *Order without Design*; and Wyatt and Phillips, *Studying Organizational Communication.*

54. The literature is reviewed in J. Michael Sproule, "Propaganda and American Ideological Critique," in *Communication Yearbook 14* (Newbury Park, Calif.: Sage, 1991), 211-238.

C H A P T E R **10**

Reflections of the Future

The title of this final chapter suggests the main characteristic of all visions of the future. The crystal ball that holds the future must reflect the past to a large extent. Like reflections of the surrounding landscape in a pond, the images of the future are unstable, resembling a fleeting mutation one moment and a slightly different one the next. There may be temporary, seemingly major upheavals. But just as a stone tossed into the water will produce major distortions that ripple out over a large area but subside quickly, so the effects of most upheavals in organizational communication patterns fade rapidly. For our purposes, the analogy suggests that despite the vast changes in communication technologies, communication in the public sector in the future will strongly reflect the patterns of the past. It also means that there are no clearly defined patterns for the future. Rather, there are ranges of possible patterns. In these final pages, I will try to sketch out some of the possibilities.

Links to the Past

The Persistence of Theories

In Chapter 9, we discussed four packages of theories, each resting on a different set of assumptions and each directed toward examining different aspects of organizational communication. It is unlikely that this broad spectrum of theoretical approaches, which is far from being fully explored, will expand in the foreseeable future. Rather, we seem to be on the threshold of an era of exploring the mechanistic, psychological, interpretive-symbolic, and systems-interaction approaches more fully as well as integrating them. The reasons for adaptation rather than innovation are twofold. Communication theories, like those in other fields, have tended to move from crude initial statements to refinements that modify the crude general concepts in light of knowledge gained from testing the theories under specific conditions. That is happening now. The second reason for foreseeing only small changes is that attempts to merge existing theories have been only modestly successful. The precise configuration of merged theories has remained fluid. More needs to be done. It is reasonable to expect continued efforts to capture the richness of organizational communication phenomena in correspondingly complex theoretical formulations.

Practical concerns are also spurring the merger of theories. For example, currently several mid-level theories about the nature and goals of bureaucracies conflict, making it difficult to specify operational goals. Initially, public agencies in the U.S. context were viewed largely as tools of the executive branch. Since they were primarily agents rather than principals, communication with public sector agencies, aside from services to clients, was routed through officials elected to direct and supervise these agencies. In recent years, public sector agencies have been viewed increasingly from the perspectives of theories of pluralist democracy. This suggests that they should communicate directly with the public and be responsive to pressures and proposals by their clients and by a variety of lobby groups. Their programs should become more diversified and geared to the needs of the constituencies communicating with the agency.

Obviously, no agency can be primarily both a tool of the executive branch and of the agency's clientele since these perspectives are often antagonistic. An integrative model needs to be developed that combines the best features of each while minimizing their deficiencies. This will require identifying the aspects of each agency's work that benefit most from direct communication and those where openness and responsiveness are most likely to impair operational and cost effectiveness. Developing sound integrative theories involves quintessentially political issues such as defining the meaning of "public interest" and "public opinion."

Human Factors

Aside from theory stability, there are many contextual reasons for questioning the likelihood of developing distinctively new patterns of public sector organizational communication. Primary among them is the fact that the characteristics of human behavior that shape organizational reality in the public sector are ingrained. They include a general reluctance to change, which has been discussed in previous chapters, and the various psychological barriers to altering established views, discussed in Chapter 4, which lead to communication distortions. The American military's flawed decisions that led to the bombing of the U.S. naval base at Pearl Harbor on

December 7, 1941, during World War II, epitomizes these endemic flaws that hamper information use and lead to poor decisions.

Because Admiral Husband Edward Kimmel, the Pacific Fleet Commander, and his staff had concluded that the Japanese would prefer sabotage of the Pearl Harbor naval base rather than an outright assault, defensive preparations were geared largely to preventing sabotage. As is common when people hold strong opinions, all contrary information that might upset their painstakingly reached conclusions was ignored or misinterpreted. The Navy had warned the admiral about a possible Japanese assault and had described a series of Japanese activities that obviously portended an attack.[1] These warnings, typically, fell on deaf ears.

There were also other problems, which recur in various forms in organizations. For example, intensive interservice rivalries prevented adequate intelligence coordination between the Navy and its Army counterparts. As is typical of members of competing organizations, each considered its own information sources to be superior and deprecated rival sources. Information available through cracking Japanese secret codes was not adequately utilized because it became embroiled in a battle over professional turf. The War Plans Division, in an attempt to extend its influence, successfully fought for the right to interpret the codes, even though it lacked Japanese linguists and specialists. Documents containing long-range plans by the State Department's Policy Planning Staff, including those relating to defense against the type of attack that actually occurred, were ignored because, like other organizations, it concentrated on current rather than future problems. Aerial reconnaissance of enemy activities, which might have detected the attackers before they reached their targets, had been neglected because other organizational goals were given higher priorities.

Plus ça change, plus c'est la même chose—the more things change, the more they remain the same. Fifty years later, when America was involved in a war in the Persian Gulf, General H. Norman Schwarzkopf, the victorious commanding officer in the field, complained about information transmission problems across organizational boundaries. Schwarzkopf charged that the analyses of intelligence reports about the effects of bombing that were provided to him by specialists in Washington were warped by their preconceived notions. These experts, said the general, "felt that they were in a better position to judge battle damage assessment from pure analysis of things like photography and that sort of thing alone, rather than allowing the theater commander—who is the person that really, in the final analysis, has to make the ultimate assessment—to apply good military judgment to what he's seen."[2] Estimates of damage to Iraqi military targets made by the general's aides were three to four times greater than the estimates of experts at the Central Intelligence and Defense Intelligence agencies. These experts discounted front-line information because the estimates were based partly on reports from pilots. The preconception was that pilots overstate the damage that they have inflicted.

Human frailties that lead to defective communication and cloud judgments made by individuals and groups cannot be eliminated. Nonetheless, greater awareness may help in controlling their damaging effects on decision making. When people recognize the harmful effects of miscommunication on their own goals and operations, they become more open to suggestions for behavior modification.

Another barrier to change that will be difficult to overcome is the pressure within large organizations to develop and maintain standard operating procedures. Such procedures become ingrained because, as James Q. Wilson points out, they "represent an internally defined equilibrium that reconciles the situational imperatives, professional norms, bureaucratic ideologies, peer group expectations, and (if present) leadership demands unique to the agency." [3] Even when new approaches seem indicated, an organization or individuals within it tend to repeat established patterns of communication in situations where they are not appropriate. It requires very major alterations in some of the component elements of organizational life to create a receptivity for changes. When new patterns do develop, they, too, become frozen very quickly.

Public sector organizations are particularly prone to inflexibility. Compared with major private sector organizations, they generally offer fewer incentives for developing and applying new approaches and provide little support if and when innovations fail. The failure of new procedures often leads to well-publicized condemnation of the unlucky agency and its leaders. The lack of incentives and the prevalence of disincentives discourage public employees from experimenting with new strategies for interpreting their missions and carrying them out. Little change can be expected as long as failures are not accepted by bureaucracy watchers, including the public, as part of the cost of progress. The chances of that happening are slim.

Previous chapters have described the many institutions and institutional processes that also serve as anchors to the past and obstacles to change because they have become vested interests for various groups. To protect their interests, these groups are likely to oppose changes in the established ways that serve their needs. They strongly defend the status quo, including the familiar operating procedures. Even when some groups welcome change, it is unlikely because the ripple effects of change in an interconnected organizational system will touch numerous recalcitrant groups.

However, some changes do occur when new claimants enter the fray, such as the many vocal interest groups that have sprung to life in the waning decades of the twentieth century. For example, it may no longer be possible for health-impaired constituencies to shield their health records from public disclosure. These rights of privacy may be forced to yield to the demands for disclosure brought by groups concerned about the spread of AIDS and groups concerned about curbing escalating medical costs. Once the barriers are lowered for one disease, they may fall for others as well.

Institutional Factors

The very nature of American political institutions diffuses pressures for change. The principles on which these institutions are based, which have had a major impact on communication activities in public sector organizations, mandate fragmentation of governmental authority through the separation of powers and federalism. A system of checks and balances further divides authority. Fragmentation forces organizations to spend considerable time and effort in communicating with diverse institutional levels and bargaining for advantageous treatment. Successful bargaining also involves nurturing diverse constituency relationships by remaining in frequent touch with various groups. The agency's objectives must be blended with its numerous political constraints. The need for compromise and flexibility makes it difficult to keep decision making rational and consistent. Little change can be expected because the American pattern of divided government is here to stay.

Public sector officials will continue to be torn between the claims of professionalism and the necessity for political adaptation. They will be forced to say things that they do not mean and disguise what they mean in order to pass political muster. They will continue to battle the problem of interpreting ambiguous, often conflicting goals that have been set for their agencies for political reasons. Their efforts to manage their agencies effectively will be further hampered by prescribed structures, limited control over personnel, incessant demands for public reports of their activities, and limited information about the resources that will be available for the long-range conduct of their work. As pointed out, similar problems exist in the private sector to a degree because politics and fragmentation of authority are ubiquitous. However, the magnitude of the problems, and hence their effect on organizational communications and operations, is considerably less in the private sector.

The large size of the American administrative sector, the vast array of its activities, and the intertwining of these activities and concerns make long-range planning well-nigh impossible. Serious problems are likely to arise suddenly, totally altering the assumptions on which prior decisions have been based. If one is to judge from past experience, this will not change. The unexpected will continue to happen without fail, either propelled by physical events or the currents of politics. Decision makers then must react to these problems without the careful research that ought to precede important determinations. They may be forced to alter previous decisions, causing major hardships. For example, in the wake of the collapse of Communist regimes in Eastern Europe since 1990, various U.S. agencies began to make plans for increased spending on domestic affairs because they fully expected to reap a "peace dividend" from the reduced financial needs of the military establishment. Alas, it was not long before the visions of such a dividend vanished. They were obliterated by demands from the military for resources to fight a war in the Middle East and to provide accompanying social services abroad and at home.

Administrative Philosophies

As discussed in Chapter 6, organizations develop unique cultures consisting of written and unwritten, explicit and implicit rules of behavior as well as unique myths and symbols. Some of these become part of the organization's basic philosophy and values, so that the chances for changing ingrained beliefs are minimal. In the American context, the requirements for open communication that are widely observed by nonsecurity related agencies are a good example of a permanent cultural constraint that has profound, persistent effects.

As we have seen, the requirements for openness constitute a mixed bag of benefits and disadvantages. On the negative side, for example, the requirements create concerns about exposing important public sector communications to hostile, prying eyes. Top agency personnel feel that they are living in glass houses, constantly exposed to the public gaze. They may feel hounded by reporters. They may spend large amounts of time in symbolic activities to create good images for their agency and for themselves. Openness also tends to discourage innovation because administrators do not wish to be caught out on the proverbial limb. They know that bold proposals are likely to encounter many nay-sayers and that they are likely to be killed through premature exposure to public scrutiny.

Fear of disclosing sensitive information or subjecting themselves to criticism may restrain bureaucrats from acting in ways that may be perfectly appropriate but do not comport with the idealistic image that they feel compelled to portray. For example, to maintain the image of the impartial official who works strictly by the rules, a welfare bureaucrat, against her better judgment, may deny the request of an elderly husband to receive payment for serving as his ailing wife's full-time nurse because payments to relatives are prohibited. This decision may force the couple to divorce, so that the husband becomes an unrelated caretaker, or it may lead to placing the wife in a public institution where nursing care is far more expensive.

On the positive side, openness does prevent misconduct by public officials and enhances accountability. Despite strong support for a policy of candor, it has been imperfectly implemented, and the resulting problems are likely to continue. Many bureaucratic agencies at the national, state, and local levels escape public scrutiny at all times or intermittently. Despite, or perhaps because of, the many requirements that public agencies submit reports to legislatures and other agencies, the monitoring processes rarely operate effectively. Reports are far more likely to gather dust than gain adequate attention. For the most part, the media, which serve as the informal monitor of governmental operations, pay little attention to the routine operations of most public sector agencies. Usually it is only the extraordinary scandal that catches the attention of the media, who are usually tipped off about it by disgruntled insiders. When formal and informal oversight is lax, the discovery of major problems becomes a matter of accident rather than design.

Cultural attitudes about the need for openness also influence the choices open to decision makers when new situations arise. For example, they play, or should play, a role in the debate about privatization in the public sector. Many public administration experts are now recommending that numerous public sector tasks be performed by private sector contractors who bid competitively for the work. Presumably privatization will reduce waste and red tape, resulting in greater efficiency and lower costs. However, when services are in private hands, they are almost invariably less exposed to public scrutiny than when they are operated by the public sector. Private companies are not subject to the Freedom of Information Act or other laws that make it possible to force public sector officials to release information that they would prefer not to divulge.

Depending on the nature of the service, privatization may or may not be a beneficial trade-off. It may be a good idea for running a cafeteria for public employees or providing janitorial services. It may not be appropriate for running a prison or a hospital, where controversial policy decisions must be made about the kinds of services that best satisfy public needs and expectations. In these situations, openness to public scrutiny may be more important than cost control. Demands for economic efficiency may have to yield to demands for democratic governance. Hence, questions about the need for openness in public sector activities may determine the choices of decision makers when issues of privatization arise.

Openness means not only that the business of public agencies is exposed to public scrutiny, but also that agencies are accessible to communication from clients and many special interest groups. The number and diversity of these groups and the intensity and sophistication of their operations have mounted steadily. As discussed, when the claims of these various groups conflict, agencies face serious problems. Attempts to satisfy the demands of powerful, or even weak, pressure groups may be detrimental to the agency's goals and the interests of unorganized clienteles. There is an inherent conflict between the goal of openness and responsiveness on the one hand and the goal of well-planned, efficient performance, judged by economic criteria. The groups that benefit most from the current system can be expected to oppose major changes.

Because of the human, institutional, and cultural contexts in which agencies operate, problems in public sector communication are likely to persist. In addition to pleasing diverse constituencies, agencies must strive to cope with information and communication overloads, as well as the great difficulties in framing messages appropriately and routing them through the most advantageous channels. There are also major difficulties in gathering appropriate information, including selecting the best sources and interrogating them successfully. An unresolved and seemingly unresolvable problem is keeping communication open, fully accessible to the media and the public, without damaging public sector organizations. There are no formulas for resolving these problems, and none seem on the horizon. However, as discussed, there are various strategies for coping with them. Deciding on the right course in specific situations will remain a question for human wisdom to resolve at each particular time and place.

Opportunities for Change

Structural Reorganization

Despite many unyielding problems, there are a number of areas in which substantial changes seem possible or even likely. When communication problems are created by organizational principles underlying bureaucratic structure and operations, such as hierarchy, centralization, and specialization, there are opportunities for reform. For instance, barriers arising from specialization can be reduced by funneling specialized decisions through channels that are controlled by generalists. The overall size of bureaucracies can be curbed, as can the proliferation of levels in hierarchical structures. However, when control over services becomes decentralized and hierarchies are flattened, the benefits may be bought at the expense of reduced coordination and uniformity.

James Wilson recommends placing the authority over public sector services at the lowest level at which information essential for sound decisions is available.[4] Bureaucracies differ greatly in this respect. When uniformity of treatment and precision are important, as in Internal Revenue matters or in prison administration, control must be centralized at the top. When many decisions are made at the street level, or when they are highly unpredictable, as happens in much police work, control should be at the street level.

Problems posed by structural reorganization may be solved more readily than ever before through careful network analyses of communication flows. Evolving network analysis techniques hold promise for depicting human communication in more realistic ways than in earlier models based on hierarchical flow charts or communications between individual senders and receivers. The computer difficulties that have plagued this type of analysis when it involved large data sets seem to be yielding to new techniques.

The ability to analyze larger networks than is currently feasible should be beneficial in detecting and resolving boundary-spanning problems. In fact, it may be possible to move beyond the analysis of actual networks to a projection of potential networks. Such projections may suggest how a particular organization can make the most fruitful kinds of connections with the fewest overload problems. Experimental networks could also provide information about changing network requirements to meet the needs of particular communication situations. As indicated in Chapter 2, mathematical formulas are available to compute the incremental value provided by additional information.

Harnessing Computer Power

Computer capabilities hold the potential for solving a number of major organizational communication problems. One of the most difficult and vexing of these problems concerns the spotting of crucial information that may have entered the system at lower levels. As the Pearl Harbor example demonstrates, such information is often available in time to avert disaster, but is useless if its importance is not recognized. With the help of advanced computers, future communication analysts should be able to devise more systematic ways to identify the characteristics of noise that should be discarded and the characteristics of important information that must be speeded along. Computers can quickly scan huge amounts of electronically submitted raw data and identify key words and concepts as well as patterns. Computers can also be used to simulate situations and detect various patterns better and faster than humans can. Technical monitoring of the performance of complicated machinery and many simulations conducted by the Defense Department provide precedents for programming computers to detect problems.

Computer programs may also make it possible to bring greater rationality to decision making during crises as well as in more ordinary times. There has been a tremendous increase in the capability of computer programs to handle large data sets and reduce them to key indicators that may be useful to decision makers. These increased capabilities may allow the inclusion of more political factors in decision-making models than has hitherto been possible. Such factors are crucial in public sector communication and must play a part in any viable model.

Harnessing computer power to the fullest will require training top-level bureaucrats appropriately. Decision makers who were trained in the pre-computer age may feel overwhelmed by the vast amounts of information now at their fingertips. They may find it difficult to determine at what point information searches should be concluded and decisions made. When decision-making models are tested under a variety of assumptions, so many possibilities may surface that bureaucrats may find themselves riding off in many different directions, putting out small brushfires while the main blaze grows in intensity. It will be the task of the educational establishment to analyze such problems and devise ways of teaching future bureaucrats how to cope with them. It is not enough to teach the technical capabilities of advanced electronic tools. Training must also include instruction in the new ways in which computerization can help to conceptualize and solve problems.

Since computers can handle more incoming and more stored information than was previously possible, decision makers will face a growing universe of data from which information must be selected for making a decision. To cope with this complexity and to construct effective computer models, decision makers will have to pay more attention to clarifying and specifying their assumptions and perceptions of the basic facts of each situation. That requirement is bound to add rigor to decision making. The fact that decisions are apt to be more solidly grounded and that computerized results are seen as "scientific" and "objective" may make them more widely acceptable and less vulnerable to challenges.

Deciding on the nature of the factors to be considered for making decisions requires securing the agreement of parties who must be consulted. In the process, all participants are apt to develop a clearer understanding of the basic factors involved and the perceptions and preferences of the contributors to the decision-making process. Decision makers who see the situation most clearly and whose data and models become the basis for discussion will be the winners in the game.

Improving Climates and Cultures

Just as the public sector tends to ignore structural factors that are important in human communication, so it ignores factors of climate and culture in general terms. As economists have long contended, when enterprises exceed their optimal size, they function less effectively. Many public sector agencies are far too large to attain and maintain a sound organizational climate in which individuals are happy and work well. Reorganization could reduce their size. The current movement to transfer certain functions to the state and local levels may provide some remedies if—and it is a big if—the federal government also reassigns the necessary resources to perform these functions. However, when structures become decentralized, the need for boundary-spanning communication grows by leaps and bounds.

Organizational cultures, and often climates as well, seem to evolve more or less haphazardly. It should be possible to design some aspects of cultures and climates more deliberately. The last decade of the twentieth century is a particularly challenging time for guided changes because many of the new communication technologies have the potential to alter organizational cultures. Reallocating decision-making authority in the wake of network analysis and permitting people to work at dispersed locations instead of in large offices are examples. Thus far, this potential for changing cultures has not been realized because of the tendency to use the new horses of computer technology to pull old wagons of organizational structures and functions. As one astute analyst of bureaucracy points out, changing a culture resembles moving a cemetery. "It is always difficult and some believe it is sacrilegious." [5] Nonetheless, adjustments are being made, particularly if they can be justified as benefiting task efficiency, narrowly conceived, rather than concern with reshaping organizational cultures.

Among changes that can be justified on the grounds of efficiency are improvements in the physical settings in which public sector organizational communication takes place. In the past, public sector bureaucratic cultures have generally striven for an image of austerity in physical settings that would convey frugality and a concern for not spending taxpayers' money on "frills." Little consideration was given to the part that well-planned physical settings can play in the success of organizational transactions. The impact of interpretive theories, with their stress on human feelings and concerns, has made it easier to shift thinking toward constructing climates conducive to raising the comfort levels. If such concerns become dominant, offices may be designed with an eye to making them attractive to office personnel as well as to clients.

Cultural differences between bureaucrats and clients often make the communication climate in public sector agencies seem harsh and even hostile to the participants. Computers can help to ease several currently serious encounter problems. For instance, communicating with people who do not speak English may become manageable because of the rapid growth of computer capabilities for translating written and even spoken language. This should make it possible to translate government forms and explanatory materials into many more languages. Desktop publishing will then permit inexpensive duplication of these forms. It will also make it far easier to revise documents that do not conform to the cultural norms of the target clientele. For example, the commanding tone in many State Department documents directed to foreign consulates has been criticized as demeaning by various Asiatic clients who are used to more deferential language.

Computer capabilities can also create a better climate for outreach efforts. Messages can be framed to meet the needs of hard-to-reach populations and can be disseminated through a broader array of channels. If technical advances are accompanied by greater efforts to understand the many cultures represented in an increasingly diverse citizenry, and by attempts to respond sensitively to cultural differences, client communication will improve greatly. Social pressures at the turn of the century seem to augur well for major improvements along these lines.

Efforts to improve client communication are particularly important because many features of bureaucracy militate against sensitive treatment of clients. When Max Weber stressed the importance of standardization and routinization, his main concern was bureaucratic efficiency. Pleasing clients was not considered an objective. Moreover, bureaucracies enjoy a monopoly position for most of the services that they provide, so that clients are forced to deal with them on the bureaucrats' terms.

Clients often do not have the choice to forgo a service. If they fail to deal with agencies under these circumstances, they can be forced to cooperate, and severe penalties may be imposed for noncompliance. The Internal Revenue and Environmental Protection agencies are examples. When public agencies wield such great powers, often providing no opportunity to challenge their edicts and procedures, it seems only right to mandate that client needs must be taken into account. Such mandates require a delicate balancing act, so that the rights of individuals are as fully protected as possible without unduly sacrificing the rights of the collectivity.

The private sector has learned that it is sound business to study clients' perceptions and to accommodate them. Elements of what is broadly called "service" are as important as quality and price for many people. Physicians have discovered that a good "bedside manner" makes the patient more likely to follow instructions and to have confidence in the physician's skill. Good interpersonal relations may actually speed recovery and deter costly malpractice suits against physicians whose treatments fail. There is no reason why comparable benefits should not ensue if public officials were to have better "office manners."

One way to hasten greater concern about creating an empathetic climate is to build scrutiny of climate factors into the many formal audits and analyses of organizational communication that have come into vogue, as well as into performance appraisals of public sector personnel. If high quality in client interactions becomes a factor in these appraisals, and if public servants are rewarded for good performance, improved behavior is likely. The incentive structure is currently skewed toward the welfare of public agencies rather than client concerns. However, the improvements in meeting client needs may not be huge because many officials, cognizant of the importance of good client communication, already perform well on that score.

Coping with Image Problems

Whenever the work of public sector agencies suffers because of demonstrably false myths, there is more than a glimmer of hope that reasoned discourse will destroy the false myth or at least weaken its hold on people.

Public relations activities are a case in point. Public scorn has made them difficult to undertake. Hiding such activities behind various euphemisms will not dispel existing negative attitudes; rather, the perception of public relations must be explicitly dissociated from the notion of intentionally deceptive persuasion. It must and can be shown that public relations messages, properly done, do not involve deception. A more positive attitude toward public relations activities will mean that the subterfuges often used to conceal their nature can be replaced by openness. If that happens, public relations activities can be planned and carried out much more carefully.

As pointed out in Chapter 7, exaggerated public expectations about what is achievable in the public sector make it necessary for agencies to engage in image building. These agencies are supposed to perform their work flawlessly at the lowest costs, often with underpaid personnel. Astronauts have joked about the fact that the safety of their missions hinges on perfect performance by the hundreds of thousands of parts that make up their multimillion dollar equipment. Yet assurance of high quality is not the top priority. It ranks behind the demand that contracts be given to the lowest-cost bidders who meet the stipulated specifications, as well as a number of political considerations that have nothing to do with quality.

Public agencies inevitably fall far short of the idealized performance against which they are measured. The resulting image problem is made worse by the fact that "bureaucracy" has become a pejorative term, so that bureaucrats are presumed to be plodding poor managers, enmeshed in red tape and swollen with their own importance. They no longer enjoy the trust and public respect that they held in years past.

Suspicion and hostility have been fed by the greater intrusiveness of government into the lives of private citizens, by the failure to find satisfactory and widely acceptable solutions to pressing social problems with which government has not dealt in the past, and by a series of widely publicized scandals involving high-level bureaucrats in such agencies as the CIA, the FBI, the Environmental Protection Agency, and the Department of Housing and Urban Development. Moreover, in recent election campaigns, including presidential elections, attacks on the bureaucracy have been prominently featured. Rather than pointing with pride to the many achievements of bureaucrats, presidential candidates have disparaged their service. The presidential campaign rhetoric of Jimmy Carter is a prime example.

To create a sound data base for setting the record straight and placing it in proper perspective, a number of comparative studies might be undertaken; conditions under which U.S. public agencies work could be compared with similar agencies in other countries and also with comparable enterprises in the private sector. Such studies might make it more apparent that the public sector often works under constraints that almost guarantee major failures. They would show that the private sector does not work as smoothly and efficiently as the idealized version has suggested. Studies would also show that, given appropriate conditions and resources, the public service often performs very well indeed when expert analysts judge accomplishments in the light of resources and constraints. The achievements of the Forest Service and the Social Security Administration are prime examples that merit being brought to the public's attention. Comparative studies may also permit American officials to learn from the experiences of the bureaucrats in other domestic and foreign jurisdictions.

In addition to clearing the atmosphere generally and improving the effectiveness of agencies in dealing with their many constituencies, a better image for the public service would enhance employee morale. As James Wilson observes, "Most people do not like working in an environment in which every action is second-guessed, every initiative viewed with suspicion, and every controversial decision denounced as malfeasance." [6] If such a hostile climate can be improved, higher morale may also spell better performance and the ability to attract and retain qualified personnel.

In the field of public relations, much remains to be learned about various social marketing efforts. The somewhat disappointing results of campaigns to inform the public about AIDS and its prevention point to the vast stakes involved in effective social marketing. It is therefore likely that research to improve social marketing campaigns will accelerate, especially as it has been shown that they can succeed.[7] Technical issues, such as market segmentation, timing, and choice of media, have been explored in the past, but much more work remains to be done to test the findings in diverse circumstances. Ethical issues have received less attention. It is not clear what limitations, if any, should be imposed on public social marketing campaigns. For example, is the graphic depiction of condom use appropriate in a publicly financed brochure? Is it appropriate to require children to be exposed to such information at the grade-school level? At what age? Given the importance of effective social marketing, such issues need to be resolved.

Setting Goals for the Public Service

One of the biggest obstacles to planning organizational communication development in the public sector is the lack of agreement on goals and priorities, beyond cost effectiveness and rationality. Even when lawmakers have defined an agency's missions, the precise nature of these organizational goals and their order of priorities require interpretation. Conflicting goals must be reconciled. Administrators have been admonished to be responsive to their superiors in the agency and to elected officials, but they must also be responsive to diverse interest groups and to the public at large. They must treat all citizens impartially, yet remain sensitive to individual differences. They must be loyal to the goals of the agency while safeguarding national interests. They must maintain standards and obey the letter of the law, yet be willing to bargain and to compromise.

Agencies and their personnel must choose among these contradictory goals. They must try to reach some kind of agreement internally about which norms should prevail or receive preferred status. Concern about societal needs in the twenty-first century should guide these choices. However, it is unclear whether such decisions can be made categorically or whether they must remain forever flexible, depending on specific circumstances and the predilections of officials involved in a particular decision. The need to compromise may require expressing goals in vague, flexible terms that permit different claimants to see them in ways that suit each claimant's purposes. Still, it is essential to clarify goals, even for the short run.

In the past, the goal of public service has primarily been to accomplish the agency's mission with the support of dedicated public servants. Major criteria for effectiveness have been relatively low costs for accomplishing tasks, speed, accuracy, and the ability to serve all rightful claimants to the service. The authors of the President's Private Sector Survey on Cost Control—which came to be known as the Grace Commission Report— argued in 1984 that the government should be run according to private sector business principles to avoid waste and inefficiency.[8]

The welfare of employees and the welfare of clients, from each group's perspective, have been secondary. One can argue that criteria expressed in terms of the performance of a businesslike service also benefit workers as well as the public, which pays for the services with its tax money. That argument, while partly valid, misses an important point. Even by the end of the nineteenth century, critics of Taylorism had demonstrated that the average person does not measure the worth of life by monetary rewards alone. Workers care about more than the economic benefits of their jobs or the speed with which tasks can be performed, permitting them to turn to other pursuits. Human communication aspects of jobs are equally and often more important than material rewards. The same holds true for clients of public services, who would often gladly trade speed and even cost for services better geared to human needs. How people feel about the goals and quality of public sector services is as important, or more important, than the objective achievements recorded in official reports.

Two yardsticks may be used to measure the desirability of improving climates of interaction in public sector agencies. One can argue that costs will pay for themselves because of improved communication and attitudes of the parties involved in the transaction. One can also argue that citizen satisfaction is an important element in a democratic society, so that some increased monetary costs are fully justified. This is the reasoning that has been used to justify other important social policies, such as affirmative action.

Whether or not such changes will be made and their direction will, of course, depend heavily on the general political climate within the nation. When the emphasis is on retrenchment and general cost cutting, new ventures, even if they promise ultimate cost saving, are not likely to be undertaken. Much depends, too, on the climate for the work of particular agencies. There was a time when NASA was a public favorite, which made it comparatively easy to obtain the resources it desired. That time perished with the *Challenger* explosion. The CIA, during the years when it was headed by Allen Dulles, and the FBI, in the J. Edgar Hoover era, were other favorites that were allowed to manage their business with a great deal of support and relatively little intrusion. Those eras are gone. As we head into the twenty-first century, there seem to be no favorites, not even the Defense Department, which once had easy sailing whenever it asked for support.

The Research Agenda

If ours is, indeed, the Age of Communication, in which information is acknowledged as the predominant resource, then it seems clear that concern about communication and information management will remain high. In fact, concern will probably rise since it is the nature of information to increase in significance the more it is exchanged and shared. With the passing of time, ever larger numbers of organizations become drawn into communication networks, with all sharing information and contributing new data that must be integrated into the existing data bases.

Given the importance of abundant good information, if organizations are to function well, whatever their goals might be, it is clear that more resources, in both time and money, will have to be devoted to communication tasks and research. That involves more than extra appropriations for computers. It also means more time for the gathering and analysis of information and for experimenting with new information practices and patterns. It means more time to study information flows within organizations and between organizations and their environment.

There is still much to learn about information flows in the public sector. For example, current knowledge of the interactions between public agencies and the news media is still rudimentary. Analysts and practitioners agree that the media play an important role in creating the images of agencies and of public policies, and that public administrators play an important role in the process. However, the details of the interactions remain obscure. It is my hope that additional studies and experiments in public sector organizational communication will be among the research priorities of social scientists. If this book galvanizes the academic and professional research community into greater action in this emerging field, it will have fulfilled its purpose.

Notes

1. Graham Allison, *Essence of Decision: Explaining the Cuban Missile Crisis* (Boston: Little, Brown, 1971), 88-95.
2. Michael Wines, "Gulf Intelligence Draws Complaint by Schwarzkopf," *New York Times,* June 13, 1991.
3. James Q. Wilson, *Bureaucracy: What Government Agencies Do and Why They Do It* (New York: Basic Books, 1989), 375.
4. Ibid., 372.
5. Ibid., 368.
6. Wilson, *Bureaucracy,* 369.
7. Rice and Atkin, eds. *Public Communication Campaigns.*
8. President's Private Sector Survey on Cost Control, *A Report to the President,* 47 vols. (Washington, D.C.: Government Printing Office, 1984).

A P P E N D I X 1

The Privacy Act

Public Law 93-579:
The Privacy Act of 1974

Be it enacted by the Senate and House of Representatives of the United States of America in Congress assembled, That this Act may be cited as the "Privacy Act of 1974."

Sec. 2.

(a) The Congress finds that—

    (1) the privacy of an individual is directly affected by the collection, maintenance, use, and dissemination of personal information by Federal agencies;

    (2) the increasing use of computers and sophisticated information technology, while essential to the efficient operations of the Government, has greatly magnified the harm to individual privacy that can occur from any collection, maintenance, use, or dissemination of personal information;

    (3) the opportunities for an individual to secure employment, insurance, and credit, and his right to due process, and other legal protections are endangered by the misuse of certain information systems;

    (4) the right to privacy is a personal and fundamental right protected by the Constitution of the United States; and

    (5) in order to protect the privacy of individuals identified in information systems maintained by Federal agencies, it is necessary and proper for the Congress to regulate the collection, maintenance, use, and dissemination of information by such agencies.

(b) The purpose of this Act is to provide certain safeguards for an individual against an invasion of personal privacy by requiring Federal agencies, except as otherwise provided by law, to—

    (1) permit an individual to determine what records pertaining to him are collected, maintained, used, or disseminated by such agencies;

    (2) permit an individual to prevent records pertaining to him obtained by such agencies for a particular purpose from being used or made available for another purpose without his consent;

    (3) permit an individual to gain access to information pertaining to him in

Federal agency records, to have a copy made of all or any portion thereof, and to correct or amend such records;

(4) collect, maintain, use, or disseminate any record of identifiable personal information in a manner that assures that such action is for a necessary and lawful purpose, that the information is current and accurate for its intended use, and that adequate safeguards are provided to prevent misuse of such information;

(5) permit exemptions from the requirements with respect to records provided in this Act only in those cases where there is an important public policy need for such exemption as has been determined by specific statutory authority; and

(6) be subject to civil suit for any damages which occur as a result of willful or intentional action which violates any individual's rights under this Act.

Sec. 3.

Title 5, United States Code, is amended by adding after section 552 the following new section:
"552a. Records maintained on individuals

"(a) DEFINITIONS.—For purposes of this section—

"(1) the term 'agency' means agency as defined in section 552(e) of this title;

"(2) the term 'individual' means a citizen of the United States or an alien lawfully admitted for permanent residence;

"(3) the term 'maintain' includes maintain, collect, use, or disseminate;

"(4) the term 'record' means any item, collection, or grouping of information about an individual that is maintained by an agency, including, but not limited to, his education, financial transactions, medical history, and criminal or employment history and that contains his name, or the. identifying number, symbol, or other identifying particular assigned to the individual, such as a finger or voice print or a photograph.

"(5) the term 'system of records' means a group of any records under the control of any agency from which information is retrieved by the name of the individual or by some identifying number, symbol, or other identifying particular assigned to the individual;

"(6) the term 'statistical record' means a record in a system of records maintained for statistical research or reporting purposes only and not used in whole or in part in making any determination about an identifiable individual, except as provided by section 8 of title 13; and

"(7) the term 'routine use' means, with respect to the disclosure of a record, the use of such record for a purpose which is compatible with the purpose for which it was collected.

"(b) CONDITIONS OF DISCLOSURE.—No agency shall disclose any record which is contained in a system of records by any means of communication to any person, or to another agency, except pursuant to a written request by, or with the prior consent of, the individual to whom the record pertains, unless disclosure of the record would be—

"(1) to those officers and employees of the agency which maintains the record who have a need for the record in the performance of their duties;

"(2) required under section 552 of this title;

"(3) for a routine use as defined in subsection (a)(7) of this section and described under subsection (e)(4)(D) of this section;

"(4) to the Bureau of the Census for purposes of planning or carrying out a census of survey or related activity pursuant to the provisions of title 13;

"(5) to a recipient who has provided the agency with advance adequate written assurance that the record will be used solely as a statistical research or reporting record, and the record is to be transferred in a form that is not individually identifiable;

"(6) to the National Archives of the United States as a record which has sufficient historical or other value to warrant its continued preservation by the United States Government, or for evaluation by the Administrator of General Services or his designee to determine whether the record has such value;

"(7) to another agency or to an instrumentality of any governmental jurisdiction within or under the control of the United States for a civil or criminal law enforcement activity if the activity is authorized by law, and if the head of the agency or instrumentality has made a written request to the agency which maintains the record specifying the particular portion desired and the law enforcement activity for which the record is sought;

"(8) to a person pursuant to a showing of compelling circumstances affecting the health or safety of an individual if upon such disclosure notification is transmitted to the last known address of such individual;

"(9) to either House of Congress, or, to the extent of matter within its jurisdiction, any committee or subcommittee thereof, any joint committee of Congress or subcommittee of any such joint committee;

"(10) to the Comptroller General, or any of his authorized representatives, in the course of the performance of the duties of the General Accounting Office; or

"(11) pursuant to the order of a court of competent jurisdiction.

"(c) ACCOUNTING OF CERTAIN DISCLOSURES.—Each agency, with respect to each system of records under its control, shall—

"(1) except for disclosures made under subsections (b)(1) or (b)(2) of this section, keep an accurate accounting of—

"(A) the date, nature, and purpose of each disclosure of a record to any person or to another agency made under subsection (b) of this section; and

"(B) the name and address of the person or agency to whom the disclosure is made;

"(2) retain the accounting made under paragraph (1) of this subsection for at least five years or the life of the record, whichever is longer, after the disclosure for which the accounting is made;

"(3) except for disclosures made under subsection (b)(7) of this section, make the accounting made under paragraph (1) of this subsection available to the individual named in the record at his request; and

"(4) inform any person or other agency about any correction or notation of dispute made by the agency in accordance with subsection (d) of this section of any record that has been disclosed to the person or agency if an accounting of the disclosure was made.

"(d) ACCESS TO RECORDS.—Each agency that maintains a system of records shall—

"(1) upon request by any individual to gain access to his record or to any information pertaining to him which is contained in the system, permit him and upon his request, a person of his own choosing to accompany him, to review the record and have a copy made of all or any portion thereof in a form comprehensible to him, except that the agency may require the individual to furnish a written statement authorizing discussion of that individual's record in the accompanying person's presence;

"(2) permit the individual to request amendment of a record pertaining to him and—

"(A) not later than 10 days (excluding Saturdays, Sundays, and legal public holidays) after the date of receipt of such request, acknowledge in writing such receipt; and

"(B) promptly, either—

"(i) make any correction of any portion thereof which the individual believes is not accurate, relevant, timely, or complete; or

"(ii) inform the individual of its refusal to amend the record in accordance with his request, the reason for the refusal, the procedures established by the agency for the individual to request a review of that refusal by the head of the agency or an officer designated by the head of the agency, and the name and business address of that official;

"(3) permit the individual who disagrees with the refusal of the agency to amend his record to request a review of such refusal, and not later than 30 days (excluding Saturdays, Sundays, and legal public holidays) from the date on which the individual requests such review, complete such review and make a final determination unless, for good cause shown, the head of the agency extends such 30-day period; and if, after his review, the reviewing official also refuses to amend the record in accordance with the request, permit the individual to file with the agency a concise statement setting forth the reasons for his disagreement with the refusal of the agency, and notify the individual of the provisions for judicial review of the reviewing official's determination under subsection (g)(1)(A) of this section;

"(4) in any disclosure, containing information about which the individual has filed a statement of disagreement, occurring after the filing of the statement under paragraph (3) of this subsection, clearly note any portion of the record which is disputed and provide copies of the statement, and if the agency deems it appropriate, copies of a concise statement of the reasons of the agency for not making the amendments requested, to persons or other agencies to whom the disputed record has been disclosed; and

"(5) nothing in this section shall allow an individual access to any information compiled in reasonable anticipation of a civil action or proceeding.

"(e) AGENCY REQUIREMENTS.—Each agency that maintains a system of records shall—

"(1) maintain in its records only such information about an individual as is relevant and necessary to accomplish a purpose of the agency required to be accomplished by statute or by executive order of the President;

"(2) collect information to the greatest extent practicable directly from the subject individual when the information may result in adverse determinations about an individual's rights, benefits, and privileges under Federal programs;

"(3) inform each individual whom it asks to supply information, on the form which it uses to collect the information or on a separate form that can be retained by the individual—

"(A) the authority (whether granted by statute, or by executive order of the President) which authorizes the solicitation of the information and whether disclosure of such information is mandatory or voluntary;

"(B) the principal purpose or purposes for which the information is intended to be used;

"(C) the routine uses which may be made of the information, as published pursuant to paragraph (4)(D) of this subsection; and

"(D) the effects on him, if any, of not providing all or any part of the requested information;

"(4) subject to the provisions of paragraph (11) of this subsection, publish in the *Federal Register* at least annually a notice of the existence and character of the system of records, which notice shall include—

"(A) the name and location of the system;

"(B) the categories of individuals on whom records are maintained in the system;

"(C) the categories of records maintained in the system;

"(D) each routine use of the records contained in the system, including the categories of users and the purpose of such use;

"(E) the policies and practices of the agency regarding storage, retrievability, access controls, retention, and disposal of the records;

"(F) the title and business address of the agency official who is responsible for the system of records;

"(G) the agency procedures whereby an individual can be notified at his request if the system of records contains a record pertaining to him;

"(H) the agency procedures whereby an individual can be notified at his request how he can gain access to any record pertaining to him contained in the system of records, and how he can contest its content; and

"(I) the categories of sources of records in the system;

"(5) maintain all records which are used by the agency in making any determination about any individual with such accuracy, relevance, timeliness, and completeness as is reasonably necessary to assure fairness to the individual in the determination;

"(6) prior to disseminating any record about an individual to any person other than an agency, unless the dissemination is made pursuant to subsection (b)(2) of this section, make reasonable efforts to assure that such records are accurate, complete, timely, and relevant for agency purposes;

"(7) maintain no record describing how any individual exercises rights guaranteed by the First Amendment unless expressly authorized by statute or by the individual about whom the record is maintained or unless pertinent to and within the scope of an authorized law enforcement activity;

"(8) make reasonable efforts to serve notice on an individual when any record on such individual is made available to any person under compulsory legal process when such process becomes a matter of public record;

"(9) establish rules of conduct for persons involved in the design, development, operation, or maintenance of any system or records, or in maintaining any record, and instruct each such person with respect to such rules and the requirements of this section, including any other rules and procedures adopted pursuant to this section and the penalties for noncompliance;

"(10) establish appropriate administrative, technical, and physical safeguards to insure the security and confidentiality of records and to protect against any anticipated threats or hazards to their security or integrity which could result in substantial harm, embarrassment, inconvenience, or unfairness to any individual on whom information is maintained; and

"(11) at least 30 days prior to publication of information under paragraph (4)(D) of this subsection, publish in the *Federal Register* notice of any new use or intended use of the information in the system, and provide an opportunity for interested persons to submit written data, views, or arguments to the agency.

"(f) AGENCY RULES.—In order to carry out the provisions of this section, each agency that maintains a system of records shall promulgate rules, in accordance with the requirements (including general notice) of section 553 of this title, which shall—

"(1) establish procedures whereby an individual can be notified in response to his request if any system of records named by the individual contains a record pertaining to him;

"(2) define reasonable times, places, and requirements for identifying an individual who requests his record or information pertaining to him before the agency shall make the record or information available to the individual;

"(3) establish procedures for the disclosure to an individual upon his request of his record or information pertaining to him, including special procedure, if deemed necessary, for the disclosure to an individual of medical records, including psychological records, pertaining to him;

"(4) establish procedures for reviewing a request from an individual concerning the amendment of any record or information pertaining to the individual, for making a determination on the request, for an appeal within the agency of an initial adverse agency determination, and for whatever additional means may be necessary for each individual to be able to exercise fully his rights under this section; and

"(5) establish fees to be charged, if any, to any individual for making copies of his record, excluding the cost of any search for and review of the record.

The Office of the Federal Register shall annually compile and publish the rules promulgated under this subsection and agency notices published under subsection (e)(4) of this section in a form available to the public at low cost.

"(g) —

"(1) CIVIL REMEDIES.—Whenever any agency

"(A) makes a determination under the subsection (d)(3) of this section not to amend an individual's record in accordance with his request, or fails to make such review in conformity with that subsection;

"(B) refuses to comply with an individual request under subsection (d)(1) of this section;

"(C) fails to maintain any record concerning any individual with such accuracy, relevance, timeliness, and completeness as is necessary to assure fairness in any determination relating to the qualifications, character, rights, or opportunities of, or benefits to the individual that may be made on the basis of such record, and consequently a determination is made which is adverse to the individual; or

"(D) fails to comply with any other provision of this section, or any rule promulgated thereunder, in such a way as to have an adverse effect on an individual, the individual may bring a civil action against the agency, and the district courts of the United States shall have jurisdiction in the matters under the provisions of this subsection.

"(2) —

"(A) In any suit brought under the provisions of subsection (g)(1)(A) of this section, the court may order the agency to amend the individual's record in accordance with his request or in such other way as the court may direct. In such a case the court shall determine the matter *de novo*.

"(B) The court may assess against the United States reasonable attorney fees and other litigation costs reasonably incurred in any case under this paragraph in which the complainant has substantially prevailed.

"(3) —

"(A) In any suit brought under the provisions of subsection (g)(1)(B) of this section, the court may enjoin the agency from withholding the records and order the production to the complainant of any agency records improperly withheld from him. In such a case the court shall determine the matter *de novo*, and may examine the contents of any agency records *in camera* to determine whether the records or any portion thereof may be withheld under any of the exemptions set forth in subsection (k) of this section, and the burden is on the agency to sustain its action.

"(B) The court may assess against the United States reasonable attorney fees and other litigation costs reasonably incurred in any case under this paragraph in which the complainant has substantially prevailed.

"(4) In any suit brought under the provisions of subsection (g)(1)(C) or (D) of this section in which the court determines that the agency acted in a manner which was intentional or willful, the United States shall be liable to the individual in an amount equal to the sum of—

"(A) actual damages sustained by the individual as a result of the refusal or failure, but in no case shall a person entitled to recovery receive less than the sum of $1,000; and

"(B) the costs of the action together with reasonable attorney fees as determined by the court.

"(5) An action to enforce any liability created under this section may be brought in the district court of the United States in the district in which the complainant resides, or has his principal place of business, or in which the agency records are situated, or in the District of Columbia, without regard to the amount in controversy, within two years from the date on which the cause of action arises, except that where any agency has materially and willfully misrepresented any information required under this section to be disclosed to an individual and the information so misrepresented is material to establishment of liability of the agency to the individual under this section, the action may be brought at any time within two years after discovery by the individual of the misrepresentation. Nothing in this section shall be construed to authorize any civil action by reason of any injury sustained as the result of a disclosure of a record prior to the effective date of this section.

"(h) RIGHTS OF LEGAL GUARDIANS.—For the purposes of this section, the parent of any minor, or the legal guardian of any individual who has been declared to be incompetent due to physical or mental incapacity or age by a court of competent jurisdiction, may act on behalf of the individual.

"(i) —

"(1) CRIMINAL PENALTIES.—Any officer or employee of an agency, who by virtue of his employment or official position, has possession of, or access to, agency records which contain individually identifiable information the disclosure of which is prohibited by this section or by rules or regulations established thereunder, and who knowing that disclosure of the specific material is so prohibited, willfully discloses the material in any manner to any person or agency not entitled to receive it, shall be guilty of a misdemeanor and fined not more than $5,000.

"(2) Any officer or employee of any agency who willfully maintains a system of records without meeting the notice requirements of subsection (e)(4) of this section shall be guilty of a misdemeanor and fined not more than $5,000.

"(3) Any person who knowingly and willfully requests or obtains any record concerning an individual from an agency under false pretenses shall be guilty of a misdemeanor and fined not more than $5,000.

"(j) GENERAL EXEMPTIONS.—The head of any agency may promulgate rules, in accordance with the requirements (including general notice) of sections 553(b)(1), (2), and (3), (c), and (e) of this title, to exempt any system of records within the agency from any part of this section except subsections (b), (c)(1) and (2), (e)(4)(A) through (F), (e)(6), (7), (9), (10), and (11), and (i) if the system of records is—

"(1) maintained by the Central Intelligence Agency; or

"(2) maintained by an agency or component thereof which performs as its principal function any activity pertaining to the enforcement of criminal laws, including police efforts to prevent, control, or reduce crime or to apprehend criminals, and the activities of prosecutors, courts, correctional, probation, pardon, or parole authorities, and which consists of (A) information compiled for the purpose of identifying individual criminal offenders and alleged offenders and consisting only of identifying data and notations of arrests, the nature and disposition of criminal charges, sentencing, confinement, release, and parole and probation status; (B) information compiled for the purpose of a criminal investigation, including reports of informants and investigators, and associated with an identifiable individual; or (C) reports identifiable to an individual compiled at any stage of the process of enforcement of criminal laws from arrest or indictment through release from supervision.

At the time rules are adopted under this subsection, the agency shall include in the statement required under section 553(c) of this title, the reasons why the system of records is to be exempted from a provision of this section.

"(k) SPECIFIC EXEMPTIONS.—The head of any agency may promulgate rules, in accordance with the requirements (including general notice) of sections 553(b)(1), (2), and (3), (c), and (e) of this title, to exempt any system of records within the agency from subsections (c)(3), (d), (e)(1), (e)(4)(G), (H), and (I) and (f) of this section if the system of records is—

"(1) subject to the provisions of section 552(b)(1) of this title;

"(2) investigatory material compiled for law enforcement purposes, other than material within the scope of subsection (j)(2) of this section: *Provided, however,* That if any individual is denied any right, privilege, or benefit that he would otherwise be entitled by Federal Law, or for which he would otherwise be eligible, as a result of the maintenance of such material, such material shall be provided to such individual, except to the extent that the disclosure of such material would reveal the identity of a source who furnished information to the Government under an express promise that the identity of the source would be held in confidence, or, prior to the effective date of this section, under an implied promise that the identity of the source would be held in confidence;

"(3) maintained in connection with providing protective services to the President of the United States or other individuals pursuant to Section 3056 of title 18;

"(4) required by statute to be maintained and used solely as statistical records;

"(5) investigatory material compiled solely for the purpose of determining suitability, eligibility, or qualifications for Federal civilian employment, military service, Federal contracts, or access to classified information, but only to the extent that the disclosure of such material would reveal the identity of a source who furnished information to the Government under an express promise that the identity of the source would be held in confidence, or, prior to the effective date of this section, under an implied promise that the identity of the source would be held in confidence;

"(6) testing or examination material used solely to determine individual qualifications for appointment or promotion in the Federal service the disclosure of which would compromise the objectivity or fairness of the testing or examination process; or

"(7) evaluation material used to determine potential for promotion in the armed services, but only to the extent that the disclosure of such material would reveal the identity of a source who furnished information to the Government under an express promise that the identity of the source would be held in confidence, or, prior to the effective date of this section, under an implied promise that the identity of the source would be held in confidence.

At the time rules are adopted under this subsection, the agency shall include in the statement required under section 553(c) of this title, the reasons why the system of records to be exempted from a provision of this section.

"(l) ARCHIVAL RECORDS.—

"(1) Each agency record which is accepted by the Administrator of General Services for storage, processing, and servicing in accordance with section 3103 of title 44 shall, for the purposes of this section, be considered to be maintained by the agency which deposited the record and shall be subject to the provisions of this section. The Administrator of General Services shall not disclose the record except to the agency which maintains the record, or under rules established by that agency which are not inconsistent with the provisions of this section.

"(2) Each agency record pertaining to an identifiable individual which was transferred to the National Archives of the United States as a record which has sufficient historical or other value to warrant its continued preservation by the United States Government, prior to the effective date of this section, shall, for the purposes of this section, be considered to be maintained by the National Archives and shall not be subject to the provisions of this section, except that a statement generally describing such records (modeled after the requirements relating to records subject to subsections (e)(4)(A) through (G) of this section) shall be published in the *Federal Register*.

"(3) Each agency record pertaining to an identifiable individual which is transferred to the National Archives of the United States as a record which has sufficient historical or other value to warrant its continued preservation by the United States Government, on or after the effective date of this section, shall, for the purposes of this section, be considered to be maintained by the National Archives and shall be exempt from the requirements of this section except subsections (e)(4)(A) through (G) and (c)(9) of this section.

"(m) GOVERNMENT CONTRACTORS.—When an agency provides by a contract for the operation by or on behalf of the agency of a system of records to accomplish an agency function, the agency shall, consistent with its authority, cause the requirements of this section to be applied to such system. For purposes of subsection (i) of this section any such contractor and any employee of such contractor, if such contract is agreed to on or after the effective date of this section, shall be considered to be an employee of an agency.

"(n) MAILING LISTS.—An individual's name and address may not be sold or rented by an agency unless such action is specifically authorized by law. This provision shall not be construed to require the withholding of names and addresses otherwise permitted to be made public.

"(o) REPORT ON NEW SYSTEMS.—Each agency shall provide adequate advance notice to Congress and the Office of Management and Budget of any proposal to establish or alter any system of records in order to permit an evaluation of the probable or potential effect of such proposal on the privacy and other personal or property rights of individuals or the disclosure of information relating to such individuals, and its effect on the preservation of the constitutional principles of federalism and separation of powers.

"(p) ANNUAL REPORT.—The President shall submit to the Speaker of the House and the President of the Senate, by June 30 of each calendar year, a consolidated report, separately listing for each Federal agency the number of records contained in any system of records which were exempted from the application of this section under the provisions of subsections (j) and (k) of this section during the preceding calendar year, and the reasons for the exemptions, and such other information as indicates efforts to administer fully this section.

"(q) EFFECT OF OTHER LAWS.—No agency shall rely on any exemption contained in section 552 of this title to withhold from an individual any record which is otherwise accessible to such individual under the provisions of this section."

Sec. 4.

The Chapter analysis of chapter 5 of title 5, United States Code, is amended by inserting:

"552a. Records about individuals."

immediately below:

"552. Public information; agency rules, opinions, orders, and proceedings."

[S]ection 5 of the Privacy Act established a Privacy Protection Study Commission for a period of two years. Its term has now expired. Among other things, the Commission was charged with the responsibility of assessing the effectiveness of privacy protections throughout the society. In July 1977, it issued a report entitled "Personal Privacy in an Information Society" which proposed a series of recommendations directed toward safeguarding personal privacy in both the public and private sector. This report can be obtained from the Superintendent of Documents, Government Printing Office, Washington, D.C. 20420 for a charge of $5.]

Sec. 6.

The Office of Management and Budget shall—

(1) develop guidelines and regulations for the use of agencies in implementing the provisions of section 552a of title 5, United States Code, as added

　　　　by section 3 of this Act; and
　　(2) provide continuing assistance to and oversight of the implementation of
　　　　the provisions of such section by agencies.

Sec. 7.

　(a) —
　　(1) It shall be unlawful for any Federal, State or local government agency to
　　　　deny to any individual any right, benefit, or privilege provided by law
　　　　because of such individual's refusal to disclose his social security account
　　　　number.
　　(2) The provisions of paragraph (1) of this subsection shall not apply with
　　　　respect to—
　　　　(A) any disclosure which is required by Federal statute, or
　　　　(B) the disclosure of a social security number to any Federal, State, or
　　　　　　local agency maintaining a system of records in existence and
　　　　　　operating before January 1, 1975, if such disclosure was required
　　　　　　under statute or regulation adopted prior to such date to verify the
　　　　　　identity of an individual.
　(b) Any Federal, State, or local government agency which requests an individual
　　　to disclose his social security number to any Federal, State, or local agency
　　　maintaining a system of records in existence and operating before January 1,
　　　1975, if such disclosure was required under statute or regulation adopted
　　　prior to such date to verify the identity of an individual.
　(c) Any Federal, State, or local government agency which requests an individual
　　　to disclose his social security account number shall inform that individual
　　　whether that disclosure is mandatory or voluntary, by what statutory or other
　　　authority such number is solicited, and what uses will be made of it.

Sec. 8.

The provisions of this Act shall be effective on and after the date of enactment,
except that the amendments made by section 3 and 4 shall become effective 270
days following the day on which this Act is enacted.

Sec. 9.

There is authorized to be appropriated to carry out the provisions of section 5 of this
Act for fiscal years 1975, 1976, 1977 the sum of $1,500,000, except that not more
than $750,000 may be expended during any such fiscal year.

Approved December 31, 1974

Freedom of Information Act

Freedom of Information Act

The Freedom of Information Act as Amended in 1974 by Public Law 93-502
§ 552. Public information: agency rules, opinions, orders, records, and proceedings

(a) Each agency shall make available to the public information as follows:
(1) Each agency shall separately state and currently publish in the Federal Register for the guidance of the public—
   (A) descriptions of its central and field organization and the established places at which, the employees (and in the case of a uniformed service, the members) from whom, and the methods whereby, the public may obtain information, make submittals or requests, or obtain decisions;
   (B) statements of the general course and method by which its functions are channeled and determined, including the nature and requirements of all formal and informal procedures available;
   (C) rules of procedure, descriptions of forms available or the place at which forms may be obtained, and instructions as to the scope and contents of all papers, reports, or examinations;
   (D) substantive rules of general applicability adopted as authorized by law, and statements of general policy or interpretations of general applicability formulated and adopted by the agency; and
   (E) each amendment, revision, or repeal of the foregoing.
Except to the extent that a person has actual and timely notice of the terms thereof, a person may not in any manner be required to resort to, or be adversely affected by, a matter required to be published in the Federal Register and not so published. For the purpose of this paragraph, matter reasonably available to the class of persons affected thereby is deemed published in the Federal Register when incorporated by reference therein with the approval of the Director of the Federal Register.
(2) Each agency, in accordance with published rules, shall make available for public inspection and copying—
   (A) final opinions, including concurring and dissenting opinions, as well as orders, made in the adjudication of cases;
   (B) those statements of policy and interpretations which have been adopted by the agency and are not published in the Federal Register; and

(C) administrative staff manuals and instructions to staff that affect a member of the public; unless the materials are promptly published and copies offered for sale. To the extent required to prevent a clearly unwarranted invasion of personal privacy, an agency may delete identifying details when it makes available or publishes an opinion, statement of policy, interpretation, or staff manual or instruction. However, in each case the justification for the deletion shall be explained fully in writing. Each agency shall also maintain and make available for public inspection and copying current indexes providing identifying information for the public as to any matter issued, adopted, or promulgated after July 4, 1967, and required by this paragraph to be made available or published. Each agency shall promptly publish, quarterly or more frequently, and distribute (by sale or otherwise) copies of each index or supplements thereto unless it determines by order published in the Federal Register that the publication would be unnecessary and impracticable, in which case the agency shall nonetheless provide copies of such index on request at a cost not to exceed the direct cost of duplication. A final order, opinion, statement of policy, interpretation, or staff manual or instruction that affects a member of the public may be relied on, used, or cited as precedent by an agency against a party other than an agency only if—

(i) it has been indexed and either made available or published as provided by this paragraph; or

(ii) the party has actual and timely notice of the terms thereof.

(3) Except with respect to the records made available under paragraphs (1) and (2) of this subsection, each agency, upon any request for records which (A) reasonably describes such records and (B) is made in accordance with published rules stating the time, place, fees (if any), and procedures to be followed, shall make the records promptly available to any person.

(4) (A) In order to carry out the provisions of this section, each agency shall promulgate regulations, pursuant to notice and receipt of public comment, specifying a uniform schedule of fees applicable to all constituent units of such agency. Such fees shall be limited to reasonable standard charges for document search and duplication and provide for recovery of only the direct costs of such search and duplication. Documents shall be furnished without charge or at a reduced charge where the agency determines that waiver or reduction of the fee is in the public interest because furnishing the information can be considered as primarily benefiting the general public.

(B) On complaint, the district court of the United States in the district in which the complainant resides, or has his principal place of business, or in which the agency records are situated, or in the District of Columbia, has jurisdiction to enjoin the agency from withholding agency records and to order the production of any agency records improperly withheld from the complainant. In such a case the court shall determine the matter *de novo*, and may examine the contents of such agency records *in camera* to determine whether such records or any part thereof shall be withheld under any of the exemptions set forth in subsection (b) of this section, and the burden is on the agency to sustain its action.

(C) Notwithstanding any other provision of law, the defendant shall serve an answer or otherwise plead to any complaint made under this pleading in which such complaint is made, unless the court otherwise directs for good cause shown.

(D) Except as to cases the court considers of greater importance, proceedings before the district court, as authorized by this subsection, and appeals therefrom, take precedence on the docket over all cases and shall be assigned for hearing and trial or for argument at the earliest practicable date and expedited in every way.

(E) The court may assess against the United States reasonable attorney fees and other litigation costs reasonably incurred in any case under this section in which the complainant has substantially prevailed.

(F) Whenever the court orders the production of any agency records improperly withheld from the complainant and assesses against the United States reasonable attorney fees and other litigation costs, and the court additionally issues a written finding that the circumstances surrounding the withholding raise questions whether agency personnel acted arbitrarily or capriciously with respect to the withholding, the Civil Service Commission shall promptly initiate a proceeding to determine whether disciplinary action is warranted against the officer or employee who was primarily responsible for the withholding. The Commission, after investigation and consideration of the evidence submitted, shall submit its findings and recommendations to the administrative authority of the agency concerned and shall send copies of the findings and recommendations to the officer or employee or his representative. The administrative authority shall take the corrective action that the Commission recommends.

(G) In the event of noncompliance with the order of the court, the district court may punish for contempt the responsible employee, and in the case of a uniformed service, the responsible member.

(5) Each agency having more than one member shall maintain and make available for public inspection a record of the final votes of each member in every agency proceeding.

(6) (A) Each agency, upon any request for records made under paragraph (1), (2), or (3) of this subsection, shall—

  (i) determine within ten days (excepting Saturdays, Sundays, and legal public holidays) after the receipt of any such request whether to comply with such request and shall immediately notify the person making such request of such determination and the reasons therefore, and of the right of such person to appeal to the head of the agency any adverse determination; and

  (ii) make a determination with respect to any appeal within twenty days (excepting Saturdays, Sundays, and legal public holidays) after the receipt of such appeal. If on appeal the denial of the request for records is in whole or in part upheld, the agency shall notify the person making such request of the provisions for judicial review of that determination under paragraph (4) of this subsection.

(B) In unusual circumstances as specified in this subparagraph, the time limits prescribed in either clause (i) or clause (ii) of subparagraph (A) may be extended by written notice to the person making such request setting forth the reasons for such extension and the date on which a determination is expected to be dispatched. No such notice shall specify a date that would result in an extension for more than ten working days. As used in this subparagraph, "unusual circumstances" means, but only to the extent reasonably necessary to the proper processing of the particular request—

 (i) the need to search for and collect the requested records from field facilities or other establishments that are separate from the office processing the request;

 (ii) the need to search for, collect, and appropriately examine a voluminous amount of separate and distinct records which are demanded in a single request; or

 (iii) the need for consultation, which shall be conducted with all practicable speed, with another agency having a substantial interest in the determination of the request or among two or more components of the agency having substantial subject-matter interest therein.

 (C) Any person making a request to any agency for records under paragraph (1), (2), or (3) of this subsection shall be deemed to have exhausted his administrative remedies with respect to such request if the agency fails to comply with the applicable time limit provisions of this paragraph. If the Government can show exceptional circumstances exist and that the agency is exercising due diligence in responding to the request, the court may retain jurisdiction and allow the agency additional time to complete its review of the records. Upon any determination by an agency to comply with a request for records, the records shall be made promptly available to such person making such request. Any notification of denial of any request for records under this subsection shall set forth the names and titles or positions of each person responsible for the denial of such request.

(b) This section does not apply to matters that are—

(1) (A) specifically authorized under criteria established by an Executive order to be kept secret in the interest of national defense or foreign policy and (B) are in fact properly classified pursuant to such Executive order;

(2) related solely to the internal personnel rules and practices of an agency;

(3) specifically exempted from disclosure by statute;

(4) trade secrets and commercial or financial information obtained from a person and privileged or confidential;

(5) inter-agency or intra-agency memorandums or letters which would not be available by law to a party other than an agency in litigation with the agency;

(6) personnel and medical files and similar files the disclosure of which would constitute a clearly unwarranted invasion of personal privacy;

(7) investigatory records compiled for law enforcement purposes, but only to the extent that the production of such records would (A) interfere with enforcement proceedings, (B) deprive a person of a right to a fair trial or an impartial adjudication, (C) constitute an unwarranted invasion of personal privacy, (D) disclose the identity of a confidential source and, in the case of a record compiled by a criminal law enforcement authority in the course of a criminal investigation, or by an agency conducting a lawful national security intelligence investigation, or confidential information furnished only by the confidential source, (E) disclose investigative techniques and procedures, or (F) endanger the life or physical safety of law enforcement personnel;

(8) contained in or related to examination, operating, or condition reports prepared by, on behalf of, or for the use of an agency responsible for the regulation or supervision of financial institutions; or

(9) geological and geophysical information and the data, including maps, concerning wells.

Any reasonably segregable portion of a record shall be provided to any person requesting such record after deletion of the portions which are exempt under this subsection.

(c) This section does not authorize withholding of information or limit the availability of records to the public, except as specifically stated in this section. This section is not authority to withhold information from Congress.

(d) On or before March 1 of each calendar year, each agency shall submit a report covering the preceding calendar year to the Speaker of the House of Representatives and President of the Senate for referral to the appropriate committees of the Congress. The report shall include—

(1) the number of determinations made by such agency not to comply with requests for records made to such agency under subsection (a) and the reasons for each such determination;

(2) the number of appeals made by persons under subsection (a)(6), the result of such appeals, and the reason for the action upon each appeal that results in a denial of information;

(3) the names and titles or positions of each person responsible for the denial of records requested under this section, and the number of instances of participation for each;

(4) the results of each proceeding conducted pursuant to subsection (a)(4)(F), including a report of the disciplinary action taken against the officer or employee who was primarily responsible for improperly withholding records or an explanation of why disciplinary action was not taken;

(5) a copy of every rule made by such agency regarding this section;

(6) a copy of the fee schedule and the total amount of fees collected by the agency for making records available under this section; and

(7) such other information as indicates efforts to administer fully this section. The Attorney General shall submit an annual report on or before March 1 of each calendar year which shall include for the prior calendar year a listing of the number of cases arising under this section, the exemption involved in each case, the disposition of such case, and the cost, fees, and penalties assessed under subsections (a)(4)(E), (F), and (G). Such report shall also include a description of the efforts undertaken by the Department of Justice to encourage agency compliance with this section.

(e) For purposes of this section, the term "agency" as defined in section 551(1) of this title includes any executive department, military department, Government corporation, Government controlled corporation, or other establishment in the executive branch of the Government (including the Executive Office of the President), or any independent regulatory agency.

Bibliography

Abelson, Robert P., and A. Levi. "Decision-making and decision theory." In Gardner Lindzey and Elliott Aronson, eds. *Handbook of Social Psychology,* vol. 1, 231-310. 3d ed. New York: Random House, 1986.

Abrams, Harvey A., and Peter Bidney. "When Clients Complain: Bureaucratic Responsiveness in Large Federal Agencies." *Journal of Sociology and Social Welfare* 6 (June 1979): 555-582.

Abramson, Jeffrey B., F. Christopher Arterton, and Gary R. Orren. *The Electronic Commonwealth: The Impact of New Media Technologies on Democratic Politics.* New York: Basic Books, 1988.

Ackerman, Bruce A., and William T. Hassler. *Clean Coal/Dirty Air.* New Haven: Yale University Press, 1981.

Albrecht, Terrance L., and Vickie A. Ropp. "Communicating about Innovation in Networks of Three U.S. Organizations." *Journal of Communication* 34 (Summer 1984): 78-91.

Allison, Graham. *Essence of Decision: Explaining the Cuban Missile Crisis.* Boston: Little, Brown, 1971.

Almond, Gabriel A., and James S. Coleman, eds. *The Politics of the Developing Areas.* Princeton, N.J.: Princeton University Press, 1960.

Altheide, David L., and John M. Johnson. *Bureaucratic Propaganda.* Boston: Allyn and Bacon, 1980.

Anderson, James E. "A Revised View of the Johnson Cabinet." *Journal of Politics* 48 (February 1986): 529-537.

Anderson, Paul. "Decision Making by Objection and the Cuban Missile Crisis." *Administrative Science Quarterly* 28 (June 1983): 201-222.

Argyris, Chris. *Personality and Organization.* New York: Harper & Row, 1957.

Axelrod, David. "New City Services Plan Threatens Political Truce," *Chicago Tribune,* May 3, 1984.

Bakke, E. Wight. *Bonds of Organization.* New York: Harper, 1957.

Bales, Robert F. *Interaction Process Analysis.* Reading, Mass.: Addison-Wesley, 1950.

Barnard, Chester L. *The Functions of the Executive.* Cambridge, Mass.: Harvard University Press, 1938.

Barnett, George A., Donna M. Hamlin, and James A. Danowski, "The Use of Fractionation Scales for Communication Audits." In Michael Burgoon, ed. *Communication Yearbook 5,* New Brunswick, N.J.: Transaction, 1982, 455-471.

Bass, Bernard. *Organizational Decision Making.* Homewood, Ill.: Richard D. Irwin, 1983.

Bauer, Raymond A., Ithiel de Sola Pool, and Lewis A. Dexter. *American Business and Public Policy.* New York: Atherton, 1963.

Bavelas, Alex. "Communication Patterns in Task-Oriented Groups." *Acoustical Society of America Journal* 22 (1950): 727-730.

Bazerman, Max, and Roy J. Lewicki. *Negotiating in Organizations.* Beverly Hills, Calif.: Sage, 1983.

Beck, Joan. "What if Taxpayers Can't Cope with New Forms and Give Up?" *Chicago Tribune,* May 25, 1987.

Bendor, Jonathan, Serge Taylor, and Roland Van Gaalen. "Politicians, Bureaucrats, and Asymmetric Information." *American Journal of Political Science* 31:4 (November 1987): 796-828.

Beniger, James R. *The Control Revolution: Technological and Economic Origins of the Information Society.* Cambridge, Mass.: Harvard University Press, 1986.

Berry, Jeffrey M. *The Interest Group Society.* 2d ed. Chicago: Scott, Foresman, 1989.

Bertalanffy, Ludwig van. *General Systems Theory.* New York: Braziller, 1968.

Best, James J. "Who Talked to the President When? A Study of Lyndon B. Johnson." *Political Science Quarterly* 103 (Fall 1988): 531-545.

Bettinghaus, Erwin. *Persuasive Communication.* New York: Holt, Rinehart and Winston, 1968.

Blau, Judith R. "Prominence in a Network of Communication: Work Relations in a Children's Psychiatric Hospital." *Sociological Quarterly* 23 (Spring 1982): 235-251.

Blau Peter. *Exchange and Power in Social Life.* New York: Wiley, 1967.

Blumenthal, W. Michael. "Candid Reflections of a Businessman in Washington." *Fortune* (January 29, 1979): 39.

Boffey, Philip M. "Three Major Research Centers Reject Censorship." *New York Times,* April 10, 1984.

Boje, David M., and David A. Whetter. "Effects of Organizational Strategies and Contextual Constraints on Centrality and Attributions of Influence in Interorganizational Networks." *Administrative Science Quarterly* 26 (September 1981): 378-395.

Bollier, David. "The Social Impact of Widespread Computer Use: Implications for East-West Relations." *Communications and Society Forum Report.* Truro, Mass.: Aspen Institute, 1989.

Bonacich, Phillip. "Power and Centrality: A Family of Measures." *American Journal of Sociology* 92 (March 1987): 1170-1182.

Boulding, Kenneth. *The Image: Knowledge in Life and Society.* Ann Arbor: University of Michigan Press, 1956.

Boynton, G. R. "When Senators and Publics Meet at the Senate Environmental Protection Subcommittee." *Discourse and Society* 2 (April 1991): 131-155.

Bozeman, Barry. *All Organizations Are Public: Bridging Public and Private Organizational Theories.* San Francisco: Jossey-Bass, 1987.

Branstad, Terry E. "Restructuring and Downsizing." In Robert D. Bohn, ed. *Governors on Governing.* Washington, D.C.: National Governors' Association, 1991, 145-155.

Brawley, Edward A. *Mass Media and Human Services: Getting the Message*

Across. Beverly Hills, Calif.: Sage, 1983.

Brodkin, Evelyn Z. "Policy Politics: If We Can't Govern, Can We Manage?" *Political Science Quarterly* 102 (Winter 1987-1988): 571-587.

Brudney, Jeffrey L., and F. Ted Hebert. "State Agencies and Their Environments: Examining the Influence of Important External Actors." *Journal of Politics* 49 (February 1987): 186-206.

Bukro, Casey. "How Accurate Was Press about Three Mile Island?" *Chicago Tribune,* March 20, 1980.

Burke, John P. "Responsibilities of Presidents and Advisers: A Theory and a Case Study of Vietnam Decision Making." *Journal of Politics* 46 (August 1984): 818-845.

Burke, Kenneth. *Language as Symbolic Action*. Berkeley: University of California Press, 1966.

Burns, Tom, and G. M. Stalker. *The Management of Innovations*. London: Tavistock, 1961.

Caldeira, Gregory A. "The Transmission of Legal Precedent: A Study of State Supreme Courts." *American Political Science Review* 79 (March 1985): 178-193.

Campbell, James. E. "Sources of the New Deal Realignment: The Contributions of Conversion and Mobilization to Partisan Change." *Western Political Quarterly* 38 (September 1985): 485-494.

Caputo, Richard K. *Management and Information Systems in Human Services*. New York: Haworth, 1988.

Carney, Tom F. "Organizational Communication: Emerging Trends, Problems, and Opportunities." In Lee Thayer, ed. *Organization—Communication: Emerging Perspectives I*. Norwood, N.J.: Ablex, 1986, 3-17.

Cassirer, Ernst. *Language and Myth*. New York: Harper, 1946.

Caudle, Sharon L. "Information Technology and Managing Public Management Choices." American Political Science Association paper, Chicago, 1987.

Chackerian, Richard, and Gilbert Abcarian. *Bureaucratic Power in Society*. Chicago: Nelson Hall, 1984.

Chi, Keon S. *State Futures Commissions: A Survey of Long-Range Planning Experiences*. Lexington, Ky.: Council of State Governments, 1983.

Cigler, Allan, and Burdett A. Loomis. *Interest Group Politics*. 2d ed. Washington, D.C.: CQ Press, 1986.

Cole, Richard L., and David A. Caputo. "The Public Hearing as an Effective Citizen Participation Mechanism: A Case Study of the General Revenue Sharing Program." *American Political Science Review* 78 (June 1978): 404-416.

Committee on Environmental Decision Making. *Decision Making in the Environmental Protection Agency*. Washington D.C.: National Academy of Sciences, 1977.

Conference Board. *Managing Federal Government Relations*. Research Report No. 905. New York: Conference Board, 1988.

"Congress Sends Bush Bill to Protect Whistle Blowers." *Chicago Tribune,* March 22, 1989.

Congressional Quarterly, Inc. *The Washington Lobby*. 5th ed. Washington, D.C.: Congressional Quarterly, 1987.

Converse, Jean M., and Howard Schuman. "The Manner of Inquiry: An Analysis of Survey Questions from Across Organizations and Over Time." In C. F. Turner and E. Martin, eds. *Surveying Subjective Phenomena*, vol. 2. New York: Russell Sage Foundation, 1984.

Cook, Karen S., Richard M. Emerson, Mary R. Gillmore, and Toshio Yamagishi.

"The Distribution of Power in Exchange Networks: Theory and Experimental Results." *American Journal of Sociology* 89 (September 1983): 275-305.

Cowan, Edward. "Problems with Government Advocacy: A Journalist's View." In Lewis M. Helm, Ray Eldon Hiebert, Michael R. Naver, and Kenneth Rabin, eds. *Informing the People*. New York: Longman, 1981, 38-50.

Cox, Martha Glenn. "Enter the Stranger: Unanticipated Effects of Communication on the Success of an Organizational Newcomer." In Lee Thayer, ed. *Organization—Communication: Emerging Perspectives I*, Norwood, N.J.: Ablex 1986, 34-50.

Crompton, John L., and Charles W. Lamb, Jr. *Marketing Government and Social Services*. New York: Wiley, 1986.

Cunningham, Robert, and Dorothy Olshfski. "Interpreting State Administrator-Legislator Relationships." *Western Political Quarterly* 39 (March 1986): 104-117.

Cutlip, Scott M. "Government and the Public Information System." In Lewis M. Helm, Ray Eldon Hiebert, Michael R. Naver, and Kenneth Rabin, eds. *Informing the People*. New York: Longman, 1981, 22-37.

Cutlip, Scott M., Allen H. Center, and Glen M. Broom. *Effective Public Relations*. 6th ed. Englewood Cliffs, N.J.: Prentice-Hall, 1985.

Cyert, Richard, and James March. *A Behavioral Theory of the Firm*. Englewood Cliffs, N.J.: Prentice-Hall, 1963.

Danowski, James A. "Organizational Infographics and Automated Auditing: Using Computers to Unobtrusively Gather as Well as Analyze Communication." In Gerald M. Goldhaber and George A. Barnett, eds. *Handbook of Organizational Communication*. Norwood, N.J.: Ablex, 1988.

—."Organizational Media Theory." In James A. Anderson, ed. *Communication Yearbook 14*. Newbury Park, Calif.: Sage, 1991, 187-207.

Danowski, James A., and Paul Edison-Swift. "Crisis Effects on Intraorganizational Computer-Based Communication." *Communication Research* 12 (April 1985): 259-270.

Danziger, James M., William H. Dutton, Rob Kling, and Kenneth L. Kraemer. *Computers and Politics*. New York: Columbia University Press, 1982.

Denhardt, Robert B. *Theories of Public Organization*. Monterey, Calif.: Brooks-Cole, 1984.

—."Toward a Critical Theory of Public Organization." *Public Administration Review* 41 (November-December 1981): 628-632.

Derthick, Martha. *Agency under Stress: The Social Security Administration and American Government*. Washington, D.C.: Brookings Institution, 1990.

—.*Policymaking for Social Security*. Washington, D.C.: Brookings Institution, 1979.

Deutsch, Karl W. *The Nerves of Government: Models of Political Communication and Control*. New York: Free Press, 1966.

DiFranceisco, Wayne, and Zvi Gitelman. "Soviet Political Culture and 'Covert Participation' in Policy Implementation." *American Political Science Review* 78 (September 1984): 603-621.

Doig, Jameson W., and Erwin C. Hargrove. *Leadership and Innovation: A Biographical Perspective on Entrepreneurs in Government*. Baltimore: Johns Hopkins University Press, 1987.

Donnellon, Anne, Barbara Gray, and Michel G. Bougon. "Communication, Meaning, and Organized Action." *Administrative Science Quarterly* 31 (March 1986): 43-55.

Downing, John D. H. "Computers for Political Change: PeaceNet and Public Data

Access." *Journal of Communication* 39 (Summer 1989): 154-162.

Downs, Anthony. *Inside Bureaucracy.* Boston: Little, Brown, 1967.

Dumas, Kitty. "Congress or the White House: Who Controls the Agencies?" *Congressional Quarterly Weekly Report,* April 14, 1990, 1130-1135.

Easton, David. *A Systems Analysis of Political Life.* New York: Wiley, 1965.

Eddy,William. *Public Organization Behavior.* Cambridge, Mass.: Winthrop, 1982.

Edelman, Murray. *The Symbolic Uses of Politics.* Urbana: University of Illinois Press, 1964.

Edwards, George C., III. *Implementing Public Policy.* Washington, D.C.: CQ Press, 1980.

Emerson, Richard M. "Power-Dependence Relations." *American Sociological Review* 27 (1962): 31-41.

Engleberg, Stephen. "Doubts on Intelligence Data: Iran Affair Renews the Issue." *New York Times,* August 31, 1987.

Etheredge, Lloyd. "Government Learning: An Overview." In Samuel L. Long, ed. *The Handbook of Political Behavior,* vol. 2. New York: Plenum, 1981.

———.*Can Governments Learn? American Foreign Policy and Central American Revolutions.* New York: Pergamon, 1985.

Eulau, Heinz. *Politics, Self, and Society.* Cambridge, Mass.: Harvard University Press, 1986.

———."The Redwood Network Project: Small-Scale Research at the Local Level." *ICPSR Bulletin* 4 (January 1984): Appendix A.

Fagen, Richard R. *Politics and Communication: An Analytic Study.* Boston: Little, Brown, 1966.

Farnham, Barbara. "Political Cognition and Decision-Making." *Political Psychology* 11 (March 1990): 83-111.

Fayon, Henri. *General and Industrial Management.* London: Pitman, 1949.

Feldman, Martha S. *Order without Design: Information Production and Policy Making.* Stanford, Calif.: Stanford University Press, 1989.

Fenno, Richard F. *Homestyle: House Members in Their Districts.* Boston: Little, Brown, 1978.

Ferguson, Kathy E. *The Feminist Case against Bureaucracy.* Philadelphia: Temple University Press, 1984.

Ferguson, Sherry Devereaux, and Stewart Ferguson. "The Physical Environment and Communication." In Sherry Ferguson and Stewart Ferguson, eds. *Organizational Communications.* 2d ed. New Brunswick, N.J.: Transaction, 1988, 165-200.

Fidler, Lori A., and J. David Johnson. "Communication and Innovation Implementation." *Academy of Management Review* 9 (October 1984): 704-711.

Fisher, James. "Is Safety NASA's Nemesis?" *Chicago Tribune,* February 7, 1988.

Frantzich, Stephen. *Computers in Congress: The Politics of Information.* Beverly Hills, Calif.: Sage, 1982.

———."Legislatures and the Revolution in Communications and Information Processing: Untangling the Linkage Between Technology and Politics." American Political Science Association paper, 1990.

Fraser, Edie, and Wes Pedersen. "Department of Agriculture: A Structural Model." In Lewis M. Helm, Ray Eldon Hiebert, Michael R. Naver, and Kenneth Rabin, eds. *Informing the People.* New York: Longman, 1981, 283-286.

Free, Lloyd A., and Hadley Cantril. *The Political Beliefs of Americans: A Study of Public Opinion.* New York: Simon & Schuster, 1968.

Frontline #602 Broadcast. "Operation Urgent Fury." Boston, WGBH Educational

Foundation, 1988.

Frost, Peter J., ed. *Organizational Culture.* Beverly Hills, Calif.: Sage, 1985.

Fulbright, J. William. *The Pentagon Propaganda Machine.* New York: Vintage Books, 1971.

Fulk, Janet, and Sirish Mani. "Distortion of Communication in Hierarchical Relationships." In Margaret L. McLaughlin, ed. *Communication Yearbook 9.* Beverly Hills, Calif.: Sage, 1986, 483-510.

Gabriel, Richard. "Scenes from an Invasion." *Washington Monthly* (February 1986): 34-41.

Gailey, Phil. "Deaver Stirs a Hornet's Nest." *New York Times,* April 5, 1986.

Gandy, Oscar H., Jr. "The Surveillance Society: Information Technology and Bureaucratic Social Control." *Journal of Communication* 39 (Summer 1989): 61-76.

Gelb, Leslie H. "Speakes Defines His Role in Shaping Events." *New York Times,* October 10, 1986.

George, Alexander L. *Presidential Decisionmaking in Foreign Policy: The Effective Use of Information and Advice.* Boulder, Colo.: Westview, 1980.

Gibson, James L., John M. Ivancevich, and James H. Donnelly, Jr., eds. *Organizations Close-up: A Book of Readings.* 5th ed. Plano, Texas: Business Publications, 1985.

Goffman, Erving. *Relations in Public: Microstudies of the Public Order.* New York: Basic Books, 1971.

Goldhaber, Gerald M. *Organizational Communication.* 3d ed. Dubuque, Iowa: Wm. C. Brown, 1983.

Goldhaber, Gerald M., and Donald P. Rogers. *Auditing Organizational Communications Systems.* Dubuque, Iowa: Kendall/Hunt, 1979.

Golembiewski, Robert T. *Humanizing Public Organizations.* Mount Airy, Md.: Lomond: 1985.

——.*Perspectives on Public Management: Cases and Learning Designs.* 2d ed. Itasca, Ill.: Peacock, 1976.

Golembiewski, Robert T., and William B. Eddy, eds. *Organizational Development in Public Administration.* Part 2. New York: Marcel Dekker, 1978.

Goodsell, Charles T. *The Social Meaning of Civic Space.* Lawrence: University Press of Kansas, 1988.

——.*The Case for Bureaucracy: A Public Administration Polemic.* Chatham, N.J.: Chatham House Publishers, 1985.

——."Conflicting Perceptions of Welfare Bureaucracy." *Social Casework: The Journal of Contemporary Social Work* 61 (June 1980): 354-360.

——."Looking Once Again at Human Service Bureaucracy." *Journal of Politics* 43 (1981): 763-778.

——.ed. *The Public Encounter: Where State and Citizen Meet.* Bloomington: Indiana University Press, 1981.

Goodsell, Charles T., Raymond E. Austin, Karen L. Hedblom, and Clarence C. Rose. "Bureaucracy Expresses Itself: How State Documents Address the Public." *Social Science Quarterly* 62 (1981): 576-591.

Gordon, Andrew C., and John P. Heinz, eds. *Public Access to Information.* New Brunswick, N.J.: Transaction, 1979.

Gormley, William T., Jr. "Intergovernmental Conflict on Environmental Policy: The Attitudinal Connection." *Western Political Quarterly* 40 (June 1987): 285-303.

——."The Representation Revolution: Reforming State Regulation through Public Representation." *Administration and Society* 18 (August 1986): 179-196.

Gormley, William, John Hoadley, and Charles Williams. "Potential Responsiveness in the Bureaucracy: Views of Public Utility Regulation." *American Political Science Review* 77 (September 1983): 704-717.

Gortner, Harold F., Julianne Mahler, and Jeanne Bell Nicholson. *Organizational Theory: A Public Perspective.* Chicago: Dorsey, 1987.

Graber, Doris A. *Mass Media and American Politics.* 3d ed. Washington, D.C.: CQ Press, 1989.

—.*Processing the News: How People Tame the Information Tide.* 2d ed. New York: Longman, 1988.

—*Verbal Behavior and Politics.* Urbana: University of Illinois Press, 1976.

Granovetter, Mark S. "The Strength of Weak Ties." *American Journal of Sociology* 78 (May 1973): 1360-1380.

Greenbaum, Howard H., Susan A. Hellweg, and Raymond L. Falcione. "Organizational Communication Evaluation: An Overview, 1950-1981." In Gerald M. Goldhaber and George A. Barnett, eds. *Handbook of Organizational Communication.* Norwood, N.J.: Ablex, Ablex, 1988, 275-317.

Greenhouse, Linda. "High Court Decides Budget Office Exceeded Power in Blocking Rules." *New York Times,* February 21, 1990.

Grimaldi, Paul L. *Supplemental Security Income: The New Federal Program for the Aged, Blind, and Disabled.* Washington, D.C.: American Enterprise Institute for Public Policy Research, 1980.

Grunig, James E. "The Message-Attitude-Behavior Relationship: Communication Behaviors in Organizations." *Communication Research* 9 (April 1982): 163-200.

Gulick, Luther, and Lyndall F. Urwick. *Papers on the Science of Administration.* New York: Columbia University, Institute of Public Administration, 1937.

Gutfeld, Rose. "Employees Pressured by Managers To Seize Property, Senate Panel Told." *Wall Street Journal,* June 23, 1987.

Habermas, Jürgen. *Towards a Rational Society: Student Protest, Science, and Politics.* Boston: Beacon, 1970.

Hage, Jerald, Michael Aiken, and Cora B. Marrett. "Organization Structure and Communications." In Daniel Katz, Robert L. Kahn, and J. Stacy Adams, eds. *The Study of Organizations.* San Francisco: Jossey-Bass, 1982, 302-315.

Hamilton, Seymour. *A Communication Audit Handbook: Helping Organizations Communicate.* New York: Longman, 1987.

Hammer, Michael, and Glenn E. Mangurian. "The Changing Value of Communications Technology." *Sloan Management Review* 28 (Winter 1987): 65-71.

Hammond, Susan Webb, Daniel P. Mulhollan, and Arthur G. Stevens, Jr. "Informal Congressional Caucuses and Agenda Setting." *Western Political Quarterly* 38 (December 1985): 583-605.

Hammond, Thomas. "Agenda Control, Organizational Structure, and Bureaucratic Politics." *American Journal of Political Science* 30 (May 1986): 379-420.

Harmon, Michael T., and Richard T. Mayer. *Organizational Theory for Public Administration.* Boston: Little, Brown, 1986.

Harrison, E. Frank. *The Managerial Decision-Making Process.* Boston: Houghton Mifflin, 1975.

Hasenfeld, Yeheskel. "Citizens' Encounters with Welfare State Bureaucracies." *Social Service Review* 59 (December 1985): 622-635.

Hasenfeld, Yeheskel, and Daniel Steinmetz. "Client-Official Encounters in Social Service Agencies." In Charles T. Goodsell, ed. *The Public Encounter.* Bloomington: Indiana University Press, 1981.

Heclo, Hugh. *A Government of Strangers: Executive Politics in Washington.* Washington, D.C.: Brookings Institution, 1977.

——."Issue Networks and the Executive Establishment." In Anthony King, ed. *The New American Political System.* Washington, D.C.: American Enterprise Institute, 1978, 87-124.

Hedge, David M., Donald C. Menzel, and George H. Williams. "Regulatory Attitudes and Behavior: The Case of Surface Mining Regulations." *Western Political Quarterly* 41 (June 1988): 323-340.

Helm, Lewis M., Ray Eldon Hiebert, Michael R. Naver, and Kenneth Rabin, eds. *Informing the People.* New York: Longman, 1981.

Henderson, J. C., and D. A. Schilling. "Design and Implementation of Decision Support Systems in the Public Sector." *MIS Quarterly* 9 (Summer 1985): 157-168.

Hershey, Robert D., Jr. "Where Personal Finances Are in the Public Eye." *New York Times,* August 22, 1988.

Hess, Stephen. *The Government/Press Connection.* Washington, D.C.: Brookings Institution, 1984.

——.*The Washington Reporters.* Washington, D.C.: Brookings Institution, 1981.

Hiebert, Ray Eldon. "A Model of the Government Communication Process." In Lewis M. Helm, Ray Eldon Hiebert, Michael R. Naver, and Kenneth Rabin, eds. *Informing the People.* New York: Longman, 1981, 3-13.

Hiemstra, Glen E. "The Electronic Organization: Communicating and Organizing in a New Age." In Lee Thayer, ed. *Organization—Communication: Emerging Perspectives I.* Norwood, N.J.: Ablex, 1986, 196-220.

Hill, Larry B. "Bureaucratic Monitoring Mechanisms." In Charles T. Goodsell, ed. *The Public Encounter.* Bloomington: Indiana University Press, 1981, 160-186.

——."The Citizen Participation-Representation Roles of American Ombudsmen." *Administration and Society* 13 (February 1982): 405-433.

Hilsman, Roger. *Strategic Intelligence and National Decisions.* Glencoe, Ill.: Free Press of Glencoe, 1956.

Holsti, Ole. *Content Analysis for the Social Sciences and Humanities.* Reading, Mass.: Addison-Wesley, 1969.

Homans, George C. *The Human Group.* New York: Harcourt Brace, 1950.

Horkheimer, Max. *Critical Theory: Selected Essays.* New York: Herder, 1972.

Horton, Forest W., Jr., and Donald A. Marchand, eds. *Information Management in Public Administration.* Arlington, Va.: Information Resources Press, 1982.

Huckfeldt, Robert, and John Sprague. "Networks in Context: The Social Flow of Political Information." *American Political Science Review* 81 (1987): 1197-1216.

Inbar, Michael. *Routine Decision-Making: The Future of Bureaucracy.* Beverly Hills, Calif.: Sage, 1979.

Ingersoll, Virginia Hill, and Guy B. Adams. "Beyond Organizational Boundaries: Exploring the Managerial Myth." *Administration and Society* 18 (November 1986): 360-381.

Janis, Irving L. *Groupthink: Psychological Studies of Policy Decisions and Fiascoes.* Boston: Houghton Mifflin, 1983.

——.*Crucial Decisions: Leadership in Policymaking and Crisis Management.* New York: Free Press, 1989.

Janis, Irving L., and Leon Mann. *Decision Making: A Psychological Analysis of Conflict, Choice, and Commitment.* New York: Free Press, 1977.

Jones, Bryan D., with Saadia Greenberg and Joseph Drew. *Service Delivery in the City: Citizen Demand and Bureaucratic Rules.* New York: Longman, 1980.

Johnson, J. David. "On the Uses of Communication Gradients." In Gerald M. Goldhaber and George A. Barnett, eds. *Handbook of Organizational Communi-*

cation. Norwood, N.J.: Ablex, 1988.

Jos, Philip H., Mark E. Tompkins, and Steven W. Hays. "In Praise of Difficult People: A Portrait of the Committed Whistleblower." *Public Administration Review* 49 (November/December 1989): 552-561.

Kanter, Rosabeth M. "Three Tiers for Innovation Research." *Communication Research* 15 (October 1988): 509-523.

——."The Middle Manager as Innovator." *Harvard Business Review* 60(4) (July-August 1982): 95-105.

Katz, Daniel, Barbara A. Gutek, Robert L. Kahn, and E. Barton. *Bureaucratic Encounters.* Ann Arbor, Mich.: Institute for Social Research, 1975.

Katz, Daniel, and Robert L. Kahn. *The Social Psychology of Organizations.* New York: Wiley, 1978.

Katz, Elihu, and Brenda Danet. *Bureaucracy and the Public.* New York: Basic Books, 1973.

——."Communication between Bureaucracy and the Public." In Ithiel de Sola Pool and Wilbur Schramm, eds. *Handbook of Communication.* Chicago: Rand-McNally, 1973, 666-697.

Katz, Elihu, Michael Gurevitch, Brenda Danet, and Tsiyona Peled. "Petitions and Prayers: A Method for the Content Analysis of Persuasive Appeals." *Social Forces* 47 (June 1969): 447-463.

Katz, Ralph. "The Effects of Group Longevity on Project Communication and Performance." *Administrative Science Quarterly* 27 (March 1982): 81-104.

Kaufman, Herbert. *The Forest Ranger: A Study in Administrative Behavior.* Baltimore: Johns Hopkins Press, 1967.

——.*The Administrative Behavior of Federal Bureau Chiefs.* Washington, D.C.: Brookings Institution, 1981.

——.*Red Tape: Its Origins, Uses, and Abuses.* Washington, D.C.: Brookings Institution, 1977.

Kelman, Steven. *Making Public Policy: A Hopeful View of American Government.* New York: Basic Books, 1987.

Kennedy, Robert F. *Thirteen Days.* New York: Norton, 1969.

Kersten, Astrid. "A Critical-Interpretive Approach to the Study of Organizational Communication: Bringing Communication Back into the Field." In Lee Thayer, ed. *Organization—Communication: Emerging Perspectives I.* Norwood, N.J.: Ablex, 1986, 133-150.

Kessel, John H. "The Structure of the Carter White House." *American Journal of Political Science* 27 (August 1983): 431-463.

——."The Structure of the Reagan White House." *American Journal of Political Science* 28 (May 1984): 231-258.

Kessler, Mark. "Interorganizational Environments, Attitudes, and the Policy Outputs of Public Agencies: A Comparative Case Study of Legal Services Agencies." *Administration and Society* 19 (May 1987): 48-73.

Kidder, Louise H. *Seltiz, Wrightsman and Cook's Research Methods in Social Relations.* 4th ed. New York: Holt, Rinehart and Winston, 1981, 191.

Kiesler, Sara. "The Hidden Messages in Computer Networks." *Harvard Business Review* 64 (January-February 1986): 46-60.

Klapp, Orrin. *Opening and Closing: Strategies of Information Adaptation in Society.* Cambridge and New York: Cambridge University Press, 1978.

Knoke, David, and James H. Kuklinski. *Network Analysis.* Beverly Hills, Calif.: Sage, 1987.

Koehler, Jerry W. *Organizational Communication: Behavioral Perspectives.* 3d ed. New York: Holt, Rinehart and Winston, 1983.

Koenig, Michael E. "The Convergence of Computers and Telecommunications: Information Management Implications." *Information Management Review* 1 (1986): 23-33.

Kraemer, Kenneth L., and J. L. King. *Municipal Information Systems: Evaluation and Policy Related Research*, vol. 1. Washington, D.C.: National Technical Information Service, 1975.

Krippendorff, Klaus. *Communication and Control in Society*. New York: Gordon and Breach, 1979.

Krone, Kathleen J., Frederic M. Jablin, and Linda L. Putnam. "Communication Theory and Organizational Communication: Multiple Perspectives." In Frederic M. Jablin, Linda L. Putnam, Karlene H. Roberts, and Lyman W. Porter, eds. *Handbook of Organizational Communication*. Newbury Park, Calif.: Sage, 1987, 18-40.

Kunde, James. "Task Force Management in Dayton, Ohio." In Robert L. Golembiewski and William B. Eddy, eds. *Organization Development in Public Administration*, part 2. New York: Marcel Dekker, 1978, 219-226.

Lamb, Chris. "Belief Systems and Decision Making in the Mayaguez Crisis." *Political Science Quarterly* 99 (Winter 1984-1985): 681-702.

Landy, Marc K., Marc J. Roberts, and Stephen R. Thomas. *The Environmental Protection Agency: Asking the Wrong Questions*. New York: Oxford, 1990.

Langer, Susan. *Philosophy in a New Key: A Study in the Sociology of Reason, Rite, and Art*. Cambridge, Mass.: Harvard University Press, 1951.

Lasswell, Harold D. "The Structure and Function of Communication in Society." In Wilbur Schramm and Donald F. Roberts, eds. *Mass Communications*. Urbana: University of Illinois Press, 1971, 84-99.

Lasswell, Harold D., and Nathan Leites et al. *The Language of Politics: Studies in Quantitative Semantics*. Cambridge, Mass.: MIT Press, 1965.

Laudon, Kenneth C. *Dossier Society: Value Choices in the Design of National Information Systems*. New York: Columbia University Press, 1986.

Laumann, Edward O. *Networks of Collective Action*. New York: Academic Press, 1976.

Laumann, Edward O., and David Knoke. *The Organizational State: Social Choice in National Policy Domains*. Madison: University of Wisconsin Press, 1987.

Lawrence, Paul R., and Jay W. Lorsch. *Organization and Environment: Managing Differentiation and Integration*. Cambridge, Mass.: Harvard University Press, 1967.

Lerner, Allan W. *The Politics of Decision-Making*. Beverly Hills, Calif.: Sage, 1976.

Lerner, Daniel. *The Human Meaning of the Social Sciences*. New York: Meridian Books, 1959.

Levine, Charles H., and James A. Thurber. "Reagan and the Intergovernmental Lobby: Iron Triangles, Cozy Subsystems, and Political Conflict." In Allan J. Cigler and Burdett A. Loomis, eds. *Interest Group Politics*. 2d ed. Washington, D.C.: CQ Press, 1986, 202-220.

Light, Paul. "Vice-Presidential Influence Under Rockefeller and Mondale. *Political Science Quarterly* 98 (Winter 1983-1984): 617-640.

Likert, Rensis. *New Patterns of Management*. New York: McGraw-Hill, 1961.

——.*The Human Organization: Its Management and Value*. New York: McGraw-Hill, 1967.

Lindblom, Charles. *The Intelligence of Democracy: Decision Making Through Mutual Adjustment*. New York: Free Press, 1965.

Lindblom, Charles E., and David K. Cohen. *Usable Knowledge: Social Science and*

Social Problem Solving. New Haven: Yale University Press, 1979.

Linsky, Martin. *Impact: How the Press Affects Federal Policymaking.* New York: Norton, 1986.

Linsky, Martin, Jonathan Moore, Wendy O'Donnell, and David Whitman. *How the Press Affects Federal Policymaking: Six Case Studies.* New York: Norton, 1986.

Lipsky, Michael. *Street-Level Bureaucracy: Dilemmas of the Individual in Public Services.* New York: Russell Sage Foundation, 1980.

Long, Samuel. *Handbook of Political Behavior,* vol. 2. New York: Plenum Press, 1981.

Lorenz, Frederick O., Betty L. Wells, Charles L. Mulford, and Daisy Kabagarama. "How Social Service Agencies React to Uncertainty: Budget Cuts Need Not Curb Creativity." *Sociology and Social Research* 71 (October 1986): 29-30.

Machlup, Fritz. *The Production and Distribution of Knowledge.* Princeton, N.J.: Princeton University Press, 1962.

MacNair, Ray H., Russell Caldwell, and Leonard Pollane. "Citizen Participants in Public Bureaucracies: Foul-Weather Friends." *Administration and Society* 14 (February 1983): 507-524.

Magat, Wesley A., Alan J. Krupnick, and Winston Harrington. *Rules in the Making: A Statistical Analysis of Regulatory Agency Behavior.* Washington, D.C.: Resources for the Future, 1986.

Maines, David R., and Joseph Palenski. "Reconstructing Legitimacy in Final Reports of Contract Research." *Sociological Review* 34 (August 1986): 575-589.

Malbin, Michael J. *Unelected Representatives: Congressional Staffs and the Future of Representative Government.* New York: Basic Books, 1980.

March, James G., and Johan P. Olsen, eds. *Ambiguity and Choice in Organizations,* 2d ed. Bergen, Norway: Universitetsforlaget, 1979.

—."The New Institutionalism: Organizational Factors in Political Life." *American Political Science Review* 78 (September 1984): 734-749.

March, James G., and Herbert A. Simon. *Organizations.* New York: Wiley, 1958.

March, James G., and Roger Weissinger-Babylon. *Ambiguity and Command.* Boston: Pitman, 1986.

Marin, Richard. "Selling Uncle Sam for a Laugh." *Insight,* February 29, 1988, 46.

Martin, Elizabeth A., and Louis P. Cusella. "Persuading the Adjudicator: Conflict Tactics in the Grievance Procedure." In Margaret L. McLaughlin, ed. *Communication Yearbook 9.* Beverly Hills, Calif.: Sage, 1986.

Maslow, Abraham H., and Norbert L. Mintz. "Effects of Esthetic Surroundings: Initial Effects of Three Esthetic Conditions upon Perceiving 'Energy' and 'Well-Being' in Faces." *Journal of Psychology* 41 (April 1956): 247-254.

Mayo, Elton. *The Social Problems of an Industrial Civilization.* Cambridge, Mass.: Harvard University Press, 1945.

McCaffrey, David P. *OSHA and the Politics of Health Regulation.* New York: Plenum Press, 1982.

McGregor, Douglas. *The Human Side of Enterprise.* New York: McGraw-Hill, 1960.

McGuire, William J. "Theoretical Foundations of Campaigns." In Ronald E. Rice and Charles K. Atkin, eds. *Public Communication Campaigns.* 2d ed. Newbury Park, Calif.: Sage 1989.

McNulty, Timothy J. "Ethics Run Weak 2d to Birth Technology." *Chicago Tribune,* October 18, 1987.

McPhee, Robert D. "Formal Structure and Organizational Communication." In

Robert D. McPhee and Phillip K. Tompkins, eds. *Organizational Communication: Traditional Themes and New Directions*. Beverly Hills, Calif.: Sage, 1985, 149-178.

McPhee, Robert D., and Phillip K. Tompkins, eds. *Organizational Communication: Traditional Themes and New Directions*. Beverly Hills, Calif.: Sage, 1985.

Meltsner, Arnold, and Christopher Bellavita. *The Policy Organization*. Beverly Hills, Calif.: Sage, 1983.

Miewald, Robert D., and John C. Comer. "Complaining as Participation." *Administration and Society*, 17 (February 1986): 481-499.

Miller, James G. "Living Systems: The Organization." *Behavioral Science* 17 (October 1982): 1-182.

Miller, Trudi C. *Public Sector Performance: A Conceptual Turning Point*. Baltimore: Johns Hopkins University Press, 1984.

Mitchell, Terence R., and James R. Larson, Jr. *People in Organizations: An Introduction to Organizational Behavior*. 3d ed. New York: McGraw-Hill, 1987.

Mladenka, Kenneth R. "Citizen Demands and Urban Services: The Distribution of Bureaucratic Response in Chicago and Houston." *American Journal of Political Science* 25 (November 1981): 693-714.

Moe, Terry M. "Control and Feedback in Economic Regulation: The Case of the NLRB." *American Journal of Political Science* 79 (December 1985): 1094-1116.

Monge, Peter R., and Eric M. Eisenberg. "Emergent Communication Networks." In Frederic M. Jablin, Linda L. Putnam, Karlene H. Roberts, and Lyman W. Porter, eds. *Handbook of Organizational Communication*. Newbury Park, Calif.: Sage, 1987.

Moore, Scott T. "The Theory of Street-Level Bureaucracy: A Positive Critique." *Administration and Society* 19 (May 1987): 74-94.

Morgan, D. *Focus Groups as Qualitative Research*. Newbury Park, Calif.: Sage, 1988.

Morgan, Gareth. *Images of Organization*, Beverly Hills, Calif.: Sage, 1986.

Morone, Joseph G., and Edward J. Woodhouse. *Averting Catastrophe: Strategies for Regulating Risky Technologies*. Berkeley: University of California Press, 1986.

Morse, Elliot R., and Robert Rich. *Government Information Management: A Counter-Report of the Commission on Federal Paperwork*. Boulder, Colo.: Westview Press, 1980.

Mumby, Dennis K. *Communication and Power in Organizations: Discourse, Ideology and Domination*. Norwood, N.J.: Ablex, 1988.

Murray, Michael A. "Comparing Public and Private Management: An Exploratory Essay." *Public Administration Review* 34 (July/August 1975): 364-371.

Murray, Michael. *Decisions: A Comparative Critique*. Marshfield, Mass.: Pitman, 1986.

Nash, Nathaniel C. "New Postal Chief Looks at the Really Big Picture." *New York Times*, July 27, 1988.

National Research Council. *Decision Making in the Environmental Protection Agency*, vol. II. Washington, D.C.: National Academy of Sciences, 1977.

Naver, Michael R. "Government Media for Internal and External Audiences." In Lewis M. Helm, Ray Eldon Hiebert, Michael R. Naver, and Kenneth Rabin, eds. *Informing the People*. New York: Longman, 1981, 130-137.

Nelson, Barbara. "Client Evaluations of Social Programs." In Charles T. Goodsell, ed. *The Public Encounter*. Bloomington: Indiana University Press, 1981, 23-42.

Neustadt, Richard. *Presidential Power.* New York: Wiley, 1960.

New York Times Co. v. U.S., 403 U.S. 713 (1971).

Nisbett, Richard E., and Lee Ross. *Human Inference: Strategies and Shortcomings of Social Judgment.* Englewood Cliffs, N.J.: Prentice-Hall, 1980.

Northrop, Alana, Kenneth L. Kraemer, Debora Dunkle, and John Leslie King. "Payoffs from Computerization: Lessons Over Time." *Public Administration Review* 50 (September/October 1990): 505-514.

O'Connor, Robert E., and Larry D. Spence. "Communication Disturbances in a Welfare Bureaucracy: A Case for Self-Management." *Journal of Sociology and Social Welfare* 4 (November 1976): 178-203.

Office of Technology Assessment. *Critical Connections: Communication for the Future.* Washington, D.C.: Government Printing Office, 1990.

——.*Defending Secrets. Sharing Data: New Locks and Keys for Electronic Information.* Washington, D.C.: Government Printing Office, 1987.

——.*Federal Government Information Technology: Management, Security, and Congressional Oversight* (Report No. OTA-CIT-297). Washington, D.C.: Government Printing Office, 1986.

——.*Informing the Nation: Federal Information Dissemination in an Electronic Age.* Washington, D.C.: Government Printing Office, 1988.

O'Reilly, Charles A., III. "The Intentional Distortion of Information in Organizational Communication: A Laboratory and Field Investigation." In Daniel Katz, Robert L. Kahn, and J. Stacy Adams, eds. *The Study of Organizations.* San Francisco: Jossey-Bass, 1982, 328-344.

Ott, J. Steven. *The Organizational Culture Perspective.* Chicago: Dorsey, 1989.

Overman, E. Sam, and Don F. Simanton. "Iron Triangles and Issues Networks of Information Policy." *Public Administration Review* 46 (November 1986): 584-589.

Pace, R. Wayne. *Organizational Communication: Foundations for Human Resource Development.* Englewood Cliffs, N.J.: Prentice-Hall, 1983.

Pace, R. Wayne, and Don F. Faules. *Organizational Communication.* 2d ed. Englewood Cliffs, N.J.: Prentice-Hall, 1989.

Paisley, William. "Public Communication Campaigns: The American Experience." In Ronald E. Rice and Charles K. Atkin, eds. *Public Communication Campaigns.* 2d ed. Newbury Park, Calif.: Sage, 1989, 15-38.

Parsons, Talcott. *The Social System.* New York: Free Press, 1951.

Pear, Robert. "Blacks and the Elitist Stereotype." *New York Times,* September 29, 1987.

Perrow, Charles. *Complex Organizations: A Critical Essay.* 2d ed. Glenview, Ill.: Scott, Foresman, 1979.

Peters, Charles. "From Ouagadougou to Cape Canaveral: Why the Bad News Doesn't Travel Up." *Washington Monthly* 18 (April 1986): 27-31.

Peterson, Steven A. "Close Encounters of the Bureaucratic Kind: Older Americans and Bureaucracy." *American Journal of Political Science* 30 (May 1986): 347-356.

Pfeffer, Jeffrey. *Power in Organizations.* Marshfield, Mass.: Pitman, 1981.

Pierce, William S. *Bureaucratic Failure and Public Expenditure.* New York: Academic Press, 1981.

Pika, Joseph A. "Interest Groups and the White House under Roosevelt and Truman." *Political Science Quarterly* 102 (Winter 1987-1988): 647-668.

Pinfield, Lawrence T. "A Field Evaluation of Perspectives on Organizational Decision Making." *Administrative Science Quarterly* 31 (September 1986): 365-388.

Plumlee, John P., Jay D. Starling, with Kenneth W. Kramer. "Citizen Participation in Water Quality Planning: A Case Study of Perceived Failure." *Administration and Society* 16 (February 1985): 455-473.

Pool, Ithiel de Sola, Wilbur Schramm et al., eds. *Handbook of Communication.* Chicago: Rand-McNally, 1973.

Poole, Marshall Scott. "Communication and Organizational Climates: Review, Critique, and a New Perspective." In Robert D. McPhee and Phillip K. Tompkins, eds. *Organizational Communication: Traditional Themes and New Directions.* Beverly Hills, Calif.: Sage, 1985, 79-108.

Porter, Roger B. "Economic Advice to the President: From Eisenhower to Reagan." *Political Science Quarterly* 98 (Fall 1983): 403-426.

Povich, Elaine. "Senate Approves Cabinet-level VA." *Chicago Tribune,* July 13, 1988.

Powers, Thomas Gid. *Secrecy and Power: The Life of J. Edgar Hoover.* New York: Free Press, 1987.

President's Private Sector Survey on Cost Control. *A Report to the President.* 47 vols. Washington, D.C.: Government Printing Office, 1984.

Prottas, Jeffrey Manditch. *People-Processing: The Street-Level Bureaucrat in Public Service Bureaucracies.* Lexington, Mass.: D.C. Heath, 1979.

Putnam, Linda L., and T. Jones. "Reciprocity in Negotiations: An Analysis of Bargaining Interactions." *Communication Monographs* 49 (1982): 171-191.

Putnam, Linda L., and Michael E. Pacanowsky, eds. *Communication and Organizations: An Interpretive Approach.* Beverly Hills, Calif.: Sage, 1983.

Pye, Lucian. *Communication and Political Development.* Princeton, N.J.: Princeton University Press, 1963.

Rainey, Hal G., Robert W. Backoff, and Charles H. Levine. "Comparing Public and Private Organizations." *Public Administration Review* 36 (March/April 1976): 233-244.

Rapoport, Anatol. "Modern Systems Theory—and Outlook for Coping with Change." *General Systems* 15 (1970): 15-26.

Rawls, John. *A Theory of Justice.* Cambridge, Mass.: Belknap Press of Harvard University Press, 1971.

Reinhold, Robert. "Courts Seeking Translators for Alien Cases." *New York Times,* August 11, 1987.

Report of the Presidential Commission on the Space Shuttle Challenger Accident (Rogers Commission). Washington, D.C., June 6, 1986.

Reuss, Carol, and Donn E. Silvis, eds. *Inside Organizational Communication,* New York: Longman, 1981.

Rice, Ronald. "Computer-Mediated Communication and Organizational Innovation." *Journal of Communication* 37 (Autumn 1987): 65-94.

Rice, Ronald E., and William J. Paisley, eds. *Public Communication Campaigns.* Beverly Hills, Calif.: Sage, 1981.

Rice, Ronald E., and Charles K. Atkin, eds. *Public Communication Campaigns.* 2d ed. Newbury Park, Calif.: Sage, 1989.

Richards, William D., Jr. "Data, Models, and Assumptions in Network Analysis." In Robert D. McPhee and Phillip K. Tompkins, eds. *Organizational Communication: Traditional Themes and New Directions.* Beverly Hills, Calif.: Sage, 1985, 109-178.

Richards, William. "The NEGOPY Network Analysis Program." Burnaby, B.C., Canada: Simon Frazier University, 1986.

Richards, William, and George Lindsey. "Social Network Analysis: An Overview of Recent Developments." In Klaus Krippendorff, ed. *Communication and Control in Society.* New York: Gordon and Breach, 1982, 59-61.

Ritti, R. Richard. "The Social Bases of Organizational Knowledge." In Lee Thayer, ed. *Organization—Communication: Emerging Perspectives I.* Norwood, N.J.: Ablex, 1986, 102-132.

Roberts, Jonathan. *Decision-Making during International Crises.* New York: St. Martin's, 1988.

Roethlisberger, Fritz J., and William J. Dickson. *Management and the Worker.* Cambridge, Mass.: Harvard University Press, 1939.

Rogers, Everett M. *Diffusion of Innovations.* 3d ed. New York: Free Press, 1983.

Rogers, Everett M., and Rekha Agarwala Rogers. *Communication in Organizations.* New York: Free Press, 1976.

Rogers, Everett M., and D. Lawrence Kincaid. *Communication Networks: Toward a New Paradigm for Research.* New York: Free Press, 1981.

Romzek, Barbara S., and Melvin Dubnick. "Accountability in the Public Sector: Lessons from the Challenger Tragedy." *Public Administration Review* 47 (May/June 1987): 227-238.

Rosenfeld, Raymond A. "An Expansion and Application of Kaufman's Model of Red Tape: The Case of Community Development Block Grants." *Western Political Quarterly* 37 (December 1984): 603-620.

Rosenthal, Robert A., and Robert S. Weiss. "Problems of Organizational Feedback Processes." In Raymond A. Bauer, ed. *Social Indicators.* Cambridge, Mass.: M.I.T. Press, 1966, 302-340.

Ross, Raymond S., and Jean Ricky Ross. *Small Groups in Organizational Settings.* Englewood Cliffs, N.J.: Prentice-Hall, 1989.

Rothenberg, Randall. "P.R. Firms Head for Capitol Hill." *New York Times,* January 4, 1991.

Rourke, Francis. *Bureaucracy, Politics, and Public Policy.* 3d ed. Boston: Little, Brown, 1984.

Rubner, Michael. "The Reagan Administration, the 1973 War Powers Resolution, and the Invasion of Grenada." *Political Science Quarterly* 100 (Winter 1985-1986): 627-647.

Sabatier, Paul A., and Neil Pelkey. "Incorporating Multiple Actors and Guidance Instruments into Models of Regulatory Policymaking." *Administration and Society* 19 (August 1987): 236-263.

Sabatier, Paul, and David Whiteman. "Legislative Decision Making and Substantive Policy Information: Models of Information Flow." *Legislative Studies Quarterly* 1 (August 1985): 395-421.

Sanger, David E. "Communications Channels at NASA: Warnings that Faded Along the Line." *New York Times,* February 28, 1986.

Sapir, Edward. *Culture, Language and Personality: Selected Essays.* David Mandelbaum, ed. Berkeley: University of California Press, 1962.

Saunders, Richard M. "Military Force in the Foreign Policy of the Eisenhower Presidency." *Political Science Quarterly* 100 (Spring 1985): 97-116.

Schachter, Hindy L. *Public Agency Communication: Theory and Practice.* Chicago: Nelson Hall, 1983.

Schall, Maryan S. "A Communication Rules Approach to Organizational Culture." *Administrative Science Quarterly* 28 (1983): 557-581.

Schneider, Keith. "Bomb Flaws Known to du Pont and U.S. for Years." *New York Times,* January 16, 1989.

Scholz, John T., and Feng Heng Wei. "Regulatory Enforcement in a Federalist System." *American Political Science Review* 80 (December 1986): 1249-1270.

Schramm, Wilbur L. *Mass Media and National Development: The Role of*

Information in Developing Countries. Stanford, Calif.: Stanford University Press, 1964.

Schulman, Paul R. "The 'Logic' of Organizational Irrationality." *Administration and Society* 21 (May 1989): 31-53.

Schutz, William. *FIRO: A Three Dimensional Theory of Interpersonal Behavior.* New York: Holt, Rinehart, and Winston, 1958.

Schwartz, Barry. *Queuing and Waiting: Studies in the Social Organization of Access and Delay.* Chicago: University of Chicago Press, 1975.

Schwartz, Donald F., and Eugene Jacobson. "Organizational Communication Network Analysis: The Liaison Communication Role." In Daniel Katz, Robert L. Kahn, and J. Stacy Adams, eds. *The Study of Organizations.* San Francisco: Jossey Bass, 1982, 345-358.

Seitz, Steven. *Bureaucracy, Policy, and the Public.* St. Louis: C. V. Mosby, 1978.

Shannon, Claude E., and Warren Weaver. *The Mathematical Theory of Communication.* Urbana: University of Illinois Press, 1949.

Sharp, Elaine B. "Citizen-Demand Making in the Urban Context." *American Journal of Political Science* 28 (November 1984): 654-670.

Shenon, Philip. "The Freedom of Information Act and Its Role in Disclosing Influence Peddling." *New York Times,* August 28, 1989.

Sidlow, Edward I., and Beth Henschen. "The Performance of House Committee Staff Functions: A Comparative Exploration." *Western Political Quarterly* 38 (September 1985): 485-494.

Sigal, Leon. *Reporters and Officials: The Organization and Politics of Newsmaking.* Lexington, Mass.: D.C. Heath, 1973.

Silverman, David. *The Theory of Organisations.* New York: Basic Books, 1971.

Simon, Herbert A. *Administrative Behavior: A Study of Decision Making Processes in Administrative Organizations.* 2d ed. New York: Macmillan, 1957.

———."Human Nature in Politics: The Dialogue of Psychology with Political Science." *American Political Science Review* 79 (June 1979): 293-304.

———.*Models of Man: Social and Rational; Mathematical Essays on Rational Human Behavior in a Social Setting.* New York: Wiley, 1956.

Singer, Benjamin D. "Organizational Communication and Social Disassembly: An Essay on Electronic Anomie." In Lee Thayer, ed. *Organization—Communication: Emerging Perspectives I.* Norwood, N.J.: Ablex, 1986.

Sproule, J. Michael. "Propaganda and American Ideological Critique." In James A. Anderson, ed. *Communication Yearbook 14.* Newbury Park, Calif.: Sage, 1991, 211-238.

Steele, Fred I. *Physical Settings and Organizational Development.* Reading, Mass.: Addison-Wesley, 1973.

Steinbruner, John D. *The Cybernetic Theory of Decision.* Princeton, N.J.: Princeton University Press, 1974.

Stephens, David. "President Carter, the Congress, the NEA: Creating the Department of Education." *Political Science Quarterly* 98 (Winter 1983-1984): 641-663.

Stevens, John M., and Robert P. McGowan. *Information Systems and Public Management.* New York: Praeger, 1985.

Stewart, David W., and Prem N. Shamdasani. *Focus Groups: Theory and Practice.* Newbury Park, Calif.: Sage, 1990.

Stone, Clarence N. "Attitudinal Tendencies Among Officials." In Charles T. Goodsell, ed. *The Public Encounter.* Bloomington: Indiana University Press, 1981, 43-68.

Strauss, Anselm. "The Articulation of Project Work: An Organizational Process."

Sociological Quarterly 29 (June 1988): 163-178.

Tarrow, Sidney. *Between Center and Periphery: Grassroots Politicians in Italy and France.* New Haven: Yale University Press, 1977.

Taylor, Frederick W. *Scientific Management.* New York: Harper, 1911.

Taylor, Serge. *Making Bureaucracies Think: The Environmental Statement Strategy of Administrative Reform.* Stanford, Calif.: Stanford University Press, 1984.

Tetlock, Philip E. "Policy-Makers' Images of International Conflict." *Journal of Social Issues* 39 (Spring 1983): 67-86.

Thayer, Lee, ed. *Organization—Communication: Emerging Perspectives I.* Norwood, N.J.: Ablex, 1986.

Thompson, Michael, and Aaron Wildavsky. "A Cultural Theory of Information Bias in Organizations." *Journal of Management Studies* 23 (May 1986): 273-286.

Toffler, Alvin. *Future Shock.* New York: Random House, 1970.

Tolchin, Martin. "Federal Aid for Destitute Reaching Just Half of Those Eligible." *New York Times,* May 10, 1988.

——."Staff Is Cut, Many Lose Social Security." *New York Times,* December 8, 1989.

——."Study Says Half of Those Eligible Get Food Stamps." *New York Times,* November 15, 1988.

Tompkins, Phillip K. "Management Qua Communication in Rocket Research and Development." *Communication Monographs* 44 (March 1977): 1-26.

——."Organizational Metamorphosis in Space Research and Development." *Communication Monographs* 45 (June 1978): 110-118.

Tompkins, Phillip K., and George Cheney. "Communication and Unobtrusive Control in Contemporary Organizations." In Robert D. McPhee and Phillip K. Tompkins, eds. *Organizational Communication: Traditional Themes and New Directions.* Beverly Hills, Calif.: Sage, 1985, 179-210.

Trainor, Bernard. "Another U.S. Study Down the Drain?" *New York Times,* January 13, 1988.

Traut, Carol Ann, and Hal G. Rainey. "The Information Gathering Practices of City Officials." American Political Science Association paper, 1989.

Tuchman, Barbara. *The March of Folly: From Troy to Vietnam.* New York: Knopf, 1984.

Tullock, Gordon. *The Politics of Bureaucracy.* Washington, D.C.: Public Affairs Press, 1965.

U.S. Congress. House. Committee on Science and Technology. *Investigation of the Challenger Accident.* Report, 99th Congress, 2d session. Washington, D.C.: Government Printing Office, 1986.

U.S. Office of Management and Budget. "Report of the General Government Team to the President's Federal Data Processing Reorganization Project, 'Information Technology: Challenges for Top Program Management in the General Government Agencies.'" *President's Reorganization Project.* Washington, D.C.: Government Printing Office, 1978.

Vandenbrouke, Lucien S. "Anatomy of a Failure: The Decision to Land at the Bay of Pigs." *Political Science Quarterly* 99 (Fall 1984): 471-491.

Vedlitz, Arnold, James A. Dyer, and Roger Durand. "Citizen Contacts with Local Governments: A Comparative View." *American Journal of Political Science* 24 (February 1980): 50-67.

Walcott, Charles, and Karen M. Hult. "Organizing the White House: Structure, Environment, and Organizational Governance." *American Journal of Political*

Science 31 (February 1987): 109-125.

Warner, W. Lloyd, and J. O. Low. *The Social System of the Modern Factory.* New Haven: Yale University Press, 1947.

Warren, James. "CBS-TV's Apple Scare is Costly to Growers." *Chicago Tribune,* May 11, 1989.

Wasby, Stephen L. *Small Town Police and the Supreme Court: Hearing the Word.* Lexington, Mass.: Lexington Books, 1976.

——."Technology and Communication in a Federal Court: The Ninth Circuit." Midwest Political Science Association paper, Chicago, 1987.

Washburn, Gary. "Red Tape Bogs Down CTA, Report Says." *Chicago Tribune,* August 17, 1988.

Washington State Commission for Efficiency and Accountability in Government. "Dollars and Sense." *Washington Journal* 2 (April 16, 1990): 1, 4-5.

Washington State Commission for Efficiency and Accountability in Government. "State Mail Operations Review." *Efficiency Quarterly* (August 1990): 2.

Weick, Karl. *The Social Psychology of Organizing.* 2d ed. Reading, Mass.: Addison-Wesley, 1979.

Weiss, Carol. *Social Science Research and Decision Making.* New York: Columbia University Press, 1980.

——."Congressional Committee Staffs as Problematic Users of Analysis," American Political Science Association paper, 1984.

Weiss, Carol H., and Alan H. Barton, eds. *Making Bureaucracies Work.* Beverly Hills, Calif.: Sage, 1980.

Weiss, Carol H., and Michael Bucuvalas. "Truth Tests and Utility Tests: Decision-Makers' Frames of Reference for Social Science Research." *American Sociological Review* 45 (April 1980): 302-303.

West, William F. "Structuring Administrative Discretion: The Pursuit of Rationality and Responsiveness." *American Journal of Political Science* 28 (May 1984): 340-360.

Whitehead, Alfred North. *Symbolism: Its Meaning and Effect.* New York: Macmillan, 1958.

Whiteman, David. "The Fate of Policy Analysis in Congressional Decision Making: Three Types of Use in Committees." *Western Political Quarterly* 38 (June 1985): 294-311.

Wigand, Rolf T. "Communication Network Analysis: History and Overview." In Gerald M. Goldhaber and George A. Barnett, eds. *Handbook of Organizational Communication.* Norwood, N.J.: Ablex, 1988.

——."A Model of Interorganizational Communication among Complex Organizations." In Klaus Krippendorff, ed. *Communication and Control in Society.* New York: Gordon and Breach, 1982.

Wiio, Osmo A., Gerald M. Goldhaber, and Michael P. Yates. "Organizational Communication Research: Time for Reflection?" In Dan Nimmo, ed. *Communication Yearbook 4.* New Brunswick, N.J.: Transaction, 1980.

Wildavsky, Aaron. *Speaking Truth to Power: The Art and Craft of Political Analysis.* Boston: Little, Brown, 1979.

Wilensky, Harold L. *Organizational Intelligence: Knowledge and Policy in Government and Industry.* New York: Basic Books, 1967.

Williams, Frederick, Ronald E. Rice, and Everett M. Rogers. *Research Methods and the New Media.* New York: Free Press, 1988.

Wilson, James Q. *Bureaucracy: What Government Agencies Do and Why They Do It.* New York: Basic Books, 1989.

Wines, Michael. "Gulf Intelligence Draws Complaint by Schwarzkopf." *New York*

Times, June 13, 1991.

Wyatt, Nancy, and Gerald M. Phillips. *Studying Organizational Communication: A Case Study of the Farmers Home Administration.* Norwood, N.J.: Ablex, 1988.

Wood, B. Dan. "Principals, Bureaucrats, and Responsiveness in Clean Air Enforcements." *American Political Science Review* 82 (March 1988): 213-234.

Woodward, Joan. *Management and Technology.* London: Her Majesty's Stationery Office, 1958.

——.*Industrial Organization: Theory and Practice.* London: Oxford University Press, 1965.

Worthley, John A., and Richard Torkelson. "Managing the Toxic Waste Problem: Lessons from the Love Canal." *Administration and Society* 13 (August 1981): 145-160.

Yamagishi, Toshio, Mary R. Gillmore, and Karen S. Cook. "Network Connections and the Distribution of Power in Exchange Networks." *American Journal of Sociology* 93 (January 1988): 833-851.

Zuckerman, Alan S., and Darrell M. West. "The Political Bases of Citizen Contacting: A Cross-National Analysis." *American Political Science Review* 79 (1985): 117-131.

Zull, C., R. Weber, and P. Mohler. *Computer-Aided Text Classification for the Social Sciences: The General Inquirer III.* Mannheim, Germany: ZUMA, 1989.

Index

Index

417